LEGAL ASPECTS
OF
HEALTH CARE
ADMINISTRATION

Fourth Edition

George D. Pozgar, MBA
Vice-President, Corporate Affairs
Episcopal Health Services, Inc.
Hempstead, New York

AN ASPEN PUBLICATION®
Aspen Publishers, Inc.
Gaithersburg, Maryland
1990

9-22-92 dmi

This publication is designed to provide accurate and authoritative information in regard to the Subject Matter covered. It is sold with the understanding that the publisher is not engaged in rendering legal, accounting, or other professional service. If legal advice or other expert assistance is required, the service of a competent professional person should be sought. (*From a Declaration of Principles jointly adopted by a Committee of the American Bar Association and a Committee of Publishers and Associations.*)

Library of Congress Cataloging-in-Publication Data

Pozgar, George D.
Legal aspects of health care administration / George D. Pozgar.
— 4th ed.
p. cm.
"An Aspen publication"
Includes bibliographical references.
ISBN: 0-8342-0161-5
1. Medical laws and legislation—United States. 2. Medical personal—Malpractice—United States. I. Title. [DNLM: 1. Delivery of Health Care—United States. 2. Legislation, Medical—United States. 3. Malpractice.
W44 P893L]KF382.1P69 1990
344.73'041—dc20
[347.30441]
DNLM/DLC
For Library of Congress
90-466
CIP

Editorial Services: Ruth Bloom

Library of Congress Catalog Card Number: 90-466
ISBN: 0-8342-0161-5

Printed in the United States of America

3 4 5

Table of Contents

Foreword

In this text the author presents a review of the medical-legal aspects of health care. There has been an ever-increasing number of malpractice suits, over-regulation, high public expectations, and skyrocketing insurance pressures. The cover title of the March 24, 1986, issue of *Time* magazine will continue to be relevant in the medical malpractice climate of the 1990s: "Sorry, America, Your Insurance Has Been Cancelled."

There is a great need to demystify the law for both students and health professionals. This text provides an excellent foundation for understanding the rapidly expanding field of law and regulation affecting the health care industry. It serves to clarify the basic medical-legal principles as well as to encourage related educational forums.

It is incumbent on health professionals to acquire a general knowledge of the potential legal hazards associated with their professions both in dealing with associates and in providing the day-to-day delivery of health care. The many risks of liability can be greatly minimized through a better understanding of the concepts presented in this book.

Unless there is a reversion to sensible understanding and application of the legal principles herein discussed, the present breakdown in the health care delivery system will continue. The unwarranted high malpractice awards presently being distributed to the few who have been harmed is extremely costly to society in general. These dollars could better serve society as a whole if they were directed toward the improvement of the health care system.

Philip A. Mantia, M.D.
Clinical Assistant Professor in Medicine
University Hospital
Stony Brook, New York

Preface

Noting that "knowledge is power," the basic purpose of this fourth edition of *Legal Aspects of Health Care Administration* is to arm the health care professional with a working knowledge of health law. Rather than frustrating the reader with confusing legal jargon, this edition provides information and explanations written in commonly understood terminology. This approach will demystify the law as it applies to health care.

Further, this edition provides health care professionals with the necessary background on a wide variety of health care topics, enabling them to deal with the common legal and practical problems facing the health care industry. The law is in a constant state of flux. The size of claims, settlements, and insurance premiums continues its upward spiral. As a result, health care professionals entering and functioning in their respective positions must possess a well-rounded knowledge of the law as it applies to their areas of responsibility in the states in which they practice. This book answers these needs and serves well as a text for the classroom and as a source for individual study. As such, it should be included in the curriculum of every health care program.

New to this edition are reviews of acquired immunodeficiency syndrome (AIDS), employee discipline and discharge, hospital waste and pollution, and criminal law and the health professional. Those chapters contained in the third edition have been extensively updated.

the delay in notification of the attending doctors of a newborn's condition had increased the likelihood of permanent damage and that adequate medical treatment had not been instituted after respiratory distress was detected. The record supported a judgment awarding $1.5 million in damages for negligent postnatal care. In *Gooden v. Tips*, 651 S.W.2d 364 (Tex. Ct. App. 1983), the plaintiff's petition alleged that the physician was negligent in failing to warn his patient not to drive an automobile while under the influence of the drug Quaalude and that this was a proximate cause of the personal injuries sustained by one plaintiff when struck by a car driven by the patient. The court of appeals held this was sufficient to state a cause of action against the physician. The decision of the district court, granting judgment for the physician, was reversed, and the case was remanded for determination.

All the elements necessary to establish negligence were well established in *Niles v. City of San Rafael*, 42 Cal. App. 3d 230, 116 Cal. Rptr. 733 (1974). On June 26, 1973, at approximately 3:30 P.M., a young boy got into an argument with another boy on the ball field and was hit on the right side of his head. He rode home on his bicycle and waited for his father who was to pick him up for the weekend. At approximately 5:00 P.M., his father arrived to pick him up. By the time they arrived in San Francisco, the son appeared to be in a great deal of pain. His father then decided to take him to Mount Zion Hospital, which was a short distance away. He arrived at the hospital emergency room at approximately 5:45 P.M. Upon admission to the emergency room, the boy was taken to a treatment room by a registered nurse. The nurse obtained a history of the injury and took the patient's pulse and blood pressure. During his stay in the emergency room the young boy was irritable, vomited several times, and complained that his head hurt. An intern who had seen the patient wrote "pale, diaphoretic, and groggy" on his chart. Skull x-rays were ordered and found to be negative except for soft tissue swelling that was not noted until later. The intern then decided to admit the patient. A second-year resident was called, and he agreed with the intern's decision. The intern was called later by an admitting clerk who indicated that the patient had to be admitted by a private attending physician. The resident went as far as to write "admit" on the chart and later crossed it out. A pediatrician who was in the emergency room at the time was asked to look at the patient. The pediatrician was also the paid director of the Mount Zion Pediatric Out-Patient Clinic. The pediatrician asked the patient a few questions and then decided to send him home. He could not recall what instructions he gave the patient's father, but he did give him his business card. The pediatrician could not recall giving the father a copy of "Head Injury Instructions," an information sheet that had been prepared for distribution to patients with head injuries. The sheet explained that an individual should be returned to the emergency room should any of the following signs appear:

- a large, soft lump on the head
- unusual drowsiness (can't be awakened)

Acknowledgments

Many thanks to those I have instructed in the legal aspects of health care administration from Molloy College, C.W. Post College, Saint Francis College, the New School for Social Research, and Saint Joseph College, as well as to those whom I have instructed through the years at various seminars, for their inspiration. Many thanks to you all.

The author wishes to acknowledge Aspen Publishers, Inc.; Robert Andrew Wild, Esq., and Norton L. Travis, Esq., of the law firm of Garfunkel, Wild & Travis, Great Neck, New York; Nicholas Fortuna, Esq., for their contributions to the chapter on labor law; Michael Jude Jannuzzi, Esq., for his contributions to the Glossary of Legal Terms; and my wife, Nina S. Pozgar, Esq., Assistant District Attorney, Suffolk County, New York, for helping to make this fourth edition a reality.

Chapter 1

Introduction to Law

Law reflects to a large degree the civilization of those that live under it.
Its progress and development are mirrors not merely of material pros-
perity but of the method of thought and of the outlook of the age.[1]

This chapter provides health care professionals with some elementary information regarding the law, the workings of the legal system, and the roles of the
various branches of government in creating, administering, and enforcing the law
in the United States.

Most definitions of law describe it as a system of principles and processes by
which people in a society deal with their disputes and problems, seeking to solve or
settle them without resort to force. Simply stated, laws are general rules of conduct
that are enforced by government, which imposes penalties when prescribed laws
are violated.

Laws govern the relationships between private individuals and organizations
and between both of these parties and government. Law that governs the relationships between private parties may be termed *private law*. *Public law* deals with
the relationships between private parties and government. Laws regulate the
activities of individuals in international situations as well as in federal, state, local,
and municipal settings.

One important segment of public law is criminal law, which prohibits conduct
deemed injurious to public order and provides for punishment of those found to
have engaged in such conduct. Public law also consists of countless regulations
designed to advance societal objectives by requiring private individuals and
organizations to adopt specified courses of action in their activities and undertakings. The thrust of most public law is to attain what society deems valid public
goals.

Private law is concerned with the recognition and enforcement of the rights and
duties of private individuals and organizations. Tort and contract actions are two
basic types of private law. In a tort action, one party asserts that the wrongful

1

conduct of another has caused harm, and the injured party seeks compensation for the harm suffered. Generally, a contract action involves a claim by one party that another party has breached an agreement by failing to fulfill an obligation. Either remuneration or specific performance of the obligation may be sought as a remedy.

SOURCES OF LAW

The basic sources of law are common law, which is derived from judicial decisions; statutory law, which emanates from the federal and state legislatures; and administrative law, prescribed by administrative agencies.

Common Law

The term *common law* is applied to that body of principles that has evolved and continues to evolve and expand from judicial decisions that arise during the trial of actual court cases. Many of the legal principles and rules applied today by courts in the United States had their origins in English common law.

Common Law in England

The law in England, prior to the Norman Conquest in A.D. 1066, was dispensed primarily on the basis of tradition and local customs and dealt, for the most part, with violent crimes. The kings during this period were concerned more with enforcing customary law, as opposed to amending it. The courts basically consisted of open-air meetings where no records were maintained. "For the Anglo-Saxons justice was a local matter, administered chiefly in the shire courts, and was largely dependent upon local customs, preserved in the memory of those persons who declared the law in the court."[2]

The Normans, following their conquest in A.D. 1066, had little regard for Anglo-Saxon laws. They considered themselves apart from such laws.

It is obviously impossible to attempt an adequate picture of Anglo-Saxon life. It was a wild time. Men lived in terror of the vast forests, where it was easy to be lost and succumb to starvation, of their fellow man who would plunder and slay, and above all of the Unknown, whose inscrutable ways seemed constantly to be bringing famine and disaster. The uncertainties of modern life pale into insignificance when regarded from the standpoint of these men. It is natural, therefore, that their law should reflect their reaction against the environment. It was conservative and harsh. Violence, robbery and death formed its background.[3]

Land disputes involved the Saxons who held the land before the conquest and the Normans who dispossessed them. Evidence in such disputes was often the result of oral testimony from neighboring landowners.

> The principal change introduced by the Norman Conquest, so far as the central jurisdiction was concerned, was that the King's court now became, for the first time, the court in which disputes relating to land-tenure among the King's tenants-in-chief were regularly decided . . . there is no hint of any professional judiciary at this period. The trials were held locally in the presence of the county court or several county courts by the king's representatives, sent out from Curia Regis (the King's Court) and the tenants-in-chief. The presiding officer was often a cleric.[4]

In A.D. 1154, following the Norman Conquest, a system of national law began to develop, based on custom, foreign literature, and the rule of strong kings. The first royal court was established in A.D. 1178. This court, enlisting the aid of a jury, heard the complaints of the kingdom's subjects. Since there were few written laws, a body of principles evolved from these court decisions, which became known as "common law." These decisions were used by judges in deciding subsequent cases. As Parliament's power to legislate grew, the initiative for developing new laws passed from the king to Parliament. "The first recorded case of medical malpractice in English common law was noted in 1329. By 1518 when the College of Physicians of London was incorporated, malpractice litigation was common enough for the charter to include disciplinary provisions for malpractice."[5]

Common Law in the United States

During the colonial period, English common law began to be applied uniformly in the colonies. However, after the Revolution each state, with the exception of Louisiana, adopted all or part of the existing English common law and added to it as needed. Louisiana civil law is based to a great extent on the French and Spanish laws and, especially, on the code of Napoleon. As a result, there is no national system of common law in the United States, and common law on specific subjects may differ from state to state. Cases are tried on common law principles unless a statute governs. Even though statutory law has affirmed many of the legal rules and principles initially established by the courts, new issues continue to arise, especially in private law disputes, which require decision making according to common law principles. Common law actions are basically initiated to recover money damages and/or possession of real or personal property.

By the 1960s, malpractice had become a major problem for the health care industry. The resulting rise in the use of malpractice insurance since that time has caused unwieldy malpractice insurance rates for both physicians and hospitals.

A decision in a case that sets forth a new legal principle establishes a *precedent*. When a common law principle has been enunciated by a higher state court, that principle must be followed by the lower courts within the state where the decision was rendered. Trial courts or those on equal footing are not bound by the decisions of other trial courts. Also, a principle established in one state does not set precedent for another state. Rather, the rulings in one jurisdiction may be used by the courts of other jurisdictions as guides to the legal analysis of a particular legal problem. Decisions found to be reasonable will be followed.

The position of a court or agency, relative to other courts and agencies, determines the place assigned to its decision in the hierarchy of decisional law. The decisions of the U.S. Supreme Court are highest in the hierarchy of decisional law with respect to federal legal questions. Because of the parties or the legal question involved, most legal controversies do not fall within the scope of the Supreme Court's decision-making responsibilities. On questions of purely state concern—such as the interpretation of a state statute that raises no issues under the U.S. Constitution or federal law—the highest court in the state has the final word on proper interpretation.

The legal principle *stare decisis* ("let the decision stand") provides that when a decision is rendered in a lawsuit involving a particular set of facts, another lawsuit involving an identical or substantially similar situation is to be resolved in the same manner as the first lawsuit. The resolution of later lawsuits will be arrived at by applying the rules and principles of preceding cases. In this manner, courts arrive at comparable rulings. Sometimes slight factual differences may provide a basis for recognizing distinctions between the precedent and the current case. In some cases, even when such differences are absent, a court may conclude that a particular common law rule is no longer in accord with the needs of society and may depart from precedent. It should be understood that principles of law are subject to change, whether they originate in statutory or in common law. Common law principles may be modified, overturned, abrogated, or created by new court decisions in a continuing process of growth and development to reflect changes in social attitudes, public needs, judicial prejudices, or contemporary political thinking.

Statutory Law

A statute is a written law emanating from a legislative body. Although a statute can abolish any rule of common law, it can do so only by express words. The principles and rules of statutory law are set in hierarchical order. The Constitution of the United States adopted at the Constitutional Convention in 1787 and ratified by the states, with its duly ratified amendments, is highest in the hierarchy of enacted law. Article VI of the Constitution declares: "This Constitution, and the Laws of the United States which shall be made in Pursuance thereof; and all Treaties made, or which shall be made, under the Authority of the United States, shall be the supreme Law of the Land. . . .'' The clear import of these words is that the U.S. Constitution, federal law, and federal treaties take precedence over the constitutions and laws of states and local jurisdictions.

Statutory law may be amended, repealed, or expanded by action of the legislature. States and local jurisdictions may enact and enforce laws that do not conflict with federal law. Statutory laws may be declared void by a court for a variety of reasons. For example, a statute may be found unconstitutional because it does not comply with a state or federal constitution, because it is vague or ambiguous, or, in the case of a state law, because it is in conflict with a federal law.

In many cases involving statutory law the court is called on to interpret how a statute applies to a given set of facts. For example, a statute may merely state that no person may discriminate against another person because of race, creed, color, or sex. A court may then be called on to decide whether certain actions by a person are discriminatory and therefore violate the law.

Administrative Law

Administrative law is an extensive body of public law issued by administrative agencies which are created by legislatures to administer the enacted laws of the federal and state governments. Administrative law takes the form of administrative rules and regulations and prescribes the procedural responsibilities and authority of administrative agencies. This body of law is particularly important to those in the health care industry as hospitals are inundated by a proliferation of administrative rules and regulations affecting every aspect of hospital operation.

Administrative agencies assist in rule making and conflict resolution in specific defined areas of national and state interests. It should be noted that resort to an administrative agency for resolution of a dispute may be a prerequisite to review of the dispute by a court. Decisions of administrative agencies may be reviewed by the courts and modified or overturned. The following federal administrative departments, divisions, and agencies are but a few of the many affecting the health care system.

Department of Health and Human Services

The Department of Health and Human Services (HHS), a cabinet-level department of the executive branch of the federal government, is concerned with people and is most involved with the nation's human concerns. The secretary of HHS, serving as the department's administrative head, advises the president with regard to health, welfare, and income security plans, policies, and programs. There are presently five operating divisions within HHS: the Social Security Administration, the Health Care Financing Administration, the Office of Human Development Services, the Public Health Service, and the Family Support Administration.

Social Security Administration

The Social Security Administration oversees the nation's social insurance program, which is funded by contributions from both employers and employees. The funds are pooled into special trusts. When the earnings of an employee are reduced or discontinued due to death or disability, social security benefits are paid to assist the employee and his or her family.

A portion of the social security contributions are placed into a separate hospital insurance trust fund. These funds are designated for hospital benefits for senior citizens (persons over 65 years of age) and their dependents. Senior citizens can receive additional benefits for other medical bills by paying a percentage of supplementary medical insurance premiums. The two health benefits programs are generally referred to as Medicare. Responsibility for administering the Medicare program has been transferred to the Health Care Financing Administration.[6]

Health Care Financing Administration

The Health Care Financing Administration (HCFA) is responsible for administering the Medicare and Medicaid programs. HCFA is also responsible for the related medical care quality assurance provisions of both Medicare and Medicaid. Under the Medicare program, HCFA develops and implements policies and procedures and guidance related to program recipients, such as hospitals, nursing homes, physicians, and the contractors who process claims such as Blue Cross and Blue Shield. Under the Medicaid program, HCFA provides grants to the states for medical care services for those who are unable to pay. HCFA is also responsible for working with the states under the Medicaid program to develop approaches toward meeting the needs of the indigent.[7]

Office of Human Development Services

The Office of Human Development Services (HDS) provides leadership and direction to programs for the aging; children, youth, and families; Native Americans; those living in rural areas; and handicapped persons. The HDS is responsible for the management and provision of leadership in planning and developing HDS programs; supervision of research; control of equal employment opportunity and civil rights policies and programs for HDS; directing public affairs, regional operations, and correspondence and assignment tracking activities; and recommendations for program improvements.[8]

Public Health Service

The mission of the Public Health Service is to promote the protection of the nation's physical and mental health. The PHS accomplishes its mission by coordinating with the states setting and implementing national health policy and pursuing effective intergovernmental relations; generating and upholding cooperative international health-related agreements, policies and programs; conducting medical and biomedical research; sponsoring and administering programs for the development of health resources, prevention and control of diseases, alcohol and drug abuse; providing resources and expertise to the states and other public and private institutions in the planning, direction, and delivery of physical and mental health care services; and enforcing laws to ensure the safety of drugs and protection against impure and unsafe foods, cosmetics, medical devices, and radiation-producing projects.[9]

Within the Public Health Service are smaller agencies responsible for carrying out the purpose of the division and HHS. The Food and Drug Administration (FDA) is one such agency. The FDA supervises and controls the introduction of drugs, foods, cosmetics, and medical devices into the marketplace and protects society from impure and/or hazardous items. Virtually every consumer product in a supermarket or a drugstore is regulated by the FDA.

The following is a list of the activities of the FDA:

- FDA inspects plants where foods, drugs, cosmetics, or other products are made or stored to make sure good practices are being observed.
- FDA reviews and approves new drug applications and food additive petitions before new drugs or new food additives can be used.
- FDA approves every batch of insulin and antibiotics, and most color additives, before they can be used.
- FDA sets standards for consumer products, such as foods that are made according to a set recipe (peanut butter, for example). FDA tests products to ensure that they meet government standards.
- FDA is conducting a review of all prescription and nonprescription medicines, biological drugs, and veterinary drugs now on the market. The goal is to make sure they are safe, effective, and properly labeled. FDA develops regulations for proper labeling. For example, FDA developed new regulations requiring cosmetic ingredient labeling and nutrition labeling on many foods.
- FDA works with the industries it regulates to help them develop better quality-control procedures.
- FDA tests drugs regularly after approval to ascertain whether they meet standards of potency, purity, and quality.
- FDA issues public warnings when hazardous products have been identified.[10]

Family Support Administration

The Family Support Administration (FSA) serves as adviser to the Secretary of Health and Human Services for children and families; provides leadership and direction to family support programs; recommends actions that improve the coordination of family support programs with other HHS programs, federal agencies, state and local governments, and private sector organizations; directs and coordinates programs with the secretary of labor for employment and training; manages and provides leadership and planning and developing FSA programs; and supervises the use of research and evaluation funds and controls equal employment opportunity programs for FSA.[11]

Department of Justice

The Department of Justice is responsible for enforcing the laws of the United States. The attorney general is the administrative head of the department, which consists of various offices, divisions (e.g., the Antitrust, Civil, Criminal, Civil Rights, and Tax divisions), bureaus (e.g., the Federal Bureau of Investigation and the Drug Enforcement Administration), and boards (e.g., the Executive Office for Immigration Review).

Department of Labor

The Department of Labor is the ninth executive department of the executive branch of government. The secretary of labor advises the president on labor policies and issues. The functions of the Department of Labor are to

> . . . foster, promote, and develop the welfare of wage earners of the United States, to improve working conditions, and to advance opportunities for profitable employment. In carrying out this mission, the department administers a variety of federal labor laws guaranteeing workers' rights to safe and healthful working conditions, a minimum hourly wage and overtime pay, freedom from employment discrimination, unemployment insurance, and workers' compensation. The department also protects workers' pension rights; provides for job training programs; helps workers find jobs; works to strengthen free collective bargaining; and keeps track of changes in employment prices and other national economic measurements. As the department seeks to assist all Americans who need and want to work, special efforts are made to meet the unique job market problems of older workers, youths, minority group members, women, the handicapped, and other groups.[12]

Within the Department of Labor are various agencies responsible for carrying out the purpose of the department. Among them is the Occupational Safety and Health Administration (OSHA), which develops and promulgates occupational safety and health standards, develops and issues regulations, conducts investigations and inspections to determine the status of compliance, and issues citations and proposes penalties for noncompliance.

National Labor Relations Board

The National Labor Relations Board (NLRB) is an agency, independent of the Department of Labor, responsible for preventing and remedying unfair labor practices by employers and labor organizations or their agents, and conducting secret ballot elections among employees in appropriate collective bargaining units to determine whether or not they desire to be represented by a labor organization. The Board conducts secret ballot elections among employees who have been covered by a union-shop agreement to determine whether or not they wish to revoke their union's authority. The General Counsel has final authority in unfair labor practice cases to investigate charges, issue complaints, and prosecute such complaints before the Board. There are 33 regional directors, under the direction of the General Counsel, that are responsible for processing representation, unfair labor practice, and jurisdictional dispute cases.[13]

In addition to the federal-level departments and agencies described above, there are counterpart departments and agencies on the state and local levels that also address public health, finance, education, welfare, labor, housing, and other needs and concerns of state residents. The number of agencies regulating the health care industry is becoming unwieldy. Hospitals in New York State, for example, are reportedly regulated by approximately 164 agencies. A study by the Hospital Association of New York State found that 96 of the 164 agencies are state controlled.[14]

GOVERNMENT ORGANIZATION

The three branches of government are the executive, legislative, and judicial branches. A vital concept in the constitutional framework of government on both the federal and the state levels is the separation of powers. Essentially, this principle provides that no one branch of government is clearly dominant over the other two; however, in the exercise of its functions, each may affect and limit the activities, functions, and powers of the others.

The concept of separation of powers—in effect, a system of checks and balances—is illustrated in the relationships among the branches of government in regard to legislation. On the federal level, when a bill creating a statute is enacted by Congress and signed by the president, it becomes law. If the president vetoes a bill, it takes a two-thirds vote of each house of Congress to override the veto. The president can also prevent a bill from becoming law by avoiding any action while Congress is in session. This procedure, known as a *pocket veto*, can temporarily stop a bill from becoming law and may permanently prevent it from becoming law if later sessions of Congress do not act favorably on it. A bill that has become law may be declared invalid by the U.S. Supreme Court if it decides that the law is in violation of the U.S. Constitution. Even though a Supreme Court decision is final regarding a specific controversy, Congress and the president may generate new, constitutionally sound legislation to replace a law that has been declared unconstitutional. The procedures for amending the Constitution are complex and often time consuming, but they can serve as a way to offset or override a Supreme Court decision.

Executive Branch

The president serves as the administrative head of the executive branch of the federal government. The primary function of the executive branch on the federal level, and in most states, is to enforce and administer the law. However, the chief executive, either the president of the United States or the governor of a state, also has a role in the creation of law through the power to approve or veto legislative proposals.

The executive branch of federal government is organized on a departmental basis. Each department is responsible for a different area of public affairs, and each enforces the law within its area of responsibility. Most states are also organized on a departmental basis. These departments administer and enforce state law concerning public affairs.

Legislative Branch

The legislative branch of the federal government consists of the Senate and the House of Representatives, together referred to as the U.S. Congress. The functions of the legislative branch are to enact laws that may amend or repeal existing legislation and to create new legislation. It is the legislature's responsibility to determine the nature and extent of the need for new laws and for changes in existing laws. Legislative proposals are assigned or referred for study to committees with special concerns or interests. The committees conduct investigations and hold hearings where interested persons may present their views; these proceedings provide information to assist committee members in their consideration of proposed bills. Some bills eventually reach the full legislative body where, after consideration and debate, they may be either approved or rejected.

The U.S. Congress and all state legislatures are bicameral (consisting of two houses), except for the Nebraska legislature, which is unicameral. Both houses in a bicameral legislature must pass identical versions of a legislative proposal before the legislation can be brought to the chief executive.

Judicial Branch

"The judicial Power of the United States, shall be vested in one supreme Court, and in such inferior Courts as the Congress may from time to time ordain and establish."[15] The function of the judicial branch of government is adjudication—resolving disputes in accordance with law. As a practical matter, most disputes or controversies that are covered by legal principles or rules are resolved without resort to the courts.

Arbitration is a common method of settling controversies between parties. However, there are times when there is no way to end a controversy without submitting to the adjudicatory process of the courts. A dispute brought before a court is decided in accordance with the applicable law; this application of law is precisely the essence of the judicial process.

The decision as to which court has jurisdiction—the legal right to hear and rule on a particular case—is determined by such matters as the locality in which each party to a lawsuit resides and the issues of a lawsuit. Each state in the United States provides its own court system, which is created by the state's constitution and/or statutes. Most of the nation's judicial business is reviewed and acted on in state courts. Each state maintains a level of trial courts that have original jurisdiction. This jurisdiction may exclude cases where the monetary value of the claim is below a specified minimum and cases involving probate matters (i.e., wills and estates) and worker's compensation. Different states have designated different names for trial courts (i.e., superior, district, circuit, or supreme courts). Also on the trial-court level are minor courts such as city, small claims, and justice of the peace courts. States such as Massachusetts have consolidated their minor courts into a statewide court system.

There is at least one appellate court in each state. Many states have an intermediate appellate court between the trial courts and the court of last resort. Where this intermediate court is present, there is a provision for appeal to it, with further review in all but select cases. Because of this format, the highest appellate tribunal is seen as the final arbiter in cases that possess importance in themselves or for the particular state's system of jurisprudence. (Figure 1-1 depicts a typical state court system.)

The trial court of the federal system is the United States district court. There are 89 district courts in the 50 states (the larger states having more than one district court) and one in the District of Columbia. The Commonwealth of Puerto Rico also has a district court with jurisdiction corresponding to that of district courts in the various states. There is generally only one judge required to sit and decide a case, although there are certain cases requiring up to three judges. The federal district courts hear civil, criminal, admiralty, and bankruptcy cases. The Bankruptcy Amendments and Federal Judgeship Act of 1984 (28 U.S.C. 151) provided that the bankruptcy judges for each judicial district shall constitute a unit of the district court to be known as the bankruptcy court.[16]

The U.S. courts of appeals (formerly called circuit courts of appeals) are appellate courts for the 11 judicial circuits. Their major purpose is to review cases tried in U.S. district courts within their respective circuits, but they also possess jurisdiction to review orders of designated administrative agencies and to issue original writs in appropriate cases. The courts of appeals are intermediate appellate courts created to relieve the U.S. Supreme Court of having to consider all appeals in cases originally decided by the federal trial courts.

The Supreme Court is the only federal court created directly by the U.S. Constitution. Eight associate justices and one chief justice sit on the Supreme

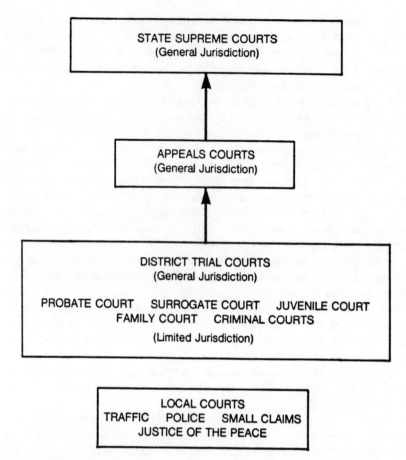

Figure 1-1 State Judicial Court System

Court. The Court has limited original jurisdiction over the lower federal courts and the highest state courts. In a few situations an appeal will go directly from a federal or state court to the Supreme Court, but in most cases today review must be sought through the discretionary *writ of certiorari*, an appeal petition. In addition to the aforementioned courts, there are special federal courts that have jurisdiction over particular subject matters. The U.S. Court of Claims has jurisdiction over certain claims against the government. The U.S. Court of Customs and Patent Appeals has appellate jurisdiction over certain customs and patent matters. The U.S. Customs Court reviews certain administrative decisions by customs officials. Also, there are a U.S. Tax Court and a U.S. Court of Military Appeals. (Figure 1-2 illustrates the federal court system.)

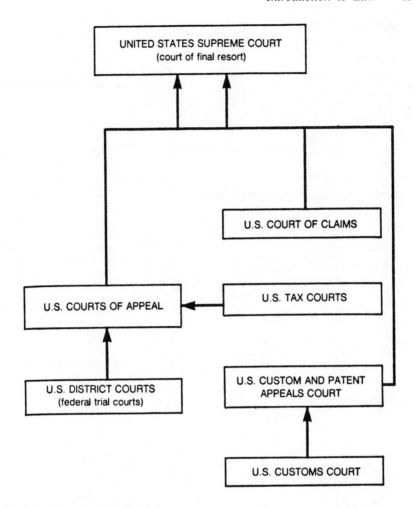

Figure 1-2 Federal Judicial Court System

NOTES

1. A.K.R. KIRALFY, POTTER'S HISTORICAL INTRODUCTION TO ENGLISH LAW, 9 (1962).

2. G.W. KEETON, ENGLISH LAW, 70 (1974).

3. KIRALFY, *supra* note 1, at 9–10.

4. KEETON, *supra* note 2, at 70.

5. U.S. DEPARTMENT OF HEALTH AND HUMAN SERVICES, TASK FORCE ON MEDICAL LIABILITY AND MALPRACTICE 3 (1987).

6. OFFICE OF THE FEDERAL REGISTER, NATIONAL ARCHIVES AND RECORDS ADMINISTRATION, THE UNITED STATES GOVERNMENT MANUAL 1988/89, at 400 (1988).

7. *Id.* at 307–08.

8. *Id.* at 293–94.

9. *Id.* at 296.

10. United States Food and Drug Administration, We Want You to Know about Today's FDA (1974).

11. The United States Government Manual, at 309–310.

12. *Id.* at 400.

13. *Id.* at 631.

14. Hospital Association of New York State, Report of the Task Force on Regulation 44 (1978).

15. U.S. Const. art. III, § 1.

16. The United States Government Manual, at 71–72.

Chapter 2

Tort Law

A tort is a civil wrong, other than a breach of contract, committed against a person or property (real or personal) for which a court provides a remedy in the form of an action for damages. The basic purposes of tort law are to keep peace between individuals by supplying a substitute for vengeance, to find fault for wrongdoing, to deter the wrongdoer (tort-feasor) from committing future torts by assessing damages to be paid to the victim(s) of the wrongdoing, and to encourage adherence to the law.

Since an adverse medical outcome generally results in some financial damage, the effect of finding fault by the court is to determine who shall bear the cost of an unfavorable outcome—the provider or the recipient of health care. To avoid cost, the plaintiff must prove the negligence of the provider. Conversely, the provider fights to avoid fault determination. Underlying this adversary proceeding is the assumption that if the provider is forced to bear the cost, it will discourage further acts of negligence by the provider and by other similarly situated providers of health care.

There are three basic categories of torts: negligent torts, intentional torts, and torts in which liability is assessed irrespective of fault (e.g., against manufacturers of defective products). Although most incidents that raise issues of liability concern harm allegedly resulting from negligence, a person may also be liable for intentional wrongs. Intentional tortious conduct (conduct implying civil wrong) that may arise in the context of patient care includes assault, battery, false imprisonment, invasion of privacy, and infliction of mental distress. Liability, irrespective of fault, may be imposed in certain situations where the activity, regardless of intentions or negligence, is so dangerous to others that public policy demands absolute responsibility on the part of the tort-feasor.

There are two major differences between intentional and negligent wrongs. The first is intent, which is present in intentional, but not in negligent wrongs. For a tort to be considered intentional, not only must the act be intentionally committed, but also the wrongdoer must realize to a substantial certainty that harm would result.

The second difference is less obvious. An intentional wrong always involves a willful act that violates another's interests; a negligent wrong may not involve committing an act at all. In certain situations involving negligence, a person may be held liable for not acting in the way that a reasonably prudent person would have acted.

NEGLIGENCE

Negligence is the omission or commission of an act that a reasonably prudent person would or would not do under given circumstances. It is a form of conduct caused by heedlessness or carelessness that constitutes a departure from the standard of care generally imposed on reasonable members of society. Negligence can occur where one has considered the consequences of an act and has exercised the best possible judgment, where one fails to guard against a risk that should be appreciated, or where one engages in certain behavior expected to involve unreasonable danger to others.

Forms of Negligence

The basic forms of negligence are the following:

- *Malfeasance*—the execution of an unlawful or improper act.
- *Misfeasance*—the improper performance of an act, resulting in injury to another.
- *Nonfeasance*—the failure to act, when there is a duty to act, as a reasonably prudent person would in similar circumstances.
- *Malpractice*—the negligence or carelessness of a professional person, such as a nurse, pharmacist, physician, accountant, etc.
- *Criminal negligence*—the reckless disregard for the safety of another. It is the willful indifference to an injury that could follow an act.

Degrees of Negligence

There are basically two degrees of negligence.

1. *Ordinary negligence*—the failure to do what a reasonably prudent person would do or the doing of that which a reasonably prudent person would not do under the circumstances of the act or omission in question.
2. *Gross negligence*—the intentional or wanton omission of care that would be proper to provide or the doing of that which would be improper to do.

Elements of Negligence

The four elements that must be present in order for a plaintiff to recover damages due to negligence are a duty to care, breach of that duty, actual injury, and proximate cause. Every element must be present in order for a plaintiff to recover for damages suffered as a result of a negligent act.

1. Duty To Use Due Care

The duty to use due care is a legal obligation which requires the actor to conform to a specific standard of care to protect others. This duty may arise from a special relationship such as that between a nurse and a patient or between a physician and a patient. The existence of this relationship implies that a nurse/patient or physician/patient relationship was in effect at the time an alleged injury occurred. Such a relationship can arise from a simple telephone conversation.

The plaintiff in *O'Neill v. Montefiore Hospital*, 11 A.D.2d 132, 202 N.Y.S.2d, 436 (1960), sought recovery against the hospital for failure to render necessary emergency treatment and a physician for his failure and refusal to treat her spouse. The deceased, Mr. O'Neill, who was experiencing pains in his chest and arms, had walked with his wife to the hospital at 5 A.M. He claimed that he was a member of the Hospital Insurance Plan (HIP). The emergency room nurse stated that the hospital had no connection with HIP and did not take care of HIP patients. After reflecting a few moments, the nurse indicated that she would try to get Mr. O'Neill a HIP doctor. The nurse called Dr. Graig, a HIP physician, and explained the patient's symptoms. She then handed the phone to Mr. O'Neill, who said, "Well, I could be dead by 8 o'clock." He concluded his phone conversation and spoke to the nurse, indicating that he had been told to go home and come back when HIP was open. Mrs. O'Neill asked that her husband be seen by a physician. The nurse again requested that they return at 8 o'clock. Mr. O'Neill again commented that he could be dead by 8 o'clock. He then left with his wife to return home, pausing occasionally to catch his breath. Upon arriving at home, Mr. O'Neill began to undress with the assistance of his wife, and he suddenly fell to the floor and died. Dr. Graig claimed that he offered to come to the emergency room, but that Mr. O'Neill said he would wait and see another HIP physician at 8 o'clock that morning. The supreme court, Bronx County, entered a judgment dismissing the complaint, and the plaintiff appealed. The supreme court, appellate division, held that a physician who undertakes to examine or treat a patient and then abandons him may be held liable for malpractice. The proof of the record in this case indicated that the physician undertook to diagnose the ailments of the deceased, by telephone, thus establishing at least the first element of negligence—duty of care. The finding of the trial court was reversed, and a new trial was ordered.

The surviving parents in *Hastings v. Baton Rouge Hospital*, 498 So. 2d 713 (La. Ct. App. 1986), brought a medical malpractice action against the hospital; the emergency room physician, Dr. Gerdes; and the thoracic surgeon on call, Dr.

McCool, for the wrongful death of their 19-year-old son who had been brought to the emergency room at 11:56 P.M. as a result of two stab wounds and weak vital signs. Dr. Gerdes decided that a thoracotomy had to be performed. He was not qualified to perform the surgery and called Dr. McCool, who was on call that evening for thoracic surgery. Dr. Gerdes described the patient's condition, indicating that he had been stabbed in one of his major blood vessels. At trial Dr. McCool claimed that he did not recall Dr. Gerdes saying that a major blood vessel could be involved. Dr. McCool asked Dr. Gerdes to transfer the patient to the Earl K. Long Hospital. Dr. Gerdes said, "I can't transfer this patient." Dr. McCool replied, "No. Transfer him." Nurse Kelly was not comfortable with the decision to transfer the patient and offered to accompany him in the ambulance. Dr. Gerdes re-examined the patient, who exhibited marginal vital signs, was restless, and was draining blood from his chest. The ambulance service was called at 1:03 A.M., and by 1:30 A.M. the patient had been placed in the ambulance for transfer. The patient began to fight wildly, the chest tube came out, and the bleeding increased. The patient virtually bled to death. An attempt to revive him from a cardiac arrest was futile, and the patient expired after having been moved back to the emergency room. The duty of care in this case cannot be reasonably disputed. Louisiana statute imposes a duty on hospitals licensed in Louisiana to make emergency services available to all persons residing in the state regardless of insurance coverage or economic status. The hospital's own bylaws provided that no patient should be transferred without due consideration for his condition and the facilities existing for his care. The Nineteenth Judicial District Court directed a verdict for the defendants, and the plaintiffs appealed. The court of appeals affirmed the district court's decision. On further appeal, the supreme court held that the evidence presented jury questions as to whether the defendants were negligent in their treatment of the victim. The findings of the lower courts were reversed, and the case was remanded for trial.

Standard of Care. The standard of care describes what conduct is expected of an individual in a given situation. It is determined by what a reasonably prudent person would do if acting under similar circumstances. A jury makes this determination if there is no prevailing statute. The "reasonably prudent person" concept describes a nonexistent, hypothetical person who is set up as the community ideal of what would be considered reasonable behavior. It is a measuring stick representing the conduct of the average person, in the community, under the circumstances facing the defendant at the time of the alleged negligence. The reasonableness of conduct is judged in light of the circumstances apparent at the time of injury and by reference to various characteristics of the actor, such as age, sex, physical condition, education, knowledge, training, mental capacity, etc. The actual performance of an individual in a given situation will be measured against what a reasonably prudent person would or would not have done. Deviation from the standard of care will constitute negligence if there is a resulting injury.

The standard of care required of physicians and surgeons was established for the first time in Michigan by statute.[1] The Michigan medical malpractice law holds general practitioners accountable for medical treatment that meets the recognized standard of care in the community in which they practice. In effect, the law also holds medical specialists accountable to the recognized standard of care within their specialty. Generally most states hold professionals and people with special skills, such as physicians, nurses, and dentists, to a standard of care that is reasonable in light of their special abilities and knowledge.

In determining what the reasonably prudent health professional should do, courts may utilize the services of an expert witness to testify regarding the professional standard of care required in the same or similar communities. This testimony is necessary because the jury is not trained or qualified to determine what the reasonably prudent professional's standard of care would be under similar circumstances. Essentially, the expert testifies to aid the judge and the jury by providing a measure for properly assessing the actual conduct required of the professional.

Because of improvements in communications, literature, and consulting, the community standard is merely one factor to be considered when applying the general professional standard. Thus, courts have moved away from reliance on the community standard of care and have applied what has been referred to as a national or ''industry'' standard. This trend has developed as a result of the view that the standard of care should not vary according to the locale where an individual receives care. The conduct of health professionals and hospitals will be increasingly compared with what is considered reasonable on a national scale in view of current professional practice.

The courts hold hospitals as well as individuals to specified standards of care. For example, in *Dickinson v. Mailliard,* 175 N.W.2d 588 (Iowa 1970), the court stated:

> Hospitals must now be licensed and accredited. They are subject to statutory regulation. In order to obtain approval they must meet certain standard requirements. . . . It is no longer justifiable, if indeed it ever was, to limit a hospital's liability to that degree of care which is customarily practiced in its own community. . . . [M]any communities have only one hospital. Adherence to such a rule, then, means the hospital whose conduct is assailed, is to be measured only by standards which it has set for itself.

Id. at 596.

It would be unreasonable for any one hospital and/or health professional to set the standard simply because there is no local basis for comparison.

The Court of Appeals of Maryland, in *Shilkret v. Annapolis Emergency Hospital Association,* 349 A.2d 245 (1975), stated:

[A] hospital is required to use that degree of care and skill which is expected of a reasonably competent hospital in the same or similar circumstances. As in cases brought against physicians, advances in the profession, availability of special facilities and specialists, together with all other relevant considerations, are to be taken into account. *Id.* at 245.

The parents in *Wickliffe v. Sunrise Hospital, Inc.,* 706 P.2d 1383 (Nev. 1985), sued the hospital for the wrongful death of their teenage daughter who suffered respiratory arrest while recovering from surgery. The Supreme Court of Nevada held that the level of care to which the hospital must conform is a nationwide standard. The hospital's level of care is no longer subject to narrow geographic limitations under the so-called locality rule; rather, the hospital must meet a nationwide standard.

Further, the Georgia Court of Appeals in *Hodges v. Effingham,* 182 Ga. App. 173, 355 S.E.2d 104 (1987), held that application of the locality rule, rather than a general standard of nursing care, was erroneous in an action against the hospital. The alleged failure of nurses to take an accurate medical history of the patient's serious condition and convey the information to the physician drew into question the professional judgment of the nurses, not the hospital's services or facilities. The jury should have been instructed as to the general standard of nursing required.

When injury has been suffered by a patient, the patient must show that the defendant failed to meet the prevailing standard of care in order for the defendant to be held liable for negligence. The fact that an injury is suffered, without proof that the defendant deviated from the practice of competent members of his or her profession, is not sufficient for imposing liability.

The ever-evolving advances in medicine, malpractice cases, and the broadening scope of governmental regulations continue to raise the standard of care required of health professionals and hospitals. Evidence of the standard of care applicable to professional activities may be found in a variety of documents, such as regulations of governmental agencies and standards established by such private organizations as the Joint Commission on Accreditation of Healthcare Organizations. The personnel of a hospital, subject to such regulations or standards, are responsible for meeting the standards of care prescribed. A professional's failure to do so provides a basis for finding the professional and the hospital liable for negligence.

In order for liability to be established, based on a defendant's failure to follow the standard of care outlined by statute, the following elements must be present: The defendant must have been within the specified class of persons outlined in the statute, the plaintiff must have been injured in a way that the statute was designed to prevent, and the plaintiff must show that the injury would not have occurred if the statute had not been violated.

Foreseeability. If the action of a defendant meets or surpasses the recognized standard of care and injury results, there has been no negligence or carelessness—just an unavoidable accident. There is no expectation that the actor can guard against events that cannot reasonably be foreseen or that are so unlikely to occur that they would be disregarded. If a defendant's actions fail to meet the standard, then there has been negligence, and the jury must make two determinations. First, was it foreseeable that harm would occur from the failure to meet the standard of care? Second, was the carelessness or negligence the proximate or immediate cause of the harm or injury to the plaintiff?

2. Breach of Duty

Breach of duty is the failure to conform to or the departure from a required duty of care owed to the patient. Evidence of a breach of duty can be offered through direct testimony, circumstantial evidence, *res ipsa loquitur*, etc. The test of breach of duty relies on the reasonably prudent person doctrine: Did the defendant act reasonably under the circumstances? A review of the *Hastings* case discussed above indicates a severe breach of duty where hospital regulations provide that when a physician cannot be reached or refuses a call, the chief of service is to be notified so that another physician can be obtained. This was not done. It is not necessary to prove that a patient would survive if proper treatment had been administered, but only that the patient would have had a chance of survival. As a result of Dr. Gerdes' failure to obtain another physician and Dr. McCool's failure to perform the necessary surgery, the patient had no chance of survival.

3. Injury/Actual Damages

A defendant may be negligent and still not incur liability if no injury or actual damages result to the plaintiff. The term *injury* includes more than physical harm. It may include mental anguish and other invasions of a plaintiff's rights and privileges.

4. Proximate Cause/Causation

There must be a reasonable, close, and causal relationship between the defendant's negligent conduct and the resulting damages suffered by the plaintiff. The breach of duty must be the *proximate cause* of the resulting injury. The mere departure from a proper and recognized procedure is not sufficient to enable a patient to recover damages unless the plaintiff can show that the departure was unreasonable and the proximate cause of the patient's injuries. Causation in the *Hastings* case was well established. In the ordinary course of events, a man does not bleed to death in a hospital emergency room over a two-and-one-half-hour period without some surgical intervention to save his life.

Causation was adequately established in *Northern Trust Co. v. Louis A. Weiss Memorial Hospital,* 493 N.E.2d 6 (Ill. App. Ct. 1986), by expert testimony that

- forceful or repeated vomiting
- a fit or convulsion (jerking or spells)
- clumsy walking
- bad headache
- one pupil larger than the other

The patient was taken back to his father's apartment at about 7:00 P.M. A psychiatrist friend dropped by at approximately 8:45 P.M. He examined the patient and noted that one pupil was larger than the other. Since the pediatrician could not be reached, the patient was taken back to the emergency room. A physician on duty noted an epidural hematoma during his examination and ordered that a neurosurgeon be called.

Today, the patient can move only his eyes and neck. A lawsuit against Mount Zion and the pediatrician amounting to $5 million was instituted. The city of San Rafael and the public school district were also included in the lawsuit as defendants. Expert testimony by two neurosurgeons during the trial indicated that the patient's chances of recovery would have been very good if he had been admitted promptly. This testimony placed the proximate cause of the injury with the hospital. The final judgment was $4 million against the medical defendants, $2.5 million for compensatory damages, and another $1.5 million for pain and suffering. The pediatrician's insurance carrier paid $100,000, and the hospital's insurance carrier paid the balance. The school district was liable for $25,000.

In summary, a physician who fails to make a thorough examination and order appropriate tests and who then makes an erroneous diagnosis leading to the premature dismissal of a case can be liable for negligence.

INTENTIONAL TORTS

Assault and Battery

An assault is the deliberate threat, coupled with the apparent present ability, to do physical harm to another. No actual contact is necessary. It is the deliberate threat and/or attempt to injure another or the attempt by one to make bodily contact with another without his or her consent. An act that otherwise would be considered to be an assault may be permissible if proper consent has been given (e.g., for invasion of the body through surgery) or if it is in defense of oneself or of a third party. The injured party must be aware of the defendant's act at the time it is committed.

A battery is an unconsented-to, intentional touching of another's person, in a socially impermissible manner, without that person's consent. The receiver of the battery does not have to be aware that a battery has been committed (e.g., a patient who is unconscious and has surgery performed on him/her without his/her consent, either expressed or implied, is the object of a battery). The law provides a remedy to the individual if consent to a touching has not been obtained or if the act goes beyond the consent given. Therefore, the injured person may initiate a lawsuit against the wrongdoer for damages suffered. Punitive damages in *Peete v. Blackwell*, 504 So. 2d 22 (Ala. 1986), in the amount of $10,000 were awarded to a nurse in her action against a physician for assault and battery. Evidence showed that the nurse, while assisting the physician, was struck on the arm and cursed at by the physician when ordering her to turn on the suction. Although there were no injuries, $1 in compensatory damages and $10,000 in punitive damages were awarded by the jury.

In the health context, the principle of law concerning battery and the requirement of consent to medical and surgical procedures is critically important. Liability of hospitals and health care professionals for acts of battery is most common in situations involving lack of or improper patient consent to medical and surgical procedures. It is inevitable that a patient in a hospital will be touched by many persons for many reasons. Procedures ranging from bathing to surgery involve some touching of a patient. Therefore, medical and surgical procedures must be authorized by the patient. If they are not authorized, the person performing the procedure could be subject to an action for battery.

It is of no legal importance that a procedure constituting a battery has improved a patient's health. If the patient did not consent to the touching, the patient may be entitled to such damages as can be proven to have resulted from commission of the battery. The Supreme Court of New Jersey in *Perna v. Pirozzi*, 457 A.2d 431 (N.J. 1983), held that a patient who consents to surgery by one surgeon, but who is actually operated on by another has an action for medical malpractice or battery. Proof of unauthorized invasion of the plaintiff's person, even if harmless, entitles him/her to nominal damages.

Not only must individual staff members be aware of assault and battery hazards for fellow employees, as well as themselves, but also they must be alert to potential problems between patients (e.g., problems caused by smoking, racial and/or religious bias, and emotional conflicts).

False Imprisonment

False imprisonment is the unlawful restraint of an individual's personal liberty or the unlawful restraining or confining of an individual. Actual physical force is not necessary to constitute false imprisonment. All that is necessary is that an individual who is physically "confined" to a given area experience a reasonable fear that force, which may be implied by words, threats, or gestures, will be used to detain the individual or to intimidate him or her into complying with orders.

In certain cases, preventing a patient from leaving the hospital may constitute false imprisonment. For example, detaining a patient until the bills are paid would qualify as false imprisonment. Protocols should be instituted for handling patients diagnosed as having contracted a highly contagious disease. Detaining such patients, without statutory protection, constitues false imprisonment. State health codes generally provide guidelines for caring for such patients. For example, Title 10, Part 2, Section 29, of the New York State Sanitary Code states, "Whenever a case of a highly communicable disease . . . comes to the attention of the city, county, or district health officer, he shall isolate such patients as in his judgment he deems necessary." In addition, statutes in many states allow mentally ill and intoxicated individuals to be detained by a hospital if they are found to be dangerous to themselves or others. Those who are mentally ill, however, can be restrained only to the degree necessary to prevent them from harming themselves or others.

The patient in *Davis v. Charter by the Sea, Inc.*, 358 S.E.2d 865 (Ga. Ct. App. 1987), was found not to be entitled to a directed verdict on a false imprisonment claim arising from her overnight, involuntary detention at a hospital. Evidence that the patient was highly intoxicated, confused, incoherent, and experiencing a low diastolic blood pressure raised a jury question as to the existence of a medical emergency that authorized her detention.

A patient's insistence on leaving should be noted on the medical record. The patient should also be informed of the possible harm in leaving against medical advice. If a patient ultimately decides to leave the hospital against medical advice, he or she should be requested to sign a discharge against advice and release form.

Excessive force used to restrain a patient may produce liability for both false imprisonment and battery. If a mentally ill patient cannot be released, procedures should be followed to provide commitment to an appropriate institution for the patient's care. In this situation, it is important to note that a patient does not actually have to be constrained to be falsely imprisoned. A threat of restraint which a patient may reasonably expect to be carried out may be enough to constitute false imprisonment. In order to recover for damages, a plaintiff must be aware of the confinement and have no reasonable means of escape. Availability of a reasonable means of escape may bar recovery. No actual damage need be shown in order for liability to be imposed.

Defamation of Character

Defamation of character is oral or written communication to someone other than the person defamed that tends to hold that person's reputation up to scorn and ridicule in the eyes of a substantial number of respectable people in the community. By tradition, libel results from the written word and slander from the spoken word. Libel can be presented in the form of signs, photographs, letters, etc. To be an actionable wrong, defamation must be communicated to a third person. Defamatory statements communicated only to the injured party are not grounds for an action.

No proof of special damage is needed in order for libel "on its face" to be actionable. Rather, in certain cases, a court will presume that the words caused injury to the person's reputation. With slander, on the other hand, special damages must be proved by the person bringing suit. There are four generally recognized exceptions where no proof of actual harm to reputation is required in order to recover damages: (1) accusing someone of a crime; (2) accusing someone of having a loathsome disease; (3) using words that affect a person's profession or business; and (4) calling a woman unchaste. Professionals are legally protected against libel when complying with a law that requires the reporting of venereal or other diseases, which could be considered loathsome.

There are few defamation of character lawsuits because of the difficulty in proving defamation, the small awards, and the high legal fees. The Georgia case of *Barry v. Baugh,* 111 Ga. App. 813, 143 S.E.2d 489 (1965), involved a nurse who brought a defamation action, charging that a physician had slandered her in the course of a consultation concerning the commitment of her husband to a mental institution. The nurse requested damages for mental pain, shock, fright, humiliation, and embarrassment. The nurse alleged that if the physician's statement were made known to the public, her job and reputation would be adversely affected. The court held that the physician's statement concerning the nurse did not constitute slander because the physician was not referring to the nurse in a professional capacity.

When any allegedly defamatory words refer to a person in a professional capacity, the professional need not show that the words caused damage. It is presumed that any slanderous reference to someone's professional capacity is damaging; the plaintiff therefore has no need to prove damages. In this case, however, since the court held that the physician's statement did not refer to the nurse in her professional capacity, the plaintiff had to demonstrate damages in order to recover. The plaintiff was unable to show damages.

Professionals who are called incompetent in front of others have a right to sue to defend their reputation. However, it is difficult to prove an individual comment injurious. If the person making an injurious comment cannot prove the comment is true, that person can be held liable for damages. Therefore, health professionals should not make disparaging remarks about other health professionals.

Essentially, there are two defenses to a defamation action: truth and privilege. When a person has said something that is damaging to another person's reputation, the person making the statement will not be liable for defamation if it can be shown that the statement was true. A privileged communication is one that might be defamatory under different circumstances, but is not because of a higher duty with which the person making the communication is charged. For example, many states have statutes providing immunity to doctors and hospitals in connection with peer review proceedings. The person making the communication must do so in good faith, on the proper occasion, in the proper manner, and to persons who have a legitimate reason to receive the information.

There are two types of privilege that may provide a defense to an action for defamation. The first, absolute privilege, attaches to statements made during judicial and legislative proceedings as well as to confidential communications between spouses. Qualified privilege, on the other hand, such as a statement made as a result of a legal or moral duty to speak in the interests of third persons, may provide a successful defense only when such statements are made in the absence of malice. If it can be shown that a statement was made as a result of some hatred, ill will, or spite on the part of the speaker, the law will not permit that speaker to hide behind the shield of privilege and avoid liability for defamation.

The defense of privilege is illustrated in the case of *Judge v. Rockford Memorial Hospital,* 17 Ill. App. 2d 365, 150 N.E.2d 202 (1958), where a nurse brought an action for libel based on a letter written to a nurses' professional registry by the director of nurses at the hospital where the nurse had been assigned by the registry. In the letter the director of nurses stated that the hospital did not wish to have the nurse's services available to them as a result of certain losses of narcotics during times when this particular nurse was on duty. The court refused the nurse recovery. Since the director of nurses had a legal duty to make the communication in the interests of society, the director's letter constituted a privileged communication. Therefore, the court held that the letter did not constitute libel because it was privileged.

A defendant nurse who was employed by a Veterans Administration hospital was directed by her superior to submit a Report of Contact concerning a disagreement with the plaintiff nurse who was also employed by the Veterans Administration hospital. The defendant nurse was found to have been acting within the parameter of her duties in submitting such a report. The court held that the report could not be the basis for a cause of action in libel. Statements made by a federal officer in the course of disciplinary proceedings, evaluations, complaints, and related investigations that the official was under a duty to complete are within the scope of the official's duties. Therefore, such statements cannot be the basis for a cause of action in libel. *Malone v. Longo,* 463 F. Supp. 139 (E.D. N.Y. 1979).

Public figures have more difficulty in pursuing defamation litigation than does the average individual. The chairman of a publicly owned and operated county hospital in *Drew v. KATV Television, Inc.,* 293 Ark. 555, 739 S.W.2d 680 (1987), brought a suit against a television station for defamation on two separate occasions. It had been reported during one news broadcast that the board chairman had been charged with a felony when in fact he had been charged with two misdemeanor counts of solicitation to tamper with evidence. These charges were dismissed at trial. The second news report implied that he was involved in a drug investigation being conducted at the hospital where he served as chairman of the board. The plaintiff occupied a position of considerable public responsibility, and he was considered a public figure for the purposes of the law of defamation. The circuit court dismissed the case on the defendant's motion for summary judgment, and the plaintiff appealed. The Supreme Court of Arkansas held that summary dismissal of the plaintiff's action against the television station was properly ordered by the trial court in the absence of any showing of malice in connection with the allegedly defamatory references to the plaintiff during the news broadcasts.

Fraud

Fraud is defined as willful and intentional misrepresentation that could cause harm or loss to a person or property. Intentional misrepresentation in many states gives rise to an action for deceit. Physicians who know they have no foundation for believing a statement to be true, and make it anyway, can be held liable for misrepresentation. For example, a physician who claims that a certain surgical operation will cure a patient's ailment, when the physician knows it is not so, would be considered misrepresentation.

Invasion of Privacy

Invasion of privacy is a wrong that invades the right of a person to personal privacy. Absolute privacy has to be tempered with reality in the medical or nursing care of any patient, and this fact is recognized by the courts. However, negligent disregard for patients' rights of privacy is intolerable and legally actionable, particularly when patients are unable to adequately protect themselves because of unconsciousness or immobility. Unfortunately, familiarity with the hospital environment tends to diminish the conscious concern that hospital personnel should have for the protection of the privacy of patients.

The right of privacy is recognized by the law as the right to be left alone—the right to be free from unwarranted publicity and exposure to public view, as well as the right to live one's life without having one's name, picture, or private affairs made public against one's will. Hospitals and health professionals may become liable for invasion of privacy if, for example, they divulge information from a patient's medical record to improper sources or if they commit unwarranted intrusions into a patient's personal affairs.

The information on a patient's chart is confidential and should not be disclosed without the patient's permission. Those who come into possession of the most intimate personal information about patients have both a legal and an ethical duty not to reveal confidential communications. The legal duty arises because the law recognizes a right to privacy. To protect this right, there is a corresponding duty to obey. The ethical duty is broader and applies at all times.

There are occasions when there is a legal obligation or duty to disclose information. The reporting of communicable diseases, gunshot wounds, child abuse, and other matters is required by law.

The liberty extended to the publication of personal matters, names, or photographs varies. Many public figures will not be heard to complain if their lives are given publicity, and ordinary citizens who voluntarily adopt a newsworthy course of conduct have no grounds for complaint if the activity is reported along with their names and pictures. Generally, the subject of a newsworthy occurrence cannot complain if his or her identity is exposed and exploited by unwarranted publication.

The news media should be accommodated within the limitations placed on such communications by the administration of the hospital and applicable statutes and/or regulations pertaining to the release of information. In any event, a patient's right of privacy must be protected. Public relations officers and other health care professionals should restrict their interviews and releases to avoid any injury to the reputation of a patient.

The press should not be given detailed statements about the physical condition of a patient. Health care professionals are in no position to make any comments concerning the occurrence that led to a patient's hospitalization. Comments concerning a patient's physical condition should come from the physician. Since such matters do involve protected information, disclosure should be with the patient's permission.

Infliction of Mental Distress

The willful infliction of mental distress is a civil wrong for which a tort-feasor can be held liable for damages. It includes mental suffering resulting from painful emotions, such as grief, public humiliation, despair, shame, wounded pride, etc. Liability for the wrongful infliction of mental distress may be based on either intentional or negligent misconduct. The courts generally bar recovery for damages unless there is a physical injury. Recovery is permitted in those cases where it can be shown that there has been an intentional infliction of mental distress.

One circuit court found that the intentional infliction of emotional distress was committed by a physician and hospital through certain of its employees. The mother of a premature infant, who died shortly after birth, had gone to her physician for a six-week check-up. She noticed a report in her medical chart which stated that the child was past the fifth lunar month in development and that hospital rules and state law prohibited disposal of it as a surgical specimen. The mother had understood that the body had been disposed of by common traditions of human dignity. Upon questioning her physician, he requested that his nurse take her to the hospital. At the hospital, she was taken by a hospital employee to a freezer which was opened, and she was handed the jar containing her premature infant. The circuit court entered a judgment in favor of the plaintiffs, and the defendants appealed. The court of appeals, in *Johnson v. Women's Hospital,* 527 S.W.2d 133 (Tenn. Ct. App. 1975), held that the jury could properly find that the hospital agreed to properly handle the infant's body and failed to do so. The jury could properly find that the hospital's conduct in displaying the infant was outrageous. There was no proof that the physician or his nurse was guilty of outrageous conduct. The award of compensatory damages in the amount of $100,000 was not so excessive as to shock the conscience of the court.

An action was brought by a patient and his wife against a physician for the intentional infliction of emotional distress. The superior court entered summary judgment for the physician, and the plaintiff appealed. The defendant physician was covering for the attending doctor who was on vacation. The patient, Mr. Greer, was in the hospital and had not seen the covering physician for several days, so he called the physician's office to complain. The physician later entered the patient's room, in an agitated manner, and became verbally abusive in the presence of Mrs. Greer and a nurse. He said to the patient: "Let me tell you one damn thing, don't nobody call over to my office raising hell with my secretary . . . I don't have to be here every damn day checking on you because I check with physical therapy . . . I don't have to be your damn doctor." When the physician left the room, Mrs. Greer began to cry, and Mr. Greer experienced episodes of uncontrollable shaking for which he had psychiatric treatment. The Court of Appeals of Georgia held that the physician's abusive language willfully caused emotional upset and precluded summary judgment for the defendant. *Greer v. Medders,* 336 S.E.2d 329 (1985).

PRODUCTS LIABILITY

Products liability is the liability of a manufacturer, seller, or supplier of chattels to a buyer or other third party for injuries sustained due to a defect in a product. An injured party may proceed with a lawsuit against a seller, manufacturer, or supplier on three legal theories: negligence, breach of warranty (express or implied), and/or strict liability.

Negligence

Negligence, as applied to products liability, requires the plaintiff to establish duty, breach, injury, and causation. An action in *Airco, Inc. v. Simmons National Bank, Guardian, et al.,* 638 S.W.2d 660 (Ark. 1982), was brought against physician partnership that provided anesthesia services to the hospital and Airco, Inc., the manufacturer of an artificial breathing machine used in the administration of anesthesia. It was alleged that the patient suffered irreversible brain damage because of the negligent use of the equipment and its unsafe design. The machine had been marketed despite prior reports that there was a foreseeable danger of human error brought about by the presence of several identical black hoses and the necessity of connecting them correctly to three ports of identical size that had been placed too close together and lacked adequate labels and warnings. The jury awarded $1,070,000 in compensatory damages against the physician partnership and Airco, Inc. Punitive damages in the amount of $3 million were awarded against Airco, Inc. On appeal of the punitive damages award, the Supreme Court of Arkansas held that the evidence for punitive damages was sufficient for the jury. The manufacturer had acted in a persistent reckless disregard of the foreseeable dangers in the machine by continuing to sell it with the known hazardous design.

Negligence, as well as breach of warranty and strict liability, were not established in the well publicized case of the 1980s involving a woman who had died from the ingestion of Tylenol capsules tainted with potassium cyanide. The decedent's estate in *Elsroth v. Johnson & Johnson,* 700 F.Supp. 151 (S.D.N.Y. 1988), sued the manufacturer and the retail grocery store, which sold the over-the-counter drug. The defendants moved for a summary judgment. The United States District Court held that the retailer did not have a "duty" to protect the decedent from acts of tampering by an unknown third party. The manufacturer was not liable under an inadequate warning theory. Manufacturers are under a duty to warn of the dangers that may be associated with the normal and lawful use of their products They, however, need not warn that their products may be susceptible to criminal misuse.

The negligent use of a Bovie plate led to liability in *Monk v. Doctors Hospital,* 403 F.2d 580 (D.C. Cir. 1968). The patient was admitted to the hospital for abdominal surgery. Before surgery the patient asked the surgeon to also remove three moles from the right arm and one from the right leg. The surgeon instructed a hospital nurse to prepare a Bovie machine, but was not present while the machine was set up. The nurse placed the contact plate of the Bovie machine under the patient's right calf in a negligent manner, and the patient suffered burns. The patient introduced instruction manuals, issued by the manufacturer, supporting a claim that the plate was improperly placed. These manuals had been available to the hospital. The trial court directed a verdict in favor of the hospital and the doctor. The appellate court found that there was sufficient evidence from which the jury could conclude that the Bovie plate was applied in a negligent manner. There was also sufficient evidence, including the manufacturer's manual and expert testimony, from which the jury could find that the physician was independently negligent.

This case demonstrates the necessity for a hospital to require conformity to the safety standards provided by the manufacturers of hospital supplies and equipment. As evidenced in the above case, such failure can cause a hospital and its staff to be held liable for negligence. This case should also alert manufacturers of the necessity to provide appropriate safety instructions to the users of their products. It can be assumed that failure to provide such instructions could be considered negligence on the part of the supplier.

Breach of Warranty

To recover under a cause of action based on a breach of warranty theory, the plaintiff must first establish whether there was an express or implied warranty. An express warranty includes specific promises or affirmations made by the seller to the buyer, such as that expressed in *Crocker v. Winthrop Laboratories,* 514 S.W.2d 429 (Tex. 1974). The patient, Mr. Crocker, had been admitted to the hospital for a hernia operation. His physician prescribed both Demerol and Talwin for pain. Following discharge from the hospital, Mr. Crocker developed an addiction to Talwin and was able to obtain prescriptions from several physicians to support his habit. He was eventually admitted to the hospital for detoxification. After six days, Mr. Crocker walked out of the hospital and went home. He became agitated and abusive, threatening his wife, and she eventually called a physician at his request. The physician went to Mr. Crocker's home and gave him an injection of Demerol. Mr. Crocker retired to bed and expired. Action was brought against the drug company for the suffering and subsequent wrongful death which occurred as the proximate result of the decedent's addiction to Talwin. The district court rendered a judgment for the plaintiff, and the court of appeals reversed. Upon further appeal, the Supreme Court of Texas held that when a drug company positively and specifically represents its product to be free and safe from all dangers of addiction and when the treating physician relies on such representation, the drug company is liable when the representation proves to be false and injury results.

Implied warranties are in effect where the law implies that one exists "by operation of law as a matter of public policy for the protection of the public." *Jacob E. Decker & Sons v. Capps,* 139 Tex. 609, 164 S.W.2d 828 (1942). This case involved the question of the liability of a manufacturer of food products to the consumer for damages sustained by ingestion of contaminated sausage. One member of the family died, and others became seriously ill as a result of eating the contaminated food. The jury found that the sausage had been contaminated before it was packaged by the defendant and that it was unfit for human consumption. The Supreme Court of Texas decided that the defendant was liable for the injuries sustained by the consumers of the contaminated food under an implied warranty. Liability in such a case is based neither on negligence nor on a breach of the usual implied contractual warranty. It is based on the broad principle of the public policy to protect human health and life.

The patient in *Perlmutter v. Beth David Hospital,* 308 N.Y. 100, 123 N.E.2d 793 (1955), contracted serum hepatitis from a blood transfusion and relied on an implied sales warranty as the basis of her suit. The court denied recovery, pointing out that even though a separate charge of $60 was made for the blood, the charge was incidental to the primary contract with the hospital for services. Since there was no claim of negligence, the pronouncement of the court that blood provided by the hospital was a service, rather than a sale, barred recovery by the patient. The rationale of this case did not extend to relieve commercial blood banks from liability on the basis of strict liability warranty theories. Action could have been instituted against the hospital if it had been shown that the hospital was negligent in handling the blood.

Strict Liability

Strict liability refers to liability without fault. Neither care nor negligence nor ignorance will save the defendant from liability. Strict liability makes possible an award of damages without any proof of negligence on the part of the manufacturer. The plaintiff needs only to show that he/she suffered injury while using the manufacturer's product in the prescribed way.

The following elements must all be present in order for a plaintiff to proceed with a case on the basis of strict liability:

- The product must have been manufactured by the defendant.
- The product must have been defective at the time it left the hands of the manufacturer or seller. A defect in a product normally consists of
  —a manufacturing defect,
  —a design defect in the product, and/or
  —an absence or inadequacy of warnings for the use of the product.
- The plaintiff must have been injured by a specific product.
- The defective product must have been the proximate cause of injury to the plaintiff.

A blood bank in *Weber v. Charity Hospital of Louisiana at New Orleans*, 487 So. 2d 148 (La. Ct. App. 1986), was held strictly liable to a hospital patient who developed hepatitis from a transfusion of defective blood during surgery. Evidence established that the blood bank collected, processed, and sold the blood to the hospital. Although the hospital administered the blood, absent any negligence in its handling or administration it was not liable for the patient's injury. Many states have enacted statutes to exempt blood from the product category, and thus remove blood products from the theory of strict liability.

In *Mulligan v. Lederle Laboratories*, 786 F.2d 859 (8th Cir. 1986), the plaintiff, a medical laboratory technician, brought an action against the drug manufacturer as the result of the side effects of the drug Varidase. The plaintiff developed several chronic health problems including mouth sores, microscopic hematuria, and red cell cast, indicating kidney disease. The U.S. District Court for the Eastern District of Arkansas awarded $50,000 in compensatory damages and $100,000 in punitive damages for failure of the drug manufacturer to warn of the side effects of the drug Varidase. On appeal by the manufacturer, the court of appeals held that the products liability action was not barred by a three-year statute of limitations contained in an Arkansas products liability act and that the evidence was sufficient to award punitive damages. Evidence presented at trial indicated that a number of side effects were associated with the drug.

Strict liability may be imposed on the manufacturer of a device that causes injury to a plaintiff, even though he or she was not the purchaser of the device, if the product was defective and that defect was the actual and proximate cause of his or her injury or damages. A case in point is *Kimberly Gerringer v. Gordon A. Runnells,* (Cal., Sacramento City Super. Ct. Nov. 13, 1973), in which a seven-year-old child suffered permanent brain damage as a result of convulsions caused by the leaking of an intravascular dose of a local anesthetic, Xylocaine, beyond the cuff (a medical device, similar to a blood pressure cuff, used to control the flow of blood). This leaking was allegedly a hazard of the procedure about which the manufacturer failed to notify the medical public. Damages awarded against the manufacturer of the automatic cuff amounted to $30,000.

Liability may be also based on the concept of *res ipsa loquitur* ("the thing speaks for itself") by showing all of the following:

- The product did not perform in the way intended.
- The product was not tampered with by the buyer or third persons.
- The defect existed at the time it left the defendant manufacturer.

Products Liability Defenses

Defenses against recovery in a products liability case include contributory negligence (e.g., use of a product in a way that it was not intended to be used), assumption of the risk (e.g., voluntary exposure to such risks as radiation treatments, chemotherapy treatments, cigarette smoking, and alcoholic beverages), intervening cause (e.g., an IV solution contaminated by the negligence of the product user, rather than that of the manufacturer), and disclaimers (e.g., manufacturers' inserts and warnings regarding usage and contraindications of their products).

A products liability action was brought against a cigarette manufacturer by an individual suffering from severe peripheral vascular disease. It was alleged that the proximate cause of the disease was cigarette smoking. The claim stated that the warnings on the cigarette packages were inadequate and that the cigarettes were defective and unreasonably dangerous. The district court held that cigarettes could not be found to be unreasonably dangerous in light of the common knowledge of their characteristics. Tobacco has been smoked for over 400 years, and its characteristics have been fully explored. Knowledge that cigarette smoking is harmful to one's health is widespread and can be considered as a part of common knowledge. *Roysdon v. R.J. Reynolds Tobacco Co.,* 623 F. Supp. 1189 (D. Tenn. 1985).

Conclusion

Successful products liability cases tend to have a negative impact on the development and use of new drugs. In addition, manufacturers tend to remove older technologies from the marketplace in order to decrease their exposure to liability and potential financial risks.

On the positive side, the slipshod manufacture of products is discouraged. This is increasingly evident in the sale of food products where consumers are demanding full disclosure of the contents of packaged products.

NOTE

1. Hosp. Week, January 6, 1978, at 1.

Chapter 3

Hospital Liability

A hospital operates through a governing board in which its authority is vested. The existence of this authority creates certain duties and liabilities for governing boards and their individual members.

Although hospitals may operate as sole proprietorships or partnerships, most hospitals function as corporations. Thus, an important source of law applicable to hospital governing boards and to the duties and responsibilities of their members is found in state corporation laws. This chapter discusses some of the major responsibilities as well as legal risks facing hospitals and their boards.

AUTHORITY OF HOSPITAL CORPORATIONS

Hospital corporations—governmental, charitable, or proprietary—have certain powers expressly or implicitly granted to them by state statutes. Generally, the authority of a corporation is expressed in the law under which the corporation was chartered and in the corporation's articles of incorporation. Members of the board of directors of a hospital have both express and implied corporate authority.

Express Corporate Authority

A hospital corporation derives its authority to act from the laws of the state in which it is incorporated. Express corporate authority is derived from state statutes, corporate articles of incorporation, and public health laws as well as from other state laws and regulations. The articles of incorporation set forth the purpose(s) of the corporation's existence and the powers the corporation is authorized to exercise in order to carry out its purposes.

Implied Corporate Authority

Implied corporate authority arises from situations where such authority is required or suggested as a result of a need for corporate powers not specifically granted in the articles of incorporation. A board of directors, at its own discretion, may enact new bylaws, rules, and regulations; purchase or mortgage property; borrow money; purchase equipment; select personnel; etc. Generally, these powers are enumerated in the articles of incorporation and, in such cases, would be categorized as express rather than implied corporate authority.

Generally, implied corporate authority is the authority to perform any and all acts necessary to exercise a corporation's expressly conferred authority and to accomplish the purpose(s) for which it was created. Much of the litigation concerning excesses of corporate authority involve questions of whether a corporation has the implied authority, incidental to its express authority, to perform a questioned act.

A hospital was permitted to construct a medical office building on land that had been donated for maintaining and carrying on a general hospital even though its certificate of incorporation did not specifically authorize such an act. The court, in recognizing a trend to encourage charitable hospitals to provide private offices for rental to staff members, held that such an act was within the implied powers of the hospital and that such offices aid in the work of a general hospital even though it went beyond the hospital corporation's express powers. *Hungerford Hospital v. Mulvey*, 225 A.2d 495 (Conn. 1966).

Ultra Vires Acts

A board can be held liable for acting beyond its scope of authority expressed, for example, in its articles of incorporation or implied in law. Acts of this nature are referred to as *ultra vires acts*.

The court of appeals in *Queen of Angels Hospital v. Younger*, 66 Cal. App. 3d 359, 136 Cal. Rptr. 36 (1977), held that the primary purpose of the corporation was the operation of a hospital and that the corporation could not abandon its operation in favor of neighborhood clinics. The hospital's board intended to use a substantial portion of funds it received from leasing the hospital to establish and operate additional medical clinics. Services provided by the Franciscan Sisters, from the inception of the hospital, were considered donated with the exception of certain compensated services, and no future remuneration was expected. The sisters' mother house had requested funds for a retirement plan. The court of appeals held that the retirement plan was not a proper exercise of either sound business judgment or the fiduciary duties of the Queen of Angels Hospital board. It is clear in this case that a board is acting beyond its scope of authority if it diverts funds to support activities not provided for in the hospital's articles of incorporation.

Members of a hospital's governing board, as well as corporate officers, may in certain circumstances be individually responsible for ultra vires acts. This might be true, for example, if a member of a governing board or corporate officer exceeded the powers of the corporation for individual benefit.

THE *DARLING* CASE

The benchmark case in the health care field that has had a major impact on the liability of hospitals and physicians cocurred in 1965 when the U.S. Supreme Court denied review of the Illinois case of *Darling v. Charleston Community Memorial Hospital*, 33 Ill. 2d 326, 211 N.E.2d 253 (1965), *cert. denied*, 383 U.S. 946 (1966).

This case involved an 18-year-old college football player who was preparing for a career as a teacher and coach. The patient, a defensive halfback for his college football team, was injured during a play. He was rushed to the emergency room of a small, accredited community hospital where the only physician on emergency room duty that day was a general practitioner who had not treated a major leg fracture for three years.

The physician examined the patient and ordered an x-ray that revealed that the tibia and the fibula of the right leg had been fractured. The physician reduced the fracture and applied a plaster cast from a point three or four inches below the groin to the toes. Shortly after the cast had been applied, the patient began to complain continually of pain. The physician split the cast and continued to visit the patient frequently while he remained in the hospital. He did not call in any specialist for consultation because he did not think it was necessary.

After two weeks, the student was transferred to a larger hospital and placed under the care of an orthopedic surgeon. The specialist found a considerable amount of dead tissue in the fractured leg. During a period of two months he removed increasing amounts of tissue in a futile attempt to save the leg until it became necessary to amputate the leg eight inches below the knee. Darling's father did not agree to a settlement and filed suit against the physician and the hospital. Although the physician settled out of court for $40,000, the case continued against the hospital.

The documentary evidence that was relied on to establish the standard of care included (1) the Rules and Regulations of the Illinois Department of Public Health under the Hospital Licensing Act; (2) the Standards for Hospital Accreditation of the Joint Commission on Accreditation of Hospitals; and (3) the Bylaws, Rules and Regulations of Charleston Hospital. These documents were admitted into evidence without objection. No specific evidence was offered that the hospital had failed to conform to the usual and customary practices of hospitals in the community.

The trial court instructed the jury to consider those documents, along with all other evidence, in determining the hospital's liability. Under the circumstances in which the case reached the Illinois Supreme Court, it was held that the verdict against the hospital should be sustained if the evidence supported the verdict on any one or more of the 20 allegations of negligence. The two allegations specified asserted that the hospital was negligent in its failure to provide a sufficient number of trained nurses for bedside care of all patients at all times—in this case, capable of recognizing the progressive gangrenous condition of the plaintiff's right leg— and in the failure of its nurses to bring the condition to the attention of the hospital administration and staff so that adequate consultation could be secured and the condition rectified.

Although these generalities provided the jury with no practical guidance for determining what constitutes reasonable care, they were considered relevant to aid the jury in deciding what was feasible and what the hospital knew or should have known concerning hospital responsibilities for the proper care of a patient. There was no expert testimony characterizing when the professional care rendered by the attending physician should have been reviewed, who should have reviewed it, or whether the case required consultation.

Evidence relating to the hospital's alleged failure to require proper nursing care and consultation or examination by specialists was found to be sufficient to support a verdict for the patient. Judgment was eventually returned against the hospital in the amount of $100,000.

The Illinois Supreme Court held that the hospital could not limit its liability as a charitable corporation to the amount of its liability insurance. "We agree that the doctrine of charitable immunity can no longer stand . . . a doctrine which limits the liability of charitable corporations to the amount of liability insurance that they see fit to carry permits them to determine whether or not they will be liable for their torts and the amount of that liability, if any." 211 N.E.2d at 260. In effect, the hospital was liable as a corporate entity for the negligent acts of its employees and physicians.

CORPORATE NEGLIGENCE

Corporate negligence occurs when a hospital fails to perform those duties it owes directly to a patient. If such a duty is breached and a patient is injured as a result of that breach, the institution can be held culpable under the theory of corporate negligence. The court of appeals in *Elam v. College Park Hospital*, 183 Cal. Rptr. 156 (Ct. App. 1982), held that a hospital is liable to a patient under the doctrine of corporate negligence for the negligent conduct of independent physicians and surgeons who are neither employees nor agents of the hospital. The hospital generally owes a duty to ensure the competency of its medical staff and to evaluate the quality of medical treatment rendered on its premises.

Traditionally, hospitals were institutions that provided the tools and a place where physicians could practice their trade. Hospitals are no longer solely responsible for providing room and board, but have a duty and responsibility to properly select and monitor physicians. The Supreme Court of Arizona in *Fridena v. Evans*, 127 Ariz. 516, 622 P.2d 463 (1980), affirmed that the hospital could be held liable for the negligent supervision of a physician where it has actual or constructive knowledge of the procedures carried on within the hospital. The patient in this case was involved in a motorcycle-automobile accident when she was 15 years old. She suffered a serious injury to her right leg, which required surgery. Following surgery by Dr. Fridena, it was noted that the patient's right leg was 1½ inches shorter than her left leg. The surgeon later attempted to lengthen the leg, which resulted in its being three inches shorter than before. The second operation gave rise to the malpractice suit, resulting in a $300,000 jury award to the patient.

A hospital cannot be held liable under the doctrine of corporate negligence for granting privileges to a nonemployee doctor who commits malpractice while in his or her private office off hospital premises. A hospital's independent duty to select and maintain a competent medical staff does not require a hospital, in order to fulfill its duty of reasonable care, to supervise a physician's office practice. *Pedroza v. Bryant*, 101 Wash. 2d 226, 677 P.2d 166 (1984).

A hospital is responsible for failing to meet the standard of care required within the hospital. An action was brought against Morton Canton (who was masquerading as a physician, Dr. LaBella), a hospital, and others in *Insinga v. LaBella*, 543 So. 2d 209 (Fla. 1989), for the wrongful death of a 68-year-old woman Canton had admitted. The patient died while she was a patient in the hospital. Canton was found to be a fugitive from justice in Canada where he was under indictment for the manufacture and sale of illegal drugs. He fraudulently obtained a medical license from the state of Florida and staff privileges at the hospital by using the name of Dr. LaBella, a deceased Italian physician. Canton was extradited to Canada without being served process. The U.S. District Court for the Southern District of Florida directed a verdict in favor of the hospital. On appeal, the U.S. Court of Appeals for the Eleventh Circuit certified a question to the Florida Supreme Court, asking whether Florida law recognizes the corporate negligence doctrine and whether it would apply under the facts of this case. The Florida Supreme Court held that the corporate negligence doctrine imposes on hospitals an implied duty to patients to select and retain competent physicians who, although they are independent practitioners, would be providing in-hospital care to their patients through their hospital staff privileges. Hospitals are in the best position to protect their patients and consequently have an independent duty to select and retain competent independent physicians seeking staff privileges.

An officer or a director of a corporation is not, merely as a result of his or her position, personally liable for the torts of corporate employees. To incur liability, the director or the officer must ordinarily be shown to have in some way authorized, directed, or participated in a tortious act. The administrator of the estate of the deceased in *Hunt v. Rabon*, 272 S.E. 2d 643 (S.C. 1980), brought a malpractice action against hospital trustees and others for the wrongful death of the deceased during an operation at the hospital. A contractor had incorrectly crossed the oxygen and nitrous oxide lines of a newly installed medical gas system leading to the operating room. The trustees demurred to the complaint on the grounds that it failed to present facts sufficient for an action against them individually as trustees. The lower court sustained the demurrer, and the plaintiff appealed. On appeal, the Supreme Court of South Carolina held that the allegations presented were insufficient to hold the trustees liable for the wrongs alleged.

DUTY TO SUPERVISE AND MANAGE

The duty to supervise and manage is applicable to the trustees of a hospital as it is to the managers of any other business corporation. In both instances there is a duty to act as a reasonably prudent person would act under similar circumstances. The hospital board must act prudently in administering the affairs of the hospital and exercise its powers in good faith.

The basic management functions of the governing board include

- selection of corporate officers and agents
- general control over the compensation of such agents
- delegation of authority to the CEO/administrator and the administrator's subordinates for administrative actions
- selection and monitoring of the medical staff members and the delineation of clinical privileges
- establishment of institutional goals, policies, and procedures
- supervision and vigilance over the welfare and assets of the corporation

Specific management duties peculiar to hospitals include (1) determining the policies of the hospital in connection with community health needs, (2) maintaining proper professional standards in the hospital, (3) assuming a general responsibility for adequate patient care throughout the institution, and (4) providing adequate financing of patient care and assuming businesslike control of expenditures.

MEDICAL STAFF

Granting of Medical Staff Privileges and Disciplining

Appointment and the granting of medical staff privileges should be given only after the appropriate committees of the hospital's medical staff have made an effective and thorough investigation of the applicant. The medical staff is responsible to the board of managers for the quality of care rendered by members of the medical staff. The delineation of privileges should be hospital specific, based on appropriate predetermined criteria that adhere to a national standard.

Most state laws, as well as the standards set forth by the Joint Commission on Accreditation of Healthcare Organizations, clearly state that the governing board of a hospital is ultimately responsible for the selection of medical staff members and the delineation of clinical privileges. Hospital trustees have a duty and obligation to protect patients from physicians they know, or should have known, were unqualified to practice medicine at their hospitals.

The duty to select members of the medical staff is legally vested in the governing board as the body charged with managing the hospital and maintaining a satisfactory standard of patient care. While cognizant of the importance of hospital staff membership to physicians, the governing board must meet its obligation to maintain standards of good medical practice in dealing with matters of staff appointment, credentialing, and the disciplining of physicians for such things as disruptive behavior, incompetence, psychological problems, criminal actions, and abuse of alcohol and/or drugs.

Credentialing

An action was brought against a hospital in *Rule v. Lutheran Hospitals & Homes Society of America*, 835 F.2d 1250 (8th Cir. 1987), for birth injuries sustained during an infant's breech delivery. The action was based on allegations that the hospital had negligently failed to investigate the qualifications of the attending physician before granting him privileges. The jury's verdict of $650,000 was supported by evidence that the hospital administrator failed to check with other hospitals where the physician had practiced. The physician's privileges at one hospital had been limited in that breech deliveries had to be performed under supervision. A finding of causation likewise was permissible on the basis of evidence that there was sufficient time to summon a qualified physician once discovering that the infant was in a breech position.

The surgeon in *Purcell & Tucson General Hospital v. Zimbelman*, 500 P.2d 335 (Ariz. Ct. App. 1972), performed inappropriate surgery because of his misdiagnosis of the patient's ailment. Prior malpractice suits against the surgeon revealed that the hospital had reason to know or should have known that the surgeon apparently lacked the skill to treat the patient's condition. The court held that the hospital had a clear duty to select competent physicians; to regulate the privileges granted to staff physicians; to ensure that privileges are conferred only for those procedures for which the physician is trained and qualified; and to restrict, suspend, or require supervision when a physician has demonstrated an inability to handle a certain type of problem. The hospital had assumed the duty of supervising the competence of its physicians. The Department of Surgery was acting for and on behalf of the hospital in fulfilling this duty. If the department was negligent in not taking action against the surgeon or recommending to the board of trustees that action be taken, then the hospital would be negligent. The court noted that it is reasonable to conclude that had the hospital taken some action against the surgeon, the patient would not have been injured.

The governing board bears the responsibility for ensuring that applicants to the hospital's medical staff are qualified to perform the clinical procedures set forth in the delineation of privileges. Otherwise, a hospital may be liable for the negligent acts of its physicians. If a hospital is to be responsible for each physician's conduct, it must be permitted to determine the nature and extent of the privileges granted physicians to practice in the institution. However, in light of the importance of staff appointments to physicians, the courts have prohibited hospital governing boards from acting unreasonably or capriciously in rejecting physicians for staff appointments or in limiting their privileges.

Osteopaths were properly denied privileges in *Silverstein v. Gwinnett Hospital Authority*, 672 F. Supp. 1444 (D. Ga. 1987), where principles of due process and equal protection were not violated by the bylaws of a county hospital. These bylaws effectively excluded osteopathic physicians from medical staff membership by limiting staff privileges to physicians who had completed allopathic training requirements for certification by the appropriate American Specialty Board and who had completed a postgraduate training program approved by the Accreditation Council for Graduate Medical Education. The differences between the two schools and their approaches to medical treatment provided a rational basis for a public hospital to deny staff privileges to those who do not meet the hospital's bylaw requirements for obtaining medical staff privileges.

Doctors of osteopathy in *Hull v. Board of Commissioners of Halifax Hospital Medical Center*, 453 So. 2d 519 (Fla. Dist. Ct. App. 1984), filed a complaint against members of the hospital's board, alleging that the eligibility requirements for medical staff membership were discriminatory against osteopaths. The Fifth District Court of Appeals of Florida held that the hospital's refusal to allow noneligible and noncertified medical board applicants positions on its staff was not an abuse of its discretion and was not done arbitrarily or unreasonably. It is of interest that the court also held that the fact the hospital did not make a detailed evaluation of every applicant who failed to meet basic minimum bylaw requirements did not violate any statute.

Hospitals have responded to lawsuits in this area by demonstrating that they have followed pre-established policies and procedures. The board may exercise its authority to fix these policies for the hospital through the promulgation of rules and regulations for the conduct of the hospital, or, like other responsibilities of the board, policy making may be delegated. This delegation may be broad or narrow as determined by the board. It may take the form of permission for the administrator, the administrator's subordinates, or committees in the hospital to make policies or formulate rules and regulations, subject to the review of the board. Policies made in this way (which do not contravene statute, charter, or bylaws) bind the hospital; they will be effective in determining the rights of beneficiaries of the hospital, its employees, and its professional staff.

The governing board is under no obligation to delegate any of its management or its policy-making functions. Those that are delegated are subject to revocation by the governing board at any time. In other words, there is no obligation to delegate any part of a board's function, and there is no obligation to continue such delegation once it is made.

Physician Monitoring

The court in *Darling v. Charleston Community Memorial Hospital*, 33 Ill. 2d 326, 211 N.E.2d 253 (1965), *cert. denied*, 383 U.S. 946 (1966), decided that the hospital governing board has a duty to establish mechanisms for the medical staff to evaluate, counsel, and, where necessary, take action against an unreasonable risk of harm to a patient arising from the patient's treatment by a personal physician. Because the hospital has a responsibility for the quality of medical care afforded the patient in the institution, appropriate mechanisms for evaluating the competency of candidates for staff appointments and the privileges given physicians must exist.

A hospital cannot defend itself on the ground that the medical staff is independent and self-governing. In *Gonzales v. Nork and Mercy Hospital*, No. 228566, (Cal., Sacramento Co. Super. Ct. 1973), *reversed on other grounds*, 60 Cal. App. 3d 835, 131 Cal. Rptr. 717 (1976), the hospital was found negligent for failing to protect the patient, a 27-year-old man, from acts of malpractice by an independent, privately retained physician. The patient had been injured in an automobile accident and was operated on by Dr. Nork, an orthopedic surgeon. The plaintiff's life expectancy was reduced as a result of an unsuccessful and allegedly unnecessary laminectomy. It was found that the hospital knew or should have known of the surgeon's incompetence since the surgeon had previously performed numerous operations either unnecessarily or negligently. Evidence was presented showing that the surgeon had performed more than three dozen similar operations unnecessarily or in a negligent manner. Even if the hospital was not aware of the surgeon's acts of negligence, an effective monitoring system should have been in place for monitoring his abilities.

The patient in *Johnson v. Misericordia Community Hospital*, 294 N.W.2d 501, 301 N.W.2d 156 (Wis. 1981), brought a malpractice action against the hospital and its liability insurer for alleged negligence in granting orthopedic privileges to a physician who performed an operation to remove a pin fragment from the patient's hip. The Wisconsin Court of Appeals found the hospital negligent for failing to scrutinize the physician's credentials before approving his application for orthopedic privileges. The hospital failed to adhere to procedures established under both its own bylaws and state statute. The measure of quality and the degree of quality control exercised in a hospital are the direct responsibilities of the medical staff. Hospital supervision of the manner of appointment of physicians to its staff is mandatory, not optional. On appeal by the hospital, the Wisconsin

Supreme Court affirmed the appellate court's decision, finding that if the hospital had exercised ordinary care, it would not have appointed the physician to the medical staff.

Disruptive Physicians

Criteria other than academic credentials—for example, the applicant's ability to work with others—should be considered prior to granting medical staff privileges. That factor was considered by the appellate court in *Ladenheim v. Union County Hospital District*, 76 Ill. App. 3d 90, 36 Ill. Dec. 568, 394 N.E.2d 770 (1979), which held that the physician's inability to work with other members of the hospital staff was in itself sufficient grounds to deny him staff privileges. The physician's record was replete with evidence of his inability to work effectively with other members of the hospital staff. As stated in *Huffaker v. Bailey*, 273 Or. 273, 278, 279, 540 P.2d 1398, 1400 (1975), most other courts have found that the ability to work smoothly with others is reasonably related to the hospital's object of ensuring patient welfare. The conclusion seems justified since health care professionals are frequently required to work together or in teams. A staff member who, because of personality characteristics or other problems, is incapable of getting along with others could severely hinder the effective treatment of patients.

The court of appeal in *Pick v. Santa Ana–Tustin Community Hospital*, 130 Cal. App. 3d 970 (1982), held that the petitioner's demonstrated lack of ability to work with others in the hospital setting was sufficient to support the denial of his application for admission to the medical staff. There was evidence that the petitioner presented a real and substantial danger to patients treated by him and that they might receive other than a high quality of medical care.

Summary Suspension and Termination of Privileges

The commissioner of health was authorized by New York's Public Health Law to summarily suspend a petitioner ophthalmologist for a period of 60 days pending disciplinary hearings and determination of charges against him. The physician had been suspended on the ground that he posed an imminent danger to the public. Proceedings against the opthalmologist had been delayed since 1977; meanwhile, he had continued to practice, and 11 new charges had been filed against him. *John P. v. Axelrod*, 97 A.D.2d 950, 468 N.Y.S.2d 951, 462 N.E.2d 1192 (1984).

A physician whose privileges are either suspended or terminated must exhaust all remedies provided in a hospital's bylaws, rules, and regulations prior to commencing a court action. The physician in *Eidelson v. Archer*, 645 P.2d 171 (Alaska 1982), failed to pursue the hospital's internal appeal procedure prior to bringing suit. As a result, the Supreme Court of Alaska reversed a superior court's judgment for the physician in his action for compensatory and punitive damages.

A hospital that denies a physician due process as provided in its medical staff bylaws could find itself involved in a lawsuit. The U.S. court of appeals in *Northeast Georgia Radiological Associates v. Tidwell*, 670 F.2d 507 (5th Cir. 1982), held that a contract with the hospital's radiologists, which incorporated the medical staff bylaws, sustained the plaintiffs' claim to a protected property interest entitling them to a hearing before the medical staff and the hospital authority.

Unnecessary Surgery

The hospital that employs a physician who commits malpractice will not escape liability in a negligence action naming the physician. A hospital owes its patients a duty of care, and this duty includes the obligation to protect them from negligent and fraudulent acts of those physicians with a propensity to commit malpractice. The courts will not permit hospitals to hide behind the cloak of ignorance in this responsibility.

For example, an orthopedic surgeon in California performed fraudulent, negligent, and/or unnecessary surgery on 38 patients. The defendant produced false and inadequate findings as well as false positive myelograms. He deceived his patients with this information and caused them to undergo surgery. The court held the surgeon and the hospital jointly liable for damages suffered by the plaintiffs. *Gonzales v. Nork and Mercy Hospital*, No. 228566 (Cal., Sacramento City Super. Ct. Nov. 27, 1973); *Hendricks v. Nork*, 16 A.T.L. NEWSLETTER 25 (Feb. 1973).

DUTY TO PROVIDE PROPITIOUS TREATMENT

Hospitals can be held liable for delays in treatment that result in injuries to their patients. For example, the patient in *Heddinger v. Ashford Memorial Community Hospital*, 734 F.2d 81 (1st Cir. 1984), filed a malpractice action against a hospital and its insurer, alleging that a delay in treating her left hand resulted in the loss of her little finger. Medical testimony presented at trial indicated that if proper and timely treatment had been rendered, the finger would have been saved. The U.S. district court entered judgment on a jury verdict for the plaintiff in the amount of $175,000. The hospital appealed, and the U.S. court of appeals held that even if the physicians who attended the patient were not employees of the hospital, but were independent contractors, the risk of negligent treatment was clearly foreseeable by the hospital. The court also held that although the award of damages was high, it was not so excessive as to require appellate reversal.

SELF-DEALING/CONFLICT OF INTEREST

There should be full disclosure to the hospital board of each board member's dealings with the hospital. Transactions between a board member and a hospital must be just and reasonable. Board members must refrain from self-dealing and avoid conflict-of-interest situations. Membership on the board or its committees should not be used for private gain. Board members are expected to disclose potential conflict-of-interest situations and withdraw from the board room at the time of voting. Board members who suspect a conflict-of-interest situation have a right and a duty to raise pertinent questions regarding any potential conflict. Conflict of interest is presumed to exist when a board member or a firm with which he or she is associated may benefit or lose from the passage of a proposed action.

Membership on the board of a hospital is deemed a public service. Neither the court nor the community expects or desires such public service to be turned to private profit. Thus, the standards imposed on hospital board members regarding the investment of trust funds, self-dealing transactions, or personal compensation may be stricter than are those for directors of business corporations. The essential rules regarding self-dealing are clear. Generally, a contract between a hospital and a trustee financially interested in the transaction is voidable by the hospital in the event that the interested trustee spoke or voted in favor of the arrangement or did not fully disclose the material facts regarding his or her interest. This resolution of the self-dealing problem is based on the belief that if an interested board member does not participate in the board's action and does make full disclosure of his or her interest, the disinterested remaining members of the board are able to protect the hospital's interests. If the fairness of the transaction is questioned, the burden of establishing fairness falls on the trustee involved.

Underlying the controversy of self-dealing is the knowledge that sometimes the most advantageous contract for the hospital would be with one of its trustees or with a company in which the director is interested. These considerations are of great importance when dealings between a charitable corporation and a member of the board are involved. A rule denying this opportunity to the corporation would be too severe. However, statutory provisions in some states specifically forbid self-dealing transactions altogether, irrespective of disclosure or the fairness of the deal. The California Court of Appeals, interpreting a state conflict-of-interest statute in *Franzblau v. Monardo*, 166 Cal. Rptr. 610 (Ct. App. 1980), ruled that a president of a private nonprofit hospital was ineligible to hold office as a director of a public hospital district serving the same area.

Under Sections 1877(b) and 1909(b) of the Social Security Act, it is considered a felony for anyone to knowingly and willfully offer, pay, solicit, or receive any payment in return for referring an individual to another for the furnishing, or the arranging for the furnishing, of any item or service that may be paid for by the Medicare or Medicaid programs. Persons convicted under these provisions are subject to fines of up to $25,000 and/or imprisonment of up to five years. The inspector general of the U.S. Department of Health and Human Services has identified the following arrangements as examples of potential violations of the Social Security Act:

- Payment of a "finder's fee" to respiratory therapists, physical therapists, or other therapists working in the hospital for referring patients to durable medical equipment suppliers who supply oxygen equipment, wheelchairs, or other equipment or supplies to patients.

• Payment to hospital social workers or discharge planners by home health agencies for referring hospital patients in need of home health services once they are discharged from the hospital.

DUTY TO PROVIDE ADEQUATE STAFF

The court of appeal in *Leavitt v. St. Tammany Parish Hospital*, 396 So. 2d 406 (La. Ct. App. 1981), held that the hospital owed a duty to respond promptly to patient calls for help. The hospital breached its duty by having less than adequate staff on hand and by failing to at least verbally answer an assistance light to inquire what the patient needed.

The patient in *Czubinsky v. Doctors Hospital*, 188 Cal. Rptr. 685 (Ct. App. 1983), appealed a judgment of the superior court that granted the hospital's motion for judgment notwithstanding the verdict after the jury had returned a verdict in favor of the patient. The patient recovering from anesthesia went into cardiac arrest, which resulted in permanent damages to the patient. The court of appeal held that the injuries sustained by the patient were the direct result of the hospital personnel's failure to properly monitor and render aid when needed in the immediate postoperative period. The registered nurse assigned to the patient had a duty to remain with her until she was transferred to the recovery room. The nurse's absence was the patent proximate cause of the patient's injuries. Failure of the hospital to provide adequate staff to assist the patient in the immediate postoperative period was an act in dereliction of duty—a failure that resulted in permanent damages, a readily foreseeable result.

DUTY TO PROVIDE ADEQUATE FACILITIES AND EQUIPMENT

A hospital is under a duty to exercise reasonable care to furnish adequate equipment, appliances, and supplies for use in the diagnosis or treatment of patients. The general rule seems to be that equipment furnished by a hospital should be fit for the purposes and uses intended.

Within its duty to provide adequate facilities and equipment, a hospital board must exercise reasonable care and skill in supervising and managing hospital property. This obligation includes protecting hospital property from destruction and loss.

DUTY TO PROVIDE ADEQUATE INSURANCE

One basic protection for tangible property is adequate insurance against fire and other risks. This duty extends to keeping the physical plant of the hospital in good repair and appropriating funds for such purpose when necessary.

The duty of a hospital board is to purchase insurance against various risks. Hospitals face as much risk of losing their tangible and intangible assets through judgments for negligence as they do through fires or other disasters. Where this is true, the duty to insure against the risks of negligence is as great as the duty to insure against fire, and the amount of insurance must be adequate for the circumstances.

DUTY TO PROVIDE SATISFACTORY PATIENT CARE

The most important aspect of a governing board's duty to operate a hospital with due care and diligence is its responsibility to provide satisfactory patient care. It is only through the fulfillment of this duty that the basic purpose of the hospital will be accomplished; this duty includes the maintenance of a satisfactory standard of medical care through supervision of the medical, nursing, and ancillary staffs of the hospital.

While the provision of satisfactory patient care clearly fulfills the purpose of nonprofit hospitals (since they exist for this purpose alone), it might be asked whether this duty applies equally to proprietary hospitals where the corporation's additional purpose is to provide a return on investment. The duty does apply equally, and the proprietary hospital's liability for failure to provide satisfactory care is clear. State licensing laws and regulations impose the same standards on both proprietary and nonprofit hospitals, despite the fact that proprietary hospitals are permitted to retain a profit.

DUTY TO SELECT A COMPETENT ADMINISTRATOR

Members of the governing board are responsible for selecting an administrator to act as their agent in the management of the hospital. The individual selected must show the competence and the character necessary to maintain satisfactory standards of patient care within the institution. Minimum qualifications for administrators are contained in several hospital licensing statutes as well as in the rules and regulations promulgated under them. Where minimum qualifications exist, the governing board must at least satisfy these requirements in the appointment of an administrator. If the circumstances of a particular hospital necessitate employing an administrator of a higher level of qualification and competency, the governing board, at its discretion, may select an administrator that meets that need.

The failure to remove an incompetent administrator or any other incapable agent of the hospital is as much a breach of a board's duty as is its failure to appoint competent employees. Termination of an administrator due to incompetence must be in accordance with hospital bylaws, which should set forth the administrator's due process rights. These rights should be included in an appropriately written contract for the administrator.

The general duty of a governing board is to exercise due care and diligence in supervising and managing the hospital. This duty does not cease upon the selection of a competent administrator. A governing board can be liable if the level of patient care becomes inadequate because of the board's failure to properly supervise the administrator's management of a hospital.

Administrators, as is the case with board members, can be personally liable for their own acts of negligence that injure others.

DUTY TO REQUIRE COMPETITIVE BIDDING

Many states have developed regulations requiring competitive bidding for work or services commissioned by public hospitals. The fundamental purpose of this requirement is to eliminate, or at least reduce, the possibility that such abuses as fraud, favoritism, improvidence, or extravagance will intrude into an institution's business practices. Contracts made in violation of a statute are considered illegal and could result in personal liability for board members, especially if the members become aware of a fraudulent activity and allow it to continue. It should be noted that the mere appearance of favoritism toward one contractor over another could give rise to an unlawful action. For example, a board member's pressing the administrator to favor one ambulance transporter over others because of his/her social acquaintance with the owner is suspect and would most likely ring a bad note in the ears of the courts. A hospital board should avoid even the appearance of wrongdoing by requiring competitive bidding.

DUTY TO PROVIDE A SAFE WORKING ENVIRONMENT

Hospitals are liable for work-related injuries to their employees and must therefore provide them with safe working conditions. Employees should be warned of any unusual hazards related to their jobs. For example, pregnant employees may abort because of exposure to anesthetic gases in the operating or delivery room; the fetus of a pregnant employee may suffer cell damage because of exposure to radiation in the radiology, nuclear medicine, or cobalt therapy department. No warnings are usually necessary where the danger is obvious.

Although one cannot guard against the unforeseeable, a hospital is liable for injuries resulting from dangers that it knowingly failed to guard against or those that it should have known about and failed to guard against.

Floors

Floors are often a major source of lawsuits for hospitals. In order to reduce liability due to falls, floors should be properly maintained. Specifically:

- Floors should not contain a dangerous amount of wax.
- "Slippery Floor" signs should be utilized where appropriate.
- Floors should be properly cared for and maintained on rainy and/or snowy days.
- Broken floor tiles should be reported.
- Foreign matter should be quickly and completely wiped from the floor.
- Signs, ropes, and lights should be used where appropriate.
- Appropriate precautions should also be taken for outdoor walkways, such as icy conditions and construction hazards.

Windows

Hospitals are required to exercise reasonable care and diligence in safeguarding a patient, measured by the capacity of the patient to provide for his or her own safety. The plaintiffs in *Horton v. Niagara Falls Memorial Medical Center*, 51 App. Div. 2d 152, 380 N.Y.S.2d 116 (1976), sought recovery against the hospital for injuries sustained by the plaintiff/patient's fall from a second story hospital window. The patient had been admitted to the hospital with a fever of unknown origin and was noted to be lacking in coordination and to have blurred vision. The patient had been placed in a private room with a single window which opened to a small balcony encircled by a 2-3 foot high railing. Prior to the patient's fall, construction workers had notified hospital personnel that the patient was standing on his balcony calling for a ladder. The patient had been confused and disoriented. The attending physician upon learning of the incident advised a nurse to keep the patient under restraint and to keep an eye on him. The patient's wife was called and she indicated that her mother would come to the hospital in 10-15 minutes to watch her husband. The patient's fall occurred shortly before the mother's arrival. The Niagara Supreme Court had entered judgment for the plaintiffs and the hospital appealed. The Supreme Court, Appellate Division, held that the hospital had a duty to supervise the patient and prevent him from injuring himself.

PATIENT VALUABLES

It should be noted that a nurse and hospital can be held liable for the negligent handling of a patient's valuables. The following points should be remembered and followed when handling the personal belongings and valuables of patients:

1. Send the belongings home when feasible
2. Deposit jewelry, wallets and other appropriate items in the hospital safe
3. Select one department to handle valuables
4. Provide proper communication between the department handling lost and found articles and the department holding patient valuables for safekeeping
5. Encourage patients to keep with them as little money, jewelry, and other valuables as possible while in the hospital
6. Establish a valuables procedure for deceased patients, patients entering the emergency room, and patients scheduled to go to the operating room and/or other areas of the hospital for treatment or diagnostic procedure
7. Provide prenumbered envelopes that list those items placed in each valuables envelope. Verification of the contents should be made between the nursing employee delivering an envelope and the business office employee accepting the envelope. A receipt should be given to the patient making a deposit. Strike outs or corrections should not be permitted on the envelope; this will help prevent claims of mishandling.

COMPLIANCE WITH FEDERAL, STATE, AND LOCAL RULES AND REGULATIONS

The governing board in general and its agents (assigned representatives) in particular are responsible for compliance with federal, state, and local rules and regulations regarding the operation of the hospital. Depending on the scope of the wrong committed and the intent of the board, failure to comply could subject the board members and/or their agents to civil liability and even, in rare instances, to criminal prosecution.

JOINT COMMISSION ON ACCREDITATION OF HEALTHCARE ORGANIZATIONS STANDARDS

The governing board through its agents is responsible for compliance with the standards of the Joint Commission. Noncompliance could cause a hospital to lose accreditation, which in turn would provide grounds for third-party reimbursement agencies (e.g., Medicare) to refuse payment for treatment rendered to patients.

FEE SPLITTING

Hospitals and nursing homes in search of alternate sources of income must do so scrupulously and not find themselves in what could be construed as questionable corporate activities.

A triable claim of illegal fee splitting in *Hauptman v. Grand Manor Health Related Facility, Inc.*, 502 N.Y.S.2d 1012 (App. Div. 1986), was stated by the allegations of a psychiatrist that a nursing home had barred him from continuing to treat its patients unless he joined a professional corporation the members of which included owners of the nursing home. Under the proposed agreement, the nursing home would retain 20 percent of the fees collected on his behalf. Although Section 6509-(a) of the New York State Education Law did not prohibit members of a professional corporation from pooling fees, the statute did not apply to forced conscription into a corporation at the price of surrendering a portion of one's fees unwillingly. Likewise, 8 NYCRR Section 29.1 [b][4] expressly forbids a professional corporation from charging a fee for billing and office expenses based on a percentage of income from a practice. The psychiatrist's allegations also showed possible violation of Public Health Law Section 2801-b, which prohibited exclusion of a practitioner on grounds not related to reasonable objectives of the institution.

DOCTRINE OF *RESPONDEAT SUPERIOR*

Respondeat superior ("let the master respond") is the legal doctrine holding employers liable, in certain cases, for the wrongful acts of their employees. In the health care setting, a hospital is liable for the negligent acts of its employees. The question of liability frequently rests on whether or not persons treating a patient are independent agents (responsible for their own acts) or employees of the hospital. The answer to this depends on whether or not the hospital can exercise control over the particular act that was the proximate cause of the injury.

Liability predicated on *respondeat superior* may be imposed on an employer only if a master-servant relationship exists between the employer and the employee and if the wrongful act of the employee occurs within the scope of employment. The doctrine has also been referred to as *vicarious liability* whereby an employer is answerable for the torts committed by employees.

Since the law holds negligent persons responsible for their negligent acts, employees are not absolved from liability when the hospital is held liable through the application of *respondeat superior*. Not only may the injured party sue the employee directly, but also the employer, if sued, may seek indemnification—that is, compensation for the financial loss occasioned by the employee's act—from the employee.

In the instance of wrongful conduct by an independent contractor, the doctrine of *respondeat superior* does not apply. An independent contractor relationship is established when the principal has no right of control over the manner in which the agent's work is to be performed. The independent contractor is therefore responsible for his or her own negligent acts. There are, however, some cases that indicate a hospital may be held liable for an independent contractor's negligence. For example, in *Mehlman v. Powell*, 46 U.S.L.W. 2227 (Md. Ct. App. 1977), the court held that a hospital may be found vicariously liable for the negligence of an emergency room physician who was not a hospital employee, but who worked in the emergency room in the capacity of an independent contractor. The court reasoned that the hospital maintained control over billing procedures; maintained an emergency room in the main hospital building; and represented to the patient that the members of the emergency room staff were its employees, which may have caused the patient to rely on the skill and competence of the staff.

The doctrine of *respondeat superior* may impose liability on a hospital for a nurse's acts or omissions that result in injury to a hospital patient. Whether such liability attaches depends on whether the conduct of the nurse was wrongful and whether the nurse was subject to the control of the hospital at the time the act in question was performed. Determination of whether the nurse's conduct was wrongful in a given situation depends on the standard of conduct to which the nurse is expected to adhere. In liability deliberations, the nurse who is subject to the control of the hospital at the time of the negligent conduct is considered a hospital employee and is not the borrowed servant of a staff physician or surgeon.

An officer or director of a corporation is not, merely as a result of his or her position, personally liable for the torts of corporate employees. To incur liability, the director or officer must ordinarily be shown to have in some way participated in or directed the tortious act. See *Hunt v. Rabon*, 272 S.E.2d 643 (S.C. 1980).

BLOOD TRANSFUSIONS

The administration of blood is considered to be a medical procedure. It results from the exercise of professional medical judgment that is composed of two parts: (1) diagnosis, deciding the need for blood; and (2) therapy, the actual administration of blood. The most common occurrences that lead to lawsuits in the administration of blood involve the transfusion of mismatched blood and serum hepatitis, which can be caused by the use of an unsterile needle or contaminated blood. The unnecessary administration of blood and improper handling procedures (i.e., inadequate refrigeration and storage) are also potential legal risks.

The blood donor in *Brown v. Shannon West Texas Memorial Hospital*, 222 S.W.2d 248 (Tex. 1949), sought to recover from a serious injury allegedly caused by the use of an unsterile needle. The court held that the burden of proof was on the plaintiff to show, by competent evidence, that the needle was contaminated when used and that it was the proximate cause of the alleged injury. The mere proof, said the court, that infection followed the use of the needle or that the infection could possibly be attributed to the use of an unsterile needle was insufficient.

The Maryland Court of Special Appeals held in *Roberts v. Suburban Hospital Association, Inc.*, 532 A.2d 1081 (Md. Ct. Spec. App. 1987), that a blood transfusion constituted provision of a service (i.e., the rendering of health care, rather than the sale of a product) and was subject to the exhaustion of Maryland's Health Claims Arbitration Act. It followed then that the complaint should have been dismissed for failure to follow the required administrative remedy. The *Roberts* case involved the contraction of AIDS by a hemophiliac through the transfusion of contaminated blood. The court stated: "A transfusion is not just a sale of blood which the patient takes home in a package. The transfusion of the blood—the injecting of it into the patient's bloodstream, is what he really needs and pays for, and that involves the application of medical skill." *Id.* at 1088.

EMERGENCY ROOM

The courts do not look kindly on hospitals with emergency rooms that deny patients emergency care. If the public is aware that a hospital furnishes emergency services and relies on that knowledge, the hospital has a duty to provide those services to the public. The standards of the Joint Commission on Accreditation of Healthcare Organizations, state licensing regulations, and health department regulations, among others, may be considered by the courts as showing a duty of hospital emergency rooms to provide emergency care to those who present themselves with the need for such care.

Some states have enacted regulations requiring that all patients presenting themselves to emergency rooms must be rendered emergency treatment. The New York State Emergency Medical Services Act of 1983 provides that every general hospital shall admit any person who is in need of immediate hospitalization. Any licensed medical practitioner who refuses to treat a person arriving at a general hospital for emergency medical treatment will be guilty of a misdemeanor and subject to up to one year in prison and a fine not to exceed $1,000. Emergency medical technicians, paramedics, and ambulance drivers are expected to report any refusals by general hospitals to treat emergency patients. Patients may be transferred after they have been stabilized if it is deemed by the attending physician to be in the best interest of the patient.

The original Hill-Burton legislation required each state to submit a plan that would provide adequate hospitals and other facilities for all persons residing within its boundaries. The 1970 amendments to the act placed a special emphasis on emergency service. Legislation in many states imposes a duty on hospitals to provide emergency care. The statutes implicitly, and sometimes explicitly, require hospitals to provide some degree of emergency service.

A hospital antidumping provision, approved by Congress, forbids hospitals from turning away emergency room patients or dumping them on other institutions for fear they can't pay. The provision is part of a section of the reconciliation bill approved on March 20, 1986. Failure to follow the new rule could result in civil penalties of up to $25,000 per occurrence. Under the bill, patients can be transferred once they are stabilized and clearance is received from a receiving institution.

No matter how trivial a complaint, each patient should be examined. If a patient rejects treatment, he or she should be asked to sign a release. Transfer of patients should be made only upon approval of the physician. Appropriate emergency room policies and procedures, medical and administrative, should be developed. The objectives of emergency care are the same regardless of severity. Treatment should begin as rapidly as possible, function is to be maintained or restored, scarring and deformity are to be minimized, etc.

Not only must hospitals accept, treat, and transfer emergency room patients if such is necessary for the patients' well-being, but also hospitals must adhere to the standards of care they have set for themselves, as well as to national standards. Treatment rendered by hospitals is expected to be commensurate with that available in the same or similar communities or in hospitals generally. The Supreme Court of South Dakota in *Fjerstad v. Knutson*, 271 N.W.2d 8 (S.D. 1978), found that a hospital could be held liable for the failure of an on-call physician to respond to a call from the emergency room. An intern who attempted to contact the on-call physician and was unable to do so for three and one-half hours treated and discharged the patient. The hospital was responsible for assigning on-call physicians and assuring that they would be available when called. The patient had expired during the night in a motel room as a result of asphyxia resulting from a swelling of the larynx, tonsils, and epiglottis that blocked the trachea. Testimony from the medical director of laboratories indicated that the emergency room on-call physician was to be available for consultation and was assigned that duty by the hospital. Expert testimony was also offered that someone with the decedent's symptoms should have been hospitalized and that such care could have saved the decedent's life. The jury could have believed that an experienced physician would have taken the necessary steps to save the decedent's life.

In *Wilmington General Hospitals v. Manlove*, 54 Del. 15, 174 A.2d 135 (1961), the parents of a four-month-old boy suffering from diarrhea sought the assistance of their family physician, who prescribed medication. After the child became feverish, the parents took the infant to the doctor's office where he was examined and treated. During the night, he seemed to grow worse. The next morning, knowing that the doctor was not in his office that day and believing that the child needed immediate medical attention, the parents took him to Wilmington General. The parents presented themselves at the emergency ward, described the baby's illness and past treatment to the nurse, and requested help. The nurse inquired as to whether or not they had an admission slip from their doctor and was told that they did not. The nurse tried calling the doctor, but to no avail; she then indicated to the parents that she could not admit the child, but that they could return the next day to the pediatric clinic. The parents returned home with the child, but by midafternoon the child had expired from bronchial pneumonia. Judgment against the hospital was appealed to the state supreme court; it was found that while a nongovernmental hospital may not have a duty to admit any and all comers, the rule would not necessarily apply in the case of persons applying for emergency treatment. The court indicated that a hospital's liability may be predicated on the refusal of service to a patient in a case of an unmistakable emergency if the patient has relied on a well-established custom of the hospital to render aid.

In *Stanturf v. Sipes*, 447 S.W.2d 558 (Mo. 1969), the Missouri Supreme Court reversed a judgment that originally favored the defendant, a hospital administrator who had refused to allow a patient to be admitted because of inability to pay a $25 admission charge. The patient had suffered frostbite of both feet. In its reversal, the court held that the evidence would have sustained findings that the hospital "was the only hospital in the immediate area, it maintained an emergency service, and . . . plaintiff applied for emergency treatment and was refused. . . . The members of the public . . . had reason to rely on the [hospital], and in this case it could be found that plaintiff's condition was caused to be worsened by the delay resulting from the futile efforts to obtain treatment from the [hospital]. In addition, it could also be found that it was the long established rule of the hospital to accept all persons for treatment upon payment of a $25 admittance fee, that the fee was offered, but admission was refused." *Id.* at 562.

In *Thomas v. Corso*, 265 Md. 84, 288 A.2d 379 (1972), a Maryland court sustained a verdict against a hospital and a physician. The patient had been brought to the hospital emergency room after he was struck by a car. He was not personally attended to by a physician although he was in shock, as indicated by dangerously low blood pressure. There was some telephone contact between the nurse in the emergency department and the physician who was providing on-call coverage. The physician failed to come to the hospital until the patient was close to death.

The court reasoned that expert testimony was not even necessary to establish what common sense made evident: that a patient who had been struck by a car may have suffered internal injuries and should have been evaluated and treated by a physician. Lack of attention in such cases is not reasonable care by any standard. The concurrent negligence of the nurse, who failed to contact the on-call physician after the patient's condition had worsened, did not relieve the physician of liability for his failure to come to the emergency department at once. Rather, under the doctrine of *respondeat superior* the nurse's negligence was a basis for holding the hospital liable as well.

Another automobile accident emergency case, *Citizens Hospital Association v. Schoulin*, 48 Ala. 101, 262 So. 2d 303 (1972), reached a conclusion similar to that of the *Thomas* case. This accident victim sued the hospital and the attending physician for their negligence in failing to discover and properly treat his injuries. The court held that there was sufficient evidence to sustain a jury verdict that the hospital's nurse was negligent in failing to inform the doctor of all the patient's symptoms, in failing to conduct a proper examination of the plaintiff, and in failing to follow the directions of the physician. Thus, as the nurse was the employee of the hospital, the hospital was liable under the doctrine of *respondeat superior*.

Two Mexican children, burned in a fire at home, were refused admission or first aid by a local hospital. A lawsuit was filed, claiming that additional injury occurred as a result of the failure to render care. The suit was dismissed by the trial court. The Arizona Court of Appeals found the defendants liable, claiming that it was the custom of the hospital to render aid in such a case. On appeal, the Arizona Supreme Court also held the defendants liable. It reasoned that state statutes and licensing regulations mandate that a hospital may not deny a patient emergency care. *Guerrero v. Copper Queen Hospital*, 112 Ariz. 104, 537 P.2d 1329 (1975).

It is important to note that not only are hospitals required to care for emergency patients, but also they are to do so in a timely fashion. A Florida trial court in *Marks v. Mandel*, 477 So. 2d 1036 (Fla. Dist. Ct. App. 1985), was found to have erred in directing a verdict against the plaintiff. It was decided that the relevant inquiry in this case was whether the hospital and the supervisor should bear ultimate responsibility for failure of the specialty on-call system to function properly. Jury issues had been raised by evidence that the standard for on-call systems was to have a specialist attending the patient within 30 minutes of being called.

CONCLUSION

There is a need for a new legal definition of the duties and responsibilities of hospital board members. A board meeting is not a social function, and board members must not delegate all decision making to the CEO or make decisions too slowly or hastily. *Smith v. Van Gorkum*, 488 A.2d 858 (Del. 1985), involved a board of directors that authorized the sale of its company through a cash-out merger for a tendered price per share nearly 50 percent over the market price. That might sound like a good deal; however, the board did not make any inquiry to determine if it was the best deal available. In fact, it made no decision during a hastily arranged, brief meeting in which it relied solely on the CEO's report regarding the desirability of the move.

The traditional business judgment doctrine is too vague in light of the goals and missions of today's modern health care institutions. Attending a monthly meeting of the board and serving on several committees are not sufficient commitment in light of the complexities and difficulties in operating multimillion-dollar health care systems. Perhaps it is time to compensate board members in light of the time commitment they are required to make and the legal risks they are exposed to. "[B]y examining the functions of corporate boards and their members, it is possible to create a new, more practical legal standard based upon the flow of responsibility, rather than on any single decision or action."[1]

NOTE

1. Manning, *The Director's Duty of Attention*, CORPORATE BOARD, Sept.–Oct. 1984, at 1(21).

Chapter 4

Physicians' Liability

Each state has enacted a medical practice act that permits those individuals who meet the necessary qualifications to practice medicine. The practice of medicine includes three basic functions: diagnosis, treatment, and prescription. A physician's license demonstrates that the state, as the representative of the public, is satisfied that the physician has the basic training and ability to make diagnostic judgments and prescribe courses of treatment that will alleviate or cure a patient's ailment.

The wide range of authority in treating patients has brought with it a broad range of lawsuits. The single most sued group of professionals is physicians. This chapter discusses many of those areas where physicians tend to be most vulnerable to lawsuits.

ABANDONMENT

The professional relationship that exists between physician and patient continues, for the most part, until it is terminated with the consent of both parties. However, a relationship can be discontinued through dismissal of the physician by the patient, or through physician withdrawal from the case, or at such time when the physician's services are no longer required. Failure to follow up after the acute stage of illness has subsided or neglect to provide a patient with necessary instructions could involve the physician in serious legal difficulties. Premature termination of treatment is quite often the subject of a legal action for abandonment, defined as the unilateral termination of a physician-patient relationship by the physician without notice to the patient. Closely related to this type of problem is one that occurs when the physician, though not intending to end the relationship with the patient, fails to ensure the patient's understanding that further treatment of the complaint is necessary.

All of the following elements must be established in order for a patient to recover damages for abandonment:

• Medical care was unreasonably discontinued.
• The discontinuance of medical care was against the patient's will. (Termination of the physician-patient relationship must have been brought about by a unilateral act of the physician. There can be no abandonment if the relationship is terminated by mutual consent or by dismissal of the physician by the patient.)
• The physician failed to arrange for care by another physician. (Refusal by a physician to enter into a physician-patient relationship by failing to respond to a call or render treatment is not considered a case of abandonment. A plaintiff will not recover for damages unless he or she can prove that a physician-patient relationship had been established.)
• Foresight indicated that discontinuance might result in physical harm to the patient.
• Actual harm was suffered by the patient.

The relationship between a physician and a patient, once established, continues until it is ended by the mutual consent of the parties, the patient's dismissal of the physician, the physician's withdrawal from the case, or the fact that the physician's services are no longer needed. A physician who decides to withdraw his or her services must provide the patient with reasonable notice so that the services of another physician can be obtained.

AGGRAVATION OF A PRE-EXISTING CONDITION

Aggravation of a pre-existing condition through negligence may cause a physician to be liable for malpractice. If the original injury is aggravated, liability will be imposed only for the aggravation, rather than for both the original injury and its aggravation.

In *Nguyen v. County of Los Angeles*, C538628 (Super. Ct. L.A. Co.), an eight-month-old baby girl went to the hospital for tests on her hip. She had been injected with air for a hip study and suffered a respiratory arrest. She later went into cardiac arrest and was resuscitated but suffered brain damage that was aggravated by further poor treatment. The Los Angeles Superior Court jury found evidence of medical malpractice, ordering payments for past and future pain and suffering as well as medical and total care costs that projected to the child's normal life expectancy totaling $54,000,000 without interest.

Patient Falls

Patient falls are major sources of lawsuits for both physicians and hospitals. The plaintiff in *Favalora v. Aetna Casualty & Surety Co.*, 144 So. 2d 544 (La. Ct. App. 1962), sued the hospital and the radiologist for injuries she sustained when she fell while undergoing an x-ray examination. The patient had been admitted to the hospital by her personal physician for a general checkup and a gastrointestinal (GI) series. She had complained about stomach pains, general fatigue, and fainting. The morning following her admission to the hospital, she was taken from her room in a wheelchair to the radiology department. When preparations for the GI series were complete, two technicians brought the patient to the x-ray room. She then waited for the arrival of the radiologist. When he arrived, she was instructed to walk to the x-ray table and stand on the footboard. The technician instructed her to drink a glass of barium. A second cup of barium was handed to her by the technician who then took the exposed film to a nearby pass box leading to the adjacent darkroom, obtained a new film, and repeated the x-ray process. While the technician was depositing the second set of exposed film in the pass box, the patient suddenly fainted and fell to the floor. The radiologist did not see the plaintiff fall, nor did he detect any evidence of distress. The technician heard a noise, immediately turned on the lights, and found her lying on the floor. The radiologist instantly began administering to the patient, while the technician summoned additional assistance. The patient was placed on the x-ray table, and x-rays were taken of those portions of her anatomy that indicated the possibility of injury. The x-rays revealed a fracture of the neck and of the right femur that subsequently required open reduction and the insertion of a metal pin by an orthopedic surgeon. As a result, a pre-existing vascular condition was aggravated, causing a pulmonary embolism, which, in turn, necessitated additional surgery. The failure of the radiologist to secure the patient's medical history prior to the x-ray examination was considered negligence constituting the proximate cause of the patient's injuries.

A defendant is generally only required to compensate a patient for the amount of aggravation caused. However, it is often difficult to determine what monetary damages should be awarded to a plaintiff. Aggravation in many instances is a matter of conjecture.

Wrongful Death

Death resulting from a negligent injury by a defendant gives rise to an action for wrongful death by the survivors. Most states have enacted wrongful death statutes allowing recovery by a defined group of persons for damages suffered through the loss of the decedent.

Damages were awarded in *Argus v. Scheppegrell*, 489 So. 2d 392 (La. Ct. App. 1986), for the wrongful death of a teenage patient with a pre-existing drug addiction. It was determined that the physician had wrongfully supplied the patient with prescriptions for controlled substances in excessive amounts, with the result that the patient's pre-existing drug addiction had worsened, causing her death from a drug overdose. The Louisiana Court of Appeals held that the suffering of the daughter due to drug addiction and deterioration of her mental and physical condition warranted an award of $175,000. Damages of $120,000 were to be awarded for the wrongful death claims of the parents, who not only suffered during their daughter's drug addiction caused by the physician in wrongfully supplying the prescription, but also were forced to endure the torment of their daughter's slow death in the hospital.

ANESTHESIOLOGY

Administration of Anesthetics

A physician's medical license was suspended for one year in *Kearl v. Division of Medical Quality*, 236 Cal. Rptr. 526 (Ct. App. 1986), due to gross negligence in the manner in which he administered anesthesia to a patient during spinal surgery. The finding was based on evidence that the physician failed to record the patient's vital signs at five-minute intervals, as required by prevailing community standards. The record further supported the conclusion that he was negligent and demonstrated a lack of knowledge and ability when in administering a spinal block to another patient who was undergoing a Caesarian section, he selected an isobaric, rather than a hyperbaric, solution of anesthetic, permitted surgery to begin before the anesthetic was fixated, and allowed the patient to be placed in a head-down position, with the result that the patient suffered oxygen deprivation secondary to a "high spinal."

Captain of the Ship

Summary dismissal was properly ordered for those portions of a patient's medical malpractice action that sought to hold a surgeon vicariously liable for throat injuries suffered by his patient because of the negligent manner in which an endotracheal tube was inserted during the administration of anesthesia. *Thomas v. Raleigh*, 358 S.E.2d 222 (W. Va. 1987). The patient's allegations that the surgeon had exercised control over the administration of anesthesia were rebutted by evidence to the contrary. Liability of the surgeon could not be premised on the captain of the ship doctrine since that doctrine would not be recognized in West Virginia. The trend in medicine has created situations where surgeons do not always have the right to control all persons within the operating room. An assignment of liability based on the theory of actual control more realistically reflects the actual relationship that exists in a modern operating room.

Failure To Maintain an Airway

On appeal by the defendant anesthesiologist in *Ward v. Epting*, 351 S.E.2d 867 (S.C. Ct. App. 1987), the issues of deviation from the standard of care and proximate cause were found to have been properly submitted to the jury. The anesthesiologist had failed to establish and maintain an adequate airway and properly resuscitate a post-surgical 22-year-old female patient which resulted in her death from lack of oxygen. Expert testimony based on autopsy and blood gas tests showed that the endotracheal tube had been removed too soon following surgery and that the anesthesiologist, in an attempt to revive the patient, reinserted the tube into the esophagus. The record contained ample evidence that the anesthesiologist failed to conform to the standard of care and that such deviation was the proximate cause of the patient's death. The plaintiff was awarded $400,000 in damages.

ALTERNATIVE PROCEDURES

The potential for liability affects the choice of treatment a physician will follow in treating his/her patient. Use of unprecedented procedures that create an untoward result may cause a physician to be found negligent even though due care was followed. However, if a physician can show that the treatment used was approved by a respectable minority of medical opinion, recovery will be denied unless the plaintiff can prove that the treatment was applied in a negligent manner. A physician's efforts do not constitute negligence simply because they were unsuccessful in a particular case. *Gielski v. State*, 216 N.Y.S.2d 85 (Ct. App. 1961).

The trial court in *Bagherzadeh v. Roeser*, 825 F.2d 1000 (6th Cir. 1987), instructed the jury that a physician could not be "required to guarantee the results" of his treatment and that "the mere fact that an adverse result may occur following orthopedic treatment is not in of itself any evidence of professional negligence." *Id.* at 1001. Innovation in the treatment for minor ailments would more likely be questioned than would innovation in the treatment of a major disease. A doctor treating a patient with a new procedure for an ordinary cold runs a greater risk of liability than does a doctor treating a patient with a new procedure for an acute and painful disease.

It is assumed by law that medicine has not become so standardized that it is unreasonable for two physicians to have differing opinions on the proper method of treating injuries or illnesses. If there is reason for the difference, the courts have held that neither side can be proven erroneous by the "proof" of the other. In *Coon v. Shields*, 39 P.2d 348, (1934), the plaintiff sustained a fracture of both bones of the leg immediately above the ankle. Gas gangrene set in, and it became necessary to amputate the leg. The plaintiff claimed that the surgeon was careless and negligent.

> [T]he real controversy between the parties arises over expert testimony offered by the plaintiff to the effect that iodine is not a disinfectant; that cultures should have been taken as an initial step to the treatment; that scrubbing with a stiff scrub brush was injurious and not beneficial to the wound; that the leg should have been exposed to the air in order to kill the gas bacilli; and that, in the opinion of the expert offered by the plaintiff, Dr. Shields, treatment was improper. This evidence was rejected by the court. In a case such as this confusion often arises over a failure to distinguish between the expert's opinion as to the proper method of treatment and his opinion as to whether or not the treatment applied conforms to what is generally accepted to be the proper method. The practice of medicine or surgery has not become so standardized that it is unreasonable for the two doctors to have different opinions as to the proper method of treating injuries.

Id. at 349.

DELAY IN TREATMENT

A patient afflicted with lung cancer was awarded damages in *Blackmon v. Langley*, 737 S.W.2d 455 (Ark. 1987), because of the failure of the examining physician to inform the patient in a timely manner that a chest x-ray showed a lesion in his lung. The lesion was eventually diagnosed as cancerous. The physician contended that because the evidence showed the patient had less than a 50 percent chance of survival at the time of the alleged negligence, he could not be the proximate cause of injury. The Arkansas Supreme Court found that the jury was properly entitled to determine that the patient suffered and lost more than would have been the case had he been promptly notified of the lesion.

FAILURE TO RESPOND TO AN EMERGENCY ROOM CALL

Physicians on call for a specific service in a hospital's emergency room are expected to respond to requests for emergency assistance when such is considered necessary by designated hospital staff. Failure to respond is grounds for negligence should a patient suffer injury as a result of a physician's failure to respond.

Issues of fact in *Dillon v. Silver*, 520 N.Y.S.2d 751 (App. Div. 1987), precluded summary dismissal of an action charging that a woman's death from complications of an ectopic pregnancy occurred because of a gynecologist's refusal to treat her despite a request for aid by a hospital emergency room physician. Although the gynecologist contended that no physician-patient relationship had ever arisen, the hospital bylaws not only mandated that he accept all patients referred to him, but also stated that the emergency room physician had authority to decide which service physician should be called and required the service physician to respond to such a call.

FAILURE TO FOLLOW UP

Breast Cancer

The Tennessee Supreme Court in *Truan v. Smith*, 578 S.W.2d 73 (Tenn. 1979) entered judgment in favor of the plaintiffs who had brought action against a treating physician for damages alleged to have been the result of malpractice by the physician in the examination, diagnosis, and treatment of breast cancer. In January or February of 1974 the patient noticed a change in the size and firmness of her left breast, which she attributed to an implant. She later noticed discoloration and pain on pressure. While being examined by the defendant on March 25, 1974, for another ailment, the patient brought her symptoms to the physician's attention, but received no significant response, and no examination of the breast was made by the physician at that time. The patient brought her symptoms to the attention of her physician for the second time on May 6, 1974. She had been advised by the defendant to observe her left breast for 30 days for a change in symptoms, which at the time of the examination included discomfort, discoloration, numbness, and sharp pain. She was given an appointment for one month later. The patient, on the morning of her appointment, June 3, 1974, called the physician's office and informed the nurse that her symptoms had not changed and that she would like to know if she should keep her appointment. The nurse indicated that she would pass on her message to the physician. The patient assumed she would be called back if it was necessary to see the physician. By late June the symptoms became more acute, and the patient made an appointment to see the defendant physician on July 8, 1974. The patient was also scheduled to see a specialist on July 10, 1974, at which time she was admitted to the hospital and was diagnosed as having a malignant mass. A radical mastectomy was performed. Expert witnesses expressed the opinion that the mass had been palpable seven months prior to the removal, when the defendant undertook to give the plaintiff a complete physical examination, and that having embarked on a "wait and see" program as an aid in diagnosis, the doctor should have followed his patient, who expired prior to the conclusion of the trial. The supreme court held that the evidence was sufficient to support a finding that the defendant was guilty of malpractice in failing to inform his patient that cancer was a possible cause of her complaints and in failing to make any effort to see his patient at the expiration of the observation period instituted by him.

Hospitals, as well as physicians, are subject to legal action for failure to follow up. As an example, patients presenting themselves to emergency rooms for care are often prescribed x-rays. The emergency room physician on duty will make a preliminary reading if there is no radiologist available. A second reading is made the following day when a radiologist is on duty. Periodically the two findings conflict in that the emergency room physician reads the x-ray as negative and the radiologist finds a fracture. The failure generally occurs when the hospital staff does not inform the patient of the conflicting diagnosis. Failure to notify the patient can result in aggravation of a patient's initial injury if it is not treated in a timely fashion. A system of checks and balances must be in place to prevent such events from occurring.

FAILURE TO DISCLOSE/INFORMED CONSENT

A physician may be held liable for malpractice if, in rendering treatment to a patient, he or she does not make a proper disclosure to the patient of the risks involved in a procedure. A lawsuit was brought against Dr. Hargiss, an ophthalmologist, and others in *Gates v. Jensen*, 595 P.2d 919 (Wash. 1979), for his failure to disclose to a patient that her test results for glaucoma were borderline and that her risk of glaucoma was increased considerably by her high blood pressure and myopia. Dr. Hargiss failed to perform a field vision test and to dilate and examine the eye. He wrote off the patient's problem of difficulty in focusing and gaps in vision as being related to difficulties with her contact lenses. Mrs. Gates visited the clinic 12 times during the following two years with complaints of blurriness, gaps in her vision, and loss of visual acuity. Mrs. Gates was eventually diagnosed as having open-angle glaucoma. By the time Mrs. Gates was properly treated, her vision had deteriorated from almost 20/20 to 20/200. The Supreme Court of Washington held that a duty of disclosure to a patient arises whenever a physician becomes aware of an abnormality that may indicate risk or danger. The facts that must be disclosed are those facts the physician knows or should know that a patient needs to be aware of in order to make an informed decision on the course that future medical care will take.

FAILURE TO ORDER DIAGNOSTIC TESTS

As medical technology becomes more advanced, it is likely that patients will claim that physicians should have ordered certain diagnostic procedures as opposed to the ones actually ordered by the physician. So long as the physician can demonstrate that the diagnostic procedure selected was consistent with the medical practice in the community, these claims will be difficult to sustain.

Judicial Notice and X-rays

The use of x-rays as a diagnostic aid in cases of fracture can be considered a matter of common knowledge of which a court, in the absence of expert testimony, could take judicial notice (the act by which a court, in conducting a trial or forming a decision, will of its own motion and without evidence recognize the existence and truth of certain facts bearing on the controversy at bar). Should a patient have a serious fall and a fracture is indicated, under the foregoing rule it is a matter of common knowledge that the ordinary physician in good standing, in the exercise of ordinary care and diligence, would have ordered x-rays.

Inadequate X-ray Examination

The failure to order a proper set of x-rays is as legally risky as the failure to order any x-rays. In *Betenbaugh v. Princeton Hospital*, 50 N.J. 390, 235 A.2d 889 (1967) (per curiam), the plaintiff had been taken to a hospital when she injured the lower part of her back. One of the defendant physicians directed that an x-ray be taken of her sacrum. No evidence of a fracture was found. This finding was confirmed by the head of the hospital's radiology department. When the patient's pain did not subside, the family physician was consulted. He found that the films taken at the hospital did not include the entire lower portion of the spine and sent her to a radiologist for further study. On the basis of additional x-rays, a diagnosis of a fracture was made, and the patient was advised to wear a lumbosacral support. Two months later, the fracture was healed. The radiologist who had taken x-ray films on the second occasion testified that it was customary to take both an anterior-posterior and a lateral view when making an x-ray examination of the sacrum. In his opinion, the failure at the hospital to include the lower area of the sacrum was a failure to meet the standard required. The family physician testified that if the patient's fracture had been diagnosed at the hospital, appropriate treatment could have been instituted earlier, the patient would have suffered less pain, and recovery time would have been reduced. The evidence was sufficient to support findings that the physicians and the hospital were negligent by not having taken adequate x-rays and that such negligence was the proximate cause of the patient's additional pain and delay in recovery.

Ruptured Appendix

The following two cases involve the failure to order diagnostic tests and the misdiagnosis of appendicitis. The similarities and differences between two cases must be considered in light of the fact that the first was decided 24 years before the second.

In *Lawless v. Calaway*, 24 Cal. 2d 81, 147 P.2d 604 (1944), a 12-year-old boy was brought to the defendant physician with complaints of stomach pains. The child's guardian told the defendant that the child had eaten some spoiled bologna the day before. The defendant diagnosed the problem as ptomaine poisoning and treated it accordingly. The child's condition deteriorated, and the defendant finally referred him to a surgeon who diagnosed appendicitis and operated. However, the child's appendix had already ruptured, and he died of peritonitis. The defendant was found not to be liable. The court held that failure to render a proper diagnosis was not actionable negligence because the physician had followed the usual standard of practice prevalent in his area. Testimony by expert witnesses for the defense indicated that taking a blood cell count was not required by normal standards of due care and that failure to do so did not constitute departure from usual practice. The mere fact that another physician might have followed a different procedure in arriving at a diagnosis does not in itself establish negligence as long as there is some substantial support within the medical profession for the procedures followed by the defendant.

Twenty-four years later in *Steeves v. United States*, 294 F. Supp. 466 (D. S.C. 1968), physicians who failed to order the appropriate diagnostic tests for a child who was referred to a Navy hospital with a diagnosis of possible appendicitis were found guilty of malpractice. Judgment in this case was entered against the United States, on behalf of the U.S. Navy, for medical expenses and for pain and suffering. The child had been referred by an Air Force dispensary where a test indicated a high white blood cell count. A consultation sheet had been given to the mother, indicating the possible diagnosis. The physician who examined the child at the Navy hospital performed no tests, failed to diagnose the patient's condition, and sent him home at 5:02 P.M., some 32 minutes after his arrival on July 21. The child was returned to the emergency room on July 22 at about 2:30 A.M., only to be sent home again by an intern who diagnosed the boy's condition as gastroenteritis. Once again, no diagnostic tests were ordered. The boy was returned to the Navy hospital on July 23, at which time diagnostic tests were performed. The patient was subsequently operated on and found to have a ruptured appendix. Holding the Navy hospital liable for the negligence of the physicians who acted as its agents, the court pointed out that a wrong diagnosis will not in and of itself support a verdict of liability in a lawsuit. However, a physician must use ordinary care in making a diagnosis. Only where a patient is adequately examined is there no liability for an erroneous diagnosis. In this instance, the physician's failure to perform further laboratory tests the first two times the child was brought to the emergency room was found to be a breach of good medical practice.

Diagnostic Testing—An Acceptable Standard

Physicians must conform to accepted standards. A plaintiff who claims that a physician has failed to order proper tests must show the following:

- It is a standard practice to employ a certain diagnostic test under the circumstances of the case.
- The physician failed to utilize the test and therefore failed to diagnose the patient's illness.
- The patient suffered injury as a result.

No damages can be awarded unless it can be shown that an incorrect therapeutic act or omission either caused injury to the patient or deprived the patient of a substantial chance for a cure.

FAILURE TO SEEK CONSULTATION OR TO REFER TO A MEDICAL SPECIALIST

The medical ethics statement of the American Medical Association indicates that physicians should seek consultations upon a patient's request, when the physician is in doubt, in difficult cases, or when it appears that the quality of medical service may be thereby enhanced.[1] Violation or failure to abide by medical ethics does not in and of itself constitute malpractice.

Whether or not the failure to refer constitutes negligence depends on whether referral is demanded by accepted standards of practice. In order to recover damages, the patient must show that the failure to refer resulted in injury.

Not every treatment of a patient that falls short of complete success is malpractice because the attending physician has failed to consult a specialist. Before malpractice may be imputed to physicians, it must be shown that they knew or should have known that a condition to be treated was beyond their ability, knowledge, and/or capacity to treat. *Manion v. Tweedy*, 257 Minn. 59, 100 N.W.2d 124 (1959).

A California Court of Appeals found that expert testimony is not necessary where good medical practice would require a general physician to suggest a specialist's consultation. The court ruled that since specialists were called in after the patient's condition grew worse, it is reasonable to assume that they could have been called in sooner. The jury was instructed by the court that a general practitioner has a duty to suggest calling in a specialist if a reasonably prudent general practitioner would do so under similar circumstances. *Valentine v. Kaiser Foundation Hospitals*, 194 Cal. App. 2d 282, 15 Cal. Rptr. 26 (1961) (dictum).

A physician is in a position of trust, and it is his or her duty to act in good faith. If a preferred treatment in a given situation is outside a physician's field of expertise, it is his or her duty to advise the patient. Failure to do so and continuance of a less desirable treatment constitute a breach of duty. Today, with the rapid methods of transportation and easy means of communication, the duty of a doctor is not fulfilled merely by utilizing the means at hand in a particular area of practice.

In *Doan v. Griffith*, 402 S.W.2d 855 (Ky. Ct. App. 1966), an accident victim was admitted to the hospital with serious injuries, including multiple fractures of his facial bones. The patient contended that the physician was negligent in not advising him at the time of discharge that his facial bones needed to be realigned by a specialist before the bones became fused. As a result, his face became disfigured. Expert testimony demonstrated that the customary medical treatment of the patient's injuries would have been to realign his fractured bones surgically as soon as the swelling subsided and that such treatment would have restored the normal contour of his face. The appellate court held that the jury could reasonably have found that the physician failed to provide timely advice to the patient on his need for further medical treatment and that such failure was the proximate cause of the patient's condition.

When a physician feels that medication, further office visits, or diet restrictions are indicated, the sufficiency of such instructions to the patient is a subjective, not an objective, matter. Physicians cannot assume that instructions are adequate just because a reasonably prudent person would understand them. They must make orders clear for each patient, given his or her experience, education, and general knowledge and the nature of the disease. *Everts v. Worrell*, 58 Utah 238, 197 P. 1043 (1921). In general, instructions to children must be given to parents as well. *Sharpe v. Pugh*, 270 N.C. 598, 155 S.E.2d 108 (1967). If a patient is incompetent, instructions must be given to an appropriate member of the family or other responsible person (e.g., a guardian or committee).

If a consulting physician has suggested a diagnosis with which the treating physician does not agree, it would be prudent to consider obtaining the opinion of a second consultant who could either confirm or disprove the first consultant's theory. Failure to diagnose and properly treat a suspected illness is an open door to liability.

INFECTIONS

The mere fact that a patient contracted an infection following an operation will not, in and of itself, cause a surgeon to be liable for negligence. The reason for this, according to the Nebraska Supreme Court in *McCall v. St. Joseph's Hospital*, 165 N.W.2d 85, 89 (Neb. 1969), is as follows:

Neither authority nor reason will sustain any proposition that negligence can reasonably be inferred from the fact that an infection originated at the site of a surgical wound. To permit a jury to infer negligence would be to expose every doctor and dentist to the charge of negligence every time an infection originated at the site of a wound. We note the complete absence of any expert testimony or any offer of proof in this record to the effect that a staphylococcus infection would automatically lead to an inference of negligence by the people in control of the operation or the treatment of the patient.

The district court of appeal held in *Gill v. Hartford Accident & Indemnity Co.*, 337 So. 2d 420 (Fla. Dist. Ct. App. 1976), that the physician who performed surgery on a patient in the same room as the plaintiff should have known that the infection the patient had was highly contagious. The failure of the physician to undertake steps to prevent the spread of the infection to the plaintiff and his failure to warn the plaintiff led the court to find that hospital authorities and the plaintiff's physician caused an unreasonable increase in the risk of injury to the plaintiff. As a result of the defendant's negligence, the plaintiff suffered injuries causally related to the negligence of the defendant.

A jury verdict in the amount of $300,000 was awarded in *Langley v. Michael*, 710 S.W.2d 373 (Mo. Ct. App. 1986), for damages arising from the amputation of the plaintiff's infected thumb. Evidence that the orthopedic surgeon failed to deeply cleanse, irrigate, and debride the injured area of the patient's thumb constituted proof of a departure from that degree of skill and learning ordinarily used by members of the medical profession, and that failure directly contributed to the patient's loss of the distal portion of his thumb.

LACK OF DOCUMENTATION

The importance of maintaining records of treatment rendered to a patient must not be underestimated. It may be many years after a patient has been treated before litigation is initiated; therefore, it is imperative that records of treatment in the physician's office, as well as in the hospital, be maintained. A jury may consider lack of documentation as sufficient evidence for finding a physician guilty of negligence.

In *Foley v. Bishop Clarkson Memorial Hospital*, 185 Neb. 89, 173 N.W.2d 881 (1970), a man sued the hospital for the death of his wife. During her pregnancy the patient was under the care of a private physician. She gave birth in the hospital on August 20, 1964 and died the following day. She had been treated by her physician for a sore throat during July and August. Several days after her death, one of her children was treated in the hospital for a strep throat. There was no evidence in the hospital record that the patient had complained about a sore throat while in the hospital. The hospital rules required a history and physical examination to be written promptly (within 24 hours of admission). No history had been taken, although the patient had been examined several times in regard to the progress of her labor. The trial judge directed a verdict in favor of the hospital. On appeal the appellate court held that the case should have been submitted to the jury for determination. A jury might reasonably have inferred that if the patient's condition had been properly treated, the infection could have been successfully combated and her life saved. It might also have been reasonably inferred that if a history had been promptly taken when she was admitted to the hospital, the cold and throat condition would have been discovered and the hospital personnel alerted to watch for possible complications of the nature that later developed. Quite possibly this attention would also have helped in diagnosing the patient's condition, especially if it had been apparent that she was exposed at home to a strep throat condition. The court held that a hospital must guard not only against known physical and mental conditions of patients, but also against conditions that reasonable care should have uncovered.

The standards and regulations fixed by the state department of health and by such organizations as the American Hospital Association, as well as the hospital's own rules, standards, and regulations, may be used to develop the standard of care.

LIABILITY FOR THE ACTS OF OTHERS

In *Martin v. Perth Amboy General Hospital*, 104 N.J. Super. 335, 250 A.2d 40 (N.J. Super., App. Div. 1969), a patient sued the hospital, cardiovascular surgeon, and nurses for leaving a laparotomy pad in his stomach. The surgeon who performed the operation was assisted by two other physicians as well as by a scrub nurse and a circulating nurse. When the lap pads were brought into the operating room, metal rings were attached to them. Sometime before the pads were used, the rings were removed at the direction of the operating surgeon. The essential reason for having the rings attached to the lap pads was to prevent errors in counts made by the nurses. The surgeon ordered the nurses to remove the rings, and they did so. By exercising control over the nurses to the extent of directing them to remove the rings, and thus eliminating the safeguards provided by the hospital to ensure a proper count by its employees, the surgeon became the nurses' "temporary or special employer" with regard to their duties involving the lap pads used during the operation. Thus, the surgeon was equally liable with the hospital for the nurses' subsequent negligence in counting the pads.

The concept of holding a physician liable for the acts of nurses or other hospital employees is commonly referred to as the borrowed servant or captain of the ship doctrine. However, many authorities are rejecting this doctrine as the role of nurses and other health care professionals and paraprofessionals becomes more specialized and independent. The physician in *Karas v. Jackson*, 582 F. Supp. 43 (E.D. Pa. 1983), was not held vicariously liable under either the captain of the ship doctrine or the general theory of *respondeat superior*. Dr. Jackson, who was the director of medical genetics at Thomas Jefferson University Hospital, did not at any time exercise or possess the right of control over an alleged negligent amniocentesis procedure conducted by another physician, which resulted in the death of the patient. Dr. Jackson did not perform the amniocentesis, nor was he present at any time during the procedure.

MISDIAGNOSIS

Misdiagnosis is the most frequently cited injury event in malpractice suits against physicians. Although diagnosis is a medical art and not an exact science, early detection is important to a patient's well-being.

Appendicitis

Misdiagnosis does not always end in a verdict for the plaintiff. Summary judgment was properly entered in dismissing an action alleging that a physician had been negligent in failing to diagnose a pregnant patient's appendicitis in *Fiedler v. Steger*, 713 P.2d 773 (Wyo. 1986). The testimony of expert witnesses for both parties established that diagnosis of appendicitis during pregnancy is difficult, that it probably would not have been diagnosed on the dates in question, and that the appendix had probably ruptured postpartum.

Breast Cancer

The patient in *DeBurkarte v. Louvar*, 393 N.W.2d 131 (Iowa 1986), brought a medical malpractice action against her family physician, an osteopathic general practitioner, for his failure to diagnose in a timely manner a patient's breast lump as cancerous. The district court had entered a verdict in favor of the patient, and the physician appealed. The supreme court held that the findings of negligence and proximate cause were adequately supported by the evidence presented at trial. The patient's husband was entitled to recover for loss of consortium, and the award of $405,000 in damages to the patient was not excessive.

Diabetic Acidosis

A case in the Mississippi Supreme Court, *Hill v. Stewart*, 209 So. 2d 809 (Miss. 1968), involved a patient who became ill and was admitted to the hospital. The physician was advised of the patient's recent weight loss, frequent urination, thirst, loss of vision, nausea, and vomiting. Routine lab tests were ordered, including a urinalysis, but not including a blood glucose test. On the following day, a consultant diagnosed the patient's condition as severe diabetic acidosis. Treatment was given, but the patient failed to respond to therapy and expired. The attending physician was sued for failing to test for diabetes and for failing to diagnose and treat the patient on the first day in the hospital. The attending physician said in court that he had suspected diabetes and admitted that when diabetes is suspected, a urinalysis and a blood sugar test should be performed. An expert medical witness testified that failure to do so would be a departure from the skill and care required of a general practitioner. The witness also stated that the patient in this case would probably have had a good chance of survival if properly treated. The state supreme court reversed the directed verdict for the physician by a lower court and remanded the case for retrial. There was sufficient evidence presented to permit the case to go to the jury for decision.

Once a physician concludes that a particular test is indicated, it should be performed and evaluated as soon as practicable. Delay may constitute negligence. The law imposes on a physician the same degree of responsibility in making a diagnosis as it does in prescribing and administering treatment.

Heart Problem

The federal government in *Lauderdale v. United States*, 666 F. Supp. 1511 (D.C. Ala. 1987), was held liable under the Federal Tort Claims Act for the death of a patient whose mitral valve malfunction was misdiagnosed at a military medical clinic. Under the applicable Alabama law the physician failed to conduct the necessary tests to determine the cause of a suspected heart problem. The physician never indicated to the patient that the problem was severe, that the treatment with digoxin was tentative, and that his well-being mandated that he return in a week. The patient subsequently died. He was found not to have been contributorily negligent by failing to return to the clinic. The patient had not been sufficiently told of the urgency of a return visit. This failure was considered the proximate cause of the patient's death since his illness might have been treated successfully.

Hyperparathyroidism

The jury found in *Koster v. Greenberg*, 502 N.Y.S.2d 395 (App. Div. 1986), that a physician was responsible for a patient's death due to his failure to diagnose her condition of hyperparathyroidism, which was supported by the record. Expert testimony demonstrated that death occurred because of a number of causes, including renal failure secondary to hyperparathyroidism.

Perforated Bowel

A clinic was found liable in *Gegan v. Backwinkel*, 417 N.W.2d 44 (Wis. Ct. App. 1987), for failing to diagnose a patient's perforated bowel. It was determined that the patient's chance of survival would have been better than 90 percent if the patient's condition had been properly diagnosed and treated by the clinic's physicians. The plaintiff was awarded $150,000 for the patient's mental anguish and suffering, which occurred during hospitalization as a result of unnecessary surgeries, and $250,000 was awarded to cover potential pecuniary losses for the financial support, college funds, and inheritance of the patient's children.

Pregnancy

A physician's license was suspended for 30 days in *Livingston v. Arkansas State Medical Board*, 701 S.W.2d 361 (Ark. 1986), for repeatedly diagnosing a patient as being pregnant over a period of 4 months when in reality she was not pregnant.

Skull Fracture

In *Ramberg v. Morgan*, 218 N.W. 492 (Iowa 1928), a police department physician, at the scene of an accident, examined an unconscious man who had been struck by an automobile. The physician concluded that the patient's insensibility was a result of alcohol intoxication, not the accident, and ordered the police to remove him to jail instead of the hospital. The man, to the physician's knowledge, remained semiconscious for several days and was finally taken from the cell to the hospital at the insistence of his family. The patient subsequently died, and the autopsy revealed massive skull fractures. The court said that any physician should reasonably anticipate the presence of head injuries when a person is struck by a car; failure to refer an accident victim to another physician or a hospital is actionable neglect of the physician's duty. While a physician does not insure the correctness of the diagnosis or treatment, a patient is entitled to such thorough and careful examination as his or her condition and attending circumstances permit, with such diligence and methods of diagnosis as are usually approved and practiced by medical people of ordinary or average learning, judgment, and skill in the community or similar localities.

Testicular Cancer

The hospital in *Brickner v. Osteopathic Hospital, Inc.*, 746 S.W.2d 108 (Mo. Ct. App. 1988), was held vicariously liable for a surgical resident's failure to diagnose testicular cancer during exploratory surgery performed under the supervision of a staff physician. The hospital was not insulated from liability under the borrowed servant doctrine even though the supervising surgeon had authority over the resident during the operation. The hospital never relinquished control over the resident, who was required under the hospital's training program to assist in diagnosis and who could have taken a biopsy without express instructions of the operating surgeon. Liability was not precluded because of the hospital's lack of actual control over the resident's medical decision not to perform a biopsy. The resident was performing a service for which he had been employed.

MISTAKEN IDENTITY

In *Southwestern Kentucky Baptist Hospital, Inc. v. Bruce*, 539 S.W.2d 286 (Ky. 1976), a patient admitted for conization of the cervix was mistakenly taken to the operating room for a thyroidectomy. The physician was notified early during surgery that he had the wrong patient on the operating room table. The operation was immediately terminated. The thyroidectomy was not completed, and the incision was sutured. The patient filed an action for malpractice and recovered $10,000 from the physician and $90,000 from the hospital. The fact that the patient mistakenly answered to the name of another patient who had been scheduled for a thyroidectomy did not excuse the failure of the surgeon, the anesthesiologist, and the surgical technician to determine the identity of the patient by examining his identification bracelet. The supreme court held that the verdict was not excessive in view of the injuries, which consisted of a four-inch incision along the patient's neck, which became infected and would require cosmetic surgery.

OBSTETRICS

One of the most vulnerable medical specialties with tremendous risk exposure to malpractice suits is obstetrics. The following cases illustrate why the risks are high.

Failure To Perform a Caesarian Section

A medical malpractice action was brought against two obstetricians, a pediatrician, and the hospital in *Ledogar v. Giordano*, 505 N.Y.S.2d 899 (App. Div. 1986), due to a newborn infant's prenatal and postnatal hypoxia which allegedly caused brain damage, resulting in autism. The record contained sufficient proof of causation to support a verdict in favor of the plaintiff where an expert obstetrician testified that both obstetricians were negligent in failing to perform a Caesarian section at an earlier time, that the hospital staff departed from proper medical standards of care by not monitoring the fetal heartbeat at least every 15 minutes, and that with a reasonable degree of medical certainty, it was probable that the fetus had suffered hypoxia during labor.

Failure To Attend

The plaintiff in *Lucchesi v. Stimmell*, 149 Ariz. 76, 716 P.2d 1013 (1986), brought an action against a physician for intentional infliction of emotional distress, claiming that the physician had failed to be present during unsuccessful attempts to deliver her premature fetus and that he had thereafter failed to disclose to her the fact that the fetus was decapitated during attempts to achieve delivery by pulling on the hip area in order to free the head. The judge instructed the jury that it could conclude that the physician had been guilty of extreme and outrageous conduct for staying at home and leaving delivery in the hands of a first-year intern and a third-year resident, neither of whom was experienced in breech deliveries.

Injury to the Brachial Plexus Nerves

The attending physician in *Jackson v. Huang*, 514 So. 2d 727 (La. Ct. App. 1987), was negligent in failing to perform a timely Caesarian section. The attending physician had applied too much traction when he was faced with shoulder dyscotia, a situation where a baby's shoulder hangs under the pubic bone, arresting the progress of the infant through the birth canal. As a result, the infant suffered permanent injury to the brachial plexus nerves of his right shoulder and arm. On appeal of this case, there was no error found in the trial court's finding of fact where such finding was supported by testimony of the plaintiff's expert witness. The trial judge accepted the testimony of Dr. Forte, the expert witness, who testified that the defendant did possess the necessary skill and knowledge relevant to the practice of obstetrics and gynecology. The defendant, because of prolonged labor and weight of the baby, should have anticipated the possibility of shoulder dyscotia and performed a timely caesarian section. 514 So.2d at 727.

Joint Liability

An obstetrician and a pediatrician were held jointly liable in *Ravo by Ravo v. Rogatnick*, 514 N.E.2d 1104 (N.Y. 1987), for injuries suffered by a newborn child which resulted in mental retardation. Expert witnesses were unable to segregate the effects of the trauma and hypoxia allegedly caused by the obstetrician's negligence from the hyperbilirubinemia and an excessively high hematocrit level which had been inadequately addressed by the pediatrician. Damages in the amount of $2,750,000 were awarded the plaintiff. The jury apportioned the fault by assigning 80 percent to the obstetrician and 20 percent to the pediatrician. This judgment did not affect the plaintiff's right to collect the entire amount from either defendant. The 80 percent/20 percent apportionment between the obstetrician and the pediatrician defined the contribution that the defendants might claim from each other.

Nurse Assessment

The defendant physicians in *Cignetti v. Camel*, 692 S.W.2d 329 (Mo. Ct. App. 1985), ignored a nurse's assessment of a patient's diagnosis, which contributed to a delay in treatment and injury to the patient. The nurse had testified that she told the physician that the patient's signs and symptoms were not those associated with indigestion. The defendant physician objected to this testimony, indicating that such a statement constituted a medical diagnosis by a nurse. The trial court permitted the testimony to be entered into evidence. Missouri Revised Statutes Section 335.016(8) (as revised in 1975) authorizes a registered nurse to make an assessment of persons who are ill and to render a "nursing diagnosis." On appeal, the Missouri Court of Appeals affirmed the lower court's ruling, holding that evidence of negligence presented by a hospital employee, for which an obstetrician was not responsible, was admissible to show the events that occurred during the patient's hospital stay.

Wrongful Death of a Viable Unborn Fetus

Summary dismissal was found to have been improperly ordered in *Lobdell v. Tarrant County Hospital District*, 710 S.W.2d 811 (Tex. Ct. App. 1986), in an action by the parents of a stillborn child against the physician and hospital on the theory that no cause of action lay for the wrongful death of a viable unborn fetus. A child capable of independent life outside the mother's womb had an independent existence as a person apart from its mother, and damages were recoverable for the wrongful death. Under the Texas Wrongful Death Act, the parents had a right to recover for the negligent conduct proximately causing the intrauterine death of a viable fetus.

A medical malpractice action was filed against the physician in *Modaber v. Kelley*, 348 S.E.2d 233 (Va. 1986), for personal injuries and mental anguish due to the stillbirth of a child. The circuit court entered judgment on a jury verdict against the obstetrician, and an appeal was taken. The supreme court held that the evidence was sufficient to support a finding that the obstetrician's conduct during the patient's pregnancy caused direct injury to the patient. Evidence at trial showed that the physician failed to treat the mother's known condition of toxemia, including the development of high blood pressure and the premature separation of the placenta from the uterine wall, and that the physician had thereafter failed to respond in a timely fashion when the mother went into premature labor. The supreme court also held that injury to the unborn child constituted injury to the mother and that she could recover for the physical injury and mental anguish associated with the stillbirth. The court found that the award of $750,000 in compensatory damages was not excessive.

PREMATURE DISMISSAL OF A CASE

Physicians and hospitals run the risk of liability for the premature dismissal of a patient. It is better to be cautious than to regret prematurely dismissing a patient's complaint. One cannot be too circumspect even if a patient is well known by the treating physician.

PRESCRIPTIONS

The Board of Registration in *Keigan v. Board of Registration*, 506 N.E.2d 866 (Mass. 1987), was found not to have acted arbitrarily or capriciously when it suspended a physician's license for one year and placed the physician on probation for four years. The physician was found to have improperly prescribed controlled substances for 13 drug-dependent individuals and to have failed to report their names and addresses and to maintain proper medical records with respect to such patients. The physician's arguments that such a sanction was overly severe because of his advanced age, that his actions had been well motivated, and that there was a lack of medical services for his indigent patients had no merit.

The Board of Regents in *Moyo v. Ambach*, 523 N.Y.S. 645 (App. Div. 1988), determined that a physician had fraudulently and with gross negligence prescribed methaqualone to 20 patients. The Board of Regents found that the physician did not prescribe methaqualone in good faith or for sound medical reasons. His abuse in prescribing controlled substances constituted the fraudulent practice of medicine. Expert testimony established that it was common knowledge in the medical community that methaqualone was a widely abused and addictive drug. Methaqualone should not have been utilized for insomnia without first trying other means of treatment. On appeal, the court found that there was sufficient evidence to support the board's finding.

PSYCHIATRY

The major risk areas of psychiatry include commitment, electroshock, duty to warn, and suicide. Matters relating to admission, consent, and discharge are governed by statute in most states. The outcomes in the cases presented below are generally governed both by the statutes involved and common law principles. As with any review of case law, it must be remembered that a court's decision in one state is not binding in another.

Commitment

Physicians who participate in the commitment of a patient should do so only after first examining the patient and reaching his/her own conclusions. Reliance on another's examination and recommendation for commitment could give rise to a claim of malpractice.

Involuntary

Proof of dangerousness in *In re Detention of Meistrell*, 733 P.2d 1004 (Wash. Ct. App. 1987), was found adequate to support an order of involuntary commitment. There was testimony that on two occasions the patient had jumped off a teeter-totter, causing his two small children to fall to the ground. A substantial risk of physical harm to others was also demonstrated by testimony that the patient had threatened his wife's ex-husband.

The likelihood of future harm was found sufficient in *In re Burmeister*, 391 N.W.2d 89 (Minn. Ct. App. 1986), to commit a patient suffering from paranoid schizophrenia. The record indicated that the patient, while living with his mother, had stuffed the family fireplace with a large amount of paper, lighted the fire, scorched the front of the fireplace, and then closed the damper while the fire continued to burn.

A psychiatrist filed a petition for additional detention of a person previously ordered admitted to a state hospital for pretrial psychiatric examination. The circuit court, after hearing testimony from the appellant's son, a social worker at the hospital, and the psychiatrist, ordered detention, and the detainee appealed. The court of appeals in *In the Matter of Todd*, 767 S.W.2d 589 (Mo. Ct. App. 1988), held that the testimony of the psychiatrist established clear and convincing evidence to meet a required standard that the detainee's actions presented risk of serious harm to herself or others. The episode giving rise to the involuntary commitment occurred when the appellant threw eggs at a house and various businesses and broke some windows at a house with a tire iron. She lightly bumped a police car and was charged with second-degree property damage. During her involuntary detention she refused to take her medications, which were necessary because of her illness. The psychiatrist indicated his concern that she might harm her invalid husband upon release. Additional detention was considered necessary until such time as the detainee's illness could be controlled by drugs.

A New York supreme court found a patient to be mentally ill and authorized his involuntary retention. On appeal the supreme court, appellate division, held in *In the Matter of Carl C.*, 511 N.Y.S.2d 144 (App. Div. 1987), that the state had not shown by clear and convincing evidence that the patient's instability caused him to pose a substantial threat of physical injury to himself or others. The examining physician's testimony indicated that the patient did not pose a direct threat of physical harm to himself or others, but that it was questionable whether he would be able to provide for the essentials of life. The patient had testified that he was aware of food needs, of where to get food, and how he would pay for it. He indicated that he would not sleep outside and that he had a bed in a rooming house where he had been paying rent for two years.

By Spouse

In *Bencomo v. Morgan*, 210 So. 2d 236 (Fla. Dist. Ct. App. 1968), the plaintiff's husband filed a petition to have his wife declared incompetent. In a letter supporting the petition, the defendant physician, who had treated the wife ten years previously, stated that she was badly in need of a psychiatric examination. The plaintiff wife attempted to sue the physician for libel and slander. The court held that the plaintiff had no cause for action since it was her husband who initiated the commitment procedures.

By Parent

The U.S. Supreme Court, in *Parham v. J.R.*, 442 U.S. 584 (1979), held that the risk of error inherent in a parental decision to have a child institutionalized for mental health care is sufficiently great that an inquiry should be made by a neutral fact finder to determine whether statutory requirements for admission are satisfied. Although a formal or quasi-formal hearing is not required and an inquiry need not be conducted by a law-trained judicial or administrative officer, such inquiry must carefully probe a child's background, using all available sources. It is necessary that a decision maker have the authority to refuse to admit a child who does not satisfy medical standards for admission. A child's continuing need for commitment must also be reviewed periodically by a similarly independent procedure.

Patient Due Process Rights

The principles of due process were violated in *Birl v. Wallis*, 619 F. Supp. 481 (D. Ala. 1985), when an involuntarily committed patient was conditionally released and reconfined without notice and opportunity for a hearing. Remand was required to permit the drafting of reconfinement procedures that would adequately protect the patient's due process rights.

Electroshock

Most states have laws and regulations governing the use of electroshock and other drastic treatments for psychiatric patients. Failure to abide by these statutory and regulatory guidelines may result in liability both to the hospital and to the treating physician.

Appropriate precautions should be taken to reduce the risks of fractures or other potential harm that might occur to patients. If appropriate precautions are taken, the likelihood of successful malpractice suits in this area will be limited. In *Collins v. Hand*, 431 Pa. 378, 246 A.2d 398 (1968), the court pointed out that fractures are a recognized risk of electroshock therapy and that negligence would have to be established by expert testimony.

Duty To Warn

In *Tarasoff v. Regents of the University of California*, 17 Cal. 3d 425, 551 P.2d 334, 131 Cal. Rptr. 14 (1976), a former patient allegedly killed a third party after revealing his homicidal plans to his therapist. His therapist made no effort to inform the victim of the patient's intentions. The California Supreme Court held that where a therapist determines or reasonably should have determined that a patient poses a serious danger of violence to others, there is a duty to exercise reasonable care to protect the foreseeable victims and to warn them of any impending danger. Discharge of this duty may also include notifying the police or taking whatever steps are reasonably necessary under the circumstances.

Under Nebraska law, the relationship between a psychotherapist and a patient gives rise to an affirmative duty to initiate whatever precautions are reasonably necessary to protect the potential victims of a patient. This duty develops when a therapist knows or should know that a patient's dangerous propensities present an unreasonable risk of harm to others (see, e.g., *Lipari v. Sears, Roebuck & Co.*, 497 F. Supp. 185 (D. Neb. 1980)).

Exceptions to the Duty To Warn

The Maryland Court of Special Appeals, in *Shaw v. Glickman*, 415 A.2d 625 (Md. Ct. Spec. App. 1980), held that a plaintiff could not recover against a psychiatric team on the theory that they were negligent in failing to warn the plaintiff of the patient's unstable and violent condition. The court held that making such a disclosure would have violated statutes pertaining to privilege against disclosure of communications relating to treatment of mental or emotional disorders. The court found that a psychiatrist may have a duty to warn the potential victim of a dangerous mental patient's intent to harm; however, the duty could be imposed only if the psychiatrist knew the identity of the prospective victim. *Furr v. Spring Grove State Hospital*, 454 A.2d 414 (Md. App. 1983).

The psychiatrist in *Currie v. United States*, 836 F.2d 209 (4th Cir. 1987), was found not to have had a duty to seek the involuntary commitment of a patient who evidenced homicidal tendencies. Absent control over the patient, the federal government could not be held liable for a murder which the patient committed at his former place of employment. The psychiatrist had warned the patient's former employer and law enforcement officials about his dangerousness.

There was no duty on the part of the hospital or treating psychiatrists in *Sharpe v. South Carolina Department of Mental Health*, 354 S.E.2d 778 (S.C. Ct. App. 1987), to warn the general public of the potential danger that might result from a psychiatric patient's release from a state hospital. There was no identifiable threat to a decedent who was shot by the patient approximately two months following the patient's release from voluntary commitment under a plan of outpatient care. In addition, there was nothing in the record that indicated that the former patient and the decedent had known each other prior to the patient's release.

Suicide

The attendant in *Fernandez v. State*, 15 A.D.2d 125, 356 N.Y.S.2d 708 (1974), left the room for five minutes when the patient appeared to be asleep. During the attendant's absence, the patient injured herself in a repeated suicide attempt. The court found that even if the hospital had assumed a duty to continually observe the patient, such a five-minute absence would not constitute negligence. Therefore, the hospital could not be held liable for the patient's injuries.

A patient with a 14-year history of mental problems escaped from a hospital and committed suicide by jumping off a roof. Notations had been made in the record that the patient was to be checked every 15 minutes. There was no evidence that such checks had been made. The appellate court ruled that the facts showed a prima facie case of negligence. *Fatuck v. Hillside Hospital*, 45 A.D.2d 708, 356 N.Y.S.2d 105 (1974), *aff'd*, 36 N.Y.2d 736, 328 N.E.2d 791, 368 N.Y.S.2d 161 (1975) (no opinion).

The supreme court, appellate division, in *Eady v. Alter*, 380 N.Y.S.2d 737 (App. Div. 1976), held that an intern's notation on the hospital record that the patient tried to jump out the window was sufficient to establish a prima facie case against the hospital. The patient succeeded in committing suicide by jumping out the window approximately ten minutes after having been seen by the intern. Testimony had been given that the patient was inadequately restrained following the reported incident.

SURGERY/ASSISTANT SURGEON

A physician who merely refers a patient to another physician—who is not an associate, employer, or employee—and who lends casual assistance at an operation is not jointly liable for the negligence of the physician operating. In *Graddy v. New York Medical College*, 19 A.D.2d 426, 243 N.Y.S.2d 40 (1963), the court ruled that referral of a patient to another physician—absent partnership, employment, or agency—does not impose liability on the referring physician.

TREATMENT OUTSIDE THE FIELD OF COMPETENCE

A physician should practice discretion when treating a patient outside his or her field of expertise or competence. The standard of care required in a malpractice case will be that of the specialty in which a physician is treating, whether or not he or she has appropriate credentials in that specialty.

In a California case, *Carrasco v. Bankoff*, 220 Cal. App. 2d 230, 33 Cal. Rptr. 673 (1963), a small boy suffering third-degree burns over 18 percent of his body was admitted to a hospital. During his initial confinement, there was little done except to occasionally dress and redress the burned area. At the end of a 53-day confinement, the patient was suffering hypergranulation of the burned area and muscular-skeletal dysfunction. The surgeon treating him was not a board-certified plastic surgeon and apparently not properly trained in the management of burn cases.

At trial, the patient's medical expert, a plastic surgeon who had assumed responsibility for care after the first hospitalization, outlined the accepted medical practice in cases of this nature. The first surgeon acknowledged this accepted practice. The court held that there was substantial evidence to permit a finding of professional negligence due to the defendant surgeon's failure to perform to the accepted standard of care and that such failure resulted in the patient's injury.

FAILURE TO READ X-RAYS

The patient in *Tams v. Lotz*, 530 A.2d 1217 (D.C. 1987), had to undergo a second surgical procedure to remove a laparotomy pad that had been left negligently in the patient during a previous surgical procedure. The trial court was found to have properly directed a verdict with respect to the patient's assertion that the surgeon who performed the first operation had failed to read a postoperative x-ray report which allegedly would have put him on notice both that the pad was present and that there was a need for emergency surgery to remove the pad, therefore averting the need to remove a portion of his intestine.

The plaintiffs in *Killebrew v. Johnson*, 404 N.E.2d 1194 (Ind. Ct. App. 1980), had filed a complaint to recover damages from the physician, alleging that he was negligent by failing to inform himself of the results of x-rays he ordered to determine the possible location of an intrauterine contraceptive device. The superior court granted the physician's motion for judgment. The court of appeals held that the testimony of the plaintiff's medical witness and the treating physician's admission that he did not inform himself of the contents of the x-rays or the x-ray reports were sufficient to place before the jury the applicable standard of care.

The failure of a radiologist to properly read an x-ray does not necessarily constitute negligence. This is especially true in those cases where the treatment rendered to the patient would have been the same regardless of the radiologist's findings.

FAILURE TO NOTIFY OF X-RAY RESULTS

The court of appeals in *Washington Healthcare Corporation v. Barrow*, 531 A.2d 226 (D.C. 1987), held that evidence was sufficient to sustain a finding that the hospital was negligent in failing to provide a radiology report demonstrating pathology on a patient's lung in a timely manner. An x-ray of the patient taken on April 4, 1982, disclosed a small nodular density in her right lung. Within a year the cancerous nodule had grown to the size of a softball. The most significant testimony at trial was that of Theresa James, a medical student who worked for Dr. Oweiss until and including April 23, 1982. Ms. James testified that her job entailed combing through Dr. Oweiss's mail and locating abnormal x-ray reports, which she would then bring to his attention. Emphasizing that she had come to know the patient personally, Ms. James said that she would have been upset if she had come across an abnormal report on her. Ms. James claimed that she received no such report while working for the physician, thus accounting for 19 days after the x-ray was taken. Ms. James stated that the x-ray reports were usually received within four or five days after being taken. There was testimony to corroborate her testimony by Dr. Odenwald, who dictated the patient's report on April 4, 1982. Dr. Odenwald of Groover, Christie and Merritt, PC (GCM), which operated the radiology department at the Washington Hospital Center (WHC), stated that the x-ray reports were usually typed and mailed the same day they were dictated. The jury could have determined that if the report did not reach Dr. Oweiss by April 23, 1982, it did not reach him by May 3, 1982. The patient's record was eventually found; however, it was not in the patient's regular folder. One could infer that the record was therefore negligently filed. Questions also arise as to why Dr. Oweiss did nothing to follow up on the matter in ensuing months. Dr. Oweiss testified that he did receive the report by May 3, 1982, and that he informed Mrs. Barrow of its contents. Mrs. Barrow stated that although her folder was on the physician's desk at the time of her visit, he did not relay to her any information regarding an abnormal x-ray. Dr. Oweiss, however, was severely impeached at trial, and the jury chose not to believe him. Considering the entire record, there was reasonable probability that WHC was negligent and that Dr. Oweiss had not received the report. The plaintiff had settled with Dr. Oweiss, the patient's personal physician, in the amount of $200,000 during pendency in the district court, and the action against him was dismissed with prejudice. The record did not support WHC's request of indemnification from Dr. Oweiss. The trial court had directed a verdict in favor of GCM, leaving WHC as the sole defendant. The court of appeals remanded WHC's crossclaim for indemnification from GCM for further findings of fact and conclusions by the trial court.

THE PHYSICIAN-PATIENT RELATIONSHIP

The suggestions below, if followed, will help to decrease the probability of malpractice suits.

- Do not guarantee treatment outcome.
- Provide for cross-coverage during days off.
- Maintain timely, complete, and accurate records. Do not make erasures.
- Personalize your treatment. A patient is more inclined to sue an impersonal physician than one with whom he or she has developed a good relationship.
- Do not overextend your practice.

- Provide sufficient time and care to each patient. Take the time to explain treatment plans and follow-up care to the patient, his or her family, and other professionals caring for your patient.
- Prescribing over the telephone is generally not advisable.
- Do not become careless because you know the patient.
- Request consultations when indicated, and refer if necessary.
- Seek the advice of counsel should you suspect the possibility of a malpractice claim.

NOTE

1. AMERICAN MEDICAL ASSOCIATION, OPINIONS AND REPORTS OF THE JUDICIAL COUNCIL (1966).

Chapter 5

Nurses' Liability

This chapter describes many of the legal risks of nurses. The acts and omissions that may constitute negligence on the part of a nurse often render a hospital liable under the doctrine of *respondeat superior*.

ADMINISTRATION OF DRUGS

Nurses are required to handle and administer a vast variety of drugs that are prescribed by physicians and dispensed by hospital pharmacies. Medications may range from aspirin to esoteric drugs that are administered via IV solutions. These medications must be administered in the prescribed manner and dose in order to prevent serious harm to patients.

The practice of pharmacy essentially includes preparing, compounding, dispensing, and retailing medications. These activities may be carried out only by a pharmacist with a state license or by a person exempted from the provisions of a state's pharmacy statutes. Nurses are exempted from the various pharmacy statutes when administering a medication upon the oral or written order of a physician.

The Wrong Dosage

A nurse is responsible for making an inquiry if there is uncertainty about the accuracy of an order in a patient's record. In the Louisiana case of *Norton v. Argonaut Insurance Co.*, 144 So. 2d 249 (La. Ct. App. 1962), the court focused attention on the responsibility of a nurse to obtain clarification of an apparently erroneous order from the patient's physician. The medication order of the attending physician, as entered in the chart, was incomplete and subject to misinterpretation. Believing the order to be incorrect because of the dosage, the nurse asked two physicians present in the ward whether the medication should be given as ordered.

The two physicians did not interpret the order as the nurse did and therefore did not share the same concern. They advised the nurse that the attending physician's instructions did not appear out of line. The nurse did not contact the attending physician, but instead administered the misinterpreted dosage of medication. As a result, the patient died from a fatal overdose of the medication.

The court upheld the jury's finding that the nurse had been negligent in failing to get in contact with the attending physician before administering the medication. The nurse was held liable, as was the physician who wrote the ambiguous order that led to the fatal dose. In discussing the standard of care expected of a nurse who encounters an apparently erroneous order, the court stated that not only was the nurse unfamiliar with the medication in question, but also she violated the rule generally followed by the members of the nursing profession in the community, which requires that the prescribing physician be called when there is doubt about an order for medication. The court noted that it is the duty of a nurse, in such instances, to make absolutely certain what the doctor intended, regarding both dosage and route. In this case, the evidence leaves no doubt that while nurses do at times consult any available physician when unsure of another physician's orders, the nurses who testified agreed that the better practice is to consult the prescribing physician about doubtful orders for medication. This clarification was not sought from the physician who wrote the order, and the departure from the standard of competent nursing practice provided the basis for holding the nurse liable for negligence.

Negligent Injection

In *Bernardi v. Community Hospital Association*, 166 Colo. 280, 443 P.2d 708 (1968), a seven-year-old patient was in the hospital after surgery for the drainage of an abscessed appendix. The attending physician had left a written postoperative order at the hospital that the patient was to be given an injection of tetracycline every 12 hours. During the evening of the first day following surgery, the nurse, employed by the hospital and acting under this order, injected the prescribed dosage of tetracycline in the patient's right gluteal region. It was claimed that the nurse negligently injected the tetracycline into or adjacent to the sciatic nerve, causing the patient to permanently lose the normal use of the right foot. The court did not hold the physician responsible. It concluded that if the plaintiff could prove the nurse's negligence, the hospital would be responsible for the nurse's act under the doctrine of *respondeat superior*. The physician did not know which nurse administered the injection since he was not present when the injection was given, and he had no opportunity to control its administration. The hospital was found liable under the doctrine of *respondeat superior*. The appellate court said: "The hospital was the employer of the nurse. Only it had the right to hire and fire her. Only it could assign the nurse to certain hours, designated areas and specific patients."

The Wrong Route

The nurse in *Fleming v. Baptist General Convention of Oklahoma,* 742 P.2d 1087 (Okla. 1987), negligently injected the patient with a solution of Talwin and Atarax subcutaneously, rather than intramuscularly. The patient suffered tissue necrosis as a result of the improper injection. The suit against the hospital was successful. On appeal, the court held that the jury's verdict for the plaintiff found adequate support in the testimony of the plaintiff's expert witness on the issues of negligence and causation.

Failure To Note an Order Change

Failure to review a patient's record before administering a medication to ascertain whether an order has been modified may render a nurse liable for negligence. The case of *Larrimore v. Homeopathic Hospital Association,* 54 Del. 449, 181 A.2d 573 (1962), concerned a female patient who had been receiving a drug by injection over a period of time. There came a time when the physician wrote an instruction on the patient's order sheet changing the method of administration from injection to oral medication. When a nurse on the patient unit who had been off duty for several days was preparing to medicate the patient by injection, the patient objected and referred the nurse to the physician's new order. The nurse, however, told the patient she was mistaken and gave the medication by injection. Perhaps the nurse had not reviewed the order sheet after being told by the patient that the medication was to be given orally; perhaps the nurse did not notice the physician's entry. Either way, the nurse's conduct was held to be negligent. The court went on to say that the jury could find the nurse negligent by applying ordinary common sense to establish the applicable standard of care.

Failure To Administer Medication

In *Kallenberg v. Beth Israel Hospital,* 45 A.D.2d 1977, 357 N.Y.S.2d 508 (1974), a patient died after her third cerebral hemorrhage due to the failure of the physicians and staff to administer necessary medications. When the patient was admitted to the hospital, her physician determined that she should be given a specific drug to reduce her blood pressure and make her condition operable. For an unexplained reason the drug was not administered. The patient's blood pressure rose, and after the final hemorrhage, she died. The jury found the hospital and physicians negligent in failing to administer the drug and ruled that the negligence had caused the patient's death. The appellate court found that the jury had sufficient evidence to decide that the negligent treatment had been the cause of the patient's death.

Failure To Discontinue Medication

A hospital will be held liable if a nurse continues to inject a solution after noticing its ill effects. In the Florida case of *Parrish v. Clark*, 107 Fla. 598, 145 So. 848 (1933), the court held that a nurse's continued injection of saline solution into an unconscious patient's breast after the nurse noticed ill effects constituted negligence. Thus, once something was observed to be wrong with the administration of the solution, the nurse had the duty to discontinue its use.

BURNS

Burns by hot water bottles, sitz baths, heating pads, etc., are major causes of liability suits against hospitals. The plaintiff in *Quinby v. Morrow*, 340 F.2d 584 (2d Cir. 1965), sought damages against the hospital, the instrument nurse, and the surgeon for third-degree burns sustained by her ward during a tonsillectomy. A hot metal gag had been placed in the patient's mouth, causing the severe burn. There was testimony that it was the duty of the circulating nurse, a hospital employee not named in the suit, to have a basin of water available to cool sterilized surgical instruments before their use. The surgeon testified that the basin was missing or at least not in its usual place and that this was a serious omission. The jury returned a verdict holding the hospital liable for $30,000, but found the surgeon and the instrument nurse not liable. These verdicts were affirmed by the appellate court, which held that evidence was sufficient to allow the jury to affix responsibility to the hospital, based on the acts of the circulating nurse, and to exonerate the surgeon and the instrument nurse.

DUTY TO FOLLOW ESTABLISHED NURSING PROCEDURES

The following cases present potential hazards to nurses who fail to follow established nursing procedures.

Isolation Techniques

Failure to follow proper isolation techniques, such as proper hand washing and prevention of cross-contamination, is a major area of concern for hospitals. The patient in *Helmann v. Sacred Heart Hospital*, 62 Wash. 2d 136, 381 P.2d 605 (1963), had sustained chest injuries, a left hip dislocation, and multiple fractures in the area of the left hip socket and was paralyzed from the waist down. The patient was returned to his room following hip surgery. The patient's roommate complained of a boil under his right arm. Eight days later a culture was taken of drainage from the wound. Three days later the laboratory identified the infection as

Staphylococcus aureus. The infected roommate was immediately transferred to an isolation room. Up until this time, ward nurses and hospital attendants administered to both patients regularly, moving from one patient to another without washing their hands as they changed dressings, gave back rubs, and carried out routine procedures. On the day the roommate was placed in isolation, the plaintiff's wound erupted, discharging a large amount of purulent drainage. A culture of the drainage showed it to have been caused by the presence of Staphylococcus aureus. The infection penetrated into the patient's hip socket, destroying tissue and requiring a second operation. In the second operation, the patient's hip was fused in a nearly immovable position. The Supreme Court of Washington affirmed a judgment for the patient. The court ruled that there was sufficient circumstantial evidence from which the jury could have found that the patients were infected with the same Staphylococcus aureus strain and that the infection was caused by the hospital's negligence in that its personnel failed to follow sterile techniques in ministering to its two patients.

In Staphylococcus infection cases, one must demonstrate negligence of the defendant and injury resulting from that negligence. The burden of proof is on the plaintiff to establish a causal relationship between the injury and the hospital's deviation from the accepted standard of care. Negligence on the part of hospitals usually arises from their failure to follow appropriate isolation procedures. Sterile technique must be followed even where a patient is suspected to have a Staphylococcus infection, though it has not been confirmed. Negligence often arises from failure to make a proper diagnosis and/or to treat properly.

A practical nurse's license was revoked in *Homes v. Department of Professional Regulation Board of Nursing*, 504 So. 2d 1338 (Fla. Dist. Ct. App. 1987), because of the nurse's failure to utilize proper aseptic techniques in inserting a catheter in a female patient who was observed to be in distress. The nurse had failed to properly assess and report a broken area on the patient's coccyx. The nurse's conduct constituted unprofessional conduct in violation of Florida statutes and was considered justification for revocation of her license. The revocation order by the Board of Nursing stated that the nurse was prohibited permanently from petitioning the board for reinstatement of her license. This was held to be improper because it conflicted with Florida statutes and with the rules of the Department of Professional Regulation.

Staphylococcus infections can be prevented by requiring the staff to have periodic physicals including cultures, maintaining an active infections committee, following predetermined isolation procedures (which should be maintained in writing), and taking other reasonable precautions.

DUTY TO FOLLOW THE PHYSICIAN'S ORDERS

In *Toth v. Community Hospital at Glen Cove*, 239 N.E.2d 368, 292 N.Y.S.2d 635 (Ct. App. 1968), twin girls were administered oxygen. One became completely blind, and the other suffered severe damage to one eye. It was established that the attending pediatrician, who was sued along with the hospital, had ordered administration of six liters of oxygen per minute for the first 12 hours and four liters per minute thereafter. The nurses in the nursery, however, had given six liters per minute continuously over a period of several weeks. The jury found that the defendant physician was not negligent in ordering the oxygen and that he was not negligent for failure to reduce the level of oxygen himself. However, the hospital was liable for the negligence of its employees—the nurses in charge of the nursery—who failed to follow the physician's orders. The court of appeals, emphasizing that it is the duty of the nurse to follow the physician's orders, held it was an error for the case against the hospital to have been dismissed. It was wrong to preclude a jury from determining if there had been a deviation from normal practice that was the proximate cause of the patient's injuries. This question was to be considered in a new trial.

DUTY TO REPORT PHYSICIAN NEGLIGENCE

A hospital can be liable for the failure of nursing personnel to take action when a patient's personal physician is clearly unwilling or unable to cope with a situation that threatens the life or health of the patient. In a California case, *Goff v. Doctors General Hospital,* 166 Cal. App. 2d 314, 333 P.2d 29 (1958), a patient was seriously bleeding following childbirth because the physician failed to suture her properly. The nurses testified that they were aware of the patient's dangerous condition and that the physician was not present in the hospital. Both nurses knew the patient would die if nothing was done, but neither contacted anyone except the physician. The hospital was liable for the nurses' negligence in failing to notify their supervisors of the serious condition that caused the patient's death. Evidence was sufficient to sustain the finding that the nurses who attended the patient and who were aware of the excessive bleeding were negligent and that their negligence was a contributing cause of the patient's death. The measure of duty of the hospital toward its patients is the exercise of that degree of care used by hospitals generally.

DUTY TO QUESTION PATIENT DISCHARGE

A nurse has a duty to question the discharge of a patient if he or she has reason to believe that such discharge could be injurious to the health of the patient. Jury issues were raised in *Koeniguer v. Eckrich,* 422 N.W.2d 600 (S.D. 1988), by expert testimony that the nurses had a duty to attempt to delay the patient's discharge if her condition warranted continued hospitalization and by permissible inferences from the evidence that the delay in treatment that resulted from the premature discharge contributed to the patient's death. Summary dismissal of this case against the hospital by a trial court was found to have been improper.

FAILURE TO REPORT CHANGES IN A PATIENT'S CONDITION

Nurses have the responsibility to observe the conditions of patients under their care and report those findings that may adversely affect a patient's well-being to the attending physician. If the physician in charge fails to respond, there is a further duty to report the matter to the nursing supervisor and/or the appropriate departmental chairperson. Hospital policy and procedure should prescribe the guidelines for staff members to follow when confronted with a physician or other health professional whose action or inaction jeopardizes the well-being of a patient. Guidelines in place, but not followed, are of no value, as the following case illustrates. The plaintiff in *Utter v. United Hospital Center, Inc.*, 236 S.E.2d 213 (W. Va. 1977), suffered an amputation that the jury determined resulted from the failure of the nursing staff to properly report the patient's deteriorating condition. The nursing staff, according to written procedures in the nursing manual, was responsible for reporting such changes. It was determined that deviation from hospital policy constituted negligence. In *Goff v. Doctors General Hospital*, 166 Cal. App. 2d 314, 333 P.2d 29 (1958), the court held that nurses who knew that a woman they were attending was bleeding excessively were negligent in failing to report the circumstances so prompt and adequate measures could be taken to safeguard her life.

As nursing procedures become more complicated, and as nurses work more closely with physicians in the performance of medical and surgical procedures, it is mandatory that the nursing staff promptly notify the patient's physician of significant changes in his/her condition. If a physician should fail to respond to a call for assistance and if such failure is likely to jeopardize a patient's health, the matter must be brought to the attention of the nursing supervisor, chief of service, or administration. Failure to exercise that duty can lead to liability of the nurse as well as the hospital under the doctrine of *respondeat superior*.

On appeal by the hospital and the nurse, the Supreme Court of Kansas in *Hiatt v. Grace*, 215 Kan. 14, 523 P.2d 320 (1974), held that there was sufficient evidence to authorize the jury to find that a nurse was negligent in failing to timely notify the physician that delivery of the plaintiff's child was imminent. This delay resulted in an unattended childbirth with consequent injuries. The plaintiff had been awarded $15,000 by the trial court.

FAILURE TO REPORT DEFECTIVE EQUIPMENT

Failure to report defective equipment can cause a nurse to be held liable for negligence if the failure to report is the proximate cause of a patient's injuries. The defect must be known and not hidden from sight.

FAILURE TO TAKE CORRECT TELEPHONE ORDERS

Failure to take correct telephone orders can be just as serious as failure to follow, understand, and/or interpret correctly a physician's orders. Telephone orders are necessary due to the nature of a physician's practice. Nurses must be alert in transcribing orders since there are periodic contradictions between what physicians claim they ordered and what nurses allege they ordered. Orders should be repeated, once transcribed, for verification purposes. Verification of an order by another nurse on a second phone is helpful, especially if an order is questionable. Any questionable orders must always be verified with the physician initiating the order. Physicians must countersign all orders—this should be a firm rule of the hospital. Nurses who disagree with a physician's order should not carry out an obviously erroneous order. In addition, they should confirm the order with the prescribing physician and report to the supervisor any difficulty in resolving a difference of opinion with the physician.

PATIENT FALLS

Bedside Rails

The plaintiff in *Polonsky v. Union Hospital*, 418 N.E.2d 620 (Mass. App. 1981), suffered a fall and fractured her hip following the administration of a sleeping medication, commonly known by the trade name Dalmane. The superior court awarded damages in the amount of the statutory limit of $20,000, and the hospital appealed. The appeals court held that from the Dalmane warning provided by the drug manufacturer and the hospital's own regulation regarding "Bedside Rails," without additional medical testimony, the jury could draw an inference that the hospital's nurse had failed to exercise due care when she failed to raise the bed rails after administering Dalmane.

Examination Tables

A judgment for the plaintiff was affirmed in *Petry v. Nassau Hospital*, 267 A.D. 996, 48 N.Y.S.2d 227 (1944), which was an action to recover damages for personal injuries suffered by the plaintiff's wife. The patient had been placed on a narrow examination table in the emergency room of the defendant hospital and fell from the table. The table had no sides, and the patient had been left unattended by the nurse in charge.

Suicidal Patients

A hospital and its staff have a duty to exercise reasonable care to protect suicidal patients against foreseeable harm to themselves. This duty exists whether the patient is voluntarily admitted or involuntarily committed. In *Abille v. United States*, 482 F. Supp. 703 (N.D. Cal. 1980), the district court held that evidence supported a finding that the attending physician had not authorized a change in status of a patient who had been admitted to a U.S. Air Force Hospital in Alaska and diagnosed as being suicidal so as to permit him to leave the ward without an escort. The nursing staff allowed him to leave the ward, and he found a window from which he jumped. This constituted a breach of the standard of due care under Alaska law, where the act or omission complained of occurred.

SPONGE AND/OR INSTRUMENT MISCOUNTS IN THE OPERATING ROOM

There are a plethora of cases involving foreign objects left in patients during surgery. The hospital in *Ross v. Chatham County Hospital Authority*, 367 S.E.2d 793 (Ga. 1988), was properly denied summary dismissal of an action in which a patient sought to recover damages for injuries suffered when a surgical instrument was left in the patient's abdomen during surgery. This incident occurred as a result of the failure of the operating room personnel to conduct an instrument and sponge count following surgery. The borrowed servant doctrine did not insulate the hospital from the negligence of its nurses since the doctrine only applies to acts involving professional skill and judgment. Foreign objects negligently left in a patient's body constitute an administrative act.

A standard nursing checkoff procedure should be used to account for all sponges and/or instruments utilized in the operating room. Preventative measures of this nature will reduce a hospital's risk of liability.

NURSE PRACTITIONER

A relatively new and exciting role for nurses is that of the nurse practitioner. The nurse practitioner is a registered nurse who has completed the necessary education to engage in primary health care decision making. The nurse practitioner is trained in the delivery of primary health care and the assessment of psychosocial and physical health problems such as the performance of routine examinations and the ordering of routine diagnostic tests. The potential risks of liability for the nurse practitioner are as real as the risks for any other nurse are. The standard of care required will most likely be set by statute. If not, the courts will determine the standard based on the reasonable person doctrine—that is, what would a reasonably prudent nurse practitioner do under the given circumstances? The standard would be established through the use of expert testimony of other nurse practitioners in the field. Case law in this area is practically nonexistent. However, nurse practitioners are required to meet the standards recognized in the field as reflecting the current status of the art. Because of potential liability problems and pressure from physicians, hospitals have been reluctant to utilize nurse practitioners to the full extent of their training.

CLINICAL NURSE SPECIALIST

A clinical nurse specialist is a professional nurse with an advanced academic degree and a major in a specific clinical specialty such as pediatrics or psychiatry. The clinical nurse specialist concentrates her practice of nursing in one specialized clinical setting by applying advanced nursing procedures and techniques. The standard of care expected of the clinical nurse specialist is determined in a manner similar to that of the nurse practitioner. Hospitals do not seem to be as reluctant to utilize clinical nurse specialists as they are the nurse practitioners.

NURSE-ANESTHETIST

In *McKinney v. Tromly,* 386 S.W.2d 564 (Tex. Civ. App. 1964), a suit was instituted against a physician for the negligence of a nurse in the administration of an anesthetic to the plaintiff's nine-year-old son who was undergoing a tonsillectomy. The Texas Court of Civil Appeals held that the nurse, an employee of the hospital, was an employee of the physician while in the operating room and under his control (applying the borrowed servant doctrine). Therefore, the physician was held liable for the death caused by the nurse in administering the anesthetic to the patient. Administration of an anesthetic is not an administrative function of the hospital, but constitutes the practice of medicine.

The physician in *Weinstein v. Prostkoff,* 23 Misc. 2d 376, 191 N.Y.S.2d 310 (Sup. Ct. 1959), *rev'd,* 213 N.Y.S.2d 571 (Sup. Ct., App. Div. 1961), testified that an examination revealed that the unborn child was suffering from fetal distress. The patient was immediately prepared for delivery, taken into the delivery room, and administered an anesthetic. The nurse who responded to the delivery room call was told that the baby was in distress and that 100 percent oxygen was to be administered immediately to the mother. Although it was customary and exceedingly important to ascertain whether a patient had eaten any food within a reasonably short time before administration of the anesthesia, no such inquiries had been made. Approximately two minutes after the baby was born, the patient gave several gasps and died. The physician testified that he immediately saw large amounts of vomit coming from the patient's mouth. The immediate impression of those in attendance indicated the patient had suffocated as a result of aspirating gastric matter into the lungs.

The jury's verdict was in favor of the hospital and the nurse, but against the physician. On the basis of contradictory evidence, the supreme court set aside the jury verdict and held that if the physician could be found responsible for having failed to prepare for, direct, or supervise the anesthetic part of the delivery, then certainly the nurse, or the physician and the hospital, were equally, if not more, responsible. On retrial, verdicts in favor of the hospital and the nurse were again set aside. However, on appeal, these verdicts were reinstated.

NURSE MIDWIFE

A certified nurse midwife in *Sweeney v. Athens Regional Medical Center (ARMC)*, 705 F. Supp. 1556 (M.D. Ga. 1989), brought an action against a public hospital and certain doctors, alleging violations of the Sherman Antitrust Act and First Amendment rights and intentional infliction of emotional distress arising out of a hospital's denying her access to a patient in the hospital. The hospital motioned for summary judgment. The district court held that a public hospital was a local governmental unit within the meaning of the Local Government Antitrust Act and thus was immune from the damage claim brought under the Sherman Act. The district court further held even assuming that the hospital's decision to deny the nurse midwife access to certain patients, the hospital's interests in providing effective and safe medical care outweighed the nurse midwife's interests in exercising her right to freely speak out on matters of natural childbirth. The nurse did not state a claim for intentional infliction of emotional distress.

> ARMC found itself unavoidably involved in a dispute between those holding different philosophical beliefs on the subject of childbirth. When faced with a difficult decision it was forced to make because of no fault of its own, ARMC responded in a way that it felt would best serve its primary concern, the safety and care of its patients. This court has found no basis in the law for requiring the Hospital to go to trial to defend that decision.

Id. at 1571.

NURSING SUPERVISOR

A nursing supervisor is liable for his or her personal negligent behavior. The hospital is liable for the negligent acts of its employees, which include supervisors. A supervisor is not liable under the doctrine of *respondeat superior* for the negligent acts of the nurses being supervised. A nursing supervisor has the right to direct the nurses who are being supervised. The hospital is the employer, and the supervisor's powers are derived directly from the hospital's right of control.

Thus, if a supervisor assigns a task to an individual the supervisor knows, or should have known, is not competent to perform a particular task and if a patient suffers injury because of incompetent performance of the task, the supervisor can be held personally liable for negligence as a supervisor. The hospital will be liable under the doctrine of *respondeat superior* as the employer of both the supervisor and the individual who performed the task in a negligent manner. The supervisor is not relieved of personal liability even though the hospital is liable under *respondeat superior.*

In determining whether a nurse with supervisory responsibilities has been negligent, the nurse is measured against the standard of care of a competent and prudent nurse in the performance of supervisory duties. If charting a patient's fluid intake was assigned to a nurse's aide not instructed in performing this task and if such an assignment was not usually made until the supervisor personally ascertained the aide's ability to chart fluids satisfactorily, the departure from the standard of care that causes a patient harm would justify imposing liability for negligence.

A supervisor may ordinarily rely on the fact that a subordinate is licensed or certified as an indication of the subordinate's capabilities in performing tasks within the ambit of the license or certificate. Nonetheless, where the individual's past actions have led the supervisor to believe that the person is likely to perform a task in an unsatisfactory manner, assigning the task to that person can lead to liability for negligence on the part of the supervisor because the risk of harm to the patient is knowingly increased.

SPECIAL DUTY NURSE

A hospital is generally not liable for the negligence of a special duty nurse—a nurse hired by the patient or the patient's family to perform nursing services. Generally, the master-servant relationship does not exist between the hospital and the special duty nurse.

A special duty nurse can be compared to a staff physician. Like a staff physician, a special duty nurse may be required to observe certain rules and regulations as a precondition to working in the hospital. The observance of hospital rules is insufficient, however, to raise a master-servant relationship between the hospital and the nurse. Under ordinary circumstances a special duty nurse is employed by the patient, and the hospital has no authority to hire or fire the nurse. The hospital does have the responsibility, however, to protect the patient from incompetent or unqualified special duty nurses.

Even though a special duty nurse is employed by a patient, a hospital can be liable for damages resulting from a nurse's negligent conduct. A hospital can also be liable for damages awarded in a malpractice action if a nurse and his/her registry have inadequate insurance to cover a jury award. In such instances, a hospital would then have a right to seek recovery from the nurse and the registry. If a master-servant relationship exists between the hospital and the special duty nurse, the doctrine of *respondeat superior* may be applied to impose liability on the hospital for the nurse's negligent conduct. Even though the patient pays a special duty nurse, the existence of an employer-employee relationship, which determines the applicability of *respondeat superior,* is a matter to be determined by the jury.

A special duty nurse should carry malpractice insurance. This is especially important if the nurse is providing a service in a patient's home. If a nursing registry has inadequate insurance coverage, there is always a possibility that recovery will be sought against a nurse's estate.

STUDENT NURSES

Student nurses are entrusted with the responsibility of providing nursing care to patients. When liability is being assessed, a student nurse serving at a hospital is considered an agent of the hospital. This is true even if the student is at the hospital on an affiliation basis. Student nurses are personally liable for their own negligent acts, and the hospital is liable for their acts on the basis of *respondeat superior.*

A student nurse is held to the standard of a competent professional nurse when performing nursing duties. The courts, in several decisions, have taken the position that anyone who performs duties customarily performed by professional nurses is held to the standards of professional nurses. Each and every patient has the right to expect competent nursing services even if the care is provided by students as part of their clinical training. It would be unfair to deprive the patient of compensation for an injury merely because a student was responsible for the negligent act. Until it is clearly demonstrated that student nurses are competent to render nursing services without increasing the risks of injury to patients, they must be more closely supervised than graduate nurses are.

NURSE LICENSURE

A nurse may discover that the procedures permitted by licensing authorities differ from those required by the employer. These potential conflicts deal with issues concerning a nurse's scope of practice. Nurses have not generally faced lawsuits for exceeding their scope of practice unless negligence is involved. A nurse who exceeds the scope of practice can be found to have violated licensure provisions or to have performed tasks that are reserved by statute for a physician. However, in view of increasingly complex nursing and medical procedures, it is often difficult to distinguish the tasks that are clearly reserved for the physician from those that may be performed by the professional nurse.

Although the actual authority of nurses to act varies considerably from state to state, and that in most states that authority is limited, the expanding scope of nursing functions and licensure are clearly illustrated in the following examples:

- 1903—North Carolina enacted the first nurse registration act.
- 1938—New York enacted the first exclusive practice act. This act required mandatory licensure of everyone who performed nursing functions as a matter of employment.
- 1957—The California Nurses Association met with representatives of medical and hospital associations to draw up a statement supporting nurses in performing venipunctures.
- 1966—The Michigan Heart Association favored the use of defibrillators by coronary care nurses.
- 1968—The Hawaii nursing, medical, and hospital associations approved nurses performing cardiopulmonary resuscitation.
- 1971—Idaho revised its nurse practice act by allowing diagnosis and treatment if such is jointly promulgated by the Idaho State Board of Medicine and the Idaho Board of Nursing.
- 1972—New York expanded its nurse practice act and adopted a broad definition of nursing.
- 1975—Missouri Revised Statutes Section 335.016(8) (as revised in 1975) authorized a nurse to make an assessment of persons who are ill and to render a ''nursing diagnosis.''
- 1985—New York revised its definition of nursing by providing that a registered professional nurse who has the appropriate training and experience may provide primary health care services as defined under the statutory authority of the Public Health Law and as approved by the hospital's governing authority. Primary health services shall mean
  —taking histories and performing physical examinations,
  —selecting clinical laboratory tests and diagnostic radiology procedures, and
  —choosing regimens of treatment.
  Nothing in this section shall alter a physician's responsibility for the medical care of his or her patient. New York Public Health Law, Ch. 5, A, Art. 1, Part 400.10 (1985).
- 1989—New York allowed nurse practitioners to diagnose, treat, and write prescriptions within their area of specialty with minimum physician supervision.

Licensing Board

The common organizational pattern of nurse licensing authority in each state is to establish a separate board, organized and operated within the guidelines of specific legislation, to license all professional and practical nurses. Each board is in turn responsible for the determination of eligibility for initial licensing and relicensing; for the enforcement of licensing statutes, including suspension, revocation, and restoration of licenses; and for the approval and supervision of training institutions.

According to the Supreme Court of Idaho, a licensing board has the authority to suspend a license; however, it must do so within existing rules and regulations. In *Tuma v. Board of Nursing*, 593 P.2d 711 (1979), a statute allowing the suspension of a professional nursing license for unprofessional conduct could not be invoked to suspend the license of a nurse who allegedly interfered with the physician-patient relationship by discussing alternative treatment with the patient without some board of nursing rules or regulations to adequately warn her that such actions were prohibited.

Requirements for Licensure

Formal professional training is necessary for nurse licensure in all states. The course requirements vary, but all courses must be completed at board-approved schools or institutions.

Each state requires that an applicant pass a written examination, which is generally administered twice annually. The examinations may be drafted by the licensing board, or they may be prepared by professional examination services or national examining boards. Some states waive their written examination for applicants who present a certificate from a national nursing examination board. There are four basic methods by which boards license out-of-state nurses: reciprocity, endorsement, examination, or waiver.

Reciprocity may be a formal or informal agreement between states whereby a nurse licensing board in one state recognizes licensees of another state if the board of that state extends reciprocal recognition to licensees from the first state. To have reciprocity, the initial licensing requirements of the two states must be essentially equivalent.

While some nurse licensing boards use the term *endorsement* interchangeably with *reciprocity,* the two words actually have different meanings. In licensing by endorsement, boards determine whether the out-of-state nurse's qualifications were equivalent to their own state requirements at the time of initial licensure. Many states make it a condition for endorsement that the qualifying examination taken in the other state be comparable to their own. As with reciprocity, endorsement becomes much easier where uniform qualification standards are applied by the different states.

Licensing out-of-state nurses can also be accomplished by waiver and examination. Where applicants do not meet all the requirements for licensure, but have equivalent qualifications, the specific prerequisite of education, experience, or examination may be waived. Some states will not recognize out-of-state licensed nurses and make it mandatory that all applicants pass the regular examination. A majority of the states grant temporary licenses for nurses. These licenses may be given pending a decision by the board on permanent licensure or may be issued to out-of-state nurses who intend to be in a jurisdiction for only a limited time.

Nurse licensing boards are cautious in licensing persons educated in foreign countries. Graduates of schools in other countries are required to meet the same qualifications as are nurses trained in the United States. Many state boards have established special training, citizenship, and experience requirements for students educated abroad, and others insist on additional training in the United States. A few states have reciprocity or endorsement agreements with some foreign countries.

Suspension and Revocation

All nurse licensing boards have the authority to suspend or revoke the license of a nurse who is found to have violated specified norms of conduct. Such violations may include procurement of a license by fraud; unprofessional, dishonorable, immoral, or illegal conduct; performance of specific actions prohibited by statute; and malpractice.

Suspension and revocation procedures are most commonly contained in the licensing act; in some jurisdictions, however, the procedure is left to the discretion of the board or is contained in the general administrative procedure acts. For the most part, suspension and revocation proceedings are administrative, rather than judicial, and do not carry criminal sanctions.

Liability for Practicing without a License

Insofar as a hospital's liability is concerned, the general considerations of the doctrine of *respondeat superior* apply. The mere fact that an unlicensed practitioner was hired and utilized by a hospital would not impose additional liability unless a patient suffered harm as a result of an unlicensed nurse's negligence.

SCOPE OF PRACTICE ISSUES

A matter of concern to professional nurses is whether certain patient care activities infringe on an area of practice reserved by state licensing legislation for physicians. The question can arise in almost any patient care setting, but it has been raised most frequently in emergency rooms and special care units. A nurse who engages in activities beyond the legally recognized scope of practice runs the risk of violating a state's medical practice act, and the hospital that employs the nurse could also be held responsible under criminal law for aiding and abetting the illegal practice of medicine.

The law in some states would allow a jury to infer that a nurse was negligent if the nurse performed functions restricted by law to physicians and if harm was suffered by a patient. The burden then shifts to the nurse who must establish that his or her performance was not of a negligent character. Even where such an inference is not recognized, a patient's attorney has the opportunity to put a nurse's performance in an unfavorable light if the facts suggest an intrusion into medical practice.

The role of the nurse is rapidly expanding due to a shortage of primary physicians in certain rural and inner city areas, ever-increasing specialization, improved technology, and public demand.

Chapter 6

Liability of Health Professionals and Related Topics

A variety of health professionals are liable for harm that results from their negligent acts. Every health professional is held to the standard of care expected in his or her profession. The following pages provide a sampling of relevant cases regarding the risks for selected health professions. Many of the cases presented in this chapter could have been discussed under one or more topics. However, they were placed here to illustrate that no health care professional is exempt from the long arm of the legal system.

Cases presented in this chapter are by no means exhaustive for a specific profession. All professionals can learn from the experiences of others.

CHIROPRACTOR

Standard of Care Required

A chiropractor is required to exercise the same degree of care, judgment, and skill exercised by other reasonable chiropractors under like or similar circumstances. He or she has a duty to determine whether or not a patient is treatable through chiropractic means and to refrain from chiropractic treatment when a reasonable chiropractor would be or should have been aware that a patient's condition would not respond to chiropractic treatment. Failure to conform to the standard of care can result in liability for any injuries suffered. *Kerkman v. Hintz*, 418 N.W.2d 795 (Wis. 1988).

Suspension of License

Inflating Insurance Claims

The Court of Appeals of North Carolina held that a chiropractor's license was properly suspended for six months in *Farlow v. North Carolina State Board of*

Chiropractic Examiners, 332 S.E.2d 696 (N.C. Ct. App. 1985), for inflating the insurance claims of victims of an automobile accident. Dr. Farlow had prescribed a course of treatment for several patients that was not justified by the injuries they had received. The treatment had been prescribed to inflate insurance claims.

Deceptive Advertising

A chiropractor's license was suspended in *Langlitz v. Board of Registration of Chiropractors*, 486 N.E.2d 48 (Mass. 1985), for deceptive advertising in the Yellow Pages of a telephone directory. The Board of Registration of Chiropractors determined that the chiropractor had advertised treatment that was beyond his scope of expertise and the statutory definition of "chiropractic" in that it included the offering of therapeutic nutrition, acupuncture, weight control, etc.

DENTAL ASSISTANT

The plaintiff in *Hickman v. Sexton Dental Clinic*, 367 S.E.2d 453 (S.C. 1988), brought a malpractice action against a dental clinic for a serious cut under her tongue. The dental assistant, without being supervised by a dentist, rammed a sharp object into the patient's mouth, cutting her tongue while taking impressions for dentures. The court of common pleas entered a judgment on a jury verdict in favor of the plaintiff, and the clinic appealed. The court of appeals held the evidence presented was sufficient to infer without the aid of expert testimony that there was a breach of duty to the patient. The testimony of Dr. Tepper, the clinic dentist, was found pertinent to the issue of the common knowledge exception where the evidence permits the jury to recognize breach of duty without the aid of expert testimony. Dr. Tepper testified regarding denture impressions:

Q. You also stated that you have taken I believe thousands?
A. Probably more than that.
Q. Of impressions?
A. Yes, sir.
Q. This never happened before?
A. No, sir, not a laceration.
Q. Would it be safe and accurate to say that if someone's mouth were to be cut during the impression process, someone did something wrong?
A. Yes, sir.

Id. at 455–56.

DENTIST

The supreme court in *Everett v. State of Washington*, 99 Wash. 2d 264, 661 P.2d 588 (1983), held that despite a license to practice dentistry and considerable expertise in the field of anesthesiology, the licensee's dental license did not authorize the administration of anesthesia for nondental purposes under then-existing law. It is of interest that Dr. Everett had served a 33-month general anesthesia residency program administered through the Washington University Medical School. Following his residency, Dr. Everett had been appointed an assistant professor in the Department of Anesthesiology at the Washington Medical School. In his capacity as assistant professor and later as associate professor, Dr. Everett had taught general anesthesiology to both medical and dental students and had administered all types of anesthesia to both dental and nondental patients.

INHALATION THERAPIST

The court of appeals in *Poor Sisters of St. Francis v. Catron*, 435 N.E.2d 305 (Ind. Ct. App. 1982), held that the failure of nurses and an inhalation therapist to report to the supervisor that an endotracheal tube had been left in the plaintiff longer than the customary three- or four-day period was sufficient to allow the jury to reach a finding of negligence. The plaintiff had been admitted to the emergency room in a comatose state as a result of an unintentional drug overdose. The emergency room physician on duty had inserted an endotracheal tube, which was removed five days later. The plaintiff suffered injury to her throat and vocal cords. The patient experienced difficulty speaking and underwent several operations to remove scar tissue and open her voice box. At the time of trial, she could not speak above a whisper and breathed partially through a hole in her throat created by a tracheotomy. The hospital was found liable for the negligent acts of its employees and the resulting injuries to the plaintiff.

LABORATORY TECHNICIAN

Inferior Work Performance

A laboratory technician in *Barnes Hospital v. Missouri Commission on Human Rights*, 661 S.W.2d 534 (Mo. 1983), had been discharged because of inferior work performance. On three occasions the employee had allegedly mismatched blood. The employee filed a complaint with the Commission on Human Rights, alleging racial discrimination as a reason for his discharge by the hospital. The hospital appealed, and the circuit court reversed the commission's order. The technician appealed to the Supreme Court of Missouri, which held that the evidence did not support the ruling of racial discrimination by the Missouri Commission on Human Rights.

Refusal To Perform Chemical Examinations

A laboratory technician in *Stepp v. Review Board of the Indiana Employment Security Division*, 521 N.E.2d 350 (Ind. Ct. App. 1988), was found to have been properly dismissed from her job for refusing to perform chemical examinations on vials with AIDS warnings attached. The court of appeals held that the employee was dismissed for just cause and that the laboratory did not waive its right to compel employees to perform assigned tasks.

NURSE'S AIDE

Termination and Defamation

Dismissal was properly ordered for claims of wrongful termination and defamation in *Eli v. Griggs County Hospital and Nursing Home*, 385 N.W.2d 99 (N.D. 1986), where a nurse's aide was terminated on the basis of an incident in the hospital dining room. In the presence of patients and visitors she cursed her supervisor and complained that personnel were working short-staffed. Given the nature of her employment and the high standard of care that persons reasonably expected from a nursing care facility, such behavior justified her termination on a charge of reported breach of patient-specific and facility-specific information. No defamation resulted from the entry of such charges in the aide's personnel file since the record established that the charges were true.

Patient Neglect

The record in *Jones v. Axelrod*, 519 N.Y.S.2d 738 (App. Div. 1987), indicated that a nurse's aide, while transferring a "total care" nursing home patient to her bed from a wheelchair, left the patient sitting on the edge of the bed. The patient subsequently fell to the floor. The aide acknowledged that the patient required restraints. The supervisor testified that the act of leaving the patient unrestrained and unattended on the edge of the bed was improper and inconsistent with safe procedure. Sufficient evidence supported a determination by the commissioner of health that the conduct of the nurse's aide constituted patient neglect.

OPTOMETRIST

Optometrists brought an action challenging a medical assistance plan that reimbursed ophthalmologists, while not reimbursing optometrists, for eye care services. The Supreme Court of Louisiana held in *Sandefur v. Cherry*, 455 So. 2d 1350 (La. 1984), that state officials could not discriminate between optometrists and ophthalmologists in reimbursement for Medicaid patients. Louisiana statutes prohibited limiting or restricting the freedom of patients in choosing a particular health professional for care.

PARAMEDIC

Many states have enacted legislation that provides civil immunity to paramedics who render emergency lifesaving services. It is important for the paramedic to be sure that a life-threatening situation exists and that it is immediate.

The plaintiff in *Malone v. City of Seattle*, 600 P.2d 647 (Wash. Ct. App. 1979), alleged the defendant was negligent in providing care to the plaintiff following an automobile accident. The plaintiff, on appeal, contended that the trial court wrongfully instructed the jury regarding a 1971 civil immunity statute. The following is an excerpt from the relevant Washington statute:

> No act or omission of any physician's trained mobile intensive care paramedic . . . done or omitted in good faith while rendering emergency lifesaving service . . . to a person who is in immediate danger of loss of life shall impose any liability upon the trained mobile intensive care paramedic . . . or upon a . . . city or other local governmental unit. . . .

1971 Wash. Laws 1783.

One of the issues raised was whether or not the legislature intended the 1971 statute to apply only to the rendition of cardiopulmonary emergency treatment by a paramedic. The court of appeals indicated that while the definition contained in the statute places special emphasis on the paramedic's training in all aspects of cardiopulmonary resuscitation, the act does not limit the paramedic to cardiopulmonary resuscitation. The act implicitly recognizes that paramedics may encounter a variety of emergencies.

The Supreme Court of Pennsylvania in *Morena v. South Hills Health Systems*, 462 A.2d 680 (Pa. 1983), held that the paramedics were not negligent in transporting a victim of a shooting to the nearest available hospital, rather than to another hospital located five or six miles farther away where a thoracic surgeon was present. The paramedics were not capable, in a medical sense, of accurately diagnosing the extent of the decedent's injury. Except for the children's center and the burn center, there were no emergency trauma centers specifically designated for the treatment of particular injuries.

PHARMACIST

Medicaid Fraud

The court of appeals in the *State of North Carolina v. Beatty*, 308 S.E.2d 65 (N.C. Ct. App. 1983), upheld a superior court's finding that the evidence submitted against the defendant pharmacist was sufficient to sustain a conviction for Medicaid fraud. The state was billed for medications that were never dispensed, was billed for more medications than some patients received, and in some instances was billed for the more expensive trade name drugs when cheaper generic drugs were dispensed.

The pharmacists in *People v. Kendzia*, 103 A.D.2d 999, 478 N.Y.S.2d 209 (1984), were convicted of mishandling drugs, and they appealed. The supreme court, appellate division, held that the evidence supported a finding that the pharmacists sold generic drugs in vials with brand name labels and was sufficient to support a conviction. Investigators, working undercover, were provided with Medicaid cards and fictitious prescriptions requiring brand name drugs to be dispensed as written. Between April and October 1979 the investigators took the prescriptions to the pharmacy where they were filled with generic substitutions in vials with the brand name labels.

Revocation of License

The supreme court, appellate division, held in *Heller v. Ambach*, 78 A.D.2d 951, 433 N.Y.S.2d 281 (1980), that violation of statutes relating to the sale of controlled substances by a pharmacist amounted to unprofessional conduct and that the revocation of the defendant's license was justified for the protection of the public. [See also *Kupper v. Kentucky Board of Pharmacy*, 666 S.W.2d 729 (Ky. 1984).]

Inaccurate Records

The operator of a pharmacy, in a disciplinary proceeding before the California Board of Pharmacy, was found negligent because of inaccurate record keeping. The pharmacist had failed to keep accurate records of dangerous drugs, report thefts by employees, and report a burglary of pharmacy drugs. Such reporting was required by state statute. *Banks v. Board of Pharmacy*, 207 Cal. Rptr. 835 (Cal. Ct. App. 1984).

PHYSICAL THERAPIST

The physical therapist in *Armintor v. Community Hospital of Brazosport*, 659 S.W.2d 86 (Tex. Civ. App. 1983), was properly enjoined from entering the hospital's premises following termination of an oral contract to furnish services to hospital patients in need of physical therapy. Substantial evidence supported the court's finding that the hospital's attempt to establish a hospital-based physical therapy program would have been disrupted if the independent therapist had been permitted to continue treating patients. The court considered the exclusion of a therapist an administrative matter within the board's discretion. The therapist's entering the hospital with the permission of a staff physician would constitute trespass and would be in violation of hospital policy.

PHYSICIAN'S ASSISTANT

One of the solutions to the shortage of physicians in certain rural and inner-city areas has been to train allied health professionals such as physician's assistants to perform the more routine and repetitive medical functions. The physician's assistant functions as an extra arm for the physician, performing such tasks as suturing minor wounds, administering injections, taking histories, and performing routine physical examinations. Physician's assistants are responsible for their own negligent acts. If the assistants are hospital employees, hospitals can be held responsible on the basis of *respondeat superior*. A physician, as an employer of a physician's assistant, can also be held liable on the basis of *respondeat superior*.

Patients should be informed when a physician's assistant is assisting in their care; they must not be misled into thinking that they are being cared for by a physician.

In order to limit the potential risk of liability to a physician's assistant, the physician should closely monitor and supervise the assistant's work. Guidelines and procedures should also be established in order to provide a standard mechanism for reviewing an assistant's performance.

It is of interest that in *Washington State Nurses Association v. Board of Medical Examiners*, 605 P.2d 1269 (Wash. 1980), the nurses association brought an action challenging a regulation that authorized physician's assistants to issue prescriptions for medication and write medical orders for patient care. The superior court enjoined the board from effectuating the regulation, and the board appealed. The supreme court held that the regulation did not exceed the statutory authority of the board since statutes and regulations placed physician's assistants in the position of agent for their supervising physician, rather than of independent contractor, and thus nurses would not be exposed to statutory liability for executing prescriptions issued by physician's assistants.

PODIATRIST

Negligent Surgery

The podiatrist in *Strauss v. Biggs*, 525 A.2d 992 (Del. 1987), was found to have failed to meet the standard of care required of a podiatrist, and that failure resulted in injury to the patient. The podiatrist, by his own admission, stated that his initial incision in the patient's foot had been misplaced. The trial court was found not to have erred in permitting the jury to consider additional claims that the podiatrist had acted improperly by failing to refer the patient, stop the procedure after the first incision, inform the patient of possible nerve injury, and provide proper postoperative treatment. Testimony of the patient's experts was adequate to show that such alleged omissions had violated the standard of care.

Assumption of the Risk by the Patient

The patient in *Faile v. Bycura*, 346 S.E.2d 528 (S.C. 1986), was awarded $75,000 in damages by a jury on her allegations that a podiatrist had employed inappropriate techniques during an unsuccessful attempt to treat her heel spurs. On appeal it was held that the trial court erred in striking the podiatrist's defense of assumption of the risk. Evidence established that the patient had signed consent forms that indicated the risks of treatment as well as alternative treatment modalities.

Expert Testimony

A podiatrist in *Bethea v. Smith*, 336 S.E.2d 295 (Ga. Ct. App. 1985), was shown not competent to testify as to the standard of care required of an orthopedic surgeon in the treatment of an ankle fracture. Experts testifying regarding the defendant's specialty generally must have appropriate qualifications in the same specialty as the defendant does.

SECURITY GUARD

Celestine v. United States, 841 F.2d 851 (8th Cir. 1988), involved an individual who sought inpatient psychiatric care at a Veterans Administration (VA) hospital and became physically violent while waiting to be seen by a physician. The VA security guards were found to be justified in placing the individual in restraints and observing him for a short time until he could be examined by a psychiatrist. Under Missouri law, no false imprisonment or battery occurred in view of the common law principle that a person believed to be mentally ill could be lawfully restrained if such was considered necessary to prevent immediate injury to that person or others.

X-RAY TECHNICIAN

The x-ray technician in *Hayes v. Shelby Memorial Hospital*, 726 F.2d 1543 (11th Cir. 1984), brought an employment discrimination action against the hospital. The technician was fired by the hospital when it learned that she was pregnant. The U.S. District Court for the Northern District of Alabama found that the hospital had violated the Pregnancy Discrimination Act. On appeal by the hospital, the U.S. court of appeals, in affirming the lower court's decision, held that the hospital failed to consider less discriminatory alternatives to firing the technician.

The chief x-ray technician in *Paros v. Hoemako Hospital*, 681 P.2d 918 (Ariz. Ct. App. 1984), was dismissed because of a chronic argumentative and hostile attitude inconsistent with the performance of supervisory duties. The superior court entered a summary judgment in favor of the hospital and the administrator. On appeal, the appeals court held that the discharge was properly based on good cause and precluded recovery for breach of contract and wrongful discharge.

SEXUAL IMPROPRIETIES

A significant number of cases deal with health professionals who have been involved in sexual relationships with patients in a hospital setting and/or with clients in private offices. Such cases are being presented, in many instances, on both civil and criminal grounds. Health professionals finding themselves in such unprofessional relationships must seek help for themselves as well as refer their patients to other appropriate professionals. A defense that sexual improprieties with clients did not take place during treatment sessions will not generally be upheld by the courts. In addition to facing civil and criminal litigation by the patient/client, health professionals found guilty of such professional misconduct are subject to revocation of their licenses.

Dentist

Revocation of a dentist's license on charges of professional misconduct was properly ordered in *Melone v. State Education Department*, 495 N.Y.S.2d 808 (App. Div. 1985), on the basis of substantial evidence that while acting in a professional capacity, the dentist had engaged in physical and sexual contact with five different male patients within a three-year period. Considering the dentist's responsible position, the extended time period during which the sexual contacts occurred, the young and impressionable nature of the victims (7 to 15 years of age), and the possibility of lasting effects on the victims, the penalty was not shocking to the court's sense of fairness.

Psychologist

The license of a psychologist was revoked by the Board of Psychologist Examiners in *Gilmore v. Board of Psychologist Examiners*, 725 P.2d 400 (Or. Ct. App. 1986), for sexual improprieties with clients. The psychologist petitioned for judicial review. She argued that therapy had terminated before the sexual relationships began. The court of appeals held that evidence supported the board's conclusion that the psychologist had violated an ethical standard in caring for her patients. When a psychologist's personal interests intrude into the practitioner-client relationship, the practitioner is obliged to re-create objectivity through a third party. The board's findings and conclusions indicated that the petitioner failed to maintain that objectivity.

Physician

A hospital technologist in *Copithorne v. Framingham Union Hospital*, 520 N.E.2d 139 (Mass. 1988), alleged that she had been raped by a staff physician during the course of a house call. The technologist's claim against the hospital had been summarily dismissed for lack of proximate causation. On appeal, the dismissal was found to be improper where the record indicated that the hospital had received actual notice of allegations that the physician had assaulted patients on and off the hospital's premises. The hospital had instructed the physician to have a chaperone present when visiting female patients and had instructed nurses "to keep an eye on him." The physician's sexual assault was foreseeable. There was evidentiary support for the proposition that failure to withdraw the physician's privileges had caused the rape where the technologist asserted that it was the physician's good reputation in the hospital that had led her to seek his services.

CERTIFICATION OF HEALTH CARE PROFESSIONALS

The certification of health care professionals is the recognition by a governmental or professional association that an individual's expertise meets the standards of that group. The standards established by professional associations generally exceed those required by government agencies. Some professional groups establish their own minimum standards for certification in those professions that are not licensed by a particular state. Certification by an association or group is a self-regulation credentialing process.

LICENSING OF HEALTH CARE PROFESSIONALS

Licensure can be defined as the process by which some competent authority grants permission to a qualified individual or entity to perform certain specified activities that would be illegal without a license. As it applies to health personnel, licensure refers to the process by which licensing boards, agencies, or departments of the several states grant to individuals who meet certain predetermined standards the legal right to practice in a health profession and to use a specified health practitioner's title.

The commonly stated objectives of licensing laws are to limit and control admission to the various health occupations and to protect the public from unqualified practitioners by promulgating and enforcing standards of practice within the professions.

The authority of states to license health care practitioners is found in their regulating power. Implicit in the power to license is the authority to collect license fees, establish standards of practice, require certain minimum qualifications and competency levels of applicants, and impose on applicants other requirements necessary to protect the general public welfare. This authority, which is vested in the legislature, may be delegated to political subdivisions or to state boards, agencies, and departments. In some instances, the scope of the delegated power is made quite specific in the legislation; in others, the licensing authority may have wide discretion in performing its functions. In either case, however, the authority granted by the legislature may not be exceeded.

HOSPITAL PRIVILEGES

There is an increasing interest in the credentialing and licensing of health care professionals. The District of Columbia enacted a bill permitting nonphysician health care practitioners access to hospital privileges. The act covers psychologists, podiatrists, nurse midwives, nurse anesthetists, and nurse practitioners. No facility in the District of Columbia may deny the application of a health practitioner without first providing the applicant the right to a fair hearing.

SOME HELPFUL ADVICE TO ALL HEALTH PROFESSIONALS

- Do not criticize the professional skill of another publicly. Use appropriate, available reporting mechanisms when the skill of another is to be challenged.
- Maintain complete and adequate medical records.
- Provide the patient with good medical care comparable to national standards.
- Seek the aid of consultants when indicated.
- Obtain consent for diagnostic and therapeutic procedures.

- Do not be afraid or too proud to ask questions.
- Do not prescribe medications, blood, diagnostic tests, treatments, etc., indiscriminately.
- Inform the patient, relatives, or parents of surgical procedures and the complications that may arise.
- Practice in the fields in which you have been trained.
- Participate in continuing education programs.
- Maintain all confidential communication without violation.
- Check equipment or have it checked frequently for safety.
- In terminating a physician-patient relationship, give adequate written notice to the patient. It is preferable to send the letter by registered mail return receipt.
- Ensure that female patient examinations, conducted by a member of the opposite sex, be performed in the presence of a third person, preferably another female.
- Confirm all telephone prescriptions in writing.
- Obtain a qualified substitute when you will be absent from your practice.
- Do not be rigid or impersonal. Develop a relationship with the patient where, for example, the patient begins to say, "That is my nurse," or "That is my doctor." Likewise, the nurse or doctor should say, "That is my patient."
- Act confident and professional in the presence of patients. A professional who is not self-confident and constantly complains about coworkers, physicians, and the institution will only serve to make patients more insecure and suit prone.
- Investigate accidents rapidly. This is a must.
- Maintain incident reports separately from patients' records. Incident reports prepared by a health professional, placed in a patient's record, and given to the administration, are not protected by attorney-client privilege. If incident reports are prepared only for the attorney to provide legal services, they could be regarded as privileged communications.
- Be a good listener and allow each patient sufficient time to express fears and anxieties.
- Above all—be compassionate and understanding to each patient and one another as individuals.

Chapter 7

Consent to Medical and Surgical Procedures

Consent is the voluntary agreement by a person in the possession and exercise of sufficient mentality to make an intelligent choice to allow something proposed by another. It can be either express or implied. Express consent can take the form of a verbal agreement to undergo a medical procedure or it can be accomplished through the execution of a signed consent form. In modern health care, written consent is the preferred method of obtaining agreement from a patient to undergo medical procedures. Implied consent is that which is manifested by some action or by inaction of silence, which raises a presumption that consent has been authorized. For example, consent by a parent to the performance of a lumbar puncture to test for suspected meningitis could be implied from the life-threatening nature of the child's condition in *Plutshack v. University of Minnesota Hospitals*, 316 N.W.2d 1 (Minn. 1982). The physician had been unable to contact the infant's mother. The child's grandmother had agreed to the lumbar puncture.

Consent must first be obtained from a patient or from a person authorized to consent on a patient's behalf before any medical or surgical procedure can be performed. A touching of another without authorization to do so could be considered a battery.

Not every touching results in a battery. When a person voluntarily enters a situation in which a reasonably prudent person would anticipate a touching (for example, riding in an elevator or being transported as a patient), consent is implied. Consent is not required for the normal, routine everyday touching and bumping that occurs in life.

The law does require consent for the intentional touching that involves medical or surgical procedures to be performed on a patient, although exceptions do exist with respect to emergency situations. The question of liability for performing a medical or surgical procedure without the patient's consent is separate and distinct from any question of negligence or malpractice in performing a procedure. Liability may be imposed for a nonconsensual touching of a patient even if the procedure improved the patient's health. The eminent Justice Cardozo, in

116

Schloendorff v. Society of New York Hospital, 211 N.Y. 125, 129, 105 N.E. 92, 93 (1914), stated:

> Every human being of adult years and sound mind has a right to determine what shall be done with his own body and a surgeon who performs an operation without his patient's consent commits an assault, for which he is liable in damages, except in cases of emergency where the patient is unconscious and where it is necessary to operate before consent can be obtained.

Patients must be given sufficient information to allow them to make intelligent choices from among the various alternative courses of available treatment for their specific ailments. They have a right to refuse a specific course of treatment even if the medical procedure is advisable. Informed consent must be given despite a patient's anxiety or indecisiveness. Patients have a right to be secure in their persons from any touching, and they are free to reject recommended treatment. Informed consent requires that a patient have a full understanding of that to which he/she has consented.

The plaintiff in *Ramos v. Pyati*, 534 N.E.2d 472 (Ill. App. Ct. 1989), brought a medical malpractice action, alleging that the doctor performed surgery on his hand outside the scope of surgery to which he consented. The plaintiff had injured his thumb while at work. He was referred to the defendant after seeing three other doctors. The plaintiff was diagnosed as having a ruptured thumb tendon. The plaintiff consented to a surgical repair of the thumb. During surgery the defendant discovered that scar tissue had formed, causing the ends of the tendons in the thumb to retract. As a result, the surgeon decided to utilize a donor tendon to make the necessary repairs to the thumb. He chose a tendon from the ring finger. The plaintiff upon discovering additional disability from the surgery filed a suit alleging that his hand was rendered unusable for his employment as a mechanic and that the defendant had breached his duty by not advising him of the serious nature of the operation, by not exercising the proper degree of care in performing the operation, and by failing to discontinue surgery when he knew or should have known that the required surgery would most likely cause a greater disability than the already injured condition of the thumb. The plaintiff testified that although he signed a written consent form authorizing the surgery on his thumb, he did not consent to a graft of his ring finger tendon or any other tendon. The plaintiff's expert witness testified that the ring finger is the last choice of four other tendons that could have been selected for the surgery. The circuit court entered a judgment for the plaintiff, and the defendant appealed. The appellate court upheld the judgment for the plaintiff, finding that the plaintiff had not consented to use of the ring finger tendon for repair of the thumb tendon.

DETERMINING INFORMED CONSENT

The objective test, in determining informed consent, requires that a physician provide as much information about a proposed procedure as is ordinarily provided by other physicians in the community. The scope of a physician's duty to disclose, as noted in *Wooley v. Henderson*, 418 A.2d 1123 (Me. 1980), is to be measured by those communications that a reasonable medical practitioner in that branch of medicine would make under the same or similar circumstances. The plaintiff must ordinarily establish this standard by expert medical evidence. The court held that causation should be judged by an objective standard. The plaintiff would have to show that a reasonable person in the position of the plaintiff would have declined the treatment after being informed of a risk that could result in harm.

An action was brought for injuries sustained when the patient's heart was punctured during the performance of a pulmonary arteriogram in *Fain v. Smith*, 479 So. 2d 1150 (Ala. 1985). The trial court was found to have properly required an objective and not a subjective test of causation in its jury charge. No error resulted when it cautioned that the patient's own testimony on the issue was not determinative since it was hindsight and self-serving. The issue of proximate causation was to include the jury's assessment of whether a reasonable person in the patient's position would have withheld consent. The Supreme Court of Alabama held that the objective standard is to be applied in actions for medical malpractice where the physician fails to obtain the informed consent of the patient.

The subjective test relies on a patient's own personal understanding of the physician's explanation of the risks of treatment and the probable consequences of the procedure. The needs of each patient can vary depending on age, maturity, and mental status. A patient instituting a lawsuit would have to show that he or she was provided information insufficient for informed consent. Physicians are reminded that patients are concerned with the risks of death and bodily harm and the problems of recuperation. Taking the time to sit at a patient's bedside and explain the procedures a patient is about to undergo will produce a first-rate physician-patient relationship and most likely result in fewer lawsuits.

The Supreme Court of Oklahoma in *Scott v. Bradford*, 606 P.2d 554 (Okla. 1979), determined that a patient suing under the theory of informed consent must prove that the defendant physician failed to inform him adequately of a material risk before securing his consent to the proposed treatment; that if he had been informed of the risk, he would not have consented to surgery; that the adverse consequences that were not made known did in fact occur; and that he was injured as a result of submitting to treatment. With regard to material risk, the court noted that "'[t]here is no bright line separating the material from the immaterial, it is a question of fact. A risk is material if it would be likely to affect a patient's decision. When non-disclosure of a particular risk is open to debate, the issue is for the finder of the facts." *Id.* at 558. Since this decision imposed a new duty on physicians with respect to disclosure of the risk of treatment, the opinion was ordered to apply prospectively, affecting those causes of action arising after the date this opinion was promulgated.

HOSPITAL LIABILITY

A hospital can be held liable if a medical or surgical procedure is performed without a patient's consent. It is the hospital's duty to protect a patient when it knows or should know of a patient's objections to a medical or surgical procedure. Under the doctrine of *respondeat superior* a hospital is liable for any wrongs of its employees while they are performing their duties. Treatment of a patient without consent is clearly a battery, and if performed by hospital personnel, the hospital would be liable.

The patient's wife in *Krane v. Saint Anthony Hospital Systems*, 738 P.2d 75 (Colo. Ct. App. 1987), brought a wrongful death action against the hospital and the physicians. The patient had expired during an elective surgical procedure. The district court entered a judgment in favor of the hospital. The plaintiff appealed, arguing, on one of three issues, that the hospital failed to advise the husband of the risks of his surgery. The court of appeals held that the hospital was not liable for any failure of the physician to sufficiently advise the patient of the risks of surgery. It is the surgeon who should obtain the informed consent of a patient about to undergo surgery. The surgeon, and not the hospital, has the technical knowledge and training necessary to advise the patient of the risks of surgery.

Hospitals do not generally have a duty to inform patients regarding surgical risks unless it knows or should know of a physician's propensity to fail to obtain informed consent prior to surgery. The reason for imposing such a duty on hospitals is to protect a patient's right to be informed of the risks of surgery prior to his/her giving consent. There were no allegations in the *Krane* case that the surgeon regularly failed to obtain the informed consent of his/her patients prior to surgery.

The parents of an injured patient in *Kesyer v. St. Mary's Hospital, Inc.*, 662 F. Supp. 191 (D. Idaho 1987), brought a medical malpractice action against a physician and the hospital. The hospital moved to dismiss certain claims regarding informed consent, and the district court held on one of the claims that the hospital had no duty to obtain informed consent. The responsibility for informed consent in Idaho is statutorily placed on the physician.

A physician in *Mele v. Sherman Hospital*, 838 F.2d 923 (7th Cir. 1988), had nicked a membrane in the patient's abdomen during performance of a tubal ligation by laparoscopy. The physician then performed a laparotomy to correct the bleeding that developed. The patient brought action against the hospital on the ground that she had never consented to a laparotomy. The trial court directed a verdict in favor of the hospital. On appeal, the appeals court upheld the trial court's finding. The evidence presented at trial, which established that the consent form in question warned of the possibility of blood loss and authorized additional procedures to remedy unforeseen conditions, was considered adequate. The plaintiff argued that the bylaws of Sherman Hospital provided that, "a surgical operation will be performed only on consent of the patient . . . except in emergencies and that the hospital negligently failed to obtain her informed consent." *Id.* at 923, 924. The United States District Court was found to have correctly stated, "The bylaw does not say that the hospital has a duty to inform patients about risks. It says nothing of that sort. It is hard for me to believe that a reasonable jury could even find that the bylaws imposes, self imposes on the hospital a duty to disclose risks or conditions of every particular surgery." *Id.* at 925.

PROOF OF CONSENT

Physicians have a legal duty to inform their patients of any procedures they are ordering. This duty should not be delegated to another. Written consent provides visible proof of a patient's wishes. A valid written consent must be signed; show that the procedure was the one consented to; show that the person consenting understood the nature of the procedure, the alternatives, the risks involved, and the probable consequences of the procedure; and be dated and witnessed. Oral consent, if proven, is as binding as written consent for there is, in general, no legal requirement that a patient's consent be in writing. However, an oral consent is generally more difficult to corroborate. The nurse, as well as other health professionals, has an important role in the realm of informed consent. He or she can be instrumental in averting major lawsuits by being observant as to doubts, changes of mind, confusion, or misunderstandings expressed by a patient regarding any proposed procedures he or she is about to undergo.

Many physicians and hospitals have relied on consent forms worded in such general terms that they permit the physician to perform almost any medical or surgical procedure believed to be in the patient's best interests. This kind of form is usually signed by the patient at the time of admission, but it does not constitute valid consent. There is little difference between a surgical patient who signs no authorization and one who signs a form consenting to whatever surgery the physician deems advisable. In a lawsuit, testimony would be necessary to establish the extent of the patient's actual knowledge and understanding of the treatment rendered. It is possible for a patient, after treatment, to claim a lack of advance knowledge about the nature of a physician's treatment. And it is possible that a jury will believe the patient and impose liability on the physician and/or the hospital.

A patient's condition during surgery may be recognized as different from that which had been expected and explained to the patient, requiring a different procedure than the one to which the patient had initially consented. The surgeon may proceed to treat the new condition; however, the patient must have been aware of the possibility of extending the procedure. The patient in *Winfrey v. Citizens & Southern National Bank*, 254 S.E.2d 725 (Ga. Ct. App. 1979), brought a suit against the deceased surgeon's estate, alleging that the surgeon during exploratory surgery had performed a complete hysterectomy without her consent. The superior court granted summary judgment for the surgeon's estate, and the patient appealed. The court of appeals held that even though the patient may not have read the consent document, where no legally sufficient excuse appeared, she was bound by the terms of the consent document that she voluntarily executed. The plain wording of the binding consent authorized the surgeon to perform additional or different operations or procedures that he might consider necessary or advisable in the course of the operation. Relevant sections of the consent signed by the patient included the following:

1. I authorize the performance upon (patient's name) of the following operation—laparoscopy, possible laparotomy. . . .
2. I consent to the performance of operations and procedures in addition to or different from those now contemplated, which the above named doctor or his associates or assistants may consider necessary or advisable in the course of the operation. . . .
7. I acknowledge that the nature and purpose of the operation, possible alternative methods of treatment, the risks involved, and the possibility of complications have been fully explained to me. . . .

Id. at 727.

An admission consent form should be signed when a patient is admitted to the hospital. This records the patient's consent to routine hospital services, general diagnostic procedures, and medical treatment. A properly executed special consent form should be obtained before every risky diagnostic test and medical or surgical treatment is rendered.

General emergency care consent forms provided by school officials, teachers, or camp counselors when they bring injured students or campers to the emergency room for treatment provide limited protection in the care of a particular child. This consent indicates a parent's desire and intent to have the school official, teacher, or counselor seek emergency treatment when necessary. Such consent allows the hospital to initiate treatment while an attempt is being made to reach the family for consent. Such a consent is no panacea and certainly does not provide a hospital or physician with a right to render carte blanche care. However, it does provide the hospital with some protection against frivolous malpractice suits.

WHO MAY CONSENT

Consent of the patient is ordinarily required before treatment. However, when the patient is either physically unable or legally incompetent to consent and no emergency exists, consent must be obtained from a person who is empowered to consent on the patient's behalf. The person who authorizes the treatment of another must have sufficient information to make an intelligent judgment on behalf of the patient.

Competent Patients

A competent adult patient's wishes concerning his or her person may not be disregarded. The court in *Erickson v. Dilgard*, 44 Misc. 2d 27, 252 N.Y.S.2d 705 (Sup. Ct. 1962), was confronted with a request by the hospital to authorize a blood transfusion over the patient's objection. The court recognized that the patient's refusal might cause his death, but it would not authorize the blood transfusion, holding that a competent individual has the right to make this decision even though it may seem unreasonable to medical experts.

The court in *In the Matter of Melideo*, 88 Misc. 2d 974, 390 N.Y.S.2d 523 (Sup. Ct. 1976), held that every human being of adult years has a right to determine what shall be done with his or her own body and cannot be subjected to medical treatment without his or her consent. Where there is no compelling state interest that justifies overriding an adult patient's decision not to receive a blood transfusion because of religious belief, such transfusions should not be ordered.

In the Illinois case of *In re Estate of Brooks*, 32 Ill. 2d 361, 205 N.E.2d 435 (1965), the court held that competent adult patients without minor children cannot be compelled to accept blood transfusions that they have steadfastly refused because of religious beliefs. In this case the patient had made her beliefs known to her physician and the hospital before consenting to any medical treatment. She was aware at all times of the meaning of her decision and had signed a statement releasing the hospital and her attending physician from liability for any consequences of her refusal to accept a blood transfusion.

Only a compelling state interest will justify interference with an individual's free exercise of religious beliefs. Application of this principle in *Application of President & Directors of Georgetown College, Inc.*, 331 F.2d 1100, (D.C. Cir.), *cert. denied*, 337 U.S. 978 (1964), involved a pregnant patient at the Georgetown Hospital. The hospital was granted a court order authorizing blood transfusions because the patient's physicians said they were necessary to save her life. The patient and her husband had refused authorization because of their religious beliefs. To learn whether the woman was in a mental condition to make a decision, the judge asked her what the effect would be, in terms of her religious beliefs, if the blood transfusions were authorized. Her response was that the transfusions would no longer be her responsibility. In its decision the court stressed that the woman had come to the hospital seeking medical attention and that it was convinced she wanted to live. Furthermore, according to the woman's statement, if the court undertook to authorize the transfusions without her consent, she would not be acting contrary to her religious beliefs. The effect of the court order preserved for Mrs. Jones the life she wanted without sacrificing her religious beliefs.

The final, and compelling reason, for granting the emergency writ was that a life hung in the balance. There was no time for research and reflection. Death could have mooted the cause in a matter of minutes, if action were not taken to preserve the status quo. To refuse to act, only to find later that the law required action, was a risk I was unwilling to accept. I determined to act on the side of life.

Id. at 1009–10.

The Court of Appeals of the District of Columbia noted in *In re Osborne*, 294 A.2d 372 (D.C. 1972), that the state's concern for the welfare of the children could override a patient's decision to refuse treatment for religious reasons. However, the court found in this case that the patient had made sufficient financial provisions for the future well-being of his two young children, so they would not become wards of the state if he should die. Under the circumstances, the court held that there was no compelling state interest to justify overriding the patient's intelligent and knowing refusal to consent to a transfusion because of his religious beliefs.

The New Jersey Supreme Court took the position in *John F. Kennedy Memorial Hospital v. Heston*, 58 N.J. 576, 279 A.2d 670 (1971), that the state's power to authorize a blood transfusion does not rest on the fact of the patient's condition or competence; it rests on the fact of the state's compelling interest in protecting the lives of its citizens, which in this case was sufficient to justify overriding the patient's determination to refuse vital aid.

The Supreme Court, Suffolk County, in *Fosmire v. Nicoleau*, 536 N.Y.S.2d 492 (App. Div. 1989), issued an order authorizing blood transfusions for a patient who had refused them. The plaintiff applied for an order vacating the supreme court's order. The supreme court, appellate division, held that the patient's constitutional rights of due process were violated by the supreme court's issuing an order authorizing blood transfusions in the absence of notice or opportunity for the patient or her representatives to be heard. The rights of a competent patient to refuse medical treatment, even if premised on fervently held religious beliefs, is not unqualified and may be overridden by compelling state interests. However, a state's interest in preserving a patient's life is not inviolate and in and of itself may not, under certain circumstances, be sufficient to overcome the patient's express desire to exercise her religious belief and forgo blood transfusion. The appellate division held in part that the state's interest would be satisfied if the other parent survived. The court of appeals went further by stating that, "The citizens of the state have long had the right to make their own medical care choices without regard to their medical condition or status as parents," *Matter of Fosmire v. Nicoleau*, No. 267, January 18, 1990. The court of appeals held that a competent adult has both a common law and statutory right under Public Health Law Sections 2504 and 2805-d to refuse life-saving treatment. Citing the state's authority to compel vaccination to protect the public from the spread of disease, to order treatment for persons who are incapable of making medical decisions, and to prohibit medical procedures that pose a substantial risk to the patient alone, the court of appeals did note that the right to choose was not absolute.

Temporary Guardianship

The treating physician and the hospital administrator petitioned the court on two occasions for authority to administer blood during two separate operations in *In re Estate Dorone*, 534 A.2d 452 (Pa. 1987). A 22-year-old male patient brought to the Lehigh Valley Hospital Center by helicopter following an automobile accident was diagnosed as suffering from an acute subdural hematoma with a brain contusion. It was determined that the patient would expire unless he underwent a cranial operation. The operation required the administration of blood to which the parents would not consent because of their religious beliefs. Following a hearing by telephone, the court of common pleas appointed the hospital's administrator as temporary guardian, authorizing him to consent to the performance of blood transfusions during emergency surgery. A more formal hearing did not take place due to the emergency situation that existed. Surgery was required a second time to remove a blood clot, and the court once again granted the administrator authority to authorize administration of blood. The superior court affirmed the orders, and the parents appealed. The Supreme Court of Pennsylvania held that the judge's failure to obtain direct testimony from the patient's parents and others concerning the patient's religious beliefs was not error where death was likely to result from withholding blood. The judge's decisions granting guardianship and the authority to consent to the administration of blood were considered absolutely necessary in light of the facts of this case. Nothing less than a fully conscious contemporary decision by the patient himself would have been sufficient to override the evidence of medical necessity.

Consent of Minors

When a medical or surgical procedure is to be performed on a minor, the question arises whether the minor's consent alone is sufficient and, if not, from whom consent should be obtained. The courts have held, as a general proposition, that the consent of a minor to medical or surgical treatment is ineffective and that the physician must secure the consent of the minor's parent or someone standing *in loco parentis*; otherwise, he or she will risk liability. Although parental consent should be obtained prior to treating a minor, treatment should not be delayed to the detriment of the child.

A number of courts have held the consent of a minor to be sufficient authorization for treatment in certain situations. In any specific case, a court's determination that the consent of a minor is effective and that parental consent is unnecessary will depend on such factors as the minor's age, maturity, mental status, and emancipation and the procedure involved, as well as public policy considerations.

The Massachusetts Supreme Judicial Court took into consideration a somewhat unusual factor in determining whether a minor's consent would be effective. In *Masden v. Harrison*, No. 68651 Eq. (Mass. June 12, 1957), the court decided that a healthy twin, 19 years old, could give an effective consent to an operation in which one of his kidneys would be removed and implanted in his sick twin. After hearing a psychiatrist's report, the court found that the operation was to the healthy twin's psychological benefit even though it might not have been to his physical benefit. The court ruled that the healthy twin had sufficient capacity to understand the planned procedure and consent.

Parental consent is not necessary in certain cases where the minor is married or otherwise emancipated. Most states have enacted statutes making it valid for married and emancipated minors to consent to medical and surgical procedures. Statutes making the consent of minors effective for blood donations and obstetrical care under specified circumstances have also been enacted by various states.

The court of appeals in *Carter v. Cangello*, 164 Cal. Rptr. 361 (Ct. App. 1980), held that a 17-year-old girl who was living away from home, in the home of a woman who gave her free room and board in exchange for household chores, and who made her own financial decisions could legally consent to medical procedures performed on her. The court made this decision knowing that the girl's parents provided part of her income by paying for her private schooling and certain medical care. The physician was privileged under statute to act on the minor's consent to surgery, and such privilege insulated him from liability to the parents for treating their daughter without their consent.

Many states have recognized by legislation that treatment for such conditions as pregnancy, venereal disease, and drug dependency does not require parental consent. State legislatures have reasoned that a minor is not likely to seek medical assistance where parental consent is demanded. Insisting on parental consent for the treatment of these conditions would increase the danger that a minor would delay or do without treatment in order to avoid explanation to the parents.

Consent of the Mentally Ill

A person who is mentally incompetent cannot legally consent to medical or surgical treatment. Therefore, consent of the patient's legal guardian must be obtained. Where no legal guardian is available, a court that handles such matters must be petitioned to permit treatment.

Subject to applicable statutory provisions, when a physician doubts a patient's capacity to consent, even though the patient has not been judged legally incompetent, the consent of the nearest relative should be obtained. If a patient is conscious and mentally capable of giving consent for treatment, the consent of a relative without the consent of the competent patient would not protect the physician from liability.

Implied Consent

Implied consent generally exists when immediate action is required to save a patient's life or to prevent permanent impairment of a patient's health. If it is impossible in an emergency to obtain the consent of the patient or someone legally authorized to give consent, the required procedure may be undertaken without any liability for failure to procure consent. An emergency situation removes the need for consent. This rule also applies when conditions discovered during an operation must be corrected immediately and the consent of the patient or someone authorized to give consent is not obtainable. This privilege to proceed in emergencies without consent is accorded physicians because inaction at such times may cause greater injury to the patient and would be contrary to good medical practice.

Unconscious patients are presumed under law to approve treatment that appears to be necessary. It is assumed that such patients would have consented if they were conscious and competent. However, if a patient expressly refuses to consent to certain treatment, such treatment may not be employed after the patient becomes unconscious. Similarly, conscious patients suffering from emergency conditions retain the right to refuse consent.

In *Collins v. Davis*, 44 Misc. 2d 622, 254 N.Y.S.2d 666 (Sup. Ct. 1964), a hospital administrator sought a court order to permit a surgical operation on an irrational adult patient whose life was in jeopardy. The consent of the patient's wife had been sought, but she refused to grant authorization for the procedure for reasons that she thought were justified, although they were medically unsound. The court authorized the surgery for the reason that the patient himself had sought medical attention. The court ruled that the hospital was trying to provide the necessary medical treatment in conformity with sound medical judgment and that the spouse was interfering.

If a procedure is necessary to protect the life or health of a patient, documentation justifying the need to treat prior to obtaining informed consent should be maintained. In *Luka v. Lowrie*, 171 Mich. 122, 136 N.W. 1106 (1912), involving a 15-year-old boy whose left foot had been run over and crushed by a train, consultation by the treating physician with other doctors was an important factor in determining the outcome of the case. Upon the boy's arrival at the hospital, the defending physician and four house surgeons decided it was necessary to amputate the foot. The court said it was inconceivable that, had the parents been present, they would have refused consent in the face of a determination by five physicians that amputation would save the boy's life. Thus, in spite of testimony at the trial that the amputation may not have been necessary, professional consultation prior to the operation supported the assertion that a genuine emergency existed, and consent could be implied. In the case of an emergency where a physician fails to proceed due to lack of parental consent, the physician could be held liable if the patient suffers injury because of a failure to act.

The hospital and the physician should be able to establish that, under circumstances where the patient is unconscious, obtaining the consent of the patient or someone legally authorized to give consent could mean a delay likely to increase unnecessary risk to the patient.

Consent can also be implied in nonemergency situations. For example, a patient may voluntarily submit to a procedure, implying consent, without any explicitly spoken or written expression of consent. In the Massachusetts case of *O'Brien v. Cunard Steam Ship Co.*, 154 Mass. 272, 28 N.E. 266 (1891), a ship's passenger who joined a line of people receiving injections was held to have implied his consent to a vaccination. The rationale for this decision is that individuals who observe a line of people and who notice that injections are being administered to those at the head of the line should expect that if they join and remain in the line, they will receive an injection. Therefore, the voluntary act of entering the line and the plaintiff's opportunity to see what was taking place at the head of the line were accepted by the jury as manifestations of consent to the injection. The *O'Brien* case contains all the elements necessary to imply consent from a voluntary act: the procedure was a simple vaccination, the proceedings were at all times visible, and the plaintiff was free to withdraw up to the instant of the injection.

Whether or not a patient's consent can be implied is frequently asked when the condition of a patient requires some deviation from an agreed-on procedure. If a patient expressly prohibits a specific medical or surgical procedure, consent to the procedure cannot be implied. The same consent rule applies if a patient expressly prohibits a particular extension of a procedure even though the patient voluntarily submitted to the original procedure.

Incompetent Patients

It may be the duty of the court to assume responsibility of guardianship for a patient who is *non compos mentis* to the extent of authorizing treatment if necessary to save his/her life even though the medical treatment authorized may be contrary to the patient's religious beliefs. A hospital was entitled to a court order authorizing medical personnel to provide necessary treatment, including the administering of blood and plasma, in *University of Cincinnati Hospital v. Edmund*, 506 N.E.2d 299 (Ohio Com. Pl. 1986). The administration of blood had been determined to be medically necessary to preserve the life of a Jehovah's Witness who was unable to express her own specific wishes with respect to her treatment because of the ingestion of excessive amounts of alcohol and the effects of a gunshot to her liver. Although the patient's children and members of her church testified that her religious beliefs precluded the administering of blood and plasma, there was a compelling state interest which permitted the hospital without prior consent to administer blood and provide other necessary treatment until such time as she might personally express her wishes concerning future treatment.

Consent and Change of Mind

The husband in *Randolph v. City of New York*, 69 N.Y.2d 844, 507 N.E.2d 298 (1987), brought a wrongful death action against the city, the city health and hospital corporation, and doctors arising out of the death of his wife, a Jehovah's Witness. Although the patient had initially refused a blood transfusion because of her religious beliefs during a Caesarean section, witnesses had testified that the patient had been alive when authorization for a transfusion was later received and that her life could still have been saved if she had been properly transfused. The jury returned a verdict finding a physician and the New York City Health and Hospital Corporation 50 percent liable for the death of the patient. On appeal by the defendants, the supreme court, appellate division, dismissed the complaint on the ground that the verdict had been based on insufficient evidence. On appeal by the plaintiff, the court of appeals held that there was evidence supporting the jury verdict for the plaintiff. Action against the city was found to have been properly dismissed.

UNAUTHORIZED TREATMENT

The plaintiff in *Gaskin v. Goldwasser*, 520 N.E.2d 1085 (Ill. App. Ct. 1988), brought a suit against an oral surgeon, alleging dental malpractice. The oral surgeon had removed 19 of the teeth remaining in the plaintiff's mouth. The defendant admitted that 5 of the 19 teeth were removed without the consent of the patient. The circuit court entered a judgment for the plaintiff on a jury verdict for damages resulting from the extraction of the five lower teeth. On appeal, the appellate court held that the patient was entitled to have the allegation of willful and wanton misconduct and battery for unauthorized removal of the five lower teeth submitted to the jury. The case was remanded for a new trial.

RELEASE FORM

Adult patients who are conscious and mentally competent have the right to refuse any medical or surgical procedure to the extent permitted by law even when the best medical opinion deems it essential to life. This refusal must be honored whether it is grounded in religious belief or mere whim. Every person has the legal right to refuse to permit a touching of his or her body. Failure to respect this right can result in a legal action for assault and battery.

When a patient refuses to consent to a procedure for any reason, religious or otherwise, a release form should be completed to protect the hospital and its personnel from liability for failure to perform a procedure. A notation should be placed on the patient's medical record when treatment is refused. The completed release form provides documented evidence of a patient's refusal to consent to a recommended treatment. Should a patient refuse to sign the release form, this should be noted on the patient's medical record. A court ruling should be sought in those cases where refusal of treatment poses a serious threat to a patient's health, especially in the case of minors.

STATUTORY CONSENT

The motor vehicle laws in some states provide that accepting the privilege of driving on the highways implies a person's consent to furnishing a sample of blood or urine for chemical analysis when charged with driving while intoxicated. Generally, these statutes imply authorization of a test, and an action for assault and battery would not be upheld. A New York statute protects physicians, hospitals, and their employees from any liability for obtaining a blood sample from a nonconsenting individual when a police officer has requested the sample. Section 1194(3) of the New York Vehicle and Traffic Law (McKinney 1970) states the following in regard to chemical tests:

> b. No physician, registered nurse . . . or hospital employing such physician, registered professional nurse . . . and no other employer of such physician, registered professional nurse . . . shall be sued or held liable for any act done or omitted in the course of withdrawing blood at the request of a police officer pursuant to this section.

In the absence of statutory protection, a procedure performed despite an individual's refusal to consent would constitute a battery. However, recovery would probably be limited to nominal damages unless physical harm resulted from negligent performance.

Lack of informed consent in New York State is the failure of the person providing the professional treatment or diagnosis to disclose alternatives to the patient and to cite the reasonably foreseeable risks and benefits involved; this disclosure must parallel what a reasonable medical practitioner under similar circumstances would have disclosed, in a manner permitting the patient to make a knowledgeable evaluation. The plaintiff in *Gonzales v. Moscarella*, 530 N.Y.S.2d 218 (App. Div. 1988), failed to present expert medical testimony in support of his claim concerning the adequacy of information provided to him prior to performance of a surgical procedure. On appeal, the supreme court, appellate division, held that the trial court properly dismissed the plaintiff's action, which was based on the lack of informed consent. Although the plaintiff's expert witness did outline the risks inherent in the operative procedure performed and expressed a medical opinion that it would have been good medical practice to advise the patient of the risks and alternatives, the physician never once expressed an opinion as to the adequacy of the information provided to the patient.

The right of action to recover for damages is limited to those cases involving a nonemergency treatment, procedure, or surgery or a diagnostic procedure that involves invasion or disruption of the integrity of the body.

The burden of establishing proof is on the plaintiff. The plaintiff must also establish that (1) a reasonably prudent person in the patient's position would not have undergone the treatment or diagnosis if fully informed and (2) the lack of informed consent is a proximate cause of the injury or condition for which recovery is sought.

The following are defenses against recovery:

- The risk not disclosed is too commonly known to warrant disclosure.
- The patient assured the medical practitioner that he or she would undergo the treatment, procedure, or diagnosis regardless of the risk involved.
- The patient indicated to the medical practitioner that he or she did not want to be informed of the matters to which he or she was entitled to be informed.
- Consent by or on behalf of a patient was not reasonably possible.
- The medical practitioner, after considering all of the attendant facts and circumstances, used reasonable discretion as to the manner and extent to which such alternatives or risks were disclosed to the patient because the practitioner reasonably believed that the manner and extent of such disclosure could reasonably be expected to adversely and substantially affect the patient's condition. New York Public Health Law Section 2805-d (McKinney 1975) [amending New York Public Health Law Section 2805 (McKinney 1971)].

Chapter 8

Hospital Records and Legal Reporting Obligations

Documentation of the facts of a patient's illness, symptoms, diagnosis, and treatment is one of the most important functions in furnishing modern medical and hospital care. Nurses and physicians are primarily charged with the responsibility of keeping accurate and up-to-date medical records. All hospital personnel who have access to medical records have both a legal and an ethical obligation to protect the confidentiality of the information in the records.

Medical records are maintained primarily to provide complete information regarding the care and treatment of patients. They are the principal means of communication among the physician, the nurse, and other health professionals in matters relating to patient care.

The major purposes of the medical record are to provide a planning tool for patient care; to record the course of a patient's treatment and the changes in a patient's condition; to document the communications between the practitioner responsible for the patient and any other health professional who contributes to the patient's care; to assist in protecting the legal interests of the patient, the hospital, and the practitioner; to provide a data base for use in statistical reporting, continuing education, and research; and to provide information necessary for third-party billing.

The nurse is generally the one medical professional the patient sees more than any other. Consequently, the nurse is in a position to keep constant watch over the patient's illness, response to medication, display of pain and discomfort, and general condition. The patient's care, as well as the nurse's observations, should be recorded fully, factually, and promptly. The nurse should promptly and accurately comply with the orders the physician writes in the record and should check, in case of doubt, to make certain that the order is correct and that it has not already been completed.

CONTENTS

The medical record must be a complete, accurate, up-to-date report of the medical history, condition, and treatment of each patient. It is composed of at least

131

two distinct parts, each of which is made up of several types of forms. The first part is compiled upon admission and includes the admission record, which describes pertinent data regarding the patient's history, including name, age, address, reason for admission, etc. It also contains the general consent and authorization-for-treatment forms allowing the hospital to perform routine diagnostic testing, etc. The second part, the clinical record, contains the patient care and progress records, the patient's history and physical, temperature charts, consultation reports, laboratory reports, x-ray reports, operative reports, delivery records, anesthesia reports, discharge summaries, etc. Licensure rules and regulations contained in state statutes generally describe the requirements and standards for the maintenance, handling, signing, filing, and retention of medical records.

A hospital's or a physician's failure to maintain a complete and accurate medical record reflecting the treatment rendered may affect the ability of the hospital and/or physician to obtain third-party reimbursement (e.g., from Medicare, Medicaid, or Blue Cross). Under federal and state laws, utilization review committees are charged with the responsibility of ensuring that the medical record accurately substantiates the treatment for which the hospital or physician seeks payment. Thus, the medical record is important to the hospital for medical, legal, and financial reasons.

Various licensing regulations require prompt completion of records after the discharge of patients. Persistent failure to conform to a medical staff rule requiring the physician to complete records promptly was held in *Board of Trustees Memorial Hospital v. Pratt*, 72 Wyo. 120, 262 P.2d 682 (1953), to provide a basis for suspension of a staff member.

FINANCIAL IMPLICATIONS OF DIAGNOSIS RELATED GROUPS

Diagnosis related groups (DRGs) refer to a methodology developed by professors at Yale University for classifying patients in categories according to age, diagnosis, and treatment resource requirements. It is the basis for the Department of Health and Human Services' prospective payment system, contained in the 1983 Social Security Amendments for reimbursing inpatient hospital costs for Medicare beneficiaries. The key source of information for determining the course of treatment of each hospital patient and the proper DRG assignment is the medical record. Reimbursement is based on pre-established average prices for each DRG. As a result of this reimbursement methodology, poor record keeping can precipitate financial disaster for a hospital. The major purpose of the amendments is to hold down the rise in Medicare expenditures before the Social Security system experiences serious deficits. The potential financial savings for Medicare are substantial. Under this system of payment, if hospitals can provide quality patient care at a cost under the price established for a DRG, they may keep the excess dollars paid. This is an incentive for hospitals to keep costs under control. There is, however, a fear that patients may, to their detriment, be discharged too early for financial reasons. This in turn could lead to costly malpractice suits.

LEGAL PROCEEDINGS AND THE MEDICAL RECORD

The ever-increasing frequency of personal injury suits mandates that hospitals maintain complete, accurate, and timely medical records. Their importance as an evidentiary tool in legal proceedings cannot be overestimated. Medical records aid police investigations, provide information for determining the cause of death, and indicate the extent of injury in worker's compensation or personal injury proceedings.

When health professionals are called as witnesses in a proceeding, they are permitted to refresh their recollections of the facts and circumstances of a particular case by referring to the medical record. Courts recognize that it is impossible for a medical witness to remember the details of every patient's treatment. The record may therefore be used as an aid in relating the facts of a patient's course of treatment.

The medical record itself may be admitted into evidence in legal proceedings. In order for medical record information to be admitted into evidence, the court must be assured that the information is accurate, that it was recorded at the time the event took place, and that it was not recorded in anticipation of a specific legal proceeding. While it is recognized that witnesses may refresh their memories and that records may be admitted into evidence, there is nevertheless a need for assurance that the information is trustworthy.

When a medical record is introduced, its custodian, usually the medical records administrator, must testify as to the manner in which the record was produced and the way in which it is protected from unauthorized handling and change. It should be noted that whether such records and other documents are admitted or excluded is governed by the facts and circumstances of the particular case, as well as by the applicable rules of evidence.

Whatever the situation, it is clear that the record must be complete, accurate, and timely. If it can be shown that the record is inaccurate or incomplete or that it was made long after the event it purports to record, it will not be accepted into evidence.

CONFIDENTIAL COMMUNICATIONS

The communications between a physician and his/her patient and the information generated during the course of the patient's illness are generally accorded the protection of confidentiality. Health professionals have a clear legal and moral obligation to maintain this confidentiality. As noted above, medical records, with proper authorization, may be utilized for the purposes of research, statistical evaluation, and education. The information obtained from medical records must be dealt with in a confidential manner; otherwise, a hospital could incur liability.

There are several exceptions to the restriction on disclosing information obtained in a confidential relationship. For example, disclosure may be required where a patient is the victim of a crime. Another exception concerns waiver of privilege where the patient may waive the privilege by his/her actions or words. The hospital in *In re Brink*, 42 Ohio Misc. 2d 5, 536 N.E.2d 1202 (Ct. C.P. 1988), sought to quash a grand jury request for the medical records pertaining to the blood tests administered to a person under investigation. The court of common pleas held that the physician-patient privilege did not extend to medical records subpoenaed pursuant to a grand jury investigation. A proceeding before a grand jury is considered secret in nature; therefore, a patient's interests in preserving the confidentiality of his or her records are protected.

RELEASE OF MEDICAL RECORDS

Traditionally, medical records have been retained for the benefit of hospitals and health care professionals in treating their patients. Records have generally been protected from public scrutiny by a general practice of nondisclosure. This practice has been waived under a limited number of specifically controlled situations, such as when information is needed on hospitalization to help locate a missing person.

Health professionals and hospitals have generally held that all records are their exclusive property and have not as a rule released them to patients. The courts, however, have taken a view that patients have a right to access their medical records. Some states have enacted legislation permitting patients access to their medical records. The New York Public Health Law was amended on January 1, 1989, by adding Section 18, which provides that patients may have access to review and/or obtain copies of their medical records, x-rays, and laboratory and diagnostic tests. Access to information includes that maintained or possessed by a health care facility and/or a health practitioner who has treated or is treating a patient. Hospitals and physicians can withhold records if it is determined that the information could reasonably be expected to cause substantial and identifiable harm to the patient. A reasonable charge for inspection and copies of medical records may be made, provided the charge does not exceed the costs incurred by the provider. On application by an infant patient's mother to produce hospital records, the Supreme Court, Nassau County, in *Scipione v. Long Island Jewish-Hillside Medical Center*, 460 N.Y.S.2d 409 (Sup. Ct. 1982), held that the mother was not entitled to an order directing the hospital to produce the infant's record for copying by a commercial photocopying facility. The mother had claimed that the fee was unreasonable in that the hospital required a $15 handling fee plus $1.50 per page for 727 pages of the child's record, which totaled $1,105.50. The mother was of the opinion that a more reasonable fee would have been ten cents per page.

The court, however, decided that the infant's mother could obtain copies of the infant's medical records by either paying the full charge requested by the hospital or by renting a photocopying machine and copying the records at the hospital or another mutually agreed-on site under the direct supervision of an employee of the hospital. However, the hospital's $15 search and retrieval fee would have to be paid, as well as a fee for the hospital's employee who supervised the photocopying. The court decided that to hold a hearing on this matter would be an improvident waste of judicial time.

The law does not apply to the records of patients in psychiatric hospitals, institutions for the mentally disabled, and alcohol and drug treatment facilities and to personal notes and observations. Qualified persons who are denied access to their medical records have appeal rights first to a medical record access review committee as appointed by the commissioner of health, and ultimately to judicial review.

Failure to release a patient's record can lead to a legal action. The patient in *Pierce v. Penman*, 515 A.2d 948 (Pa. Super. Ct. 1986), brought a lawsuit seeking damages for severe emotional distress when physicians repeatedly refused to turn over her medical records. The defendants had rendered various professional services to the plaintiff for approximately 11 years. The patient moved and found a new physician, Dr. Hochman. She signed a release authorizing Dr. Hochman to obtain her records from the defendant physicians. Dr. Hochman wrote a letter for her records, but never received a response. The defendants claimed they never received the request. The patient changed physicians again and continued in her efforts to obtain a copy of the records. There came a time when the defendants' offices were burglarized, and the plaintiff's records were allegedly taken. The detective in charge of investigating the burglary stated that he was never notified that any records were taken. The court of common pleas awarded the patient $2,500 in compensatory damages and $10,000 in punitive damages. On appeal, the superior court upheld the award. The physicians' contention that they relied on the advice of legal counsel did not insulate them from liability for punitive damages.

DRUG AND ALCOHOL ABUSE RECORDS

The federal Drug Abuse and Treatment Act of 1972, 21 U.S.C. § 1175, and the federal regulations promulgated thereunder provide that patient records relating to drug and alcohol abuse treatment must be held confidential and not disclosed except as provided in these laws. Unlike other medical records, drug and alcohol abuse records cannot be released until the court has determined whether a claimed need for the records outweighs the potential injury to the patient, to the patient-physician relationship, and to the treatment services being rendered. Due to these strict requirements, the courts have been reluctant to order the release of records unless absolutely necessary.

PRIVACY ACT OF 1974

The Privacy Act of 1974, 5 U.S.C. § 552a, was enacted to safeguard individual privacy from the misuse of federal records, give individuals access to records concerning themselves that are maintained by federal agencies, and establish a Privacy Protection Safety Commission. A portion of the Privacy Act reads as follows:

Sec. 2[a] The Congress finds that (1) the privacy of an individual is directly affected by the collection, maintenance, use, and dissemination of personal information by Federal agencies; (2) the increasing use of computers and sophisticated information technology, while essential to the efficient operations of the Government, has greatly magnified the harm to individual privacy that can occur from any collection, maintenance, use, or dissemination of personal information; (3) the opportunities for an individual to secure employment, insurance, and credit, and his right to due process, and other legal protections are endangered by the misuse of certain information systems; (4) the right to privacy is a personal and fundamental right protected by the Constitution of the United States; and (5) in order to protect the privacy of individuals identified in information systems maintained by Federal agencies, it is necessary and proper for the Congress to regulate the collection, maintenance, use, and dissemination of information by such agencies. [b] The purpose of this Act is to provide certain safeguards for an individual against an invasion of personal privacy by requiring Federal agencies, except as otherwise provided by law, to—(1) permit an individual to determine what records pertaining to him are collected, maintained, used, or disseminated by such agencies; (2) permit an individual to prevent records pertaining to him obtained by such agencies for a particular purpose from being used or made available for another purpose without his consent; (3) permit an individual to gain access to information pertaining to him in Federal agency records, to have a copy made of all or any portion thereof, and to correct or amend such records; (4) collect, maintain, use, or disseminate any record of identifiable personal information in a manner that assures that such action is for a necessary and lawful purpose, that the information is current and accurate for its intended use, and that adequate safeguards are provided to prevent misuse of such information; (5) permit exemptions from the requirements with respect to records provided in this Act only in those cases where there is an important public policy need for such exemption as has been determined by the specific statutory authority; and (6) be subject to civil suit for any damages which occur as a result of willful or intentional action which violates any individual's rights under this Act.

COMPUTERIZED MEDICAL RECORDS

Computers have invaded the health care industry. They are found in the admitting office, the business office, and even the operating room. They are in the laboratory, pharmacy, x-ray, and medical records departments. They are fast and accurate and have an almost endless capacity to store data. From research to treatment, they are here to stay. Although computers are an economic necessity in the modern hospital, they are not faultless. Problems associated with computerization include the loss of confidentiality and the unauthorized disclosure of information, thus requiring the development of sophisticated security systems; equipment reliability; and the accuracy of input by computer operators.

Another potential shortcoming of computerized medical records is the lack of system responsiveness. A system must respond quickly to any request for information. Most forms of human-computer communication, such as computer keyboards and monitors, respond too slowly for effectiveness and patient safety. The need for a written patient care record will most likely be with us for a long time.

Few cases, if any, have been litigated to date involving computer negligence in the health care field. As computers become more widely utilized in the health care industry, the potential for computer-related liability will increase.

In *Whalen v. Roe*, 423 U.S. 1313 (1975), an application had been made for a stay of judgment of a three-judge court sitting in the Southern District of New York. The applicant, the commissioner of health of the state of New York, had been enjoined by a three-judge court from enforcing certain provisions of the New York State Public Health Law that required the name and address of each patient receiving a Schedule II controlled substance be reported to the applicant. Schedule II drugs are those considered to have a high potential for abuse, but also have an accepted medical use. Under the law, a doctor prescribing a Schedule II drug does so on a special serially numbered prescription form, one copy of which goes to the commissioner of health of New York, who transfers the data, including the name and address of the user, from the prescription form to a centralized computer file. The respondent claimed that mandatory disclosure of the name of a patient receiving Schedule II drugs violated the patient's right of privacy and interfered with the doctor's right to prescribe treatment for his patient solely on the basis of medical considerations.

The court held that the patient identification requirement had been the product of an orderly and rational legislative decision about the state's broad police powers. The statute does not impair any private interest on its face and does not impair the right of doctors to practice medicine free from unwarranted state interference.

Hospitals undergoing computerization must provide for ways to assess user needs, methods to design an effective system, the selection of appropriate equipment, user training programs, a disaster recovery plan (e.g., provisions for backup files and electrical shutdowns), information access, data security, and hardware and software theft. Experienced computer consulting firms can save hospitals thousands of dollars with their expertise. Computers are not difficult to understand, but minor mistakes can cost major dollars.

THE MEDICAL RECORD BATTLEGROUND

The medical record must not be utilized as a battleground against another professional or the hospital. The medical record is a document that cannot be erased once a recording has been made. It should not be utilized as an instrument for registering a complaint against another health care professional or the institution. The health care professional who utilizes a patient's medical record unwisely may have vented his/her emotions for the moment, but may have at the same time provided the basis for having to justify his/her actions to another professional, to the institution, or to a jury. It should be remembered that comments written during a time of anger may have been based on inaccurate information, which in turn could be damaging to one's credibility and future statements.

FALSIFICATION OF RECORDS

All professionals should be aware that falsification of medical and/or business records is a ground for criminal indictment, as well as for civil liability for damages suffered. In *People v. Smithtown General Hospital*, 402 N.Y.S.2d 318 (Sup. Ct. 1978), a motion to dismiss indictments against a physician and a nurse charged with falsifying business records in the first degree was denied. In each indictment it was charged that the defendant was in violation of a duty imposed on him or her by law or by the nature of his or her position. The surgeon was charged because he omitted to make a true entry in his operative report. The nurse was charged because she failed to make a true entry in the operating room log.

CHARTING—SOME HELPFUL ADVICE

The medical record is the most important document in a negligence action against the hospital and its staff. Both plaintiff and defendant utilize it as a basis for their action and defense. The following advice on documentation should prove to be helpful in charting:

- The medical record is a historical document that describes to those who read it how the hospital cared for each patient it treated. Make entries that are legible, clear, concise but complete, and meaningful to each patient's course of treatment.

- Do not write long, defensive, and/or derogatory notes about your colleagues, the hospital, and other health professionals. Stick to the facts.
- Do not make erasures or use correction fluid to cover up entries on the chart. Draw a single line through a mistaken entry, enter the correct information, and then sign and date it.
- Place charts related to pending legal action in a separate file under lock and key. Notify hospital counsel immediately of any potential lawsuit.
- If you are aware of an asserted legal action, consult the medical records administrator before charting further information. "Doctoring a chart" makes for a suspicious and unforgiving jury.
- Remember that a medical record has many authors. Do not ignore the entries made by others. After all, good patient care is a team effort.

LEGAL REPORTING OBLIGATIONS

A society wishes the best possible environment for its members. It works through government to protect its people by health regulations and statutes. Only through reliable observations and reports can proper measures be instituted to safeguard the environment of society.

Of prime importance to the health professional are health statutes requiring that certain information be transmitted to the state. Although most statutory reporting requirements do not contain an express immunity from suit for disclosure without the permission of the person affected, as a general rule a person making a report in good faith and under statutory command is protected.

Child Abuse

The physically abused or neglected child is a medical, social, and legal problem. What constitutes an abused child is difficult to determine because it is often impossible to ascertain whether a child was injured intentionally or accidentally.

There was a time when health practitioners were somewhat reluctant to report cases of possible child abuse. Given the significant level of uncertainty as to the true cause of the child's condition and the tremendous amount of social reprobation associated with such a charge or claim, physicians hesitated to act as self-appointed police. Additionally, a person who made a report of suspected child abuse to the proper authorities could have been sued by the child's parents on the claim that the report was a defamation of the parents' character or an invasion of their privacy.

Today, however, all states and the District of Columbia have enacted laws to protect abused children. Furthermore, almost all states protect the persons required to report cases of child abuse.

The various laws differ in their definition of an abused child. Generally, an abused child is one who has had serious physical injury inflicted by other than accidental means. The injuries may have been inflicted by a parent or any other person responsible for the child's care. Some states extend the definition to include a child suffering from starvation. Other states include moral neglect in the definition of abuse. For example, Arizona mentions immoral associations; Idaho includes endangering a child's morals; Mississippi incorporates location of a child in a disreputable place or association with vagrant, vicious, or immoral persons. Sexual abuse is also enumerated as an element of neglect in the statutes of a few states.

Most state laws require certain people to report suspected cases of abuse. In a few states certain identified individuals who are not required to report instances of child abuse, but who do so, are protected. The child abuse laws may or may not provide penalties for failure to report. The individuals covered by the various statutes range from physicians to "any person." Many of the statutes specifically include hospital administrators.

Any report of suspected child abuse must be made with a good faith belief that the facts reported are true. The definition of good faith as used in a child abuse statute may vary from state to state. However, when a health practitioner's medical evaluation indicates reasonable cause to believe a child's injuries were not accidental and when the health practitioner is not acting from his or her desire to harass, injure, or embarrass the child's parents, making the report will not result in liability.

Reporting laws specify the nature of what constitutes child abuse. Statutes generally require that when a person covered by statute is attending a child as a staff member of a hospital or similar institution and suspects child abuse, the staff member must notify the person in charge of the institution, who in turn makes the necessary report. Typical statutes provide that an oral report be made immediately, followed by a written report. Most states require the report to contain the following information: the name and address of the child; the persons responsible for the child's care; the child's age; the nature and extent of the child's injuries (including any evidence of previous injuries); and any other information that might be helpful in establishing the cause of the injuries, such as photographs of the injured child and the identity of the perpetrator.

An action for damages was brought by a minor child and his mother in *Awkerman v. Tri-County Orthopedic Group*, 143 Mich. App. 722, 373 N.W. 2d 204 (1985), against physicians for failing to diagnose disease and filing erroneous child abuse reports. The Wayne County Circuit Court granted the physicians' motions for partial summary judgment, and the plaintiffs appealed. The Court of

Appeals of Michigan held that the child abuse reporting statute, Michigan Compiled Laws Annotated § 722.625, provides immunity to persons who file child abuse reports in good faith even if the reports were filed due to negligent diagnosis of the cause of the child's frequent bone fractures, which was eventually diagnosed as osteogenesis imperfecta. The court of appeals also held that damages for shame and humiliation were not recoverable pursuant to Michigan statute. Immunity from liability did not extend to damages for malpractice that may have resulted from the failure to diagnose the child's disease as long as all the elements of negligence were present.

Diseases in Newborns

Most states have legislative reporting requirements for diseases in newborns. Hospitals are required to report instances of diarrhea, staphylococcal disease, and other infections. Most states provide penalties for violation of these laws.

Phenylketonuria

Phenylketonuria (PKU) is a reportable condition. The chief concern in reporting PKU is to encourage the testing and treatment of infants for PKU. A state's regulations do not automatically exempt the state from liability if it fails in its responsibility in the diagnosis of PKU. The state of Louisiana was held liable for damages in *Marcel v. Louisiana State Department of Health & Human Resources*, 492 So. 2d 103 (La. Ct. App. 1986), for the mental retardation and physical disabilities which a child suffered as a result of a state laboratory's failure to diagnose PKU. An initial Guthrie test was positive for PKU. The state was directly liable because of its institution of a substandard PKU program, where expert evidence established that a urine test was unreliable when compared with the more accurate blood tests and that a third Guthrie test should have been performed when the second screening test showed a negative. The state was also held vicariously liable for the negligence of laboratory personnel who received samples of the newborn's blood, ran a second Guthrie test, improperly found a negative test result, and closed her file.

Communicable Diseases

Most states have enacted laws that require the reporting of actual or suspected cases of communicable diseases. For example, the New York State Sanitary Code Chapter 1, Section 2.12 (1973), provides the following guidelines:

Reporting by others than physicians of cases of diseases presumably communicable. When no physician is in attendance it shall be the duty of the head of a private household or the person in charge of any institution, school, hotel, boarding house, camp or vessel or any public health nurse or any other person having knowledge of an individual affected with any disease presumably communicable, to report immediately the name and address of such person to the city, council or district health officer.

The need for statutes requiring the reporting of communicable diseases is clear. If a state is to protect its citizens' health through its power to quarantine, it must ensure the prompt reporting of infection or disease.

Births and Deaths

All births and deaths are reportable by statute. Births occurring outside of hospitals should be reported by the legally qualified physician in attendance at a delivery or, in the event of the absence of a physician, by the registered nurse or other attendant. Death certificates must be signed by the physician pronouncing a death. Statutes requiring the reporting of births and deaths are necessary in order to maintain accurate census records. Census reports are of great importance to states seeking funding of federally sponsored programs, which often grant funds based on population statistics.

Suspicious Deaths

Greater than a state's interest in the recording of all births and deaths is the state's desire to review unnatural deaths that may be the result of some form of criminal activity. Unnatural deaths must be referred to the medical examiner for review. Such cases may include violent deaths, deaths caused by unlawful acts or criminal neglect, and/or deaths that may be considered suspicious or unusual. The medical examiner may make an investigation of such cases and issue an autopsy report. The purpose of a medical examiner's investigation is to determine the actual cause of death and thereby provide assistance for any further criminal investigation that may be considered necessary.

Gunshot Wounds

Gunshot wound laws require reports where injuries are inflicted by lethal weapons or, in some cases, by unlawful acts. Some statutes even include automobile accidents within their definition of lethal weapons. The New York statute is typical.

265.25 CERTAIN WOUNDS TO BE REPORTED

Every case of a bullet wound, gunshot wound, powder burn or any other injury arising from or caused by the discharge of a gun or firearm, and every case of a wound which is likely to or may result in death and is actually or apparently inflicted by a knife, ice pick or other sharp or pointed instrument, shall be reported at once to the police authorities in the city, town or village where the person reported is located by: (a) the physician attending or treating the case; or (b) the manager, superintendent or other person in charge, whenever such case is treated in a hospital, sanitarium or other institution. . . .

N.Y.S. P.L. § 265.25.

Criminal Acts

In addition to reporting the subjects specified by statute, there may be a legal duty to report to the police such acts as attempted suicide, assault, rape, child molestation, or the unlawful dispensing or taking of narcotic drugs. Much of this information may be learned while caring for patients and therefore may be privileged communication. Without a patient's express consent to disclose such information or a statutory mandate that a report be made, it may be a violation of the patient's rights to report a suspected criminal act.

Chapter 9

Abortion

Abortion is the premature termination of pregnancy. It can be classified as spontaneous or induced. It may occur as an incidental result of a medical procedure, or it may be an elective decision on the part of the patient. As of 1985 there were 1.588 million abortions annually in the United States,[1] up from .586 million in 1972. Abortion, besides having substantial ethical, moral, and religious implications, has proven to be a major political issue in the 1980s and will continue as such well into the 1990s and beyond.

> By the end of the decade, the right to an abortion was battered but still standing. The Supreme Court had agreed to hear new abortion challenges, but there were no credible predictions on what would happen to abortion in the 1990s. The only certainties were that more laws would be proposed, more laws would be passed, and more lawsuits would wend their way up to the Supreme Court.[2]

Medical professionals are currently faced with a twofold problem regarding abortions. First, civil liability may be incurred for refusing to allow abortions or for restricting the circumstances under which an abortion may be performed on the premises. Second, criminal liability may be incurred for allowing an abortion procedure when it is prohibited by valid state statutes. Both the civil and the criminal liability aspects have been complicated by recent U.S. Supreme Court decisions regarding abortion. In part, those decisions have given further strength to a woman's right to privacy in the context of matters relating to her own body. However, the Supreme Court has also recognized the interest of the states in protecting potential life and has attempted to spell out the extent to which the states may regulate and even prohibit abortions.

SUPREME COURT DECISIONS

In *Roe v. Wade*, 410 U.S. 113, 164 (1973), the U.S. Supreme Court held the Texas penal abortion law unconstitutional, stating: "State criminal abortion statutes . . . that except from criminality only a lifesaving procedure on behalf of the mother, without regard to the stage of her pregnancy and other interests involved, is violating the Due Process Clause of the Fourteenth Amendment.''

The Court then went on to delineate what regulatory measures a state may lawfully enact during the three stages of pregnancy. In the companion decision, *Doe v. Bolton*, 410 U.S. 179 (1973), where the Court considered a constitutional attack on the Georgia abortion statute, further restrictions were placed on state regulation of the procedure. The provisions of the Georgia statute establishing residency requirements for women seeking abortions and requiring that the procedure be performed in a hospital accredited by the Joint Commission on Accreditation of Hospitals were declared constitutionally invalid. In considering legislative provisions establishing medical staff approval as a prerequisite to the abortion procedure, the Court decided that "[i]nterposition of the hospital abortion committee is unduly restrictive of the patient's rights and needs that . . . have already been medically delineated and substantiated by her personal physician. To ask more serves neither the hospital nor the State." *Id.* at 198.

The Court was unable to find any constitutionally justifiable rationale for a statutory requirement of advance approval by the abortion committee of the hospital's medical staff. Insofar as statutory consultation requirements are concerned, the Court reasoned that the acquiescence of two copractitioners has no rational connection with a patient's needs and, furthermore, unduly infringes on the physician's right to practice.

Thus, by using a test related to patient needs, the Court in *Doe v. Bolton* struck down four preabortion procedural requirements commonly imposed by state statutes: (1) residency, (2) performance of the abortion in a hospital accredited by the Joint Commission, (3) approval by an appropriate committee of the medical staff, and (4) consultations.

THE FIRST TRIMESTER

During the first trimester of pregnancy, the decision to undergo an abortion procedure is between the woman and her physician. A state may require that abortions be performed by a physician licensed pursuant to its laws. However, a woman's right to an abortion is not unqualified since the decision to perform the procedure must be left to the medical judgment of her attending physician. "For the stage prior to approximately the end of the first trimester, the abortion decision and its effectuation must be left to the medical judgment of the pregnant woman's attending physician." 410 U.S. at 164.

THE SECOND TRIMESTER

In *Roe v. Wade*, 410 U.S. 113, 164 (1973), the Supreme Court stated, "For the stage subsequent to approximately the end of the first trimester, the State, in promoting its interest in the health of the mother, may, if it chooses, regulate the abortion procedure in ways that are reasonably related to maternal health.''

Thus, during approximately the fourth to sixth months of pregnancy the state may regulate the medical conditions under which the procedure is performed. The constitutional test of any legislation concerning abortion during this period would be its relevance to the objective of protecting maternal health.

The Supreme Court of Virginia held in *Simopoulos v. Commonwealth*, 277 S.E.2d 194 (Va. 1981), that the indictment—which expressly charged that the defendant used procedures intended to initiate abortion during the second trimester of pregnancy and did so outside of a hospital licensed by the state—was valid. The court also held that a requirement that abortion during the second trimester take place in a licensed hospital is reasonably related to the commonwealth's compelling interest in preserving and protecting maternal health.

THE THIRD TRIMESTER

The Supreme Court reasoned that by the time the final stage of pregnancy has been reached, the state has acquired a compelling interest in the product of conception, which would override the woman's right to privacy and justify stringent regulation even to the extent of prohibiting abortions. In the *Roe* case the Court formulated its ruling as to the last trimester in the following words: ''For the stage subsequent to viability, the State in promoting its interest in the potentiality of human life, may, if it chooses, regulate, and even proscribe, abortion except where it is necessary, in appropriate medical judgment for the preservation of the life or health of the mother.'' 410 U.S. at 164.

Thus, during the final stage of pregnancy a state may prohibit all abortions except those deemed necessary to protect maternal life or health. The state's legislative powers over the performance of abortions increase as the pregnancy progresses toward term.

STATE REGULATION

The effect of the Supreme Court's 1973 decisions in *Roe* and *Doe* was to invalidate all or part of almost every state abortion statute then in force. The responses of state legislatures to these decisions were varied, but it is clear that a number of state laws have been enacted to restrict the performance of abortions as much as possible. Some of these laws may, in fact, restrict abortions to a greater extent than is permitted by Supreme Court decisions, and several aspects of these statutory restrictions have been challenged.

CONSENT

Spouse

A Florida statute had required written consent of the husband before a wife could be permitted to obtain an abortion. The husband's interest in the baby was held to be insufficient to force his wife to face the mental and physical risks of pregnancy and childbirth. *Poe v. Gerstein*, 517 F.2d 787 (5th Cir. 1975).

In *Doe v. Zimmerman*, 405 F. Supp. 534 (M.D. Pa. 1975), the court declared unconstitutional the provisions of the Pennsylvania Abortion Control Act, which required that the written consent of the husband of a married woman or of the parents of an unmarried minor be secured before the performance of an abortion. The court found that these provisions impermissibly permitted the husband to withhold his consent either because of his interest in the potential life of the fetus or for capricious reasons.

The natural father of an unborn fetus in *Doe v. Smith*, 486 U.S. 1308 (1988), was found not to be entitled to an injunction to prevent the mother from submitting to an abortion. Although the father's interest in the fetus was legitimate, it did not outweigh the mother's constitutionally protected right to an abortion, particularly in light of the evidence that the mother and father had never married. The father had demonstrated substantial instability in his marital and romantic life. The father was able to beget other children and, in fact, did produce other children.

Parental

The U.S. Supreme Court ruled in *Danforth v. Planned Parenthood of Central Missouri*, 428 U.S. 52 (1976), that it is unconstitutional to require all women under the age of 18 to obtain parental consent in writing prior to obtaining an abortion; however, the Court failed to provide any definitive guidelines as to when and how parental consent may be required if the minor is too immature to fully comprehend the nature of the procedure.

A Massachusetts statute that required parental consent before an abortion could be performed on an unmarried woman under the age of 18 was held to be unconstitutional in *Bellotti v. Baird*, 443 U.S. 622 (1979). Justice Stevens, joined by Justices Brennan, Marshall, and Blackmun, concluded that the Massachusetts statute was unconstitutional because under that statute as written and construed by the Massachusetts Supreme Judicial Court, no minor, no matter how mature and capable of informed decision making, could receive an abortion without the consent of either both parents or a superior court judge, thus making the minor's abortion subject in every instance to an absolute third-party veto.

However, in *H.L. v. Matheson*, 49 U.S. L.W. 4255 (U.S. Mar. 1981), the U.S. Supreme Court upheld a Utah statute that required a physician to "notify, if possible" the parents or guardian of a minor on whom an abortion is to be performed. In this case the physician advised the patient that an abortion would be in her best medical interest, but, because of the statute, refused to perform the abortion without notifying her parents. The Supreme Court ruled that although a state may not constitutionally legislate a blanket, unreviewable power of parents to veto their daughter's abortion, a statute setting out a mere requirement of parental notice where possible does not violate the constitutional rights of an immature, dependent minor.

The trial court in the *Matter of Anonymous*, 515 So. 2d 1254 (Ala. Civ. App. 1987), was found to have abused its discretion when it refused a minor's request for waiver of parental consent to obtain an abortion. The record indicated that the minor lived alone, was within one month of her 18th birthday, lived by herself the majority of the time, and held down a full time job.

Incompetent Patient

An abortion was found to have been properly authorized by a family court in *In re Doe*, 533 A.2d 523 (R.I. 1987), for a profoundly retarded woman. She had become pregnant during her residence in a group home as a result of a sexual attack by an unknown person. The record had supported a finding that if the woman had been able to do so, she would have requested the abortion. The court properly chose welfare agencies and the woman's guardian *ad litem* (a guardian appointed to prosecute or defend a suit on behalf of a party incapacitated by infancy, mental incompetence, etc.) as the surrogate decision makers, rather than the woman's mother. The mother apparently had had little contact with her daughter over the years.

HOSPITAL EMPLOYEES' REFUSAL TO PARTICIPATE

Hospital personnel have a right to refuse to participate in abortions and can abstain from involvement in abortions as a matter of conscience or religious or moral conviction. In a Missouri case, *Doe v. Poelker*, 515 F.2d 541 (8th Cir. 1975), the city was ordered to obtain the services of physicians and personnel who had no moral objections to participating in abortions. The city was also required to pay the plaintiff's attorney's fees because of the wanton disregard of the indigent woman's rights and the continuation of a policy to disregard and/or circumvent the U.S. Supreme Court's rulings on abortion.

AVAILABILITY OF SERVICES

In Nebraska a teaching hospital was permitted to limit the number of abortions to be performed at the hospital so long as the limitation was in the interest of education. *Orr v. Koefoot*, 377 F. Supp. 673 (M.D.Pa. 1974).

FUNDING

Several states have placed an indirect restriction on abortion through the elimination of funding. Under the Hyde Amendment, the U.S. Congress, through appropriations legislation, has limited the types of medically necessary abortions for which federal funds may be spent under the Medicaid program. While the Hyde Amendment does not prohibit states from funding nontherapeutic abortions, this action by the federal government opened the door to state statutory provisions limiting the funding of abortions.

In *Beal v. Doe*, 432 U.S. 438 (1977), the Pennsylvania Medicaid plan was challenged on the basis of denial of financial assistance for nontherapeutic abortions. The Supreme Court held that Title XIX of the Social Security Act (the Medicaid program) does not require the funding of nontherapeutic abortions as a condition of state participation in the program. The state has a strong interest in encouraging normal childbirth, and nothing in Title XIX suggests that it is unreasonable for the state to further that interest. The Court ruled that it is not inconsistent with the Medicaid portion of the Social Security Act to refuse to fund unnecessary (though perhaps desirable) medical services.

In *Maher v. Roe*, 432 U.S. 464 (1977), the Supreme Court considered the Connecticut statute that denied Medicaid benefits for first trimester abortions that were not medically necessary. The Court rejected the argument that the state's subsidy of medical expenses incident to pregnancy and childbirth created an obligation on the part of the state to subsidize the expenses incident to nontherapeutic abortions. In *Webster v. Reproductive Health Services*, 57 U.S.L.W. 5023 (U.S. 1989), the Court upheld against constitutional challenges a Missouri statute providing that no public facilities or employees should be used to perform abortions and that physicians should conduct viability tests prior to performing abortions.

Federal regulations that prohibit abortion counseling and referral by family planning clinics that receive funds under Title X of the Public Health Service Act were found not to violate the constitutional rights of pregnant women or Title X grantees in *New York v. Sullivan*, No. 88-6204 (2d Cir. Nov. 1, 1989). The plaintiffs argued that the regulations impermissibly burden a woman's privacy right to abortion and violate the First Amendment. *Webster* emphasized that so long as no affirmative legal obstacle to abortion services is created by a denial of the use of governmental money, facilities, or personnel, the practical effect of such a denial on the availability of such services is constitutionally irrelevant. In *Sullivan*, there was no violation of a woman's or provider's First Amendment rights. The court has extended the doctrine that government need not subsidize the exercise of the fundamental rights to free speech. The plaintiff argued that the government may not condition receipt of a benefit on the relinquishment of constitutional rights. The *Sullivan* court said that an individual employed by Title X projects remains free to say whatever he or she wishes about abortion outside the scope of his or her employment. A dissenting opinion in this case argued that by prohibiting the delivery of abortion information, even as to where such information could be obtained, the regulations deny a woman her constitutionally protected right to choose. She cannot make an informed choice between the two options when she cannot obtain information as to one of them.

It is interesting that the First U.S. Circuit Court of Appeals agreed with the dissenting opinion of the Second Circuit, "Boston—The 1st U.S. Circuit Court of Appeals here struck another blow to anti-abortion efforts with a 4-1, March 19 decision declaring unconstitutional federal regulations that block family planning clinics receiving federal funds from offering certain services such as abortion counseling and contraceptive prescriptions."[3]

There will most likely be a continuing stream of court decisions, as well as political and legislative battles in the decade of the 1990s. Given the emotional, religious, and ethical concerns, as well as those of women's rights groups, it is unlikely that this matter will be resolved any time soon.

NOTES

1. *Statistical Abstract of the United States, 1989*, 109th ed., U.S. Department of Commerce, Bureau of the Census, Washington, D.C.: U.S. Government Printing Office, 1989, p. 70.

2. *The 80's: the Year in Review*, NAT'L L.J., Dec. 25, 1989; Jan. 1, 1990, at S15.

3. Legal News Briefs, NAT'L L.J., April 2, 1990, at 6.

Chapter 10

Sterilization and Artificial Insemination

Sterilization is the termination of the ability to produce offspring. Sometimes sterilization is the primary and desired result of a surgical operation; sometimes it is a secondary consequence of an operation to remove a diseased reproductive organ or to cure a particular malfunction of such an organ. Most sterilizations are effected by the performance of a procedure known as a vasectomy for men or salpingectomy for women. A vasectomy merely shuts off the flow of a portion of the seminal fluid. A salpingectomy blocks the passage between the ovary and the uterus, reducing the likelihood that pregnancy will occur through a natural reopening of the passage.

EUGENIC STERILIZATION

The term *eugenic sterilization* refers to the sterilization of persons within certain classes or categories described in statutes, without the need for consent by, or on behalf of, those subjected to the procedures. Persons classified as insane, mentally deficient, feeble minded, and, in some instances, epileptic are included within the scope of the statutes. Several states have also included certain sexual deviates and persons classified as habitual criminals. Such statutes are ordinarily said to be designed to prevent the transmission of hereditary defects to succeeding generations, but several recent statutes have also recognized the purpose of preventing procreation by individuals who would not be able to care for their offspring.

Although there have been numerous judicial decisions to the contrary, the U.S. Supreme Court in *Buck v. Bell*, 224 U.S. 200 (1927), specifically upheld the validity of such eugenic sterilization statutes, provided that certain procedural safeguards are observed.

A number of states have laws authorizing eugenic sterilization. The decision in *Wade v. Bethesda Hospital*, 337 F. Supp. 671 (E.D. Ohio 1971), strongly suggests that in the absence of statutory authority, the state cannot order sterilization for eugenic purposes.

At the minimum, eugenic sterilization statutes provide the following:

- a grant of authority to public officials supervising state institutions for the mentally ill or prisons and to certain public health officials to conduct sterilizations
- a requirement of personal notice to the person subject to sterilization and, if that person is unable to comprehend what is involved, notice to the person's legal representative, guardian, or nearest relative
- a hearing by the board designated in the particular statute to determine the propriety of the prospective sterilization; at the hearing, evidence may be presented, and the patient must be present or represented by counsel or the nearest relative or guardian
- an opportunity to appeal the board's ruling to a court

The procedural safeguards of notice, hearing, and the right to appeal must be present in sterilization statutes in order to fulfill the minimum constitutional requirements of due process.

The image of castration is commonly evoked by the term *sexual sterilization*. However, current statutes generally do not authorize castration—in fact, many laws specifically prohibit it—and most eugenic sterilization statutes provide for vasectomy or salpingectomy. This prohibition against castration, along with provisions granting immunity only to persons performing or assisting in a sterilization that conforms to the law, is an added safeguard for persons subject to sterilization.

Civil or criminal liability for assault and battery may be imposed on one who castrates or sterilizes another without following the procedure required by law.

THERAPEUTIC STERILIZATION

If the life or health of a woman may be jeopardized by pregnancy, the danger may be avoided by terminating her ability to conceive or her husband's ability to impregnate. Such an operation is a therapeutic sterilization—one performed to preserve life or health. The medical necessity for sterilization renders the procedure therapeutic. Sometimes a diseased reproductive organ has to be removed to preserve the life or health of the individual. The operation results in sterility, although this was not the primary reason for the procedure. Such an operation technically should not be classified as a sterilization since the sterilization is incidental to the medical purpose.

STERILIZATION OF CONVENIENCE

An operation resulting in sterilization of the patient is termed a *sterilization of convenience* or *contraceptive sterilization* if no therapeutic reason for such an operation exists. Such operations raise a host of legal problems.

Civil Liability

Civil liability for performing a sterilization of convenience may be imposed if the procedure is performed in a negligent manner. The physician in *McLaughlin v. Cooke*, 774 P.2d 1171 (Wash. 1989), was found negligent for mistakenly cutting a blood vessel in the patient's scrotum while he was performing a vasectomy. Excessive bleeding at the site of the incision was found to have occurred because of the physician's negligent postsurgical care. On appeal, the jury's finding of negligence was held to have been properly supported by testimony that the physician's failure to intervene sooner and to remove a hematoma had been the proximate cause of tissue necrosis, which later required the removal of the patient's testicle.

The parents in *Goforth v. Porter Medical Associates, Inc.*, 755 P.2d 678 (Okla. 1988), brought a medical malpractice action for expenses resulting from the negligence of the physician in performing a sterilization on August 2, 1980. The physician assured the plaintiff that she was sterile. The patient subsequently became pregnant and delivered a child on October 9, 1981. The plaintiff argued that as a result of the physician's negligence, she incurred $2,000 in medical bills and will incur $200,000 for the future care of the child. The district court dismissed the case. On appeal, the Supreme Court of Oklahoma held that the parents could not recover the expenses of raising a healthy child; however, they could maintain an action for expenses resulting from the negligent performance of a sterilization and the unplanned pregnancy.

Several states have enacted specific legislation with respect to sterilizations of convenience. For example, the Virginia statute provides that upon receiving a written request from an adult and his or her spouse, and after giving a full explanation of the consequences of such an operation, a licensed physician may perform the sterilization only after waiting 30 days after the request. This requirement for the consent of the spouse is inapplicable in particular circumstances specified in the statute.

The consent of the person who is to be sterilized or subjected to an operation that may incidentally destroy the reproductive function should be obtained before the operation is performed. Even if an operation is medically necessary, in the absence of consent the performance of a sterilization constitutes a battery, as does any surgical or medical procedure for which consent has not been obtained.

In addition to the issue of whether a sterilization procedure is supported by adequate informed consent, there is substantial legal debate regarding the impact of an improperly performed sterilization. Several suits have been brought on a theory of wrongful life whereby the child born after the ineffective sterilization sues the physician who performed the operation (and sometimes the hospital). Such suits have been unsuccessful so far, primarily due to the court's unwillingness, for public policy reasons, to permit financial recovery for the "injury" of being born into the world.

However, some success has been achieved in litigation by the patient (and his or her spouse) who was allegedly sterilized and subsequently proved fertile. Although recovery has not yet been granted for the full cost of raising the child—such cost to include college education—damages have been awarded for the cost of the unsuccessful procedure, pain and suffering as a result of the pregnancy, the medical expense of the pregnancy, and the loss of comfort, companionship services, and consortium of the spouse. Again, as a matter of public policy, the courts have indicated that the joys and benefits of having the child outweigh the cost incurred in the rearing process.

Regulation of Sterilization of Convenience

Like abortion, voluntary sterilization is the subject of much debate over its moral and ethical propriety. Some health care institutions have adopted policies restricting the performance of such operations at their facilities. The U.S. Court of Appeals for the First Circuit has ruled in *Hathaway v. Worcester City Hospital*, 475 F.2d 701 (1st Cir. 1973), that a governmental hospital may not impose greater restrictions on sterilization procedures than on other procedures that are medically indistinguishable from sterilization with regard to the risk to the patient or the demand on staff or facilities. The court relied on the Supreme Court decisions in *Roe v. Wade*, 410 U.S. 113 (1973), and *Doe v. Bolton*, 410 U.S. 179 (1973), which accorded considerable recognition to the patient's right to privacy in the context of obtaining medical services. The extent to which hospitals may prohibit or substantially limit sterilization procedures is not clear, but it appears likely that such hospitals will be allowed considerable discretion in this matter.

At least one state, Kansas, has enacted legislation declaring that hospitals are not required to permit the performance of sterilization procedures and that physicians and hospital personnel may not be required to participate in such procedures or be discriminated against for refusal to participate. Such legislation, which is more frequently enacted in relation to abortion procedures, is often referred to by the term *conscience clause* and was not found objectionable in Supreme Court decisions striking down most state abortion laws.

LEGAL STATUS OF ARTIFICIAL INSEMINATION

Generally, artificial insemination is the injection of seminal fluid into a woman to induce pregnancy. The term may also include insemination that takes place outside of the woman's body, as with so-called "test tube" babies. If the semen of the woman's husband is used to impregnate her, the technique is called homologous artificial insemination (AIH), but if the semen comes from a donor other than the husband, the procedure is called heterologous artificial insemination (AID).

AID raises several problems with which legislation has begun to deal. The first state to pass a comprehensive statute dealing with the problems attendant to AID was Oklahoma. This statute provides guidelines for the physician and the hospital and resolves some of the questions arising from AID that have been litigated. Subsequent to the Oklahoma legislation, a few other states have passed laws dealing generally with the same issues.

The absence of answers to a number of questions concerning AID may have discouraged couples from seeking to utilize the procedure and physicians from performing it. Some of the questions concern the procedure itself; others concern the status of the offspring and the effect of the procedure on the marital relationship.

Consent

The Oklahoma AID statute resolves the issue of whose consent should be obtained by specifying that husband and wife must consent to the procedure. It is obvious that the wife's consent must be obtained because, without it, the touching involved in the artificial insemination would constitute a battery. In addition to the wife's consent, it is important to obtain the husband's consent in order to ensure against liability accruing if a court adopted the view that without the consent of the husband, AID was a wrong to the husband's interest for which he could sustain a suit for damages. Because AID involves the impregnation of the woman with the semen of a person other than her husband, failure to obtain the husband's consent may raise the issue of whether the woman has committed adultery.

The Oklahoma statute also deals with establishing proof of consent; it requires the consent to be in writing and to be executed and acknowledged by the physician performing the procedure and by the local judge who has jurisdiction over the adoption of children, as well as by the husband and wife.

In states without specific statutory requirements, medical personnel should attempt to avoid such potential liability by establishing the practice of obtaining the written consent of the couple requesting the AID procedure.

Legal Status of Offspring

The Oklahoma AID statute resolves the questions that have arisen with respect to the legitimacy of a child conceived by means of AID, the duty of support owed an AID child by the nondonor husband, the effect of AID birth on the child's right of intestate succession, and the right to custody of such a child. The law declares that any child born as a result of AID performed in accordance with the statute's requirements is to be considered in all respects the same as a naturally conceived, legitimate child.

Several states have enacted legislation declaring that children conceived by artificial insemination with the consent of the parents are to be considered legitimate and natural children. California has declared by statute that the husband of a woman who bears a child as a result of artificial insemination shall be liable for support of the child as though he were the natural father if he consented in writing to the artificial insemination.

Confidentiality of the Procedure

Another problem that directly concerns medical personnel involved in AID birth is preserving confidentiality. This problem is met in the Oklahoma AID statute, which requires that the original copy of the consent be filed pursuant to the rules for the filing of adoption papers and is not to be made a matter of public record.

ETHICAL AND MORAL IMPLICATIONS OF ARTIFICIAL INSEMINATION

There are a variety of religious and ethical views as to the propriety of artificial insemination. However, the present state of the law does not appear to forbid AIH or AID, and a hospital would not be liable for permitting artificial insemination to take place on its premises, provided appropriate consents are obtained from both husband and wife and statutory requirements are complied with.

WRONGFUL LIFE AND WRONGFUL BIRTH

There have been numerous cases in recent years involving actions for wrongful life and wrongful birth. Such litigation originated with a California case, *Curlender v. Bio-Science Laboratories*, 106 Cal. App. 3d 811, 165 Cal. Rptr. 477 (1980), where a court found that a genetic testing laboratory can be held liable for damages from incorrectly reporting genetic tests, leading to the birth of a child with defects. Injury due to birth had not been previously actionable at law. The court of appeals held that medical laboratories engaged in genetic testing owe a duty to parents and their as yet unborn child to use ordinary care in administering available tests for the purpose of providing information concerning potential genetic defects in the unborn. Damages in this case were awarded on the basis of the child's shortened life span.

The following cases indicate the direction of the courts since the *Curlender* case. The parents of a handicapped child stated a cause of action for wrongful birth in *Proffitt v. Bartolo*, 412 N.W. 2d 232 (Mich. Ct. App. 1987), against a physician who allegedly failed to properly interpret a rubella test performed during the mother's first trimester of pregnancy, thereby precluding the option of abortion. The physician had a duty to advise the parents so that they would have an opportunity to exercise the option of an abortion. If it could be established that the physician breached such a duty and that the parents would have terminated the pregnancy, the necessary causal connection would be demonstrated, and the parents would be entitled to recover for their extraordinary costs of raising the handicapped child and for any emotional harm they might have suffered as a result of their child's handicap.

A cause of action for wrongful life was not cognizable under Kansas law in *Bruggeman v. Schimke*, 239 Kan. 245, 718 P.2d 635 (1986). A child who was born with congenital birth defects was not entitled to recover damages on the theory that physicians had been negligent when, after a prior sibling was born with congenital anomalies, they mistakenly advised the parents that the first child's condition was not due to a known chromosomal or measurable biochemical disorder. In view of the fundamental principle of law that human life is valuable, precious, and worthy of protection, a legal right not to be born—to be dead, rather than to be alive with deformities—could not be recognized. The Supreme Court of Kansas held that there was no recognized cause for wrongful life.

A wrongful life action was brought against the physicians in *Speck v. Finegold*, 408 A.2d 496 (Pa. Super. Ct. 1979), on behalf of an infant born with defects. The court held that regardless of whether the claim was based on wrongful life or otherwise, no legally cognizable cause of action was stated on behalf of the infant even though the defendants' actions of negligence were the proximate cause of her defective birth. The parents could recover pecuniary expenses that they had borne and would bear for care and treatment of their child and that resulted in the natural course of things from the commission of the tort. The tort in this case was the failure of the urologist to properly perform a vasectomy and the failure of the obstetrician/gynecologist to properly perform an abortion. Recovery for negligence was allowed because the plaintiff parents did set forth a duty owed to them by the physicians and breached by the physicians with resulting injuries to the plaintiffs. Claims for emotional disturbance and mental distress were denied.

The California Supreme Court in *Turpin v. Sortini*, 643 P.2d 954 (Cal. 1982), denied a child born with total deafness the right to seek damages from a physician and hospital for wrongful life. However, the court did hold that either the parents or the child could recover for the extraordinary medical and other expenses incurred because of the hearing impairment.

In *Pitre v. Opelousas General Hospital*, 530 So. 2d 1151 (La. 1988), the parents of a child born with a congenital defect filed a malpractice suit seeking damages for themselves and their child, alleging that the surgeon had been negligent in performing a tubal ligation. The suit also claimed that the hospital and the physician failed to inform Mrs. Pitre that the operation was unsuccessful. A pathology report had revealed that the physician had severed fibromuscular tissue, rather than fallopian tissue, during the surgical procedure. The parents were not informed of this finding. The mother became pregnant and gave birth to an albino child. The court of appeal dismissed the child's claim for wrongful life and struck all of the parents' individual claims with the exception of expenses associated with the pregnancy and the husband's loss of consortium. On a writ of certiorari to review the ruling, the Supreme Court of Louisiana held that the physician owed a duty to warn the parents regarding the failure of the tubal ligation, the physician did not have a duty to protect the child from the risk of albinism, and the parents were entitled to damages relating to the pregnancy and the husband's consortium. Special damages relating to the child's deformity were denied.

Recovery for damages was permitted for wrongful birth, but not wrongful life, in *Smith v. Cote*, 513 A.2d 341 (N.H. 1986). The physician in this case was negligent in that he failed to test in a timely fashion for the mother's exposure to rubella and to advise her of the potential for birth defects. She was therefore entitled to maintain a cause of action for wrongful birth. However, for compelling reasons of public policy, the mother would not be permitted to assert on the child's behalf a claim for damages on the basis of wrongful life.

Chapter 11

Autopsy, Donation, and Experimentation

Section 1138, Title XI, of the Omnibus Budget Reconciliation Act of 1986 requires hospitals to establish organ procurement protocols or face a loss of Medicare and Medicaid funding. The ever-increasing success of organ transplants and demand for organ tissue require the close scrutiny of each case, making sure that established procedures have been followed in the care and disposal of all body parts. Physicians, nurses, and other paramedical personnel assigned with this responsibility are often confronted with a variety of legal issues. Liability can be limited by complying with applicable regulations and adhering to hospital procedures implementing these regulations.

LEGAL PRINCIPLES REGARDING DEAD BODIES

Consideration of legal duties regarding the utilization, handling, and disposition of dead bodies cannot be divorced from the legal questions involved in determining when death occurs. In many contexts, such as deciding rights to the property of the deceased person, the determination of death does not involve the hospital or its personnel. However, where permission has been granted for use of a patient's body or organs for the benefit of another patient or science in general, determination of the point of death becomes critical. New technology, specifically medical advancement in artificially sustaining life and transplanting vital organs, has placed in question the viability of the traditional methods of determining death. See Chapter 14 on Euthanasia, Death, and Dying.

INTERESTS IN DEAD BODIES

The rule now uniformly recognized in the United States is that the person entitled to possession of a body for burial has certain legally protected interests.

159

Interference with these rights can result in liability. Damages awarded in cases of liability through interference with the rights of a surviving spouse, or near relative, in the body of a decedent are based on the emotional and mental suffering that results from such interference. For damages to be awarded, the conduct of the alleged wrongdoer must be sufficiently disturbing to a person of ordinary sensibilities as to cause emotional harm. Cases involving the wrongful handling of dead bodies may be classified into four groups: mutilation of a body; unauthorized autopsy; wrongful detention; and miscellaneous wrongs such as unauthorized sale, refusal or neglect to bury, and unauthorized use or publication of photographs taken after death.

In many states, intentionally mutilating a dead body is a punishable crime as well as a basis for civil liability. Obviously, such acts could be said to cause substantial emotional suffering for those who loved and respected the decedent. Similarly, an unauthorized autopsy may disturb persons whose religious beliefs prohibit such a procedure as well as those persons who have a general aversion to the procedure, although autopsies have become an accepted and necessary aspect of hospital practice. Where autopsies have been performed without statutory authorization and without the consent of the decedent, the surviving spouse, or an appropriate relative, liability may be imposed.

Refusal to deliver a dead body to a person who demands custody, and is entitled to receive it, may also result in liability. There do not appear to be any such cases directly involving hospitals, but if a hospital refused to deliver a body until the decedent's bill was paid or if it retained possession of a body after receiving a proper request for delivery, such refusal could provide sufficient grounds for an action based on interference with rights to a dead body.

Unintentional as well as intentional conduct interfering with rights to a body has resulted in hospital liability. For example, in the case of *Lott v. State*, 32 Misc. 2d 296, 225 N.Y.S.2d 434 (Ct. Cl. 1962), two bodies in a hospital were mistagged. The body of a person of the Roman Catholic faith was prepared for Orthodox Jewish burial, and the person of the Orthodox Jewish faith was prepared for Roman Catholic burial. This negligent conduct interfered with burial plans and caused mental anguish, for which liability was imposed.

RIGHT OF SUIT FOR IMPROPER ACTION

Although several persons may suffer emotional stress and mental suffering because of indignities in the treatment of the body of the decedent, recovery for wrongful interference with the body and its proper burial has generally been limited to the person who has the right of possession of the body for burial. Some state statutes delineate an order of the duty to bury the decedent. Others set forth an order of persons authorized to give consent to autopsy, from which the order of devolution may be established. In states without either provision, case law must provide the guidelines. Generally, the primary right to custody of a dead body belongs to the surviving spouse. Where there is no spouse, the right passes to the adult children of the decedent, if any, and then to the decedent's parents.

AUTOPSY

Autopsies, or postmortem examinations, are conducted to ascertain the cause of a person's death, which in turn may resolve a number of legal issues. An autopsy may reveal whether death was the result of criminal activity, whether the cause of death was one for which payment must be made in accordance with an insurance contract, whether the death is compensable under worker's compensation and occupational disease acts, or whether death was the result of a specific act or a culmination of several acts. Aside from providing answers to these specific questions, the information gained from autopsies adds to medical knowledge. Autopsies may also provide a valuable source of information about the medical practice in the hospital.

Autopsy Consent Statutes

Recognizing both the need for information that can be secured only through the performance of a substantial volume of autopsies and the valid interests of relatives and friends of the decedent, most states have enacted statutes dealing with autopsy consent. Such legislation seems intended to have a twofold effect: first, to protect the rights of the decedent's relatives, and, second, to guide hospitals and physicians in establishing procedures for consent to autopsy.

Most autopsy consent statutes can be classified in two groups. One group consists of the statutes that establish an order for obtaining consent to autopsy based on the degree of family relationship. Provisions of this type furnish the most precise guidelines to the physician and the hospital, enabling them to determine, without resort to other statutes or decisions, who the proper person is to contact for autopsy authorization.

The statutes of the second group contain provisions enumerating those persons from whom consent may be obtained, but they do not provide an order of priority among them. These laws say the consent is to be obtained from any one of the enumerated persons who has assumed custody of the body for burial. In some states with such statutes there are no additional statutes concerning the devolution of the duty to bury and the right to custody. In these states a hospital must rely on case law to determine whether a person who requests custody of a body for burial is entitled to such custody and is therefore the proper person from whom consent to autopsy should be obtained. Furthermore, the assumption of custody of the body by a person enumerated in the statutes must be clear before consent to an autopsy can be relied on.

In states that have autopsy consent statutes, as well as statutes specifying the order in which duty of burial and right to custody of the body devolve on the relatives of the decedent, the two statutes taken together indicate the proper person from whom consent is to be obtained. In states without autopsy consent statutes, other statutes regarding the duty to bury and the right to custody of a body for burial (or donation of the body or body parts) may prove helpful in determining which of the decedent's relatives may give effective authorization for autopsy.

Authorization by the Decedent

Most autopsy consent statutes provide that deceased persons may authorize an autopsy on their remains. Ordinarily such consent must be in writing. While there should be no problem regarding the validity of the decedent's authorization in such states, as a practical matter it may be difficult to obtain consent because it is undesirable to bring the subject to the attention of most hospital patients. There may be legal as well as practical problems in obtaining authorization for an autopsy from a patient before death if the state does not provide by statute for such authorization. If an autopsy is desired, it would probably be simpler and more effective to obtain authorization from the relative or some other person who assumes the legal responsibility for burial, rather than from the patient before death.

Some states have no specific provision for authorization of autopsy by the deceased, but do permit donation of a person's body or parts to hospitals, universities, or other institutions that operate eye and tissue banks; such donation is usually intended for the advancement of medical science or for transplantation procedures. A court might construe the donation statute as authorizing the decedent to consent to an autopsy because one purpose for the performance of autopsies is to advance medical science.

In states where there is neither an autopsy consent statute nor a statute permitting donation that may be construed to include autopsy, it is unwise to rely exclusively on the authorization of a decedent to perform an autopsy. This is especially true where relatives of the deceased who assume custody of the body for burial object to an autopsy. Although many cases have upheld the wishes of the deceased with respect to the place of interment or the manner of disposition of the remains (by burial or cremation), it is possible that the courts will not afford the same weight to the decedent's wishes concerning autopsies. In such instances, compelling reasons presented by certain next of kin of the decedent, especially the surviving spouse, may prevail over the wishes of the decedent.

It is also possible that a patient would specifically request that no autopsy be performed on his or her body upon death. This request may stem from religious convictions or personal preference. Some state legislatures have specifically recognized this right to refuse an autopsy. For example, in New York, it is provided:

Except as required by law, no dissection or autopsy shall be performed on the body of any person who is carrying an identification card upon his person indicating his opposition to such dissection or autopsy. To be valid, this card must be signed and dated by the person opposed to the dissection or autopsy and must be notarized.

New York Public Health Law Section 4209-a; L. 1981 Chapter 982, Section 1.

Authorization by Person Other Than the Decedent

Two closely related concepts concern the determination of who may authorize the performance of an autopsy. One of these has developed in litigation when a corpse has been mutilated and a person has been permitted to bring an action to recover damages. Such cases ordinarily determine an order of priority with respect to the person who may bring an action. The second concept—responsibility for burial of the deceased body—is the basis for the right of an individual to bring an action for mutilation of a dead body.

The order of responsibility for burial is ordinarily the same as the order of preference for bringing an action for mutilation since the latter arises from the former. The person on whom the duty to bury the deceased is imposed has the right to custody of the body and the right to recover for mutilation of the corpse; authority to perform an autopsy should be obtained from this person.

Where custody of the body has been assumed by the first person in the preference order, that person's consent is sufficient to authorize the autopsy and prevent liability for mutilation of the corpse. If consent to the autopsy is refused, performance of the autopsy could lead to liability even if some other relative of the deceased sought to authorize it. What if the first person in the order of preference is deceased or mentally incompetent, or is unwilling or unable to assume the responsibility for burial of the body, or fails to do so? It is then necessary to determine who has such responsibility and the concomitant right to authorize an autopsy. Fortunately, in many states the order of responsibility for burial is set forth in statutes, and the right to authorize an autopsy is given to the person who has assumed custody of the body for burial.

Several statutes that specifically deal with authority for autopsies indicate who can give authorization when the first person in order of priority is unavailable. Such statutes enable the hospital to determine whose consent is sufficient; the chance of a successful suit by anyone claiming superior rights in the body is practically nonexistent if the statutory provisions are followed.

In the absence of statutes furnishing a preference order of responsibility for burial or for consent, the order usually followed is surviving spouse, adult children of the deceased, parents, adult brothers and sisters, grandparents, uncles and aunts, and finally cousins.

When consent for an autopsy has been obtained from a relative who assumed custody of the decedent's body, a court would be likely to consider such consent sufficient. So long as the hospital made a good faith, albeit unsuccessful, attempt to locate the closer relative and had no knowledge of an objection to the autopsy by that relative, it is unlikely that a court would hold a hospital or physician liable for mutilation of the body in the event that the closer relative, who had been unavailable or who would not assume custody for the burial, brought an action against the hospital after an autopsy was completed. A court may find that a surviving spouse's unwillingness to assume responsibility for burial is sufficient to permit the right to custody of the body to devolve on a relative who is willing to assume such responsibility.

Scope and Extent of Consent

Legal issues may arise as a result of an autopsy even if consent has been obtained from the person authorized by law to grant such consent. If autopsy procedures go beyond the limits imposed by the consent, or if the consent to an autopsy is obtained by fraud or without the formal requisites, liability may be incurred. It is a fundamental principle that a person who has the right to refuse permission for the performance of an act also has the right to place limitations or conditions on consent.

It is especially important that the hospital and its personnel adhere to any limitations or conditions placed on the permission to autopsy; if such limitations are exceeded, the physician or the hospital has no defense on the ground of emergency or medical necessity. The principle involved in limiting the scope of an autopsy has been expressed as follows:

> One having the right to refuse to allow an autopsy has the right to place any limitations or restrictions on giving consent to such procedure, and one who violates such stipulations renders himself liable.

22A Am. Jur. 2d *Dead Bodies* § 64 at 43 (1988).

While consent to autopsy may also encompass authorization for removal of body parts for examination, a separate question may arise concerning disposal of tissues and organs on completion of the examination: May the hospital and its personnel dispose of such material in a routine manner or use it for the hospital's own purposes, or must the hospital return the tissue and organs to the body before burial? In *Hendriksen v. Roosevelt Hospital*, 297 F. Supp. 1142 (1969), permission had been granted for a complete autopsy including an examination of the central nervous system by a scalp incision. Yet the court held that liability might be imposed on the hospital if the jury found that the hospital in fact retained parts of the body. Pursuant to a New York statute requiring the authorization of the next of kin, consent was given for dissection; however, the court held that this statute should be narrowly construed and that separate consent would have to be obtained to retain the internal organs of the decedent.

Consent given with the understanding that organs and tissue could be removed and retained for examination would seem to authorize the hospital to dispose of such materials in a suitable manner or to utilize them after the autopsy. However, the *Hendriksen* decision raises doubts on this matter. Where the party giving consent expressly stipulates that parts severed from the body are to be returned to the body for burial, conduct deviating from this provision may result in liability. Also, it would appear that consent to autopsy does not include authorization to mutilate or disfigure the body. Therefore, when autopsy involves the removal of exterior body parts and the physical appearance of the body cannot be restored without return of such parts, the hospital may be subject to liability for exceeding the scope of the authorization if the removed parts are not returned.

Fraudulently Obtained Consent

It is a long-accepted principle that consent obtained through fraud or material misrepresentation is not binding and that the person whose consent is so obtained stands in the same position as if no consent had been given.

This principle can apply to autopsies when facts are misrepresented to the person who has the right to consent in order to induce his or her consent. If a physician or a hospital employee states, as fact, something known to be untrue in order to gain consent, the autopsy would be unauthorized, and liability might follow.

ORGAN DONATIONS

Recent developments in medical science have enabled physicians to take tissue from persons immediately after death and use it for transplantation in order to replace or rehabilitate diseased or damaged organs or other parts of living persons. Progress in this field of medicine has created the problem of obtaining a sufficient supply of replacement body parts. Throughout the country there are eye banks, artery banks, and other facilities for the storage and preservation of organs and tissue that can be used for transplantation and for other therapeutic services.

Organs and tissues to be stored and preserved for future use must be removed almost immediately after death. Therefore, it is imperative that an agreement or arrangement for obtaining organs and tissue from a body be completed before death, or very soon after death, to enable physicians to remove and store the tissue promptly.

States have enacted legislation to facilitate donation of bodies and body parts for medical uses. Virtually all the states have based their enactments on the Uniform

Anatomical Gift Act, drafted by the Commission on Uniform State Laws, but it should be recognized that in some states there are deviations from this act or additional laws dealing with donation.

Summary of the Uniform Anatomical Gift Act

Individuals who are of sound mind and 18 years of age or older are permitted to dispose of their own bodies or body parts by will or other written instrument for medical or dental education, research, advancement of medical or dental science, therapy, or transplantation. Among those eligible to receive such donations are any licensed, accredited, or approved hospitals; accredited medical or dental schools; surgeons or physicians; tissue banks; or specified individuals who need the donation for therapy or transplantation. The statute provides that when only a part of the body is donated, custody of the remaining parts of the body shall be transferred to the next of kin promptly following removal of the donated part.

In cases of donation made by a written instrument other than a will, the instrument must be signed by the donor in the presence of two witnesses who, in turn, must sign the instrument in the donor's presence. If the donor cannot sign the instrument, the document may be signed by a person authorized by the donor at the donor's direction and in the presence of the donor and the two signing witnesses. Delivery of the document during the donor's lifetime is not necessary to make the donation valid. A donation by will becomes effective immediately upon the death of the testator, without probate, and the gift is valid and effective to the extent that it has been acted on in good faith. This is true even if the will is not probated or is declared invalid for testimonial purposes.

A donation by a person other than the decedent may be made by written, telegraphic, recorded telephonic, or other recorded consent. In the absence of a contrary intent evidenced by the decedent or of actual notice of opposition by a member of the same class or a prior class in the preference order, the decedent's body or body parts may be donated by the following persons in the order specified: (1) surviving spouse, (2) adult child, (3) parent, (4) adult brother or sister, (5) decedent's guardian, or (6) any other person or agency authorized to dispose of the body. In *Nicoletta v. Rochester Eye & Human Parts Bank*, 519 N.Y.S.2d 928 (Sup. Ct. 1987), the father of a deceased patient brought an action against a hospital for alleged emotional injuries resulting from the removal of his son's eyes for donation following a fatal motorcycle accident. The hospital was immune from liability under the provisions of the Uniform Anatomical Gift Act where the hospital had neither actual nor constructive knowledge that the woman who had authorized the donation was not the decedent's wife. The hospital was entitled to the immunity afforded by the "good faith" provisions of Section 4306(3) of the act where its agents had made reasonable inquiry as to the status of the purported wife, who had resided with the decedent for ten years and was the mother of their two children. The hospital had no reason to believe that any irregularity existed.

The father, who was present at the time his son was brought to the emergency room, failed to object to any organ donation and failed to challenge the authority of the purported wife to sign the emergency room authorization.

The statute provides several methods by which a donation may be revoked. If the document has been delivered to a named donee, it may be revoked by a written revocation signed by the donor and delivered to the donee, an oral revocation witnessed by two persons and communicated to the donee, a statement to the physician attending during a terminal illness that has been communicated to the donee, or a card or piece of writing that has been signed and is on the donor's person or in the donor's immediate effects. If the written instrument of donation has not been delivered to the donee, it may be revoked by destruction, cancellation, or mutilation of the instrument. If the donation is made by a will, it may be revoked in the manner provided for revocation or amendment of wills. Any person acting in good faith reliance on the terms of an instrument of donation will not be subject to civil or criminal liability unless there is actual notice of the revocation of the donation.

The time of death shall be determined by a physician in attendance at the donor's death, or a physician certifying death, who shall not be a member of the team of physicians engaged in the transplantation procedure.

UNCLAIMED DEAD BODIES

Persons entitled to possession of a dead body must arrange for release of the body from the hospital, for transfer to an embalmer or undertaker, and for final disposal. The recognition by the courts of a quasi-property right in the body of a deceased person imposes a duty on the hospital to make reasonable efforts to give notice to persons entitled to claim the body. When there are no known relatives or friends of the family who can be contacted by the hospital to claim the body, the hospital has a responsibility to dispose of the body in accordance with law.

Unclaimed bodies are generally buried at public expense; a public official, usually a county official, has the duty to bury or otherwise dispose of such bodies. Most states have statutes providing for the disposal of unclaimed bodies by delivery to institutions for educational and scientific purposes. The public official in charge of the body has a duty to notify the government agency of the presence of the body. The agency then arranges for the transfer of the body in accordance with the statute. If no such agency exists under the statute, the hospital or the public official may be authorized to allow a medical school or other institution or person, designated by the statute as an eligible recipient of unclaimed dead bodies, to remove the body for scientific use.

When an unclaimed dead body is in the possession of a charitable or proprietary hospital, the hospital should notify the public official charged by law with disposing of such bodies. The public official then arranges for the ultimate disposition of the body, either by burial or transfer to an institution entitled to obtain it for educational and scientific use.

Certain categories of persons are usually excluded from these provisions permitting the distribution of bodies for educational and scientific use. For public health reasons the statutes do not usually permit distribution of the bodies of persons who have died from contagious diseases. Generally, the bodies of travelers and veterans are also not to be used for educational and scientific purposes.

While the majority of these statutes quite explicitly require notification of relatives and set time limits for holding the body to allow relatives an opportunity to claim the body, strict compliance with the statutory provisions is often impossible because of the very nature of the problems that arise in the handling of dead bodies and in the required procedures themselves. Noncompliance in such instances would not appear to cause liability. An example of such a provision is the requirement that relatives be notified immediately upon death and that the body be held for 24 hours subject to claim by a relative or friend. The procedure of locating and notifying relatives may consume the greater part of the 24-hour period following death; if relatives who are willing to claim the body are located, the body should be held for a reasonable time to allow them to arrange custody for burial. It should be recognized that literal compliance may prejudice the interests of relatives of the decedent.

Similarly, when a body remains unclaimed and the hospital has no way of ascertaining that the decedent was a veteran, delivering or disposing of the body for educational or scientific purposes pursuant to the statute would not appear to cause liability should it later be proved that the decedent was a veteran. Failure to adhere to the statute in such instances is not likely to result in liability.

In some instances, a hospital may be or may want to become a recipient of cadaver material to be used for science or education. This may be true in respect to bodies of persons held by public officials and other hospitals, as well as to the unclaimed bodies of persons dying within the recipient institution. In either case, if a hospital wants to receive such materials, it must comply with the statutory provisions relating to recipients. The hospital may have to register as an eligible recipient or request that unclaimed bodies be delivered to it; it may have to post a bond to ensure proper use and disposal of the bodies. In addition, the hospital may be required to maintain equipment and facilities for the preservation and storage of cadavers.

EXPERIMENTATION

The Nuremberg Code and the Declaration of Helsinki provided guidelines for the development of federal regulations for medical research and the protection of human subjects in the United States. The federal regulations are generally triggered by the experimenter's receipt of federal grants and may apply to experiments involving new drugs, new medical devices, or new medical procedures. Generally, a combination of federal and state guidelines and regulations ensures proper supervision and control over experimentation that involves human subjects. For example, federal regulations require hospital-based researchers to obtain the approval of an institutional review board. This board functions to review proposed research studies and conduct follow-up reviews on a regular basis.

Federal and state regulations impose several other requirements on experiments involving human subjects. Institutions conducting medical research on human subjects must do the following:

- fully disclose the inherent risks to the patient
- make a proper determination that the patient is competent to consent
- identify treatment alternatives
- obtain written consent from the patient

California has enacted legislation that protects the rights of research subjects and provides for fines and imprisonment if proper consent procedures are not followed. California Health & Safety Code, §§ 24170–24179.5, 26668.4.

The district court in *Blanton v. United States*, 428 F. Supp. 360 (D. D.C. 1977), held that where a ''new drug'' of unknown effectiveness was administered to a patient at a navy medical center, despite the availability of other drugs of known effectiveness, the hospital violated the accepted medical standards and its duty of due care, so that in the absence of the patient's consent to the experiment, the United States was liable for the resulting injury.

Chapter 12

Patient Rights and Responsibilities

ADMISSION

Hospitals must not discriminate by reason of race, creed, color, sex, religion, or national origin. Those that do discriminate violate constitutionally guaranteed rights. They may also be in violation of federal, state, and local laws. Discrimination in some states can be considered a misdemeanor and may also carry a civil penalty. Funds may be withheld from hospitals that practice discrimination. Most federal, state, and local programs specifically require, as a condition for receiving funds under such programs, an affirmative statement on the part of the hospital that it will not discriminate. For example, the Medicare program, and the Medicaid program specifically require affirmative assurances by the hospitals and other health care institutions that no discrimination will be practiced.

Whether a person is entitled to admission to a particular governmental hospital depends on the statute establishing that hospital. Governmental hospitals are, by definition, creatures of some unit of government; their primary concern is service to the population within the jurisdiction of that unit. In all cases, connection with the unit operating the hospital is necessary to entitle one to use the hospital facilities. Some of the statutes cover all inhabitants of the geographic area and, in addition, are broad enough to apply to any person within the area who falls ill or suffers traumatic injury and requires hospital care. However, many of the statutes limit use of the hospital facilities to residents of the governmental unit operating the hospital.

While persons who are not within the statutory classes have no right of admission, hospitals and their employees owe a duty to extend reasonable care to those who present themselves for assistance and are in need of immediate attention. With respect to such persons, governmental hospitals are subject to the same rules that apply to private hospitals. Patients presenting themselves to a hospital with acute medical or surgical problems should not be turned away. Priority of admissions should be emergency cases (acute appendicitis, massive burns, etc.) first, followed by urgent and then elective cases.

The patient in *Stoick v. Caro Community Hospital*, 421 N.W.2d 611 (Mich. Ct. App. 1988), brought a medical malpractice action against a government physician in which she alleged the following facts. The physician determined that she was having a stroke and required hospitalization, but refused to hospitalize her. The plaintiff's daughter-in-law called the defendant Caro Family Physicians, P.C., where the patient had a 1:30 appointment. She was told to take the patient to Caro Community Hospital. Upon arriving at the hospital, there was no physician available to see the patient, and she was directed by a nurse to Dr. Loo's clinic in the hospital. Upon examination, Dr. Loo found right-side facial paralysis, weakness, dizziness, and an inability to talk. He told the patient that she was having a stroke and that immediate hospitalization was necessary. Dr. Loo refused to admit her because of a hospital policy that only the patient's family physician or treating physician could admit a patient. The plaintiff went to her physician, Dr. Quines, who instructed her to go to the hospital immediately. He did not accompany her to the hospital. At the hospital she waited approximately one hour before another doctor from Caro Family Physicians arrived and admitted her. Dr. Loo claimed that he did not diagnose the patient as having a stroke and that there was no bad faith on his part. The circuit court granted the physician's motion for summary judgment on the grounds of governmental immunity. The court of appeals reversed, holding that the plaintiffs did plead sufficient facts constituting bad faith on the part of Dr. Loo. His failure to admit or otherwise treat the patient is a ministerial act for which governmental immunity does not apply and which may be found by a jury to be negligence.

Federal and State Regulations

Civil rights are rights assured by the U.S. Constitution and by the acts of Congress and the state legislatures. Generally, the term includes all the rights of each individual in a free society.

Discriminatory practices in hospitals and other health facilities have been dealt with by Congress and the federal courts. Discrimination in the admission of patients and segregation of patients on racial grounds are prohibited in any hospital receiving federal financial assistance. Pursuant to Title VI of the Civil Rights Act of 1964, the guidelines of the Department of Health and Human Services (HHS) prohibit the practice of racial discrimination by any hospital or agency receiving money under any program supported by HHS. This includes all hospitals that are "providers of service" receiving federal funds under Medicare legislation.

According to the Fourteenth Amendment to the Constitution, a state cannot act so as to deny any person equal protection of the laws. If a state or a political subdivision of a state, whether through its executive, judicial, or legislative branch, acts in such a way as to unfairly deny to any person the rights accorded to another, the amendment has been violated. If the state supports or authorizes an activity for the benefit of the public, it is possible that a private institution engaging in such activity will be considered to be engaged in state action and subject to the Fourteenth Amendment.

The acts of the executive, judicial, and legislative branches of government encompass the acts of government agencies as well, and state action has been extended to include activities of private entities under certain circumstances.

Considering the constitutional requirement with HHS guidelines and the requirements of Title II of the Civil Rights Act of 1964, which prohibits discrimination in restaurants and other places of public accommodation and thus may include restaurants in a hospital, it is apparent that racial discrimination is prohibited in hospitals.

The Civil Rights Act of 1964 specifies that the hospital must treat nurses, along with patients, physicians, and other employees, in a nondiscriminatory manner. Title VII makes it illegal to deny equal job opportunities on the basis of race, creed, color, religion, sex, or national origin; it also prohibits discrimination against patients, physicians, or employees.

Most states have enacted laws to protect the civil rights of their citizens. Some of these statutes declare that life, liberty, and the pursuit of happiness should not be denied; others adhere closely to the language of federal civil rights legislation.

Hill-Burton Act

The Hospital Survey and Construction Act, popularly known as the Hill-Burton Act, provides that any hospital receiving funds from this program must make available a reasonable number of free services to persons unable to pay. Regulations promulgated by the Department of Health and Human Services in July 1972 established numerical guidelines for what the Hill-Burton Act refers to as a "reasonable volume of services." While these guidelines do not require that any particular person who is unable to pay be admitted, they do require that at least some amount of service be provided to this group by every hospital that has received Hill-Burton funds.

In *Hospital Center at Orange v. Cook*, 426 A.2d 526 (N.J. Super. Ct. App. Div. 1981), the hospital sued a medically indigent patient to recover payment for an unpaid bill. The Essex County District Court entered summary judgment in favor of the hospital. The superior court, appellate division, held on appeal that the patient could plead as a defense to the action the hospital's noncompliance with its obligations under the Hill-Burton Act to provide a reasonable volume of free or reduced cost care for persons unable to pay for such services. The court also held that failure of the hospital to give the required notice to the patient constituted an absolute bar to the right of the hospital to sue for its bill.

The provisions of the act, and its corresponding regulations, have been interpreted by the courts to require a policy of nondiscrimination in the administration and use of facilities constructed, renovated, or maintained under authorized, state-approved construction programs.

The following cases illustrate court decisions in the discrimination area. In *Simkins v. Moses H. Cone Memorial Hospital*, 323 F.2d 959 (4th Cir. 1963), a federal court held that two hospitals were prohibited from denying appointments to physicians on the basis of race. The court also prohibited the hospitals from refusing to admit patients or segregating patients on the basis of race. In *Smith v. Hampton Training School for Nurses*, 360 F.2d 577 (4th Cir. 1966), a federal court reviewed a case involving the dismissal of black nurses for eating in the all-white cafeteria of a hospital receiving federal assistance under the Hill-Burton Act. The court relied heavily on the *Simkins* case in deciding that the dismissal constituted unlawful discrimination on the part of the hospital.

DISCHARGE

A patient may not be detained in the hospital for inability to pay. An unauthorized detention of this nature could subject a hospital to charges of false imprisonment.

The release of a minor should be made only to a parent or authorized guardian. An incompetent should be released in the care of an appropriate family member or guardian. At times patients will refuse discharge if they have no place to go. These cases should be handled on an individual basis and in consultation with hospital counsel if necessary.

When discharging a patient, a physician should issue and sign all discharge orders. Patients in critical condition should never be discharged. If there is no need for immediate attention, the patient should be advised to seek follow-up care. The plaintiff in *Palmer v. Forney*, 429 N.W.2d 712 (Neb. 1988), brought a negligence action against the physicians and the hospital, charging that her deceased spouse was negligently discharged from the hospital at a time when his condition was worse than when he had entered the hospital. Mr. Palmer had suffered chest injuries (at least one fractured rib and a partial collapse of the lower lungs) and abdominal injuries in a car accident and was admitted to the hospital on October 29. He was discharged on November 8 and was provided follow-up care in the physician's office on November 10. Although the patient was continuing to experience some pain in his chest, Dr. Meyers, his physician, claimed that he was doing "quite well." On November 12, Mrs. Palmer called Dr. Meyers, indicating to him that Mr. Palmer was "profoundly short of breath" and was experiencing chest pains, a condition that existed the evening before. He expired en route to the hospital as the result of a pulmonary embolism. The district court entered a judgment for the defendants. On appeal, the Supreme Court of Nebraska affirmed the district court's judgment for the defendants.

Patients with communicable diseases can be held by a health officer to prevent the spread of infection. Psychiatric patients can be detained if they are considered to be dangerous to themselves or others. The decision to hold a patient on this basis must be well documented with sufficient facts.

PATIENT'S BILL OF RIGHTS

A large number of documents have been prepared on the national and state levels regarding patient rights. The following excerpt from the Rules and Regulations of New York State at 10 NYCRR 405.7(c), January 1, 1989, is generally consistent with documents regarding patients' rights in other states.

As a patient in a hospital in New York State, you have the right, consistent with law, to:

1. Understand and use these rights. If for any reason you do not understand or you need help, the hospital must provide assistance, including an interpreter.
2. Receive treatment without discrimination as to race, color, religion, sex, national origin, disability, sexual orientation, or source of payment.
3. Receive considerate and respectful care in a clean and safe environment free of unnecessary restraints.
4. Receive emergency care if you need it.
5. Be informed of the name and position of the doctor who will be in charge of your care in the hospital.
6. Know the names, positions, and functions of any hospital staff involved in your care and refuse their treatment, examination, or observation.
7. A no smoking room.
8. Receive complete information about your diagnosis, treatment and prognosis.
9. Receive all the information that you need to give informed consent for any proposed procedure or treatment. This information shall include the possible risks and benefits of the procedure or treatment.
10. Receive all the information you need to give informed consent for an order not to resuscitate. You also have the right to designate an individual to give this consent for you if you are too ill to do so. If you would like additional information, please ask for a copy of the pamphlet, Do Not Resuscitate—A Guide for Patients and Families.
11. Refuse treatment and be told what effect this may have on your health.

12. Refuse to take part in research. In deciding whether or not to participate, you have a right to a full explanation.
13. Privacy while in the hospital and confidentiality of all information and records regarding your care.
14. Participate in all decisions about your treatment and discharge from the hospital. The hospital must provide you with a written discharge plan and written description of how you can appeal your discharge.
15. Review your medical record without charge and obtain a copy of your medical record for which the hospital can charge a reasonable fee. You cannot be denied a copy solely because you cannot afford to pay.

Title 10 NYCRR 405.7(c), Jan. 1, 1989 as amended.

The following is an excerpt from the American Hospital Association's "A Patient's Bill of Rights":

1. A patient has the right to considerate and respectful care.
2. The patient has the right to obtain from his physician complete current information concerning his diagnosis, treatment, and prognosis in terms the patient can be reasonably expected to understand. When it is not medically advisable to give such information to the patient, the information should be made available to an appropriate person in his behalf. He has the right to know by name the physician responsible for coordinating his care.
3. The patient has the right to receive from his physician information necessary to give informed consent prior to the start of any procedure and/or treatment. Except in emergencies, such information for informed consent should include but not necessarily be limited to the specific procedure and/or treatment, the medically significant risks involved, and the probable duration of incapacitation. Where medically significant alternatives for care or treatment exist, or when the patient requests information concerning medical alternatives, the patient has the right to such information. The patient also has the right to know the name of the person responsible for the procedures and/or treatment.
4. The patient has the right to refuse treatment to the extent permitted by law, and to be informed of the medical consequences of his action.
5. The patient has the right to every consideration of his privacy concerning his own medical care program. Case discussion, consultation, examination, and treatment are confidential and should be conducted discreetly. Those not directly involved in his care must have the permission of the patient to be present.

The American Hospital Association's bill of rights must be viewed as a document with legal significance whether or not the state in question has adopted a similar code. Authorities generally agree that since the document has not been prepared by consumers, but has been prepared by an organization of providers, it would probably be admissible in evidence in a case where the rights of the patient were concerned. It is likely that the patient's bill of rights will find its way into proceedings and litigation involving patients, institutions, governmental organizations, and employer-employee relations. In order to avoid the impact of the American Hospital Association's bill of rights, many hospitals have seen fit to adopt their own bill of rights, especially in those states that have not adopted a bill of rights on a state level.

PATIENT RESPONSIBILITIES

Patients have responsibilities as well as rights. They must, for example, follow the instructions of their physicians and nurses. The court of appeals in *Fall v. White*, 449 N.E.2d 628 (Ind. Ct. App. 1983), affirmed the superior court's ruling that the patient had a duty to provide the physician with accurate and complete information and to follow the physician's instructions for further care or tests. Patients are expected to abide by the rules and regulations of the hospital and treat others with the respect and dignity they themselves would expect. The following is an excerpt from Cornwall General Hospital's "Rules for Patients," which were posted in that hospital in 1897:

1. Patients on admission to the Hospital must have a bath, unless orders to the contrary are given by the Attending Medical Attendant.

* * *

6. Patients must be quiet and exemplary in their behaviour and conform strictly to the rules and regulations of the Hospital, and carry out all orders and prescriptions of the various officers of the establishment.

* * *

8. No male patient shall, under any pretense whatever, enter the apartments or wards for the females, nor shall a female patient enter the apartments or wards for males, without express orders from the Medical Attendant or Lady Superintendent.

* * *

10. Every patient shall retire to bed at 9 P.M. from First May to First November, and at 8 P.M. from November to May; and those who

are able shall rise at 6 A.M. in the Summer and 7 A.M. in the Winter.

11. Such patients as are able, in the opinion of the physicians and surgeons, shall assist in nursing others, or in such services as the Lady Superintendent may require.

* * *

13. Patients must not take away bottles, labels or appliances when leaving the Hospital.
14. No patients shall enter into the basement story, operating theatre, or any of the officers' or attendants' rooms, except by permission of an officer of the Hospital.

* * *

17. Any patient bringing spirituous liquors into the Hospital or the grounds, or found intoxicated, will be discharged.
18. Whenever patients misbehave or violate any of the standing rules of the Hospital, the Attending Physician may remove or discharge them, as provided by clauses 91 and 93 of Rules for Medical Staff.

Today, patient responsibilities are stated somewhat differently than they were in 1897. The Joint Commission on Accreditation of Healthcare Organizations sets forth the following list of patient responsibilities:

Provision of Information

A patient has the responsibility to provide, to the best of his knowledge, accurate and complete information about present complaints, past illnesses, hospitalizations, medications and other matters relating to his health. He has the responsibility to report unexpected changes in his condition to the responsible practitioner. A patient is responsible for making it known whether he clearly comprehends a contemplated course of action and what is expected of him.

Compliance Instructions

A patient is responsible for following the treatment plan recommended by the practitioner primarily responsible for his care. This may include following the instructions of nurses and allied health personnel as they carry out the coordinated plan of care and implement the responsible practitioner's orders, and as they enforce the applicable hospital rules and regulations. The patient is responsible for keeping appointments and, when he is unable to do so for any reason, for notifying the responsible practitioner or the hospital.

Refusal of Treatment

The patient is responsible for his actions if he refuses treatment or does not follow the practitioner's instructions.

Hospital Charges

The patient is responsible for assuring that the financial obligations of his health care are fulfilled as promptly as possible.

Hospital Rules and Regulations

The patient is responsible for following hospital rules and regulations affecting patient care and conduct.

Respect and Consideration

The patient is responsible for being considerate of the rights of others and hospital personnel and for assisting in the control of noise, smoking, and the number of visitors. The patient is responsible for being respectful of the property of other persons and of the hospital.[1]

NOTES

1. JOINT COMMISSION ON ACCREDITATION OF HEALTHCARE ORGANIZATIONS, 1990 ACCREDITATION MANUAL FOR HOSPITALS xvi–xvii (1989).

Chapter 13

Acquired Immunodeficiency Syndrome

Acquired immunodeficiency syndrome (AIDS) is generally accepted as a syndrome—a collection of specific, life-threatening, opportunistic infections and manifestations that are the result of an underlying immune deficiency. Acquired immunodeficiency syndrome itself does not kill. AIDS destroys the body's capacity to ward off bacteria and viruses that would ordinarily be fought off by a properly functioning immune system. AIDS poses extremely serious social, ethical, economic, and health problems throughout the world.

Acquired immunodeficiency syndrome is considered to be a highly contagious disease among certain high-risk groups (homosexual males, intravenous drug users, Haitian immigrants, and those who require transfusions of blood and blood products, such as hemophiliacs).

There has been a global response to the acquired immunodeficiency syndrome. According to Jonathan Mann, Director of the World Health Organization's Global Program on AIDS, by the end of 1988 virtually every nation in the world had established an education program to educate its population about AIDS. More than 130,000 cases had been reported with as many as 400,000 new cases projected by the end of 1990.[1]

As of February 1987, there were approximately 30,000 reported cases of persons with AIDS in the U.S., according to the CDC. To date, about 54 percent of all reported cases have resulted in death. An estimated 1.5 million Americans are afflicted with the AIDS virus that causes AIDS, with a large percentage of them expected to develop the full symptoms of the disease. It is projected that cumulatively about 270,000 Americans will have contracted AIDS by 1991, with 179,000 deaths from the disease.[2]

Legal liability for transmission of the disease lies in the realm of transmission through transfusions and the failure of blood banks to properly screen for the contagion. AIDS is one of the nation's primary health concerns and most dreaded diseases.

BLOOD TRANSFUSIONS

Suits often arise as a result of a person with AIDS claiming that he or she contracted the disease as a result of a transfusion of contaminated blood or blood products. In blood transfusion cases the standards most commonly identified as having been violated concern blood testing and donor screening. An injured party must generally prove that a standard of care existed, that the defendant's conduct fell below the standard, and that this conduct was the proximate cause of the plaintiff's injury.

A summary dismissal against a hospital and the American Red Cross was properly ordered in *Kozup v. Georgetown University*, 663 F. Supp. 1048 (D. D.C. 1987), where it was alleged that the death of a premature infant was due to causes related to AIDS contracted through a blood transfusion given in January 1983 without the parent's informed consent. The case was dismissed on the basis that no reasonable jury would have found that the possibility of contracting AIDS from a blood transfusion in 1983 was a material risk. Dismissal was also justified on the basis that the transfusion was the only method of treating the child for a life-threatening condition.

The hemophiliac patient in *McKee v. Miles Laboratories, Inc.*, 675 F. Supp. 1060 (D.C. Ky. 1987), had contracted AIDS from a coagulation protein (Factor VIII), which was provided by the defendants, and subsequently died. The defendants moved for summary judgment as to the merits of the case, contending that at the time the plaintiff's decedent contracted AIDS, there were no tests that would have revealed the presence of the AIDS virus. The plaintiff argued that there was a genuine issue of material fact as to whether an alternative testing method was available when the decedent contracted AIDS in 1983. The district court held that the provision of blood and blood byproducts was a service and not a sale and that the lack of any test to purify or screen blood or blood byproducts for the AIDS virus demonstrated that the supplier did not violate industry standards.

The methods available for testing for AIDS during the early 1980s were carefully analyzed in the *Kozup* case, where the court determined that it was not until 1984 that the medical community reached a consensus as to the proposition that AIDS was transmitted by blood. The district court in *McKee* held that there was no need to rehash the same chronological medical history of AIDS that the *Kozup* case so methodically composed.

The plaintiff in *McKee* appealed the district court's decision to the U.S. Court of Appeals for the Sixth Circuit. *McKee v. Cutter Laboratories, Inc.*, 866 F.2d 219 (6th Cir. 1989). The court of appeals upheld the district court's decision that the manufacturer was not negligent.

BLOOD DONORS/CONFIDENTIALITY

A patient who was infected with Human Immunodeficiency Virus (HIV)-contaminated blood during surgery brought an action against a hospital and a blood bank. The trial court granted the patient's request to discover the identity of the blood donor, and the defendants appealed. The court of appeals, in *Doe v. University of Cincinnati*, 538 N.E.2d 419 (Ohio Ct. App. 1988), held that the potential injury to a donor in revealing his identity outweighed the plaintiff's modest interest in learning of the donor's identity. A blood donor has a constitutional right to privacy not to be identified as a donor of blood that contains the HIV virus. At the time of the plaintiff's blood transfusion in July of 1984, no test had been developed to determine the existence of AIDS antibodies. By May 27, 1986, all donors donating blood through the defendant blood bank were tested for the presence of HIV antibodies. Patients who received blood from donors that tested positive were to be notified through their physicians. The plaintiff's family in this case was notified due to the plaintiff's age and other disability.

The appeals court in *Tarrant County Hospital District v. Hughes*, 734 S.W.2d 675 (Tex. Ct. App. 1987), held that the trial court properly ordered a hospital to disclose the names and addresses of blood donors in a wrongful death action alleging that a patient contracted AIDS from a blood transfusion administered in the hospital. The physician-patient privilege expressed in Section 509 of the Texas Rules of Evidence did not apply to preclude such disclosure since the record did not reflect that any such relationship had been established. The disclosure was not an impermissible violation of the donors' right of privacy. The societal interest in maintaining an effective blood donor program did not override the plaintiff's right to receive such information. The order prohibited disclosure of the donors' names to third parties.

NEWS MEDIA

The superior court in *Stenger v. Lehigh Valley Hospital Center, Appeal of The Morning Call, Inc.*, 554 A.2d 954 (Pa. Super. Ct. 1989), upheld the court of common pleas' order denying the petition of The Morning Call, Inc., which challenged a court order closing judicial proceedings to the press and public in a civil action against a hospital and physicians. A patient and her family had all contracted AIDS after the patient received a blood transfusion. The access of the media to pretrial discovery proceedings in a civil action is subject to reasonable control by the court in which the action is pending. The protective order limiting public access to pretrial discovery material did not violate the newspaper's First Amendment rights. The discovery documents were not judicial records to which the newspaper had a common law right of access. Good cause existed for nondisclosure of information about the intimate personal details of the plaintiffs' lives, disclosure of which would cause undue humiliation.

MEDICAL RECORDS

Hospitals must be sure to adopt appropriate and effective policies and procedures for protecting the rights of patients with AIDS. As with mental health records, a higher degree of confidentiality is generally expected of the treating institution due to the negative impact on persons who have contracted AIDS.

PRISON RIGHTS

Health professionals and others working with AIDS patients have a right to know when they are caring for patients with highly contagious diseases, such as AIDS. There are times when the duty to disclose outweighs the rights of confidentiality. The U.S. Court of Appeals for the Tenth Circuit in *Dunn v. White*, No. 88-2194 (10th Cir. Aug. 1, 1989), declared that there is no Fourth Amendment impediment to a state prison's policy of blood testing all inmates for AIDS. Under the U.S. Supreme Court's drug-testing decisions, the proper analysis is to balance the prisoner's interest in being free from bodily intrusion inherent in a blood test against the prison's institutional rights in combating the disease. The U.S. Court of Appeals held that in or out of prison a person has only a limited privacy interest in not having his blood tested. The court cited *Schmerber v. California*, 384 U.S. 757 (1966), which rejected a Fourth Amendment challenge to the blood testing of a suspected drunken driver. Against the prisoner's minimal interest, prison authorities have a strong interest in controlling the spread of AIDS.

DISCRIMINATION

Discrimination against persons who have contracted the AIDS virus is often found to be in violation of their constitutional rights. The sufferings and hardships of those who have contracted the disease extend to family as well as best friends. The infringements of those afflicted with AIDS include discrimination in housing, insurance, access to health care, public benefits, military service, employment, and education.

Housing

Discrimination in housing is generally prohibited. Several municipalities have ordinances prohibiting discrimination against those who have or are perceived to have AIDS or related conditions. A number of cities have such ordinances: Berkeley, California; Los Angeles, California; San Francisco, California; and Austin, Texas;[3] among others.

Case law is developing in housing. For example, in *People of the State of New York v. 49 West 12 Tenants Corp.*, No. 43604183 (N.Y., Sup. Ct. of New York County 1983), a cooperative building in New York City sought to evict a physician who treated a number of people with AIDS. The trial court held that the physician's office was a public accommodation under the New York Human Rights Law, that the physician and the patients had standing to pursue the claim, and that AIDS is a disability under applicable state law. The court granted a temporary injunction, and the litigation was subsequently settled prior to trial.

Military Service

Although the following cases are not specifically related to AIDS, they do suggest an undercurrent of fear of contracting the AIDS virus through contact with those labeled as being in the high-risk population. This fear has had a negative impact on entire groups of people. The U.S. Court of Appeals for the Seventh Circuit ruled that a recently promulgated Army regulation that denies admitted homosexuals the right to re-enlist does not violate a soldier's First Amendment right to freedom of speech or his or her Fifth Amendment right to equal protection. The court said, "the sergeant's First Amendment claim fails because the regulation does not prohibit speech per se. Under the new regulation, the sergeant is free to say whatever she wants about homosexuality. She simply cannot claim to be a homosexual and remain in the service. It is her identity as a lesbian, not her speech, that makes her ineligible for military duty. . . ." [Ben-Shalom v. Marsh, No. 88-2771 (7th Cir. Aug. 7, 1989)]. The regulation classifies the sergeant not on the basis of her sexual preferences, but on the basis of her propensity to commit the acts it prohibits. The court reasoned that if the U.S. Supreme Court in *Bowers v. Hardwick*, 478 U.S. 186 (1986), refused to recognize that homosexuals have a fundamental right to engage in sodomy under the due process clause, then homosexuals cannot be viewed as a suspect class for equal protection purposes.

Employment

The growing consensus of case law indicates that employment-related discrimination is unlawful. The California Court of Appeals, Second District, in *Raytheon v. Fair Employment & Housing Commission*, No. BO35809 (Cal. Ct. App. Aug. 7, 1989), determined that an employee with AIDS who was admitted to and treated in a hospital was unlawfully denied his right to return to work following treatment in the hospital. The court held that AIDS is a protected physical handicap under California's Fair Employment and Housing Act and that the employer failed to prove its defense of protecting the health and safety of its other workers. The employer had ignored the advice of county health officials and communicable disease authorities that there was no risk to other employees at the plant.

Health Care Benefits

AIDS patients in *Weaver v. Reagan*, 701 F. Supp. 717 (D. Mo. 1988), were found to be entitled to summary judgment in their class action suit to require Missouri's authorities to provide Medicaid coverage for cost of AZT treatments. The U.S. Court of Appeals for the Eighth Circuit decided that states must provide Medicaid coverage for the drug AZT to HIV-infected individuals who are eligible for Medicaid and whose physicians have prescribed AZT for their treatment, whether or not those individuals meet the Food and Drug Administration's criteria for AZT treatment on its approval label for the drug. *Weaver v. Reagan*, No. 88-2560 (8th Cir. Sept. 25, 1989). The state had argued that its reliance on the Food and Drug Administration's approval statement in limiting coverage for AZT treatments was a reasonable exercise of its discretion. The Eighth Circuit disagreed. The fact that the Food and Drug Administration has not approved a drug for a particular use does not necessarily bear on uses of the drug established within the medical and scientific communities as medically appropriate.

Education

A school's refusal to admit students with the AIDS virus is generally considered an unnecessary restriction on an individual's liberty. *Board of Education v. Cooperman*, 209 N.J. Sup. 174, 507 A.2d 253 (N.J. Super. Ct. App. Div. 1986); *District 27 Community School Board v. Board of Education*, 130 Misc. 2d 398, 502 N.Y.S.2d 325 (Sup. Ct. 1986).

CRIMINAL ACTIONS

On June 24, 1987, the defendant, an inmate at the Federal Medical Center in Rochester, was convicted by a jury of assault and battery with a deadly or dangerous weapon. The indictment indicated that he had tested positive for the HIV virus antibody and that later he had assaulted two federal correctional officers with his mouth and teeth. *United States v. Moore*, No. Crim. 4-87-44 (D. Minn. Sept. 3, 1987). The defendant motioned the U.S. district court for a judgment of acquittal and for a new trial. Evidence at trial showed that AIDS can be transmitted through body fluids such as blood and semen. The defendant had been informed that he had both the AIDS virus and the hepatitis antibody and that he could potentially transmit the diseases to other persons. He bit one officer on the leg twice, leaving a 4-inch saliva stain. He bit the second officer, leaving a mark that was visible five months later at trial. Expert testimony at trial indicated that any human bite can cause a serious infection and that blood is sometimes present in the mouth, particularly if an individual has ill-fitting teeth or gum problems. In the defendant's motion for a new trial, he claimed that the court erred in denying his requested Jury Instruction 12, which would have prohibited the officers' testimony as to medical instructions they were given to avoid infecting their families from being entered into evidence. The evidence was considered probative of the dangerousness of the bites inflicted by the defendant, and the probative value outweighed any prejudicial effect. The defendant's motions for a judgment of acquittal and a new trial were denied.

REPORTING REQUIREMENTS

Because of the social stigma associated with AIDS, there is a worldwide tendency to underreport the incidence of the disease. This is particularly true in developing countries, where the problem is compounded by the lack of efficient reporting systems. For example, in Africa, for every person with AIDS, between 50 and 100 more are estimated to be infected with the HIV virus. Most cases are not reported, and some governments are unwilling to admit to the problem. Few African countries possess the medical resources to deal with this disease epidemic. Whole sectors of African economies face ruin. The social stigma is not endemic to African countries. In the United States, health information is merely more readily available due to sophisticated reporting systems.[4]

AIDS is now a reportable communicable disease in every state. . . . Physicians and hospitals must report every case of AIDS—with the patient's name—to government public health authorities. New York State does not require reports of ARC or of positive blood test for HIV antibodies, but some states do. . . . Cases reported to local health authorities are also reported to the federal Centers for Disease Control (CDC), with the patients' names encoded by a system known as Soundex. CDC records come under the general confidentiality protections of the federal Privacy Act of 1974. However, the statute permits disclosures to other federal agencies, under certain circumstances.[5]

CONCLUSION

The case of Veronica Prego, M.D., was expected to help to further define hospitals' responsibilities for protecting their workers from occupational exposure to the human immunodeficiency virus (HIV). But a $1.35 million out-of-court settlement kept the lawsuit from going to the jury—and left many questions unanswered for hospitals. . . .

AHA Senior Counsel Margaret Hardy said after the case was settled, "This just adds another reminder, from a different sector, that hospitals have to be serious about [protecting their workers]."[6]

In 1988, five years after Prego claims she was infected, the CDC [Centers for Disease Control] expanded its infection control guidelines and urged hospitals to adopt "universal precautions" to protect their workers from exposure to patients' blood and other body fluids. Currently, the Occupational Safety and Health Administration (OSHA) and virtually every U.S. hospital follow universal precautions as the accepted standard for employee protection. Recently, OSHA introduced a new proposal that goes beyond the CDC's . . . guidelines. That proposal, however, has not received total support from the hospital field.[7]

The AIDS hysteria is far more contagious than the disease itself. It exists in every corner of our society and affects lawyers, judges, court clerks, physicians, nurses, aides, orderlies, family, and friends. The answers are not simple and will be difficult to find; however, through compassion, research, and education, we can all be winners in our fight against this dreaded disease.

NOTES

1. Wagner, *The World's Struggle against AIDS*, FUTURIST, May/June 1989, at 17–20.

2. Brown, *AIDS Discrimination in the Workplace: The Legal Dilemma*, CASE AND COMMENT, Nov.–Dec. 1989, at 1.

3. LAMBDA LEGAL DEFENSE AND EDUCATION FUND, INC., AIDS LEGAL GUIDE 8-1 (1987).

4. *Incalculable Cost of AIDS*, ECONOMIST (U.K.), Mar. 12, 1988, at 44.

5. LAMBDA LEGAL DEFENSE AND EDUCATION FUND, INC., LIVING WITH AIDS 7 (1987).

6. Green, *Prego AIDS Case: Settlement Leaves Few Answers for Hospitals*, AHA NEWS 26(11), March 19, 1990, at 8.

7. Green, *Beefed-up Safeguards, Increased Knowledge Benefit Health Workers*, AHA NEWS 26(11), March 19, 1990, at 8.

Chapter 14

Euthanasia, Death, and Dying

The human struggle to survive and dreams of immortality have been instrumental in pushing mankind to develop means to prevent and cure illness. Advances in medicine and related technologies that have resulted from human creativity and ingenuity have indeed given society the power to prolong life. However, dying can also be prolonged. Those victims of long-term pain and suffering, as well as patients in irreversible comas, are the most directly affected. Today, rather than watching hopelessly as a disease destroys a person or as a body part malfunctions, causing death to a patient, physicians can implant artificial body organs. In addition, exotic machines and antibiotics are new weapons in a doctor's arsenal to help extend a patient's life. Such situations have generated vigorous debate. There seems to be an absence of controversy only when a patient who is kept alive by modern technology is still able to appreciate and maintain control over his or her life. However, when patients and their families see what they perceive as a deterioration of the quality of life and no end to unbearable pain, it is then that conflict arises between health care professionals who are trained to save lives and patients and their families who wish to end the suffering. This conflict centers around the concept of euthanasia and its place in the modern world.

From its inception, euthanasia has evolved into an issue with competing legal, medical, and moral implications, which continue to generate debate, confusion, and conflict.

DEFINING EUTHANASIA

Even the connotation of the word *euthanasia* has changed with time and those persons attempting to define it. Originating in the Greek language, euthanasia, meaning "good death," was accepted in situations where people had what were considered to be incurable diseases.[1] In the religions of Confucianism and Buddhism, suicide was an acceptable answer to unendurable pain and incurable

187

disease. The Celtic people went a step farther, believing that those who chose to die of disease or senility, rather than committing suicide, would be condemned to hell.[2] Such acceptance began to change during the nineteenth century when Western physicians refused to lessen suffering by shortening a dying patient's life. Napoleon's doctor, for example, rejected Napoleon's plea to kill plague-stricken soldiers, insisting that his obligation was to cure rather than to kill people.[3]

In the late 1870s writings on euthanasia began to appear, mainly in England and the United States. Although such works were, for the most part, written by lay authors, the public and the medical community began to consider the issues raised by euthanasia. Then defined as "the act or practice of painlessly putting to death persons suffering from incurable conditions or diseases,"[4] it was considered to be a merciful release from incurable suffering. By the beginning of the twentieth century, however, there were still no clear answers or guidelines regarding the use of euthanasia. Unlike in prior centuries when society as a whole supported or rejected euthanasia, different segments of today's society apply distinct connotations to the word, generating further confusion. Some believe euthanasia is meant to allow a painless death when one suffers from an incurable disease, yet is not dying. Others, who remain in the majority, perceive euthanasia as an instrument to aid only dying people in ending their lives with as little suffering as possible.

Since an estimated "80% of Americans now die in hospitals and nursing homes,"[5] rather than at home as in the past, therefore leading to greater involvement and participation on the part of the public, the topic of euthanasia is now openly and often vigorously discussed. The misconceptions and confusion regarding the topic have led to wide disparity among jurisdictions, both in legislation and in judicial decisions. As a result, the American Medical Association, the American Bar Association, legislators, and judges are actively attempting to formulate and legislate clear guidelines in this sensitive, profound, and as yet not fully understood area. In order to ensure compliance with the law, while serving the needs of their patients, health care providers must keep themselves informed of the legislation enacted in this ever-changing field.

CLASSIFYING EUTHANASIA

In order to properly address the topic of euthanasia, it is necessary to understand the precise meaning of the recognized forms. Rhetorical phrases such as "right to die," "right to life," and "death with dignity" have obfuscated, rather than clarified, the public's understanding of euthanasia.

The labeling of euthanasia as active or passive is, for many, the most controversial distinction. Active euthanasia is commonly understood to be the commission of an act that results in death. The act, if committed by the patient, is thought of as suicide. Moreover, if the patient cannot take his or her own life, any person who assists in the causing of the death could be subject to criminal sanction for aiding and abetting suicide.

Passive euthanasia occurs when lifesaving treatment (such as a respirator) is withdrawn or withheld, allowing the patient diagnosed as terminal to die a natural death. Passive euthanasia is generally allowed by legislative acts and judicial decisions. *In re Estate of Brooks*, 32 Ill. 2d 361, 205 N.E.2d 435 (1965); *Superintendent of Belchertown State School v. Saikewicz*, 373 Mass. 728, 370 N.E.2d 417 (1977); *In re Quinlan*, 81 N.J. 10, 355 A.2d 647 (1976). These decisions, however, are generally limited to the facts of the particular case.

The distinctions are important when considering the duty and the liability of a doctor who must decide whether or not to continue or initiate treatment of a comatose or terminally ill patient. Physicians are bound to use reasonable care to preserve health and to save lives, so unless fully protected by the law, they will be reluctant to abide by a patient's or family's wishes to terminate life-support devices. In *Barber v. Superior Ct.*, 147 Cal. App. 3d 1006, 195 Cal. Rptr. 484 (1983), the court of appeals dismissed murder charges against doctors who intentionally failed to continue treatment with the knowledge that a comatose patient would die as a result. The court found that the doctors did not deviate from normal medical practice.

Both active and passive euthanasia may be either voluntary or involuntary. Voluntary euthanasia occurs when the suffering incurable makes the decision to die. To be considered voluntary, the request or consent must be made by a legally competent adult and be based on material information concerning the possible ramifications and alternatives available. The term *legally competent* was addressed in a right to refuse treatment case, *Lane v. Candura*, 6 Mass. App. Ct. 377, 376 N.E.2d 1232 (1979). The case involved a patient who twice refused to permit surgeons to amputate her leg in order to prevent gangrene from spreading. The patient's daughter sought to be appointed as a legal guardian to enable her to consent to her mother's surgery. The appellate court, finding no evidence indicating that Mrs. Lane was incapable of appreciating the nature and consequence of her decision, overturned the trial court's holding of incompetence. Therefore, even though Mrs. Lane's decision would ultimately lead to her death, she was found to be competent, and, thus, she was allowed to reject medical treatment.

The *Lane* court and others have defined legal competence as the mental ability to make a rational decision. A patient must exhibit perception and appreciation of all relevant facts and then make decisions based on those facts. In the active euthanasia context, the patient would be demonstrating that by voluntarily requesting euthanasia, he or she would be selecting death over life. *State Department of Human Services v. Northern*, 563 S.W.2d 197, 209 (Tenn. Ct. App.), *appeal dismissed as moot*, 436 U.S. 923 (1978).

In the case of *In re Lydia Hall Hospital*, 455 N.Y.S.2d 266 (Sup. Ct. 1981), the patient, terminally ill and requiring dialysis, was taken off all medication to ensure that his mind would be clear when psychiatrists examined him to determine if he was competent. Recent case law asserts that the standard of proof required for a finding of an incurable's incompetence is that of clear and convincing evidence. *In re Lydia E. Hall Hospital*, 455 N.Y.S.2d 706, 712 (N.Y. 1982) [quoting *In re*

Storar, 438 N.Y.S.2d 266, 274 (Ct. App. 1981)]. This is a higher standard than the normal fair preponderance of the credible evidence required in civil proceedings.

Involuntary euthanasia, on the other hand, occurs when a person other than the incurable makes the decision to terminate an incompetent or an unconsenting competent person's life.[6]

The patient's lack of consent could be due to mental impairment or comatose unconsciousness. Important value questions face courts dealing with involuntary euthanasia: Who should decide to withhold or withdraw treatment? On what factors should the decision be based? Are there viable standards to guide the courts? Should criminal sanctions be imposed on a person assisting in ending a life? When does death occur?

CONSTITUTIONAL ASPECTS

In order to analyze the important questions regarding whether or not life-support treatment can be withheld or withdrawn from an incompetent patient, it is necessary to first consider what rights a competent patient possesses. Both statutory law and case law have presented a diversity of policies and points of view. Some courts point to common law and the early case of *Schloendorff v. Society of New York Hospital*, 105 N.E. 92 (N.Y. 1914), to support their belief in a patient's right to self-determination. The *Schloendorff* court stated: "Every human being of adult years has a right to determine what shall be done with his own body; and the surgeon who performs an operation without his patient's consent commits an assault for which he is liable for damages." *Id.* at 93. This right of self-determination was emphasized in *In re Storar*, 438 N.Y.S.2d 266 (Ct. App. 1981), when the court announced that every human being of adult years and sound mind has the right to determine what shall be done with his own body. *Id.* at 272.

The *Storar* case was a departure from the New Jersey Supreme Court's rationale in the case of *In re Quinlan*, 81 N.J. 10, 355 A.2d 647 (1976). The *Quinlan* case was the first to significantly address the issue of whether euthanasia should be permitted where a patient is terminally ill.[7] The *Quinlan* court, relying on *Roe v. Wade*, 410 U.S. 113 (1973), announced that a patient's right to self-determination is protected by the constitutional right to privacy. The court noted that the right to privacy "is broad enough to encompass a patient's decision to decline medical treatment under certain circumstances, in much the same way as it is broad enough to encompass a woman's decision to terminate pregnancy under certain conditions." *Id.* at 40, 355 A.2d at 663.

The majority of cases today follow the right to privacy argument. The court, in reaching its decision, applied a test balancing the state's interest in preserving and maintaining the sanctity of human life against Karen Quinlan's privacy interest. It decided that especially in light of the prognosis (doctors determined that Karen was in an irreversible coma), the state's interest did not justify interference with

Karen's right to refuse treatment. Thus, Karen's father was appointed her legal guardian, and the respirator was shut off. Opponents of euthanasia argue that before the *Quinlan* decision, any form of euthanasia was defined as murder by our legal system. Although acts of euthanasia did take place, the law was applied selectively, and the possibility of criminal sanction against active participants in euthanasia was enough to deter doctors from assisting a patient in committing self-euthanasia.

In spite of intense criticism by legal and religious scholars, the *Quinlan* decision paved the way for courts to consider extending the right to decline treatment to incompetents as well. The U.S. Supreme Court has not yet addressed this issue, but state courts have; and even though the state courts recognize the right, they differ on how this right is to be exercised.

In the same year as the *Quinlan* decision, the case of *Superintendent of Belchertown State School v. Saikewicz*, 373 Mass. 728, 370 N.E.2d 417 (1977), was decided. There the court, utilizing the balancing test enunciated in *Quinlan*, approved the recommendation of a court-appointed guardian ad litem that it would be in Mr. Saikewicz's best interests to end chemotherapy treatment. Mr. Saikewicz was a mentally retarded, 67-year-old patient, suffering from leukemia. The supreme judicial court found from the evidence that the prognosis was dim, and even though a "normal person" would probably have chosen chemotherapy, it allowed Mr. Saikewicz to die without the treatment in order to spare him the suffering.

Although the court also followed the reasoning of the *Quinlan* opinion in giving the right to an incompetent to refuse treatment, based on either the objective "best interests" test or the subjective "substituted judgment" test, which it favored since Mr. Saikewicz was always incompetent, the court departed from *Quinlan* in a major way. It rejected the *Quinlan* approach of entrusting a decision concerning the continuance of artificial life support to the patient's guardian, family, attending doctors, and a hospital "ethics committee." The *Saikewicz* court asserted that even though a judge might find the opinions of physicians, medical experts, or hospital ethics committees helpful in reaching a decision, there should be no requirement to seek out the advice. The court decided that questions of life and death with regard to an incompetent should be the responsibility of the courts, which would conduct detached, but passionate investigations. The court took a "dim view of any attempt to shift the ultimate decision-making responsibility away from duly established courts of proper jurisdiction to any committee, panel, or group, ad hoc or permanent." *Id* at 758, 370 N.E.2d at 434.

This major point of difference between the *Saikewicz* and *Quinlan* cases marked the emergence of two different policies on the incompetent's right to refuse treatment. One line of cases has followed *Saikewicz* and supports court approval before doctors withhold or withdraw life support. Advocates of this view argue that it makes more sense to leave the decision to an objective tribunal than to extend the right of a patient's privacy to a number of interested parties, as was done in *Quinlan*. They also attack the *Quinlan* method as being a privacy decision effectuated by popular vote.[8]

Six months after *Saikewicz*, the Massachusetts Appeals Court narrowed the need for court intervention in *In re Dinnerstein*, 6 Mass. App. Ct. 466, 380 N.E.2d 134 (1978), in finding that "no code" orders are valid to prevent the use of artificial resuscitative measures on incompetent terminally ill patients. The court there was faced with the case of a 67-year-old woman who was suffering from Alzheimer's disease. She was determined to be permanently comatose at the time of trial. Further, the court decided that *Saikewicz*-type judicial proceedings should take place only when medical treatment could offer "a reasonable expectation of effecting a permanent or temporary cure of or relief from the illness." 380 N.E.2d at 138.

The Massachusetts Supreme Judicial Court attempted to clarify its *Saikewicz* opinion with regard to court orders in *In re Spring*, 405 N.E.2d 115 (Mass. 1980). It held that such various factors as the patient's mental impairment and his or her medical prognosis with or without treatment must be considered before judicial approval is necessary to withdraw or withhold treatment from an incompetent patient. The problem in all three of these cases is that there is still no clear guidance as to exactly when the court's approval of the removal of life-support systems would be necessary. *Saikewicz* seemed to demand judicial approval in every case. *Spring*, however, in partially retreating from that view, stated that it did not have to articulate what combination of the factors it discussed, thus making prior court approval necessary. Recently, however, a Maine court ruled that it was within the scope of a guardian's powers and rights to request and instruct the treating physicians and hospital to stop all life support including food, water and antibiotics—without prior court approval. *In re Hallock* (Me., Kennebec County P. Ct. Sept. 26, 1988).

The inconsistencies presented by the Massachusetts cases have led the majority of courts since 1977 to follow the lead set by *Quinlan*, requiring judicial intervention. In cases where the irreversible nature of the patient's loss of consciousness has been certified by physicians, an ethics committee (actually a neurological team) could certify the patient's hopeless neurological condition. Then a guardian would be free to take the legal steps necessary to remove life-support systems. The major reason for the appointment of a guardian is to ensure that incompetents, like all other patients, maintain their right to refuse treatment. The majority of holdings indicate that since a patient has the constitutional right of self-determination, those acting on the patient's behalf can exercise that right when rendering their best judgment concerning how the patient would assert the right. This substituted judgment doctrine could be argued on standing grounds, whereby a second party has standing to assert the constitutional rights of another when that second party's intervention is necessary to protect the other's constitutional rights. Of course, the guardian's decision is more sound if based on the known desires of a patient who was competent immediately prior to becoming comatose.

Courts adhering to the *Quinlan* rationale have recognized that fact, and in 1984 the highest state court of Florida took the lead and accepted the living will as persuasive evidence of an incompetent's wishes. The Supreme Court of Florida, in *John F. Kennedy Memorial Hospital, Inc. v. Bludworth*, 452 So. 2d 925 (Fla. 1984), allowed an incompetent patient's wife to act as his guardian, and in accordance with the terms of a living will he executed in 1975, she was told to substitute her judgment for that of her husband. She asked to have a respirator removed. The court declined the necessity of prior court approval, finding that the constitutional right to refuse treatment which had been decided for competents in *Satz v. Perlmutter*, 362 So. 2d 160 (Fla. Dist. Ct. App. 1978), *aff'd*, 379 So. 2d 359 (Fla. 1980), extends to incompetents. The court required the attending physician to certify that the patient was in a permanent vegetative state, with no reasonable chance for recovery, before a family member or guardian could request termination of extraordinary means of medical treatment.

In keeping with *Saikewicz*, the decision maker would attempt to ascertain the incompetent patient's actual interests and preferences. Court involvement would be mandated only to appoint a guardian, or in one of the following cases: (1) if family members disagree as to the incompetent's wishes, (2) if physicians disagree on the prognosis, (3) if the patient's wishes cannot be known because he has always been incompetent, (4) if evidence exists of wrongful motives or malpractice, or (5) if no family member can serve as a guardian. *John F. Kennedy Memorial Hospital, Inc. v. Bludworth*, 452 So. 2d 925, 430 (Fla. 1984) [citing *In re Welfare of Colyer*, 99 Wash. 2d 114, 660 P.2d 738 (1983) where the court found prior court approval to be "unresponsive and cumbersome"].

DEATH CAN BE DEFINED

The decision in *John F. Kennedy Memorial Hospital v. Bludworth*, 452 So. 2d 925 (Fla. 1984), increased the desire of the public, courts, and religious groups to know when a patient is considered to be legally dead and what type of treatment can be withheld or withdrawn at that point. Most cases dealing with euthanasia speak of the necessity that a physician diagnose a patient as being either

- in a persistent vegetative state, *Severns v. Wilmington Medical Center*, 425 A.2d 156 (Del. Ch. 1980) (incompetent's right to refuse medical treatment may be expressed through a guardian when the patient is in a chronic vegetative state); *Leach v. Akron General Medical Center*, 68 Ohio Misc. 1, 426 N.E.2d 809 (Ohio C.P. 1980) (right to privacy includes right of a terminally ill patient in a vegetative state to determine his/her own course of treatment); or

- terminally ill, *Satz v. Perlmutter*, 379 So. 2d 359 (Fla. 1980) (constitutional right to privacy supports decision of a competent adult suffering from a terminal illness to refuse extraordinary treatment); *Superintendent of Belchertown State School v. Saikewicz*, 373 Mass. 728, 370 N.E.2d 417 (1977) (right to refuse medical treatment for terminal illness extended to incompetent patients).

This diagnostic role of the physician acts as a limitation on the decision-making role of the family or the guardian. Where death is actually present, of course, the termination of mechanical or other similar devices would be a consistent and permissible act.

Traditionally, the definition of death adopted by the courts has been the *Black's Law Dictionary* definition: "cessation of respiration, heartbeat, and certain indications of central nervous system activity, such as respiration and pulsation." *Schmitt v. Pierce*, 344 S.W.2d 120, 133 (Mo. 1961). At present, however, modern science has the capacity to sustain vegetative functions of those in irreversible comas. Machinery can actually sustain heartbeat and respiration even in the face of brain death. "With 10,000 patients existing in the twilight state at this time,"[9] every appellate court that has ruled on the question has recognized that the irreversible cessation of brain function constitutes death.

Further, ethicists who advocate the prohibition of taking action to shorten life agree that "where death is imminent and inevitable, it is permissible to forego treatments that would only provide a precarious and painful prolongation of life, as long as the normal care due to the sick person in similar cases is not interrupted."[10]

Relying on the 1968 Harvard Criteria set forth by the Ad Hoc Committee of the Harvard Medical School To Examine the Definition of Brain Death, the American Medical Association in 1974 accepted that death occurs when there is "irreversible cessation of all brain functions including the brain stem."[11] At least 38 states now recognize brain death by statute or judicial decision. New York, for example, in *People v. Eulo*, 482 N.Y.S.2d 436 (1984), in rejecting the traditional cardiopulmonary definition of death, announced that the determination of brain death need be made only according to acceptable medical standards in order to be valid. The court also repeated its holding in *In re Storar*, 438 N.Y.S.2d 266 (1981), that clear and convincing evidence of a person's desire to decline extraordinary medical care may be honored and that a third person may not exercise this judgment on behalf of a person who has not or cannot express the desire to decline treatment. Following the *Bludworth* logic, the court noted that health professionals acting within the cases should not face liability. Nearly half of the states, in response to cases since *Quinlan*, have enacted laws setting forth statutory guidelines that relieve courts of the burden of deciding on a case-by-case basis whether or not to terminate life support.

The clear and convincing evidence standard was recently more succinctly defined by the New York Court of Appeals in *In the Matter of Westchester County Medical Center*, 534 N.Y.S.2d 886 (1988). There the court determined that artificial nutrition could be withheld from Mary O'Connor, a stroke victim who was unable to converse or feed herself. The court held that ''nothing less than unequivocal proof of a patient's wishes will suffice when the decision to terminate life support is at issue.'' *Id.* at 891. The factors outlined by the court when determining the existence of clear and convincing evidence of a patient's intention to reject life prolonged by artificial means were

- the persistence of statements regarding an individual's beliefs,
- the desirability of the commitment to those beliefs,
- the seriousness with which such statements were made, and
- the inferences that may be drawn from the surrounding circumstances.

The Missouri Supreme Court has followed the *Westchester* ruling and has held that the family of a woman who has been in a persistent vegetative state since 1983 cannot order doctors to remove artificial nutrition. *Cruzan v. Harman*, No. 70813 (Mo. Nov. 12, 1988). The U.S. Supreme Court is expected to render a decision on this case by the summer of 1990, the first time it has dealt with a right-to-die case, and will decide whether there are constitutional rights to privacy and liberty to be free from unwarranted bodily intrusions by the state broad enough to allow Cruzan's family to disconnect the feeding tubes. The court's decision will have a major impact on right-to-die cases across the nation. It is anticipated that the court's reasoning will clear up some of the confusion in existing state laws.

THE LEGISLATIVE RESPONSE

California was the first state to enact what has been called a Natural Death or Living Will Act in 1976. Cal. Health & Safety Code §§ 7185–95 (West 1983). California's legislation is typical of similar laws that exist in 40 other states that allow the creation of documents that provide a legally recognized way for competent adults to express in advance their desires regarding life-crucial medical decisions in the event they become terminally ill and death is imminent. While most of the statutes fail to cover incompetents, cases like *Quinlan* and *Saikewicz* created a constitutionally protected obligation to terminate the incurable incompetent's life when the doctrine of substituted judgment is used by guardians. Further, some states provide for proxy consent in the form of durable power of attorney statutes. Generally, these involve the designation of a proxy to speak on the incompetent incurable's behalf.[12] They represent a combination of the intimate wishes of the patient and the medical recommendations of the physicians.

The oral declarations are accepted only after the patient has been declared terminally ill. Moreover, the declarant bears the responsibility of informing the doctor to ensure that the document becomes a part of the medical record. The California statute provides that the document be re-executed after five years. Other statutes differ in the length of time of effectiveness. The majority of states allow the document to be effective until revoked by the individual. To revoke, the patient must sign and date a new writing, destroy the first document himself or herself, direct another to destroy the first document in his or her presence, or orally state to the physician an intent to revoke.[13] The effect of the directive varies among the jurisdictions. However, there is unanimity in the promulgation of regulations that specifically authorize health care personnel to honor the directives without fear of incurring liability. The highest court of New York in *In re Eichner*, 52 N.Y.2d 363, 420 N.E.2d 64 (1981), complied with the request of a guardian to withdraw life-support systems from an 83-year-old brain-damaged priest. The court reached its result by finding the patient's previously expressed wishes to be determinative.

Although many interest groups hailed the enactments of natural death or living will acts as providing the solution to the difficult problems inherent in euthanasia situations, the statutes present inadequacies that must be addressed. A person drafting a living will when healthy and mentally competent cannot predict how he or she will feel at the time of a terminal illness. Moreover, unless the document is updated regularly, how can it be ascertained that the document actually reflects what the patient wishes? If a proxy is used and that proxy is a close family member, there could be the danger of a conflict of interest, emotionally or legally. Guidelines must be unified and tightened in order to offer better guidance to physicians and courts.

Now that there is increasing acceptance of the right to end what has been deemed extraordinary care for the terminally ill, a relatively new dilemma has emerged.

FEEDING TUBES

Theologians and ethicists have long recognized a distinction between ordinary and extraordinary medical care. The theological distinction is based on the belief that life as a gift from God should not be deliberately destroyed by humans. Therefore, extraordinary therapies that extend life by imposing grave burdens on the patient and family are not required. A patient, however, has an ethical and moral obligation to accept ordinary or life-sustaining treatment.[14] Although the courts have accepted decisions to withhold or withdraw extraordinary care, especially the respirator, from those who are comatose or in a persistent vegetative state with no possibility of emerging, they have been unwilling until now to discontinue feeding, which they have considered ordinary care.

However, in 1985, the case of *In the Matter of Claire C. Conroy*, 486 A.2d 1209 (N.J. Sup. Ct. 1985), was heard by the New Jersey Supreme Court. The case involved an 84-year-old nursing home patient whose nephew petitioned the court for authority to remove the nasogastric tube that was feeding her. The supreme court overturned the appellate division decision and held that life-sustaining treatment, including nasogastric feeding, could be withheld or withdrawn from incompetent nursing home patients who will, according to physicians, die within one year, in three specific circumstances.

1. when it is clear that the particular patient would have refused the treatment under the circumstances involved ("the subjective test")
2. when there is some indication of the patient's wishes (but she has not "unequivocally expressed" her desires before becoming incompetent) and the treatment "would only prolong suffering" ("the limited objective test")
3. when there is no evidence at all of the patient's wishes, but the treatment "clearly and markedly outweighs the benefits the patient derives from life" ("the pure-objective test" based on pain)

A procedure involving notification of the state Office of the Ombudsman is required before withdrawing or withholding treatment under any of the three tests. The ombudsman must make a separate decision. *Id.* at 1232.

The court also found tubal feeding to be a medical treatment, and as such, it is as intrusive as other life-sustaining measures are. The court in its analysis emphasized duty, rather than causation, with the result that medical personnel acting in good faith will be protected from liability. If physicians follow the *Quinlan/ Conroy* standards and decide to end medical treatment of a patient, the duty to continue treatment ceases; thus, the termination of treatment becomes a lawful act.

Although *Conroy* presents case-specific guidelines, there is concern that the opinion will have far-reaching repercussions. There is fear that decisions to discontinue treatment will not be based on the "balancing of interests" test, but rather that a "quality of life" test similar to that used by Hitler will be utilized to end the lives of severely senile, very old, decrepit, and burdensome people.[15]

However, at least in one recent situation, the New Jersey ombudsman denied a request to remove feeding tubes from a comatose nursing home patient.[16] In applying the *Conroy* tests, the ombudsman decided that Hilda Peterson might live more than one year, the period that *Conroy* decided was a criterion before life support can be removed.

To further complicate this issue, on March 17, 1986, the American Medical Association changed its Code of Ethics on comas. Now doctors may ethically withhold food, water, and medical treatment from patients in irreversible comas or persistent vegetative states with no hope of recovery—even if death is not imminent.[17] While doctors can consider the wishes of the patient and family or the legal representatives, they cannot intentionally cause death. The wording is permissive so those doctors who feel uncomfortable in withdrawing food and water may refrain from doing so. The AMA's decision does not comfort those who fear abuse or mistake in euthanasia decisions, nor does it have any legal value as such. There are doctors, nurses, and families who are unscrupulous and have their own, and not the patient's, interests in mind. Even with the *Conroy* decision and the American Medical Association's Code of Ethics change, the feeding tube issue is not settled.

On April 23, 1986, the New Jersey Superior Court ruled that the husband of severely brain damaged Nancy Jobes may order the removal of her life-sustaining feeding tube, which would ultimately cause the 31-year-old comatose patient, who has been in a vegetative state in a hospice for the past six years, to starve to death. *In re Jobes*, 510 A.2d 133 (N.J. App. 1986). Medical experts testified that the patient could, under optimal conditions, live another 30 years. Relieving the nursing home officials from performing the act on one of its residents, the court ruled that the patient may be taken home to die (with the removal to be supervised by a physician and medical care to be provided to the patient at home).

The nursing home had petitioned the court for the appointment of a "life advocate" to fight for continuation of medical treatment for Mrs. Jobes, which, it argued, would save her life. The court disallowed the appointment of a life advocate, holding that case law does not support the requirement of the continuation of life-support systems in all circumstances. Such a requirement, continued the court, would contradict the patient's right of privacy.

The court's decision applied "the principles enunciated in *Quinlan* and . . . *Conroy*" and the "recent ruling by the American Medical Association's Council on Judicial Affairs that the provision of food and water is, under certain circumstances, a medical treatment like any other and may be discontinued when the physician and family of the patient feel it is no longer benefiting the patient."[18]

The Illinois Supreme Court in *In re Estate Longeway*, 139 Ill. Dec. 780 (1989), agreed with the logic of the *Jobes* decision and other sister state rulings regarding the characterization of artificial nutrition and hydration as medical treatment. The Illinois court found that the authorized guardian of a terminally ill patient in an irreversible coma or persistent vegetative state has a common law right to refuse artificial nutrition and hydration. The court found that there must be clear and convincing evidence that the refusal is consistent with the patient's interest. The court also required the concurrence of the patient's attending physician and two other physicians. "Court intervention is also necessary to guard against the remote, yet real possibility that greed may taint the judgment of the surrogate decisionmaker." *Id.* at 790. Dissenting, Judge Ward said, "[t]he right to refuse treatment is rooted in and dependent upon the patient's capacity for informed decision, which an incompetent patient lacks." *Id.* at 793.

In addition, Elizabeth Bouvia, a mentally competent cerebral palsy victim, has won her struggle to have feeding tubes removed even though she is not terminally ill. *Bouvia v. Superior Court (Glenchur)*, 225 Cal. Rptr. 297 (Ct. App. 1986). The California Court of Appeals announced on April 16, 1986, that she can go home to die. The appeal court found that Miss Bouvia's decision to "let nature take its course" did not amount to a choice to commit suicide with people aiding and abetting it. The court stated that it is not "illegal or immoral to prefer a natural, albeit sooner, death than a drugged life attached to a mechanical device." *Id.* at 306. The court's finding that it was a moral and philosophical question, not a legal or medical one, leaves one wondering if the courts are opening the door to permitting "legal starvation" to be used by those who are not terminally ill, but who do wish to commit suicide.

To further complicate the issue, there are those in the health care field who are using their knowledge to develop new instruments of death to assist those who are terminally ill and want to end their lives. Dr. Jack Kevorkian of Michigan announced in October 1989 that he had developed a device that will end one's life quickly, painlessly, and humanely.[19] He described his invention as a metal pole with bottles containing three solutions that feed into a common IV line. When the IV is inserted into the patient's vein, a harmless saline solution will flow to clean the line of air. The patient can then flip a switch causing an anesthetic to render the patient unconscious. Sixty seconds later, a lethal dose of potassium chloride will flow into the patient, causing heart seizure and death. The news of this invention motivated the medical community and society at large to repeat their fear that individuals would abuse euthanasia in spite of any safeguards that are in place.

DO NOT RESUSCITATE ORDERS

Do not resuscitate (DNR) orders are written by physicians and placed on the medical charts of patients, indicating that in the event of a cardiac or respiratory arrest, no resuscitative measures should be employed to revive the patient. Many states have acknowledged the validity of DNR orders in cases involving terminally ill patients where no objections to such orders are made by the patient's family.

The official Compilation of Codes, Rules and Regulations, Title 10(c) of the State of New York provides:

> The hospital shall adopt and implement written policies and procedures governing orders not to attempt cardiopulmonary resuscitation of a patient where consent has been obtained and ensure the clarification of the rights and obligations of patients, their families, and health care providers regarding cardiopulmonary resuscitation and the issuance of orders not to resuscitate. Such policies assure that:
> (1) each patient who consents to an order not to resuscitate is informed of the range of available resuscitation measures, consistent with the hospital's equipment and facilities; and
> (2) all staff involved in the care of any person for whom an order not to resuscitate has been issued are promptly informed of the order, including any limitations or other instructions.

Chapter V, Part 400, Section 405.43, 12/31/88.

Figures 14-1 and 14-2 illustrate and summarize the numerous ramifications of euthanasia, as discussed in this chapter.

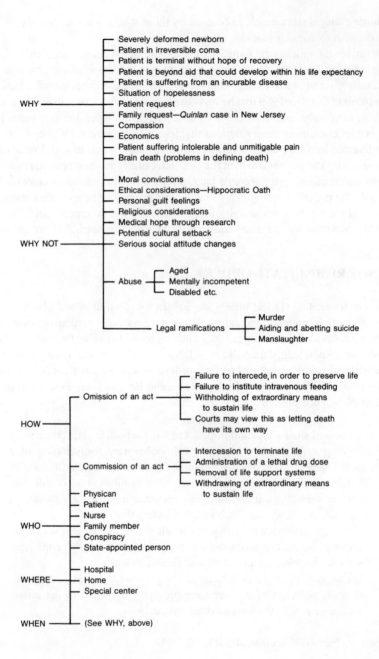

Figure 14-1 Considerations in Euthanasia

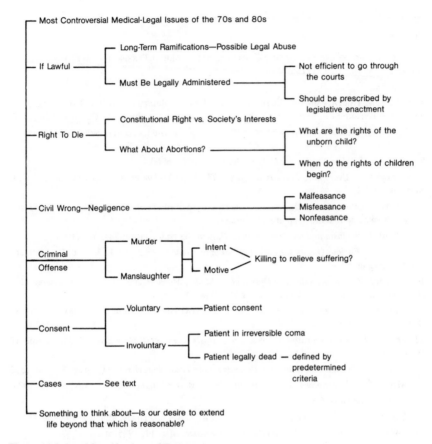

Figure 14-2 Legal Ramifications of Euthanasia

CONCLUSION

Any discussion of euthanasia obliges a person to confront a human's greatest fear—death. The courts and legislatures have faced it and have made advances in setting forth some guidelines to assist decision makers in this area. However, more must be accomplished. Society must be protected from the risks associated with permitting the removal of life-support systems. We cannot allow the complex issues associated with this topic to be simplified to the point where we accept that life can be terminated based on subjective quality-of-life considerations. The legal system must assure that the constitutional rights of the patient will be maintained, while at the same time protecting society's interests in preserving life, preventing suicide, and maintaining the integrity of the medical profession.

NOTES

1. GILLON, SUICIDE AND VOLUNTARY EUTHANASIA: HISTORICAL PERSPECTIVE IN EUTHANASIA AND THE RIGHT TO DEATH 173 (1969).

2. *Id.* at 182.

3. S. REISER, THE DILEMMA OF EUTHANASIA IN MODERN MEDICAL HISTORY: THE ENGLISH AND AMERICAN EXPERIENCE, ETHICS IN MEDICINE PERSPECTIVES AND MEDICAL CONCERNS 20 (1977).

4. WEBSTER'S THIRD NEW INTERNATIONAL DICTIONARY OF THE ENGLISH LANGUAGE UNABRIDGED 786 (1976).

5. Wallis, *To Feed or Not To Feed?* TIME, Mar. 31, 1986, at 60.

6. Sherlock, *For Everything There Is A Season: The Right To Die in the United States*, B.Y.U. L. REV. 545 (1982).

7. Karen Ann Quinlan, at age 22, was in a coma due to an overdose of valium and alcohol. As a result, she was hooked up to a life-supporting respirator.

8. Gelford, *Euthanasia and the Terminally Ill Patient*, 63 NEB L. REV. 741, 747 (1984).

9. Coyle, *Fast Furious Questioning Marks Session on Coma Case*, NAT'L L. J., Dec. 18, 1989, at 8; Wallis, *supra* note 5.

10. Connery, *Prolonging Life: The Duty and Its Limits, Moral Responsibility in Prolonging Life's Decisions*, in TO TREAT OR NOT TO TREAT 25 (1984).

11. AMA HOUSE OF DELEGATES, RESOLUTION 77—STATEMENT OF MEDICAL OPINION RE: "BRAIN DEATH" (June 1974).

12. *The Physician's Responsibility Toward Hopelessly Ill Patients*, NEW ENGL. J. MED., Apr. 12, 1984, at 955.

13. Novak, *"Natural Death Acts": Let Patients Refuse Treatment*, HOSPITALS, Aug. 1, 1984, at 72.

14. McCormick, *To Save or Let Die: The Dilemma of Modern Medicine* 229 J. A.M.A. 172 (1974).

15. Wallis, *supra* note 5.

16. Sullivan, *Ombudsman Bars Food Tube Removal*, New York Times, March 7, 1986, at 82.

17. *AMA Changes Code of Ethics on Comas*, NEWSDAY, Mar. 17, 1986, at 2.

18. *Man Wins Right To Let Wife Die*, NEWSDAY, Apr. 24, 1986, at 3.

19. Fireman, *MD Invents Mercy Death Device*, NEWSDAY, Oct. 27, 1989, at 6.

Chapter 15

Insurance

Today, almost everyone has some form of insurance. We insure our automobiles against collision and theft and our homes against fire. We insure our personal property, ourselves, and the members of our family. Professionals buy insurance to protect themselves from suit in the event that others are injured as a result of their professional services.

The upward spiral of malpractice claims and insurance premiums continues to plague the health care industry. The increase in claims has not only presented practical and professional difficulties for health care professionals, but has also significantly affected the availability, as well as the cost, of insurance. Many commercial insurance carriers have discontinued writing professional liability coverage since the mid to late 1970s. As a result, some states required insurance carriers to join a consortium of insurance companies in order to underwrite medical malpractice insurance. These consortiums were referred to as *joint underwriting associations*. According to one study, there were only 12 such consortiums in 1986.[1]

Insurance is a contract in which the insurer agrees to assume certain risks of the insured for consideration, or payment of a premium. Under the terms of the contract, also known as the insurance policy, the insurer promises to pay a specific amount of money if a specified event takes place. An insurance policy contains three necessary elements: (1) identification of the risk involved, (2) the specific amount payable, and (3) the specified occurrence.

A risk is the possibility that a loss will occur. The major function of insurance is to provide security against this loss. Insurance does not prevent or hinder the occurrence of the loss, but it does compensate for the damages.

An insured individual may be exposed to three categories of risk: (1) risk of property loss or damage, (2) personal risk or loss of life, and (3) legal liability. Property risk is the possibility that an insured's property may be damaged or destroyed by fire, flood, tornado, hurricane, or other catastrophe. Personal risk is the possibility that the insured may be injured in an accident or may become ill; the possibility of death is a personal risk covered in the typical life insurance plan. Legal liability risk is the possibility that the insured may become legally liable to pay money damages to another and includes accident and professional liability insurance. The various types of policies include (1) occurrence policies, which cover all incidents that arise during a policy year, regardless of when they are reported, and (2) claims-made policies, which cover only those claims made or reported during the policy year, regardless of when they occurred or were paid.

Insurance companies are required by the laws of the various states to issue only policies that contain certain mandated provisions and to maintain certain financial reserves to guarantee to policyholders that their expectations will be met when the coverage is needed. The basic underlying concept of insurance is the spreading of risk. By writing coverage for a large enough pool of individuals, the company has determined actuarially that a certain number of claims will arise within that pool, and if the premium structure has been established correctly and the prediction of claims made accurately, the company ought to be able to meet those claims and return a profit to its shareholders.

MANDATED MEDICAL STAFF INSURANCE COVERAGE

Many hospitals require physicians to carry their own malpractice insurance. A U.S. district court in New Orleans has ruled that a hospital has the legal right to suspend a staff physician for failing to comply with its requirement that physicians carry medical malpractice insurance coverage. The decision resulted from a suit brought against Methodist Hospital in New Orleans by a physician whose staff privileges were suspended because he failed to comply with a newly adopted hospital requirement that all staff physicians provide proof of malpractice coverage of at least $1 million. The court rejected the physician's charges that the requirement violated his civil rights and antitrust laws. *Pollack v. Methodist Hospital*, 392 F. Supp. 393 (E.D. La. 1975).

The court of appeals in *Wilkinson v. Madera Community Hospital*, 144 Cal. App. 3d 436, 192 Cal. Rptr. 593 (1983), held that a Health and Safety Code section providing that a health facility may require every member of its medical staff to have professional liability insurance as a condition to being on staff was not an unconstitutional delegation of legislative authority to hospitals as insurance companies. Dr. Wilkinson was refused reappointment because he failed to maintain malpractice insurance with a "recognized insurance company" as required by the hospital.

An interesting twist to requiring physicians to purchase malpractice insurance is that of requiring hospitals to purchase or provide excess insurance coverage for physicians and dentists. In New York State, the Medical Malpractice Law, Chapter 294 of the Laws of 1985, mandates that $1 million excess coverage be provided to physicians and dentists requesting such coverage who are primarily affiliated with a specific hospital. In order to qualify for coverage, the applicant must have a primary policy of $1 million for each claimant and $3 million aggregate. The legislation provides that hospitals be reimbursed through adjustments in their reimbursement rates.

RISK OF LIABILITY

A nurse or a physician who provides professional services to another person for pay may be legally responsible for any harm the person suffers as a result of negligence; furthermore, the nurse or the physician may be subject to a loss of money in the form of legally awarded damages. Many professionals protect themselves from the risk of a legal loss by acquiring a professional liability insurance policy. The court of appeals, on rehearing en banc, in *Jones v. Medox, Inc.*, 413 A.2d 1288, 430 A.2d 488 (D.C. 1981), held that only the nurse's insurance carrier, Globe Insurance, was liable for injuries sustained by the plaintiff while at Doctors Hospital; these injuries resulted from an injection administered by the nurse. Ms. Jones was employed by Medox, Inc., a corporation providing temporary medical personnel to Doctors Hospital. Following settlement of the claim against the nurse, the hospital, and the nurse's employer, the nurse and her insurer brought an action against Doctors Hospital, Medox, Inc., and their insurers. The superior court had granted summary judgment in favor of the hospital and its insurer and dismissed the claim against Medox, Inc., and its insurer.

The Supreme Court of New Jersey in *American Nurses Association v. Passaic General Hospital*, 98 N.J. 83, 484 A.2d 670 (1984), held that the nurse's insurance policy was primary with respect to the first $100,000 of a settlement that resulted from a malpractice action against the nurse. The National Fire Insurance Company had issued an insurance policy covering the contractual obligation of the American Nurses Association to its members. The court also held that the judgment against the nurse in excess of $100,000 was properly apportioned equally between the hospital's liability insurer and the nurses association's liability insurer.

The potential for liability is not limited to licensed professionals. Students engaged in learning a profession and paraprofessionals such as therapists, etc., who engage in activities involving the care and treatment of others face potential liability for their acts. For this reason, these individuals often obtain personal insurance coverage or assure themselves of such coverage through the institution in which they are employed or the institution in which they are enrolled to obtain their education. The process by which an institution provides coverage by pledging its assets to the defense and payment for claims against its employees or agents is known as *indemnification*.

An example of the necessity of insurance coverage for a licensed professional is provided by the private duty nurse. A private duty nurse is not an employee of an institution, but rather is engaged by the patient (or the patient's family) to provide services to that patient. As such, the nurse should obtain personal coverage. In fact, the patient engaging the nurse would be well advised to ask about the availability of such coverage, as would the institution in which the nurse is functioning on behalf of that patient.

THE PROFESSIONAL LIABILITY INSURANCE POLICY

A nurse or physician who is covered by a professional liability insurance policy must recognize the rights and duties inherent in the policy. The professional should be able to identify the risks that are covered, the amount of coverage, and the conditions of the contract.

Although the policies of different insurance companies may vary, the standard policy usually says the insurance company will "pay on behalf of the insured all sums which the insured shall become legally obligated to pay as damages because of injury arising out of malpractice error, or mistake in rendering or failing to render professional services."

A standard liability insurance policy has five distinct parts: (1) the insurance agreement, (2) defense and settlement, (3) the policy period, (4) the amount payable, and (5) conditions.

Insurance Agreement

The insurer, under the terms of the policy, has no obligation to pay any sum over and above the legal liability and will not pay a sum of money merely because the insured feels a moral obligation toward an injured party.

Under a professional liability policy, the professional is protected from damages arising from rendering or failing to render professional services. Thus, a professional who performs a negligent act resulting in legal liability or who fails to perform a necessary act (thereby incurring damages) is personally protected from paying an injured party. The actual payment of the legal money damages to the injured party is made by the insurer.

Defense and Settlement

In the defense and settlement portion of the insurance policy, the insured and the insurance company agree that the company will defend any lawsuit against the insured arising from performance or nonperformance of professional services and that the company is delegated the power to effect a settlement of any claims as it deems necessary. A policy stating that the insurer will provide a defense of all lawsuits guarantees such a defense in any suit including those that are groundless, false, or fraudulent. In the case of a professional liability policy, the duty of the insurer under this clause is limited to the defense of lawsuits against the insured that are a consequence of professional services.

The insurance company fulfills its obligation to provide defense by engaging the services of an attorney on behalf of the insured. The obligation of the attorney is to the insured directly since the insured is the attorney's client. Of course, there is, to some extent, a divided loyalty since the attorney looks to the insurance company to obtain business. Nevertheless, the attorney-client relationship exists only between the attorney and the insured, and the insured has the right to expect the attorney to fulfill the requirements of such relationship.

If an insurance company has established the right to obtain a settlement of any claim before trial, the company's only obligation is to act reasonably and not to the detriment of the insured.

Policy Period

The period of the policy is always stated in the insurance contract. The contract provides protection only for risks that occur during the time when the policy is stated to be effective. Any incident that occurs before or after the policy period would not be covered under the insuring agreement. Claims-made policies provide coverage for only those claims instituted during the policy period. Occurrence policies provide coverage for all claims that may arise out of a policy period. The actual reporting time has no bearing on the validity of the claim as long as it is filed before the applicable statute of limitations runs out. While the reporting time has no bearing on the validity of the claim from the standpoint of coverage under the policy, the conditions of the policy will require notice within a specified time, and the failure to provide such notice to the insurer within such time may void the insurer's obligation under the policy.

Amount Payable

The amount to be paid by the insurer is determined by the amount of damage suffered by the injured party. This determination may be made by a jury, or the insurance company and the injured party may reach a settlement before the lawsuit comes to trial or before the jury has determined the amount of damages.[2] In any event, the insurance company will pay the injured party no more than the maximum coverage stated in the insurance policy. The insured professional must personally pay any damages not covered by the policy.

Under a policy with maximum coverage of $40,000 for each claim and $120,000 for aggregate claims, the aggregate claims figure is the total amount payable to all injured parties. Thus, the insured is protected on each individual claim up to $40,000; when there is more than one claim, the insured is protected up to $40,000 on each claim up to three claims. Should there be more than three claims, the aggregate $120,000 is spread across all claims, but payment will not exceed $40,000 on any one claim.

Conditions of the Policy

Each insurance policy contains a number of important conditions. Failure to comply with these conditions may cause forfeiture of the policy and nonpayment of claims against it. Generally, insurance policies contain the following conditions:

- *Notice of occurrence*—When the insured becomes aware that an injury has occurred as a result of acts covered under the contract, the insured must promptly notify the insurance company. The form of notice may be either oral or written, as specified in the policy.

- *Notice of claim*—Whenever the insured receives notice that a claim or suit is being instituted, notice must be sent by the insured to the insurance company. The policy will specify what papers are to be forwarded to the company. Note that failure to provide timely notification in accordance with the terms of a policy may void the insurer's obligation under the policy. It may not matter that the insurer has in no way been prejudiced by the late notification. The mere fact that the insured has failed to carry out its obligations under the policy may be sufficient to permit the insurer to avoid its obligations. Where the insurer has refused to honor a claim because of late notice and the insured wishes to challenge such refusal, a declaratory judgment action can be brought, asking a court to determine the reasonableness of the insurer's position.

- *Assistance of the insured*—The insured must cooperate with the insurance company and render any assistance necessary to reach a settlement.

- *Other insurance*—If the insured has pertinent insurance policies with other insurance companies, the insured must notify the insurance company in order that each company may pay the appropriate amount of the claim.

- *Assignment*—The protections contracted for by the insured may not be transferred unless permission is granted by the insurance company. Because the insurance company was aware of the risks the insured would encounter before the policy was issued, the company will endeavor to avoid protecting persons other than the policyholder.

- *Subrogation*—This is the right of a person who pays another's debt to be substituted for all rights in relation to the debt. When an insurance company makes a payment for the insured under the terms of the policy, the company becomes the beneficiary of all the rights of recovery the insured has against any other persons who may also have been negligent. For example, if several nurses were found liable for negligence arising from the same occurrence and the insurance company for one nurse pays the entire claim, the company will be entitled to the rights of that nurse and may collect a proportionate share of the claim from the other nurses.

- *Changes*—The insured cannot make changes in the policy without the written consent of the insurance company. Thus, an agent of the insurance company ordinarily cannot modify or remove any condition of the liability contract. Only the insurance company, by written authorization, may permit a condition to be altered or removed.

- *Cancellation*—A cancellation clause spells out the conditions and procedures necessary for the insured or the insurer to cancel the liability policy. Written notice is usually required. The insured person's failure to comply with any of the conditions can result in nonpayment of a claim by the insurance company. An insurance policy is a contract, and failure to meet the terms and conditions of the contract may result in the penalties associated with breach of contract, such as nonpayment of claims.

MEDICAL PROFESSIONAL LIABILITY INSURANCE

The fundamental tenets of insurance law and their application to the typical liability insurance policy are pertinent to the provisions of medical professional liability insurance as applied to individuals and institutions. Professional liability policies vary in the broadness, the exclusions from coverage, and the interpretations a company places on the language of the contract.

There are three medical professional liability classes:

1. Individuals including (but not limited to) physicians, surgeons, dentists, nurses, osteopaths, chiropodists, chiropractors, opticians, physiotherapists, optometrists, and various types of medical technicians. This category may also include medical laboratories, blood banks, and optical establishments.
2. Hospitals and related institutions such as extended care facilities, homes for the aged, institutions for the mentally ill, sanitariums, and other health institutions where bed and board are provided for patients or residents.
3. Clinics, dispensaries, and infirmaries where there are no regular bed or board facilities. These institutions may be related to industrial or commercial enterprises; however, they are to be distinguished from facilities operated by dentists or physicians, which are usually covered under individual professional liability contracts.

The insuring clause will usually provide for payment on behalf of the insured if an injury arises from:

- malpractice, error, or mistake in rendering or failing to render professional services in the practice of the insured's profession during the policy period; or
- acts or omissions on the part of the insured during the policy period as a member of a formal accreditation or similar professional board or committee of a hospital or a professional society.

The injury is not limited to bodily injury or property damage. However, it must result from malpractice, error, mistake, or failure to perform acts that should have been performed.

The most common risks covered by medical professional liability insurance are (1) negligence, (2) assault and battery as a result of failing to obtain consent to a medical or surgical procedure, (3) libel and slander, and (4) invasion of privacy for betrayal of professional confidences. Coverage varies from company to company because of differences in interpretation of the same or similar language. The premium rates for each state are generally established by either the state legislature or the insurance company and the rates can differ for individuals by profession and specialty, hospitals, and clinics.

TRUSTEE COVERAGE

Hospital trustees should be covered by liability insurance just as physicians and other health professionals. In *Lynch v. Redfield Foundation*, 9 Cal. App. 3d 293, 88 Cal. Rptr. 86 (1970), a California bank refused to honor corporate drafts unless all trustees concurred. They could not agree, and the noninterest-bearing account continued to grow in principal from $4,900 to $47,000 over a five-year period. Although two trustees did try to carry on corporate functions despite the dissident trustee, their good faith did not protect them from liability in this case. The money could have been transferred to at least an interest-bearing account without the third trustee's signature. The trustees were held jointly liable to pay to the corporation the statutory rate of simple interest.

Before an insurer writing trustees' coverage (generally known as directors' and officers' liability insurance) will respond to defend and/or pay on behalf of a trustee, it must be shown that the trustee acted in good faith and within the scope of his or her responsibilities. Ordinarily, coverage would not be afforded where a trustee is accused by the hospital of acting improperly in his or her relationship with the hospital. In addition, insurance coverage for officers' and directors' liability generally excludes as a covered event the failure to obtain insurance. Thus, if the hospital is held liable in an instance where insurance coverage normally would have been available and the hospital has failed to procure such coverage, the hospital cannot take action against its trustees and through the mechanism of the officers' and directors' liability policy hope to avail itself of such coverage.

In cases involving medical staff members and hospital financial transactions, trustees can find themselves involved on a personal basis. Directors' and officers' liability coverage should be provided for trustees. Such coverage is helpful to hospitals in attracting qualified individuals to serve as directors on their boards.

MEDICAL MALPRACTICE INSURANCE ASSOCIATIONS

The difficulty that hospitals or physicians have in obtaining malpractice insurance in a number of states has caused the formation of medical malpractice insurance associations. The purpose of these associations is to provide a market for hospitals and/or physicians who are unable to obtain medical malpractice insurance on the open market at a reasonable price. Legislation generally requires all insurance carriers engaged in writing personal liability insurance within a particular state to provide coverage for physicians and hospitals.

SELF-INSURANCE

Skyrocketing medical malpractice insurance premiums have often produced situations in which the premium cost of insurance has approached and, on occasion, actually reached the face amount of the policy. Due to the extremely high cost of maintaining such insurance, some hospitals have sought alternatives to this conventional means of protecting against medical malpractice. One alternative that is becoming increasingly popular is self-insurance. When a hospital self-insures its malpractice risks, it no longer purchases a policy of malpractice insurance, but instead periodically sets aside a certain amount of its own funds as a reserve against malpractice losses and expenses. A hospital that self-insures generally retains the services of a self-insurance consulting firm and of an actuary to determine the proper level of funding that the hospital should follow.

A self-insurance program need not involve the elimination of insurance coverage in its entirety. A hospital may find it prudent to purchase excess coverage whereby the hospital self-insures the first agreed-on dollar amount of risk and the insurance carrier insures the balance. For example, in a typical program the hospital may self-insure the first $1 million of professional liability risk per year. Since the vast majority of claims against the hospital will be disposed of within such limitation, the cost of excess insurance may be quite reasonable.

Before a hospital makes a decision to self-insure, not only must it determine the economic aspects of such a decision and the necessary funding levels to maintain an adequate reserve for future claims, but also it must determine whether there are any legal impediments to such program. A hospital that has obtained funding from governmental sources or that has issued bonds or other obligations containing certain covenants may find itself unable to self-insure because of these prior commitments. Hospitals are urged to consult their counsel to review appropriate and applicable documentation before making the self-insurance decision.

OTHER INSURANCE COVERAGES

Besides insurance coverage for liability risks, a hospital is typically involved in numerous other insurance situations. For example, a hospital provides fringe benefits to its employees that may include health insurance, disability insurance, life insurance, and a pension or other retirement plan also involving insurance. These programs require appropriate administration and create rights and obligations on the part of the hospital and the hospital personnel. Many legal disputes arise within a hospital (and other employment settings) regarding the rights of employees under such programs. Such issues as eligibility for coverage, coverage for particular circumstances, termination of coverage, etc., can give rise to substantial legal problems and possibly even litigation.

Other insurance coverages in which a hospital will be involved include coverages for the hospital's physical plant, motor vehicles, and, where applicable, construction projects. In the course of a construction project, appropriate insurance coverages for liability risks, fire risks, and other similar hazards must be considered. In addition, the requirement that contractors obtain a payment and performance bond to ensure the completion of their work and the payment of all subcontractors and material suppliers is important. Substantial litigation can arise during the course of or at the conclusion of a construction project involving large sums of money because of inappropriate construction, the failure to complete construction, or the failure to follow plans and/or specifications, live up to expectations, or adhere to schedules.

Insurance is a contract that creates legal obligations on the part of both the insured and the insurer. Moreover, certain individuals (e.g., hospital employees) may be in the classification of third party beneficiaries by virtue of their relationship to the insured.

INVESTIGATION AND SETTLEMENT OF CLAIMS

An injured party may urge settlement of a claim before instituting legal action. The majority of malpractice claims are settled before reaching the courtroom. A study by the U.S. General Accounting Office indicates that approximately 90 percent of malpractice claims are settled in this manner.[3]

As a first step toward settlement of a claim, the insurance carrier may send an investigator to interview a claimant regarding the details of the alleged occurrence that led to the injury. Itemization of damages (e.g., lost wages and medical expenses) and a request for a physical examination may be made by the insurance company. Following an investigation, the insurance company may agree to a settlement if liability is questionable and the risks proceeding to trial are too great. Should settlement negotiations fail, an attorney may be employed by the injured party to negotiate a settlement. If the attorney fails to obtain a settlement, either the claim is dropped, or legal action is commenced. If the claim is settled, a general release is signed by the plaintiff, surrendering the right of action against the defendant. Should the claimant be married, a general release must also be obtained from the spouse since there may be a cause of action because of loss of the injured spouse's services, such as companionship. A parent's release surrenders only a parental claim. Approval of the court is necessary to release a child's claim. Release by a minor may in some instances be repudiated by the minor upon reaching majority.

Intoxication, the influence of drugs, shock, and/or extreme pain can prevent sufficient understanding of a general release and therefore prevent or void its execution. The same may apply in cases where the signer of a general release does not understand the language, has not had the opportunity to obtain appropriate legal consultation, or has been subjected to mental or physical duress. Misrepresentation or fraud can void an agreement. Those who are mentally incompetent cannot give a valid release. In this instance, a court-appointed guardian is required to execute a release on behalf of a mental incompetent, and a court must pass on the terms of any settlement.

NOTES

1. NATIONAL ASSOCIATION OF INDEPENDENT INSURERS, REPORT OF THE FINANCIAL SOLVENCY OF STATE MEDICAL MALPRACTICE JUAs TO THE NAII LAWS COMMITTEE, 1986.

2. Some states have provisions mandating that prior to any settlement of a negligence claim, consent of the court or, in the alternative, a medical malpractice panel to any proposed resolution must be obtained in order to best protect the minor's interests.

3. U.S. GENERAL ACCOUNTING OFFICE, MEDICAL MALPRACTICE, CHARACTERISTICS OF CLAIMS CLOSED IN 1984 (April 1987).

Chapter 16

Labor Relations

The relationship between employers and employees is regulated by both state and federal laws (and, to a lesser extent, local laws). Hospitals are not exempt from the impact of these laws and therefore are required to take into account such matters as employment practices (wages, hours, and working conditions), union activity, worker's compensation laws, occupational safety and health laws, and employment discrimination laws.[1] *Central Dispensary & Emergency Hospital*, 44 N.L.R.B. 533 (1942), *enforced*, 145 F.2d 852 (D.C. Cir. 1944), *cert. denied*, 324 U.S. 847 (1945).

Federal or state regulation generally pervades all areas of employer-employee relationships. The trend is toward greater involvement of the federal government in matters of labor relations. The most significant piece of federal legislation dealing with labor relations is the National Labor Relations Act. While federal laws generally take precedence over state laws where there is a conflict between the state and the federal laws, state laws are applicable and must be considered, especially where the state standards are more stringent than those mandated by the federal government. *San Diego Building Trades Council v. Garmon,* 359 U.S. 236 (1959).

UNIONS AND HOSPITALS

The hospital employee is likely to be more concerned with labor relations than is a person who is privately employed. Unions have only recently become a large factor in hospital-employee relations. Until the mid-1930s, union organizational activity in hospitals was minimal, and until the late 1950s, it increased relatively slowly. However, unions now play a significant role in hospital-employee relations.

A variety of labor organizations are now heavily involved in attempts to become the recognized collective bargaining representatives in the hospital field. There are craft unions which devote their primary organizing efforts to skilled employees, such as carpenters and electricians; industrial unions and unions of governmental employees, which seek to represent large groups of unskilled or semiskilled employees; and professional and occupational associations and societies, such as state nurses associations, which are interested in representing their members. To the extent that the professional organizations seek goals directly concerned with wages, hours, and other employment conditions and engage in bargaining on behalf of employees, they perform the functions of labor unions.

Union activity in the hospital field has generally been successful in the geographical areas where unions have been successful in other industries. It is not unreasonable to assume that this pattern will continue.

FEDERAL LABOR ACTS

National Labor Relations Act

The National Labor Relations Act (NLRA)[2] was enacted in 1935. It defines certain conduct of employers and employees as unfair labor practices and provides for hearings on complaints that such practices have occurred. This act was modified by the Taft-Hartley amendments of 1947 and the Landrum-Griffin amendments of 1959.

Jurisdiction

Nearly all proprietary hospitals have, for some time, been subject to the provisions of the NLRA. The National Labor Relations Board (NLRB), which is entrusted with enforcing and administering the act, has jurisdiction over matters involving proprietary and not-for-profit hospitals with gross revenues of at least $250,000 per year and nurses associations and health-care-related facilities with gross revenues over $100,000 per year.[3] *Butte Medical Properties*, 168 N.L.R.B. 52 (1967).

An exemption for governmental hospitals was included in the 1935 enactment of the National Labor Relations Act, and charitable hospitals were exempted in 1947 by the Taft-Hartley Act amendments to the NLRA.[4] However, a July 1974 amendment to the National Labor Relations Act[5] extended coverage to employees of nonprofit health care institutions that had previously been exempted from its provisions. In the words of the amendment, a health care facility is "any hospital, convalescent hospital, health maintenance organization, health clinic, nursing home, extended care facility, or other institution devoted to the care of the sick, infirm or aged."[6]

The amendment also enacted unique, special provisions for employees of health care facilities who oppose unionization on legitimate religious grounds. These provisions allow a member of such an institution to make periodic contributions to one of three nonreligious charitable funds selected jointly by the labor organization and the employing institution, rather than paying periodic union dues and initiation fees. If the collective bargaining agreement does not specify an acceptable fund, the employee may select a tax-exempt charity.

Elections

The NLRA sets out the procedures by which employees may select a labor organization as their collective bargaining representative to negotiate with the hospital over employment and contract matters.[7] A hospital may choose to recognize and deal with the union without resorting to the formal NLRA procedure. If the formal process is adhered to, the employees vote on union representation in an election held under NLRB supervision.[8] If the union wins, it is certified by the NLRB as the employees' bargaining representative. *Brooks v. NLRB*, 348 U.S. 96 (1954).

The NLRA provides that the representative, having been selected by a majority of employees in a bargaining unit, is the exclusive bargaining agent for all employees in the unit. *Montgomery Ward & Co.*, 137 N.L.R.B. 346, 50 L.R.R.M. 1137 (1962). The scope of the bargaining unit is often the subject of dispute for its boundaries may determine the outcome of the election, the employee representative's bargaining power, and the level of labor relations stability.

When the parties cannot agree on the appropriate unit for bargaining, the NLRB has broad discretion to decide the issue. But the NLRB's discretion is limited to determining appropriate units for only those employees who are classified as professional, supervisory, clerical, technical, or service and maintenance employees when they are included in units outside their particular category. This is the case unless there has been a self-determination election in which the members of a certain group vote, as a class, to be included within the larger bargaining unit. For example, nurses and other professional employees of a hospital can be excluded from a bargaining unit composed of service and maintenance employees unless the professionals are first given the opportunity to choose separate representation and reject it. Supervisory nurses have also been held to be entitled to a bargaining unit separate from the unit composed of general duty nurses.[9] *St. Francis Hospital*, 265 N.L.R.B. No. 120 (1982).

While the NLRA does not require employee representatives to be selected by any particular procedure, the act provides for the NLRB to conduct representation elections by secret ballot. The NLRB may conduct such an election only when a petition for certification has been filed by an employee, a group of employees, an individual, a labor union acting on the employees' behalf, or an employer. When the petition is filed, the NLRB must investigate and direct an election if it has reasonable cause to believe a question of representation exists. After an election, if any party to it believes that certain conduct created an atmosphere that interfered with employee free choice, that party may file objections with the NLRB.[10]

The National Labor Relations Board has held in *N.L.R.B. v. Woodview-Calabasas Hospital*, 112 L.R.R.M. 3290 (9th Cir. 1983), that strikers are eligible to vote in a decertification election even though they may be employed elsewhere during the strike.

Unfair Labor Practices

The NLRA prohibits hospitals from engaging in certain conduct classified as employer unfair labor practices.[11] For example, discriminating against an employee for holding union membership is not permitted. The NLRA stipulates that the employer must bargain in good faith with representatives of the employees; failure to do so constitutes an unfair labor practice. *NLRB v. Reed & Prince Manufacturing Co.*, 205 F.2d 131 (1st Cir.), *cert. denied*, 346 U.S. 887 (1953). The NLRB may order the employer to fulfill the duty to bargain.

If the employer dominates or controls the employees' union or interferes and supports one of two competing unions, the employer is committing an unfair labor practice. Such employer support of a competing union is clearly illustrated in a situation in which two unions are competing for members in the hospital, as well as for recognition as the employees' bargaining organization. If the hospital permits one of the unions to use hospital facilities for its organizational activities, but denies the use of the facilities to the other union, an unfair labor practice is committed. Financial assistance to one of the competing unions also constitutes an unfair labor practice.[12]

The NLRA also places duties on labor organizations and prohibits certain employee activities that are denominated as employee unfair labor practices. Coercion of employees by the union constitutes an unfair labor practice; such activities as mass picketing, assaulting nonstrikers, and following groups of nonstrikers away from the immediate area of the hospital plainly constitute coercion and will be ordered stopped by the NLRB.[13] Breach of a collective bargaining contract by the labor union is another example of a union unfair labor practice.

Labor Disputes

Congress enacted the Norris-LaGuardia Act to limit the power of the federal courts to issue injunctions in cases involving or growing out of labor disputes. The act's strict standards must be met before such injunctions can be issued. Essentially, a federal court may not apply restraints in a labor dispute until after the case is heard in open court and the finding is that unlawful acts will be committed unless restrained and that substantial and irreparable injury to the complainant's property will follow. *United States v. Hutcheson*, 312 U.S. 219 (1941).

The Norris-LaGuardia Act is aimed at reducing the number of injunctions granted to restrain strikes and picketing. An additional piece of legislation designating procedures limiting strikes in health institutions is the 1974 amendment to the National Labor Relations Act.[14]

This amendment sets out special procedures for handling labor disputes that develop from collective bargaining at the termination of an existing agreement or during negotiations for an initial contract between a health institution and its employees. The procedures were designed to ensure that the needs of patients would be met during any work stoppage (strike) or labor dispute in such an institution.

The amendment provides for creating a board of inquiry if a dispute threatens to interrupt health care in a particular community.[15] The board is appointed by the director of the Federal Mediation and Conciliation Service (FMCS) within 30 days after notification of either party's intention to terminate a labor contract. The board then has 15 days in which to investigate and report its findings and recommendations in writing. Once the report is filed with the FMCS, both parties are expected to maintain the status quo for an additional 15 days.

The board's findings provide a framework for arbitrators' decisions, while recognizing both the community's need for continuous health services and the good faith intentions of labor organizations to avoid a work stoppage whenever possible and to accept arbitration when negotiations reach an impasse.

The amendment also mandates certain notice requirements by labor groups in health care institutions: The institution must be given 90 days' notice before a collective bargaining agreement expires, and the FMCS is entitled to 60 days' notice. Previously, only 60 days' notice to the employer and 30 days' notice to the FMCS were required. However, if the bargaining agreement is the initial contract between the parties, only 30 days' notice need be given to the FMCS.

More significantly, ten days' notice is required in advance of any strike, picketing, or other concerted refusal to work, regardless of the source of the dispute.[16] This allows the NLRB to determine the legality of a strike before it occurs and also gives health care institutions ample time to ensure the continuity of patient treatment. At the same time, any attempt to utilize this period to undermine the bargaining relationship is implicitly forbidden.

The ten-day notice may be concurrent with the final ten days of the expiration notice. Any employee violation of these provisions amounts to an unfair labor practice and may automatically result in the discharge of the employee. In addition, injunctive relief may be available from the courts if circumstances warrant.

In summary, the amendment's provisions are designed to ensure that every possible approach to a peaceful settlement is fully explored before a strike is called in hospitals and other health care facilities.[17]

Labor-Management Reporting and Disclosure Act

The Labor-Management Reporting and Disclosure Act of 1959 places controls on labor unions and the relationships between unions and their members. In addition, it requires that employers report payments and loans to officials or other representatives of labor organizations or any promises to make such payments or loans. Expenditures made to influence or restrict the way employees exercise their rights to organize and bargain collectively are illegal unless they are disclosed by the employer. Agreements with labor relations consultants, under which such persons undertake to interfere with certain employee rights, must also be disclosed.

Reports required under this law must be filed with the secretary of labor and are then made public. Both charitable and proprietary hospitals that make such payments or enter into such agreements must file reports, but governmental hospitals are not subject to these provisions. Penalties for failing to make the required reports, or for making false reports, include fines up to $10,000 and imprisonment for one year.

Fair Labor Standards Act

The Fair Labor Standards Act, 29 U.S.C. Ch. 8, establishes minimum wages and maximum hours of employment. The employees of all governmental, charitable, and proprietary hospitals are covered by this act, and hospitals must conform to the minimum wage and overtime pay provisions. However, bona fide executive, administrative, and professional employees are exempted from the wage and hour provisions.

The law permits hospitals to enter into agreements with employees, establishing a work period of 14 consecutive days as an alternative to the usual 7-day week. If the alternative period is chosen, the hospital has to pay the overtime rate only for hours worked in excess of 80 hours during the 14-day period. It should be noted that the alternate 14-day work period does not relieve the hospital from paying overtime for hours worked in excess of 8 in any one day even if no more than 80 hours are worked during the period.

Equal Employment Opportunity

Title VII of the Civil Rights Act of 1964, as amended by the Equal Employment Opportunity Act of 1972, prohibits private employers and state and local governments from discriminating on the basis of race, color, religion, sex, or national origin. An exception to prohibited employment practices may be permitted when religion, sex, or national origin is a bona fide occupational qualification necessary to the operation of a particular business or enterprise. *Griggs v. Duke Power Co.*, 401 U.S. 424 (1971).

The act also exempts hospitals operated by religious corporations or societies, but only with respect to employees directly concerned with religious activities. It should be noted that practically all employment in hospitals operated by religious bodies is unrelated to religious activity.

Many states have enacted protective laws with respect to the employment of females. The Equal Employment Opportunity Commission (EEOC) guidelines on sex discrimination make it clear that state laws limiting the employment of females in certain occupations are superseded by Title VII and are no defense against a charge of sex discrimination.

Equal Pay Act of 1963

The Equal Pay Act of 1963, 29 U.S.C. Ch. 8, is essentially an amendment to the Fair Labor Standards Act and was passed to address wage disparities based on sex. The law is applicable everywhere that the minimum wage law is applicable and is enforced by the EEOC. The Equal Pay Act, simply stated, requires that employees who perform equal work receive equal pay. There are situations where wages may be unequal so long as they are based upon factors other than sex, such as in the case of a formalized seniority system or a system that objectively measures earnings by the quantity or quality of production.

Age Discrimination in Employment Act

The Age Discrimination in Employment Act of 1967, 29 U.S.C. Ch. 14, as amended, prohibits age-based employment discrimination against individuals between 40 and 70 years of age. The purpose of this law is to promote employment of older persons on the basis of their ability without regard to their age.

Rehabilitation Act of 1973

The essential purpose of the Rehabilitation Act of 1973, 29 U.S.C. Ch. 14, is to afford protection to handicapped employees. As applicable to hospitals, the law is basically administered by the Department of Health and Human Services, which derives its jurisdiction from the fact that hospitals participate in such federal programs as Medicare, Medicaid, Hill-Burton, etc. The law is therefore applied to both public and private hospitals since both participate in these programs.

Section 503 of the act applies to government contractors whose contracts exceed $2,500 in value. Section 504 applies to employers who are recipients of federal financial assistance. Section 504 states, "No . . . qualified handicapped individual in the United States . . . shall solely by reason of his handicap, be excluded from participation in, be denied the benefits of, or be subjected to discrimination under any program as actively receiving Federal financial assistance." Section 504 applies to virtually every area of personnel administration including recruitment, advertising, processing of applications, promotions, rates of pay, fringe benefits, job assignments, etc.

Since July 1977, all institutions receiving federal financial assistance from the Department of Health and Human Services have been required to file assurances of compliance forms. Each employer must designate an individual to coordinate compliance efforts. A grievance procedure should be in place to address employee complaints alleging violation of the regulation. All employment decisions must be made without regard to physical or mental handicaps that are not disqualifying (e.g., an employer is not obligated to employ a person with a highly contagious disease that can be easily transmitted to others).

Employers receiving federal funds are required to perform a self evaluation as to their compliance with section 504 of the Rehabilitation Act of 1973. If discriminatory practices are identified through the self-evaluation process, remedial steps are to be taken to eliminate the effects of any discrimination. Records of the evaluation are to be maintained on file for at least three years following the review for public inspection. 45 C.F.R. Sec. 4.6(c).

STATE LAWS

Regulation of Employee Occupational Safety and Health

Congress enacted the Occupational Safety and Health Act of 1970, 29 U.S.C. Sec. 651, to establish administrative machinery for the development and enforcement of standards for occupational health and safety.[18] The employer must comply with the occupational and health standards under the act. Employees must follow the rules, regulations, and orders issued under the act that are applicable to their actions and conduct on the job.

The Occupational Safety and Health Administration (OSHA) of the Department of Labor is responsible for administering the act, issuing standards, and conducting on-site inspections to ensure compliance with the act. Employees or their representatives have the right to file a complaint with the nearest OSHA office and request an inspection when they believe that conditions in the work place are unsafe or unhealthful. If a violation of the act is found at an inspection, the employer receives a citation stating a time frame within which a violation must be corrected.

Additionally, under the law of some states, employers are charged with the duty of furnishing employees with a safe place to work. A hospital can be liable if employees are injured because of negligence in the care of the premises or the upkeep of equipment.

In addition to provisions regarding safety, other state statutes require that certain facilities—for example, lavatories and seats for elevator operators—be provided for the employees. The city and county in which a hospital is located may also prescribe rules regarding the health and safety of employees. Many communities have enacted sanitary and health codes that require certain facilities or standards. It should be emphasized that in most instances charitable institutions are not exempt from convenience and safety laws.

Bargaining Units

A major area of concern to hospitals is the number of bargaining units allowed in any one institution. New rules and regulations issued on April 21, 1989, by the National Labor Relations Board (NLRB) would have allowed up to eight collective bargaining units. A federal court in Chicago issued a permanent injunction barring the National Labor Relations Board from utilizing its new rules and regulations. The new regulations would have allowed up to eight bargaining units as opposed to the three normally allowed prior to the regulations. The new rules and regulations had been successfully challenged in court by the American Hospital Association.[19]

State Labor-Management Relations Act

Because the National Labor Relations Act (NLRA) excludes from coverage hospitals operated by the state or its political subdivisions, regulation of labor-management relations in these hospitals is left to state law.[20] State laws vary considerably in their coverage, and often employees of state and local governmental hospitals are covered by separate public employee legislation. Some of these statutes cover both state and local employees, whereas others cover only state or only local employees.

Most states have no labor relations statutes. Unless the constitution in such a state guarantees the right of employees to organize and imposes the duty of collective bargaining on the employer, most hospitals do not have to bargain collectively with their employees. In states that do have labor relations acts, the obligation of a hospital to bargain collectively with its employees is determined by the applicable statute.

A number of states have statutes similar to the Norris-LaGuardia Act, restricting the granting of injunctions in labor disputes. There are anti-injunction acts in several other states that are different from this type, and decisions under them do not fall into an easily recognized pattern.

Some of the states that have labor relations acts granting hospital employees the right to organize, join unions, and bargain collectively have specifically prohibited strikes and lockouts and have provided for compulsory arbitration whenever a collective bargaining contract cannot otherwise be executed amicably. Anti-injunction statutes would not forbid injunctions to restrain violations of these statutory provisions.

The doctrine of federal pre-emption, as applied to labor relations, displaces the states' jurisdiction to regulate an activity that is arguably an unfair labor practice within the meaning of the NLRA. Nonetheless, the U.S. Supreme Court has ruled that states can still regulate labor relations activity that also falls within the jurisdiction of the NLRB where deeply rooted local feelings and responsibility are affected. *Amalgamated Association of Street, Electric Railway & Motor Coach Employees v. Lockridge,* 403 U.S. 274 (1971).

Union Security Contracts and Right-To-Work Laws

Labor organizations frequently seek to enter union security contracts with employers. Such contracts are of two types: the closed shop contract, which provides that only members of a particular union may be hired, and the union shop contract, which makes continued employment dependent on membership in the union, although the employee need not have been a union member when applying for the job.

More than one-third of all the states have made such contracts unlawful. Statutes forbidding such agreements are generally called right-to-work laws on the theory that they protect everyone's right to work even if a person refuses to join a union. Several other state statutes or decisions purport to restrict union security contracts or specify procedures to be completed before such agreements may be made.

Anti-Discrimination Acts

State acts that prohibit discriminatory practices in employment are important if those laws provide greater protection than does the federal counterpart. All hospitals, except governmental hospitals, are employers under the federal statute and subject to its provisions. Thus, at minimum, hospital employees have all the protections afforded by federal anti-discrimination laws.

Wage and Hour Laws

State legislation establishing minimum wage rates is also of minor importance because the 1966 amendment to the federal Fair Labor Standards Act provides hospital personnel with coverage under the act. Where state minimum wage standards are higher than federal standards, the state's standards are applicable to hospital employees.

Child Labor Acts

Many states prohibit the employment of minors below a certain age and restrict the employment of other minors. Child labor legislation commonly requires that working papers be secured before a child may be hired, forbids the employment of minors at night, and prohibits minors from operating certain types of dangerous machinery.

This kind of legislation rarely exempts charitable hospitals, although some exceptions may be made with respect to the hours when student nurses may work.

Worker's Compensation

An employee who is injured while performing job-related duties may sue the employer for injuries suffered. State legislatures have recognized that it is difficult and expensive for employees to recover from their employers and have therefore enacted worker's compensation laws.[21]

Worker's compensation laws give the employee a legal way to receive compensation for injuries on the job. The acts do not require the employee to prove that the injury was the result of the employer's negligence. Worker's compensation laws are based on the employer-employee relationship and not on the theory of negligence.

The scope of worker's compensation varies widely. Some states limit an employee's compensation to the amount recoverable by the worker's compensation law, and further lawsuits against the employer are barred. Other states permit employees to choose whether they accept the compensation provided by law or institute a lawsuit against the employer. Some acts go further and provide a system of insurance that may be under the supervision of state or private insurers. Recovery by an employee begins with a hearing on the claim before a board of commissioners. Following the hearing, the commissioners decide whether there was an employee-employer relationship, whether the injury is covered by the act,[22] and whether there is a connection between the employment and the injury. The commissioners then award compensation according to a predetermined schedule based on the nature of the injury. Generally, worker's compensation boards tend to be liberal in interpreting the law to provide compensation for employees.

MANAGEMENT AND LABOR RIGHTS

- Labor has the right to organize and bargain collectively.
- Labor has the right to solicit and distribute union information during nonworking hours (i.e., mealtimes and coffee breaks).

- Management has the right to reasonably restrict union organizers to certain locations at the hospital and to certain time periods to avoid interference with hospital operations.
- Management has the right to prohibit unionization activities during working hours.
- Management has the right to prohibit unionization activities in patient care areas of the hospital.
- Management has the right to prohibit supervisors from engaging in union organizational activity. A nursing supervisor in *Arena v. Lincoln Lutheran of Racine*, 149 Wis. 2d 35, 437 N.W.2d 538 (1989), was dismissed for her activities in attempting to form an organization to represent the nurses. The petitioner alleged in her complaint that she had become concerned with certain policies which included nurses' being treated in an arbitrary manner. The petitioner had held a meeting outside the hospital with the nurses to discuss their concerns and the possibility of forming an association to represent the collective interests of the nurses. The NLRA did not protect the nursing supervisor due to the fact that she was a supervisor, rather than an employee. Congress excluded supervisors from protection afforded rank-and-file employees engaged in concerted activity for their mutual benefit to assure management of the undivided loyalty of its supervisory personnel by making sure that no employer would have to retain as its agent one who is obligated to a union. Federal labor law pre-empted the nurse from bringing action on the theory that her discharge for organizational activities constituted a violation of Wisconsin state law.
- Patient rights take precedence over employee rights when a patient's right to privacy or well-being is in jeopardy.
- Management must bargain in good faith.
- Labor must not threaten nonstrikers.
- Management may not discharge employees in retaliation for union activity.

NOTES

1. 29 U.S.C. § 151 *et seq.*
2. *Id.*
3. NLRA Amendments of 1974, Pub. L. No. 93-360.
4. NLRB, LEGISLATIVE HISTORY OF THE LABOR-MANAGEMENT RELATIONS ACT, 1947, at 303, 359 (1949). There exists almost no debate regarding this exclusion, although Senator Tydings of Maryland did justify this approach on the rationale that nonprofit hospitals were charitable institutions subject to local governmental regulations and, at least in 1947, were in dire financial straits. NLRB, LEGISLATIVE HISTORY OF THE LABOR MANAGEMENT RELATIONS ACT OF 1947, at 1464–65 (1948).
5. NLRA, §§ 2 (2) & (14), 8(d) & (g).
6. *Id.* § 2(14).
7. *Id.* § 9.

8. *Id.*

9. *Id.* § 9(b)(1) & (b)(3).

10. Id. § 8.

11. *Id.* §§ 8, 9.

12. *Id.* § 8(a)(1) & (a)(3).

13. *Id.* § 8(b)(7); Landrum-Griffin Amendments of 1959, Pub. L. No. 86-257 (1959).

14. *Id.* § 8(g).

15. *Id.*

16. *Id.* § 8(d).

17. SUBCOMMITTEE ON LABOR OF THE SENATE COMMITTEE ON LABOR AND PUBLIC WELFARE, 93D CONG., 2D SESS., LEGISLATIVE HISTORY OF THE COVERAGE OF NON-PROFIT HOSPITALS UNDER THE NATIONAL LABOR RELATIONS ACT of 1974, at 412–14 (1974).

18. 29 U.S.C. § 651 *et seq.*

19. Burda, *Bargaining-unit Rules Struck Down*. MODERN HEALTHCARE, Jul. 28, 1989, at 11.

20. NLRA, § 2(3), 29 U.S.C. § 152(3), Pub. L. No. 93-360 (1974).

21. THE REPORT OF THE NATIONAL COMMISSION ON STATE WORKMEN'S COMPENSATION LAWS (1972). The statute that authorized the study and subsequent report was the Occupational Safety and Health Act of 1970.

22. This refers to the particular state statute in effect at the time of the injury.

Chapter 17

Employee Discipline and Discharge

Discipline and discharge actions are two of the most unpleasant management tasks that supervisors confront in their careers. Fairly balancing the rights of the employee and the needs of the organization is an extremely complex objective. This chapter provides some direction in this balancing act.

EMPLOYMENT AT WILL

The employment at will doctrine provides that employment is at the will of either the employer or the employee and that employment may be terminated by the employer or the employee at any time for any or no reason unless there is a contract in place that specifies the terms and duration of employment. A discharged employee in *Rock v. Sear-Brown Associates, P.C.*, 524 N.Y.S.2d 935 (App. Div. 1988), brought an action against his employer for wrongful discharge. The supreme court dismissed the complaint, and the employee appealed. The supreme court, appellate division, held that an employee could not state a claim for wrongful discharge. The employee manual did not contain an express limitation on the employer's right to terminate an employee at will.

The court of appeals in *O'Connor v. Eastman Kodak Co.*, 492 N.Y.S.2d 9 (1985), held that an employer had a right to terminate an employee at will at any time and for any reason or no reason. An employer's right, however, can be limited by express agreement with the employee or in a collective bargaining agreement of which the employee is a beneficiary. There was no such agreement in this case. The plaintiff did not rely on any specific representation made to him during the course of his employment interviews, nor did he rely on any documentation in the employee handbook, which would have limited the defendant's

Adapted from Pozgar, *Wrongful Discharge and Discipline*, HEALTH CARE SUPERVISOR, Oct. 1989, at 57.

common law right to discharge at will. The employee had relied on a popular perception of Kodak as a womb-to-tomb employer. The employment at will doctrine provided employees with few employment rights. Employers who experience favorable court decisions in wrongful discharge claims are often the losers due to the bad press and the negative effects a discharge has on employee morale. "Wrongful discharge claims are difficult, time consuming and expensive lawsuits to defend and, when they reach the jury, employers are losing about 75% of the time."[1]

The hospital in *Jagust v. Brookhaven Memorial Association, Inc.,* 541 N.Y.S.2d 41 (App. Div. 1989), was found to have properly dismissed a staff physician from his administrative position as director of the hospital's Family Practice Residency Program without a hearing. The hospital learned that the physician had engaged in improper billing practices by submitting bills for services that he never rendered. The physician was an employee at will as far as his administrative position was concerned. Neither the hospital's administrative procedure manual nor the employee handbook stated that the employee was subject to discharge for cause. Procedural protection was provided in the hospital's medical staff bylaws; however, the bylaws pertained to medical staff privileges and not administrative positions.

DISCRIMINATION

Legislation has been enacted that prohibits the discharge of employees on the basis of handicap, age, race, creed, color, religion, sex, national origin, pregnancy, filing of safety violation complaints with various agencies (e.g., the Occupational Safety and Health Administration), and/or union membership.

A black respiratory therapist stated a cause of action against the university medical center under 42 U.S.C. Section 1981 in *Lee v. Loyola University of Chicago,* 668 F. Supp. 1187 (D.C. Ill. 1987), when he asserted in his complaint that he was black, that the medical center had been seeking applications for the position of respiratory therapist, and that he had applied for and was qualified for the position. Despite such qualifications, the positions had remained open until the medical center had ultimately filled them with white applicants having inferior qualifications.

The Civil Service Commission in *Theodore v. Department of Health & Human Services,* 515 So. 2d 454 (La. Ct. App. 1987), was found to have acted improperly in suspending a black LPN as a result of a physical altercation with a white coworker. The white nurse had been accidentally struck by a crib being pushed by the black nurse. Evidence at trial supported the black nurse's contentions that she had apologized for the accident. The white nurse struck the first blow and spoke inflammatory slurs. The black nurse's reaction had been defensive. The facts revealed no grounds for suspension or disciplinary action against the black nurse.

In *Jones v. Hinds General Hospital*, 666 F. Supp. 933 (D.C. Miss. 1987), a prima facie case of sex discrimination was established by evidence showing that a hospital laid off female nursing assistants, while retaining male orderlies who performed the necessary functions. The court held that Title VII of the Civil Rights Act was not violated by the hospital's use of gender as a basis for laying off its employees. Gender was a bona fide occupational qualification for orderlies since a substantial number of male patients objected to the performance of catheterizations and surgical prepping by female assistants.

INTERFERENCE WITH EMPLOYMENT OPPORTUNITIES

Liability for discrimination is not limited strictly to employer-employee relationships, but can be applied in situations in which a hospital's discriminatory practices can affect the ability of a nonemployee to obtain a job with a third party. This occurred in *Pardazi v. Cullman Medical Center*, 838 F.2d 1155 (11th Cir. 1988), where the U.S. court of appeals held that the physician stated a claim for relief under Title VII of the Civil Rights Act of 1964 based on the allegation that the hospital's denial of staff privileges interfered with his employment relationship with a third party. Dr. Pardazi, an Iran-educated medical practitioner, had entered into an employment contract with an Alabama corporation that required that Dr. Pardazi become a staff member of the defendant hospital. Dr. Pardazi argued that the hospital's discriminatory practices in denying his appointment denied him the right of an attorney at rehearing, extended his observation period from four months to one year (a deviation from the medical staff bylaws), and interfered with his employment opportunities. The U.S. district court's summary judgment for the hospital was reversed and the case remanded.

PUBLISHED POLICIES AND PROCEDURES

The rights of employees have been expanding through judicial decisions in the various states and have included employee rights as described in employee handbooks as well as in administrative procedure manuals.

The provisions of a hospital employee handbook were held binding in *Duldulao v. St. Mary of Nazareth Hospital Center*, 483 N.E.2d 956 (Ill. App. Ct. 1985). The Appellate Court of Illinois held that the employee handbook imposed obligations on both the hospital and the employee. The hospital was wrong in not permitting a nurse her rights to follow the hospital's progressive disciplinary policy prior to termination. The plaintiff had argued in this case that the defendant had breached the employment relationship by not affording her the benefit of the progressive disciplinary policy established for nonprobationary employees in the employee handbook.

A nurse's aide was awarded $20,000 in *Watson v. Idaho Falls Consolidated Hospitals, Inc.*, 720 P.2d 632 (Idaho 1986), for damages when the hospital, as employer, violated the provisions of its employee handbook in the manner in which it terminated her employment. Evidence that the employee was making $1,000 a month at the time of her discharge and was not able to find suitable employment following her discharge supported the award of $20,000 in her favor for wrongful discharge. Although the nurse's aide had no formal written contract, the employee handbook and the hospital policies and procedures manual constituted a contract in view of evidence to the effect that these documents had been intended to be enforced and complied with by both employees and management. Employees read and relied on the handbook as creating terms of an employment contract and were required to sign for the handbook in order to establish receipt of a revised handbook explaining hospital policy, discipline, counseling, and termination. A policy and procedure manual placed on each floor of the hospital also outlined termination procedures.

The Supreme Court, Appellate Division, in *Battaglia v. Sisters of Charity Hospital*, 508 N.Y.S. 802 (App. Div. 1986), held that the hospital's personnel manual could not be interpreted to limit the hospital's power to terminate an at-will employee. The personnel manual contained language to the effect that it is not a contract, that it may be modified, amended or supplemented, and that the hospital retains the right to make all necessary management decisions, including the selection, direction, compensation, and retention of employees.

The plaintiff in *Blair v. CBS*, 662 F. Supp. 947 (S.D. N.Y. 1987), could not show anything other than employment at will without restriction on the employer's right to terminate her employment. Limitation on an employer's right to terminate may be imported from an express provision in the employee's handbook. The plaintiff also did not show that she would not have commenced employment or ceased her job search absent representations in the employee handbook.

Limitation on an employer's right to discharge was barred in *Weiner v. McGraw-Hill*, 57 N.Y.2d 458, 443 N.E.2d 441, 457 N.Y.S.2d 193 (1982), where the court of appeals held that although the plaintiff was not engaged by the defendant for a fixed term of employment, he pleaded a good cause of action for breach of contract. The plaintiff was allegedly discharged without the "just and sufficient cause" or the rehabilitative efforts specified in the defendants' handbook and allegedly promised at the time the plaintiff accepted employment. Furthermore, on several occasions when the plaintiff had recommended that certain of his subordinates be dismissed, he was allegedly instructed to proceed in strict compliance with the handbook and policy manuals. The employment application that the plaintiff had signed stated that his employment would be subject to the provisions of McGraw-Hill's "handbook on personnel policies and procedures."

A personnel manual, according to the supreme court, appellate division in *Battaglia v. Sisters of Charity Hospital*, 508 N.Y.S.2d 802 (App. Div. 1986), could not be interpreted to limit the hospital's power to terminate an at-will employee. Language in the manual indicated that the personnel manual is not a contract; that it may be modified, amended, or supplemented; and that the hospital retains the right to make all necessary management decisions for the delivery of patient care services and the selection, direction, compensation, and retention of employees.

No cognizable claim was stated in *Hinson v. Cameron*, 742 P.2d 549 (Okla. 1987), by a nurse's aide whose at-will employment was terminated by a hospital on the basis of a supervisor's charge that the aide failed to administer an enema to a patient. The nurse's aide had not been ordered to perform an illegal act, and thus the tort of wrongful discharge could not be made out. In this case, the hospital's employee manual could not be read as conferring tenured employment or job security. The Supreme Court of Oklahoma held that although the employee manual listed examples of some grounds for termination, it was not an exclusive listing of all grounds for termination. Even if there might be an implied covenant of good faith and fair dealing in every at-will employment relationship, that covenant does not operate to forbid employment severance except for good cause.

Employment guidelines and manuals are very helpful in obtaining employee goodwill and maintaining good employee relations. They can also be excellent tools in maintaining a union-free environment. Therefore, the use, drafting and implementation of an employment manual should be taken seriously. When drafting such manuals, employers should keep in mind the legal consequences of each provision and take care to avoid restrictive or tightly worded language. An employee handbook can be both written in accordance with the stated guidelines and help to maintain good employee communication and effective employee relations."[2]

EMPLOYMENT DISCLAIMERS

A disclaimer is the denial of a right that is imputed to a person or that is alleged to belong to him or her. Although a disclaimer is often a successful defense for employers in wrongful discharge cases, it should not be considered a license to discharge at will and at the whim of the supervisor in an arbitrary and capricious manner. Employers can help prevent successful lawsuits for wrongful discharge that are based on the premise that an employee handbook or departmental policy and procedure manual is an implied contract by incorporating disclaimers in published manuals, such as that described above in the *Battaglia* case.

TERMINATION FOR CAUSE

Financial Necessity

No breach of employment contract occurred in *Wilde v. Houlton Regional Hospital*, 537 A.2d 1137 (Me. 1987), when because of financial difficulties and overstaffing, a hospital terminated the employment of two nurses, a ward clerk, and a dietary supervisor. Even if the employees were correct in contending that their indefinite contracts of employment had been modified by virtue of a "dismissal for cause" provision in the employee's handbook and by management's oral assurances that they were permanent, full-time employees whose jobs were secure so long as they performed satisfactorily, the employees' discharge for financial or other legitimate business reasons did not offend the employment contracts as thus modified. A private employer had an essential business prerogative to adjust its work force as market forces and business necessity required, and the layoffs in question violated no compelling public policy.

Theft

A nurse's discharge in *Waara v. Mesabi Regional Medical Center*, 415 N.W.2d 362 (Minn. Ct. App. 1987), involved gross misconduct so as to deny unemployment compensation where it was based on charges that she had stolen supplies of Demerol for her own use and that she had falsified patient records to conceal such thefts.

DEFAMATION ACTIONS

Employers across the country are facing a new kind of potential liability with every employee they hire: A defamation action if the relationship doesn't work out. Observers say an increasing number of defamation claims are being brought by current and former workers, apparently because of a greater awareness by those employees—and a growing recognition by the courts—of new protections available to them.[3]

Defamation actions are being attached to—or are taking the place of—wrongful discharge suits. "[P]laintiffs must overcome an employer's qualified privilege and show malice in order to recover."[4]

The nurse's aide in *Watson v. Idaho Falls Consolidated Hospitals, Inc.*, 720 P.2d 632 (Idaho 1986) claimed that the head nurse intentionally interfered with her employment relationship with the hospital, that both the head nurse and the hospital had intentionally inflicted emotional distress, and that accusations prior to discharge constituted slander. The defendants made a motion for summary judgment which was granted in part as to the nurse's aide's claim for slander. Although the nurse's aide did not appeal the issue of slander, it seems clear that actions for defamation will appear in an ever-increasing number of cases.

RETALIATORY DISCHARGE

Threats, abuse, intimidation, and retaliatory discharge are causes for legal action. "Employees have . . . brought claims alleging abusive discharge in violation of public policy. This type of action is usually found to sound in tort, and thus in certain circumstances punitive damages have been awarded."[5] The burden of proof for establishing some hidden motive for discharge from employment rests on discharged employees.

The court of appeal in *Khanna v. Microdata Corp.*, 215 Cal. Rptr. 860 (Ct. App. 1985), held that substantial evidence supported a finding that the employer fired the employee in bad faith retaliation for bringing a lawsuit against the employer, thus violating an implied covenant of good faith and fair dealing. Under the traditional common law rule, codified in Labor Code Section 2922, an employment contract of indefinite duration is in general terminable at the will of either party. Over the past several decades, however, judicial authorities in California and throughout the United States have established the rule that under both common law and the statute, an employer does not enjoy an absolute or totally unfettered right to discharge even an at-will employee . . . ." 215 Cal. Rptr. at 865. A cause of action was stated for the employer's breach of an implied-in-fact covenant to terminate only for good cause.

In *Shores v. Senior Manor Nursing Center*, 518 N.E.2d 471 (Ill. App. Ct. 1988), a formerly employed nurse's assistant brought an action against the nursing home on the basis of retaliatory discharge. The circuit court dismissed the complaint for failure to state a cause of action. The decision was appealed. The Appellate Court of Illinois held that the former nursing home employee, who alleged that she was discharged in retaliation for reporting to the nursing home administrator that the charge nurse was improperly performing her functions as a nurse which allegedly violated the Nursing Home Care Reform Act, stated a cause of action for retaliatory discharge. The circuit court was reversed and the case remanded for further proceedings.

The former director of nursing administration brought an action against the hospital and others for breach of contract, violation of civil rights, and interference with contractual relations in *Hobson v. McClean Hospital Corp.*, 402 Mass. 413, 522 N.E.2d 975 (1988). The Supreme Judicial Court of Massachussetts held (1) the complaint stated a cause of action for breach of an employment contract and interference with the employment contract, (2) the complaint stated a cause of action for discharge in violation of public policy, but (3) the complaint did not state a cause of action under the Civil Rights Act. The director of nursing administration alleged that the hospital bylaws for professional staff conferred privileges on employees and that the hospital terminated her without good cause (" . . . wrongfully terminated employee in retaliation for her enforcement of State municipal laws . . ."). There were no counselings and no warnings.

TERMINATION FOR CAUSE ONLY CONTRACT

A termination for cause only clause in an employment contract is binding. An employment contract in *Eales v. Tanana,* 663 P.2d 958 (Alaska 1983), that provided that an employee hired up to retirement age could be terminated only for cause was upheld by the court.

The Supreme Court of New Jersey in *Pierce v. Ortho Pharmaceutical Corp.,* 417 A.2d 505 (N.J. 1980), held that an employee at will has a cause of action for wrongful discharge when the discharge is contrary to public policy; however, unless an employee identifies a specific expression of public policy, he may be discharged with or without cause. The physician in this case did not have a cause of action for wrongful discharge in opposing continued research on a particular formulation of a drug. The trial court's decision granting a summary judgment for the defendant was reinstated following the reversal of this decision by the New Jersey Supreme Court.

"The National Labor Relations Act and other labor legislation illustrate the governmental policy of preventing employers from using the right of discharge as a means of oppression." *Id.* at 509.

"Consistent with this policy, many states have recognized the need to protect employees who are not parties to a collective bargaining agreement or other contract from abusive practices by the employer." *Id.* Recently those states have recognized a common law cause of action for employees at will who were discharged for reasons that were in some way "wrongful." The courts in those jurisdictions have taken various approaches: some recognizing the action in tort, some in contract. *Id.*

The employment at will common law doctrine is not truly applicable in today's society and many courts have recognized this fact.

> In the last century, the common law developed in a laissez-faire climate that encouraged industrial growth and improved the right of an employer to control his own business, including the right to fire without cause an employee at will . . . The twentieth century has witnessed significant changes in socioeconomic values that have led to reassessment of the common law rule. Businesses have evolved from small and medium size firms to gigantic corporations in which ownership is separate from management. Formerly there was a clear delineation between employers, who frequently were owners of their own businesses and employees. The employer in the old sense has been replaced by a superior in the corporate hierarchy who is himself an employee.

Id.

TERMINATION CHECKLIST

Prior to termination of an employee, the employer should review the following questions:

* Was the termination
  —a violation of any policy or procedure outlined in the hospital's administrative manual, the employee handbook, the personnel department's policies and procedures, and/or any other hospital policies and procedures and/or regulations?
  —arbitrary and capricious?
  —discriminatory on the basis of age, disability, race, creed, color, religion, gender, national origin, or marital status?
  —a violation of any contract, oral or written?
  —a violation of any public policy—federal, state, or local?
  —consistent with the reasons for discharge?
  —discriminatory against the employee for filing a lawsuit?
  —fixed prior to any appeal actions that might be available to the employee? If so, was he/she granted an opportunity to be represented by counsel?
* Was there
  —retaliatory action because of a refusal to perform an illegal act or a questioning of a management practice?
  —defamation of character?
  —a conspiracy?
  —a personal vendetta?
  —threat or intimidation?
  —unlawful activity?
  —an attempt to bribe?
  —a denial of constitutional rights to freedom of speech?
  —an interference with an employee's rights as secured by the laws or constitution of the United States?

COMPENSATORY AND PUNITIVE DAMAGES

An employee who is wrongly discharged may maintain a cause of action in contract or tort or both. In a tort action for wrongful discharge, the court can award punitive damages. This remedy is not available under the law of contract.

Recent headlines highlight that the damages awarded in employment related litigation may not be limited to back pay, fringe benefits and other forms of compensatory relief. In June 1988, a federal jury in the Eastern District of Kentucky awarded a total of $3 million in punitive damages to two former executives of Ashland Oil, Inc. who prevailed in a wrongful termination suit. . . . The plaintiffs alleged that they were dismissed for opposing and then failing to cover up illegal payments made to foreign government representatives. The jury assessed punitive damages against the corporation, its chairman, former chairman and a senior vice president.[6]

A California Supreme Court decision that prohibits plaintiffs from seeking punitive and emotional distress damages from former employers in wrongful dismissal cases applies retroactively to thousands of cases pending in state courts. In *Newman v. Emerson Radio Corp.*, 772 P.2d 1059 (Cal. 1989), the court, by a 4–3 vote, decided that its December 29 decision in *Foley v. Interactive Data Corp.*, 765 P.2d 373, 47 Cal. Rptr. 3d 211 (1988), applies to all wrongful dismissal cases pending as of January 30. The Supreme Court of California had held in *Foley* that a wrongful discharge claim asserting a breach of an implied covenant of good faith and fair dealing may give rise to contract, but not tort, damages. As a result of this ruling, punitive damages will not ordinarily be available to successful wrongful discharge plaintiffs.

The Montana Supreme Court held that a Montana statute that limits the damages recoverable in wrongful discharge suits to four years' wages and benefits does not violate the state constitution. *Meech v. Hillhaven West, Inc.*, No. 88-410 (Mont. June 6, 1989). According to the court, the state constitution's guarantee of "full legal redress" affords the plaintiff, a former nursing home administrator, only a right to judicial access to obtain remedies, not a fundamental right to full redress. The statute abolishes common law causes of action for discharge and creates a statutory action. It is the first of its kind in the nation. Punitive damages are available only upon clear and convincing evidence that the employer acted with actual malice or committed actual fraud.

LIMITING UNFAIR DISCHARGE CLAIMS

It is possible for employers to reduce their exposure to liability for wrongful discharge by developing appropriate guidelines. The best way for the human resources manager to prevent negligent-hiring litigation for the employer is to become familiar with the risks and avoid hiring workers who are likely to become problem employees.

- Take appropriate precautions to prevent the hiring of those who might be a hazard to others.
- Develop clear policies and procedures on hiring, disciplining, and terminating employees.
- Review each applicant's background and past work behavior.

- Become familiar with any state laws that might be applicable when hiring an individual with a past criminal record.
- Develop an application that realistically determines an applicant's qualifications prior to hiring.
- Develop a two-tiered interview system for screening applicants (the interviews should be conducted first by an appropriately trained member of the personnel department and then by the department head of the service to which the applicant is applying).
- Solicit appropriate references, and follow up with a telephone call for further information.
- Develop constructive performance evaluations that reinforce good behavior and provide instruction in those areas needing improvement. The performance evaluation should include a written statement regarding the employee's performance.
- Develop a progressive disciplinary action policy.
- Provide inservice education programs for supervisors on such subjects as employee interviews, evaluations, and discipline. (Various colleges, universities, and consultants provide inservice education programs for employers.)
- Be mindful of the importance of developing appropriate employment contract language, as well as administrative manuals and employee handbooks.

Employers must clearly communicate to employees during recruitment that their employment is at will and can be terminated at any time by the employer. During the course of employment, handbooks and personnel manuals must provide a fair and unambiguous standard for employee discipline and termination . . . . At the termination of employment, the discharge decision should be carefully reviewed by a member of management familiar with the issues of wrongful discharge. At this point the employer may seek from the employee a release from all legal claims for additional consideration.[7]

Oral counseling, written counseling, written counseling with suspension, and written counseling with termination are the textbook responses to disciplinary action and discharge. Textbook theories are fine in a black and white world, but few people live in such a world. The following listing presents some alternatives to the undesirable task of terminating employees:

- Use inter- and intradepartmental transfers when indicated. Transfers are generally more effective in larger corporations such as multisite health care systems where relocation is geographically possible.
- Substitute suspension for termination when possible. Do not have the courts do it for you. An emergency department technician's termination was properly reduced to a suspension in *Ellins v. Department of Health*, 519 So. 2d 850 (La. Ct. App. 1988). The technician had been discharged for failure to

comply with emergency department procedures that required patient evaluation by a nurse. The Civil Service Commission reduced the discharge to a 60-day suspension since the technician had bypassed the hospital's triage process because of the patient's critical condition. Under the circumstances, the city department of health failed to show that the conduct of the technician was improper, had impaired the efficiency of the hospital, or bore a real and substantial relationship thereto.

- Provide an opportunity for early retirement.
- Consider a redeployment of personnel, a hiring freeze, a reduction of overtime, etc., before personnel cutbacks are made due to financial difficulties.

The employer's right to terminate an employee is not absolute. It is limited by fundamental principles of public policy and by express or implied terms of agreement between the employer and the employee.

> Formulating a standard for substantive fairness in employee dismissal law requires accommodating a number of different interests already afforded legal recognition. The legal interest of employees to be protected against certain types of unfair and injurious action . . . are at the core of any employee dismissal proposal. Arrayed against these interests are employer and societal interests in effective management of organizations, which require that employees not be shielded from the consequences of their poor performance or misconduct, and that supervisors not be deterred from exercising their managerial responsibilities by the inconvenience of litigating employees' claims.[8]

An employee, especially a supervisor, who believes he or she has been unfairly discharged will be most likely to seek access to the following information in defense of his/her claim:

- minutes of any meetings
- written reports, typed or handwritten
- personnel file
- tapes
- letters, cards, and handwritten notes written on their behalf from the public
- personnel handbook
- personnel and departmental policies and procedures books
- oral testimony from fellow employees and supervisors

Employers must carefully and fairly document any disciplinary proceedings that might be subject to discovery by a disgruntled employee. Failure to do so could place a board or a supervisor at an uncomfortable disadvantage should a complaint reach the courts.

FAIRNESS—THE ULTIMATE TEST

"Is it fair?" is the ultimate question that a supervisor must ask when deciding if termination is proper. Some courts and legislative enactments have overturned the view that employers have total discretion to terminate workers who are not otherwise protected by collective bargaining agreements or civil services regulations. Montana legislation grants every employee the right to sue the employer for wrongful discharge.

The mere fact that an employment contract is terminable at will does not give the employer an absolute right to terminate it in all cases. The court of appeals in *Cleary v. American Airlines, Inc.* 199 Cal. Rptr. 722 (Cal. 1980), held the longevity of the employee's services, together with the express policy of the employer, operated as a form of estoppel, precluding any discharge of the employee by the employer without good cause, and, thus, the employer stated a cause of action for wrongful discharge.

There is an implied covenant of good faith and fair dealing in every contract that neither party will do anything that will injure the right of the other to receive benefits from the agreement.

- Termination of employment without legal cause after an employee completed 18 years of apparently satisfactory performance offended implied-in-law covenants in good faith and fair dealing contained in all contracts, including the employment contract.

The employee in *Pugh v. See's Candies, Inc.*, 116 Cal. App. 3d 311, 171 Cal. Rptr. 917 (1981), was found to have demonstrated a prima facie case of wrongful termination in violation of an implied promise that the employer would not act arbitrarily in dealing with the employee. The employer's right to terminate an employee is not absolute. It is limited by fundamental principles of public policy and by expressed or implied terms of agreement between the employer and the employee.

Procedural issues are as important as issues of discrimination are. The Supreme Court of Michigan in *Renny v. Port Huron Hospital,* 398 N.W.2d 327 (Mich. 1986), found, as did the jury, that the employee's discharge hearing was not final and binding because it did not comport with elementary fairness. The supreme court found that there was sufficient evidence for the jury to find that the employee had not been discharged for just cause. The existence of a just-cause contract is a question of fact for the jury where the employer establishes written policies and procedures and does not expressly retain the right to terminate an employee at will. The fact that the hospital followed the grievance procedure with the plaintiff is evidence that a just-cause contract existed on which the plaintiff relied.

The employee handbook provided for a grievance board as a fair way to resolve work-related complaints and problems. This was not a mandatory procedure to which the hospital's employees had to submit. The employee was not bound by the grievance board determination that her discharge was proper in that evidence supported a finding that she was not given adequate notice of who the witnesses against her would be. She was not permitted to be present when the witnesses testified, and she was not given the right to present certain evidence.

There was sufficient evidence for the jury to conclude that the plaintiff had in fact suffered damages in the amount of $100,000. Evidence presented indicated that her subsequent professional employment did not equal her earnings prior to discharge and that she had experienced increased expenses due to the loss of her health insurance as well as other financial losses that she suffered as a result of her discharge.

CONCLUSION

Creative thinking as to what will effectively rehabilitate an employee, as opposed to terminating him or her, is critical to the smooth and effective operation of any organization. There is no magic formula that will be effective for all disciplinary cases; many cases are unique and should be treated as such. Whenever possible, whatever form of discipline is utilized, should be designed to produce a more effective and productive employee.

"Too little or too much, but never right" is often the motto of those who criticize your disciplinary actions. When is too little too little and too much too much? This is a rhetorical question whenever sentencing is handed down for wrongdoing. There are those who will argue that all discipline should be punishment. Do not get caught in this trap. You can be fair, firm, consistent, caring, and creative all at the same time.

NOTES

1. Office of General Counsel of American Hospital Association, *The Wrongful Discharge of Employees in the Health Care Industry 1* (Legal Memorandum No. 10) (1987).

2. P.I. WEINER, S.H. BOMPEY, & M.G. BRITTAIN, JR., WRONGFUL DISCHARGE CLAIMS 98 (1986).

3. *Employers Face Upsurge in Suits Over Defamation*, NAT'L L. J., May 4, 1987, at 1.

4. *Id.* at 31.

5. Furfaro & Josephson, *Punitive Damages in Employment Cases*, N.Y.L.J., Apr. 7, 1989, at 4.

6. *Id.* at 3.

7. D. HILL, WRONGFUL DISCHARGE AND THE DEROGATION OF THE AT-WILL EMPLOYMENT DOCTRINE 176 (1987).

8. H.H. PERRITT, EMPLOYEE DISMISSAL LAW AND PRACTICE 354. (1984).

Chapter 18

Trial Procedures

Today, trial by jury plays an important role in civil actions in the United States. Many of the procedures followed in a trial are discussed in this chapter.

A case is heard in the court that has jurisdiction over the subject of controversy. The parties to a controversy are the plaintiff and the defendant. The plaintiff is the person who institutes an action by filing a complaint; the defendant is the person against whom a suit is brought. Many cases have multiple plaintiffs and defendants. Although the procedures for beginning an action vary according to jurisdiction, there are procedural common denominators. An action is commenced by filing an order with a court clerk to issue a writ or summons. All jurisdictions require service of process—a summons—on the defendant and a return to the court of that process by the person who served it. Where a summons is not required to be issued directly by a court, an attorney, as an officer of the court, may prepare and cause a summons to be served without direct notice to or approval of a court. Notice to a court occurs when an attorney files a summons in a court, thereby indicating to the court that an action has been commenced.

A complaint can be served on the defendant either with the summons or within a prescribed time after the summons has been served. After service of the complaint, an action is deemed to have commenced.

Specific formalities must be observed in the service of a summons so that appropriate jurisdiction over a defendant is obtained. Such formalities dictate the manner in which a summons is to be delivered, the time period within which service must be effected, and the geographic limitations within which service must be made. For example, a summons to commence an action in a local municipal court would generally require service within the particular municipality in order for the court to obtain jurisdiction. Where such service is not possible, the action may have to be brought in a different court.

Upon delivery of a summons or a complaint, prompt notice to the defendant's attorney and insurance company is necessary. The defendant's attorney will need to investigate the complaint, decide on strategy, identify and talk to witnesses, and prepare a defense.

Malpractice insurance policies generally require prompt notice of a suit. This provides the insurance company with an opportunity to investigate the facts of a case. When notice to the insurer is required, failure to provide notification could bar any right of the insured under the policy. The mere failure to timely advise may be in and of itself a breach of the insurance contract, entitling the insurer to decline coverage.

PLEADINGS

The pleadings of a case (including the summons, complaint, answer, and counterclaims—all the allegations of each party to a lawsuit) are filed with the court. The pleadings may raise questions of both law and fact. If only questions of law are involved, the judge will decide the case on the pleadings alone. If questions of fact are involved, there must be a trial to determine those facts.

Complaint

The first pleading filed in a negligence action is the complaint. It is the first statement of a case by the plaintiff(s) against the defendant(s) and states a cause of action, notifying the defendant(s) as to the basis for a suit. In some courts and in some jurisdictions a complaint must accompany the summons.

In the preliminary objections the defendant cites possible errors that would defeat the plaintiff's case. For example, the defendant may object that a summons or a complaint was improperly served, that the action was brought in the wrong county, or that there was something technically incorrect about the complaint. The court may then permit the plaintiff to file a new or amended complaint. However, in some instances the defects in the plaintiff's case may be so significant that the case is dismissed.

Demurrer

Upon receiving a copy of the plaintiff's complaint, the defendant can file preliminary objections before answering the complaint.

Answer

Following service of a complaint, an answer is due from the defendant. If the defendant fails to answer the complaint within the prescribed time, the plaintiff can seek judgment by default against the defendant. However, in certain instances a default judgment will be vacated if the defendant can demonstrate an acceptable excuse for failing to answer. Even if a plaintiff has been granted judgment by default, he or she could be required to present the basis for damages at a hearing before a court. A defaulting defendant may be entitled to oppose the evidence presented by the plaintiff at such a hearing, at least to the extent of the damages claimed.

Personal appearance of the defendant to respond to a complaint is not necessary. The defendant's attorney, in order to prevent default, responds to the complaint with an answer. The defense attorney attempts to show through evidence that the defendant is not responsible for the negligent act. The answer generally consists of a denial of the charges made and specifies a defense or argument justifying the position taken. The defense may show that the claim is unfounded for such reasons as the following: the period within which a suit must be instituted has run out, there is contributory negligence on the part of the plaintiff, any obligation has been paid, a general release was presented to the defendant, and the contract was illegal and therefore canceled by mutual agreement. The original answer to the complaint is filed with the court having jurisdiction over the case, and a copy of the answer is forwarded to the plaintiff's attorney.

Counterclaim

In some cases the defendant may have a claim against the plaintiff and may therefore file a counterclaim. For example, the plaintiff may have sued a hospital for personal injuries and property damage caused by the negligent operation of the hospital's ambulance. The hospital may file a counterclaim on the ground that its driver was careful and that it was the plaintiff who was negligent and is liable to the hospital for damage to the ambulance.

Bill of Particulars

Since a complaint may provide very little information regarding the claim, the defense attorney may request a bill of particulars, which limits the scope and generality of the pleadings. This document requests more specific and detailed information than is provided in the complaint. If a counterclaim has been filed, the plaintiff's attorney may request a bill of particulars from the defense attorney. More specifically, a bill of particulars for a malpractice suit may request the following from the plaintiff's attorney:

- Specify the date and time of day when the alleged malpractice occurred. Does the malpractice claim include
  —misdiagnosis or failure to diagnose correctly;
  —failure to perform a test or diagnostic procedure;
  —failure to medicate, treat, or operate;

—giving a contraindicated test or performing a contraindicated test or surgical procedure; and/or

—administering a medicine or treatment or performing a test or surgical procedure in a manner contrary to accepted standards of medical practice?

- Specify where the alleged malpractice occurred.
- Specify how the occurrence of the malpractice is claimed.
- Specify all the commissions and/or omissions constituting the malpractice claimed.
- List all injuries claimed to have been caused by the defendant's alleged malpractice.
- List any witnesses to the alleged malpractice.
- State the length of time the plaintiff was confined to bed.
- State the weekly earnings of the plaintiff.
- State the name and address of the employer.

A death action rider may also be attached if the malpractice allegedly caused death. The rider may request such information as

- the length of time the decedent experienced pain
- the date, time, and place of death
- a statement setting forth the cause of death

MOTIONS

The procedural steps that occur before trial are specifically classified as pretrial proceedings. After the pleadings have been completed, many states permit either party to move for a judgment on the pleadings. When this motion is made, the court will examine the entire case and decide whether to enter judgment according to the merits of the case as indicated in the pleadings. In some states the moving party is permitted to introduce sworn statements showing that a claim or defense is false or a sham. This procedure cannot be utilized when there is substantial dispute concerning the facts presented by the affidavits.

In many states a pretrial conference will be ordered at the judge's initiative or upon the request of one of the parties to the lawsuit. The pretrial conference is an informal discussion during which the judge and the attorneys eliminate matters not in dispute, agree on the issues, and settle procedural matters relating to the trial. Although the purpose of the pretrial conference is not to compel the parties to settle the case, it often happens that cases are settled at this point.

MOTION TO DISMISS

A defendant may make a motion to dismiss a case, alleging that the plaintiff's complaint, even if believed, does not set forth a claim or cause of action recognized by law. A motion to dismiss can be made before, during, or after trial. Motions made before a trial may be made on the basis that the court lacks jurisdiction, that the case is barred by the statute of limitations, that another case is pending involving the same issues, and other similar matters. A motion during trial may be made after the plaintiff has presented his or her case on the ground that the court has heard the plaintiff's case and the defendant is entitled to a favorable judgment as a matter of law. In the case of a motion made by the defendant at the close of the plaintiff's case, the defendant will normally claim that the plaintiff has failed to present a prima facie case—that is, that the plaintiff has failed to establish the minimum elements necessary to justify a verdict even if no contrary evidence is presented by the defendant. After the trial has been completed, either party may move for a directed verdict on the ground that he or she is entitled to such verdict as a matter of law.

A plaintiff has the right to appeal a lower court's decision to an appellate court if a defendant's motion for dismissal is granted. If the court rules against the defendant's motion for dismissal, as well as any other preliminary objections and motions the defendant may have made, the defendant will then be required to file an answer to the plaintiff's complaint.

MOTION FOR SUMMARY JUDGMENT

Either party to a suit may believe that there are no triable issues of fact and only issues of law to be decided. In such event, either party may make a motion for summary judgment. This motion asks the court to rule that there are no facts in dispute and that the rights of the parties can be determined as a matter of law, on the basis of submitted documents, without the need for a trial.

EXAMINATION BEFORE TRIAL

The parties to a lawsuit have the right to *discovery*—to examine witnesses before trial. Examination before trial (EBT) is one of several discovery techniques utilized to enable the parties of a lawsuit to learn more regarding the nature and substance of each other's case. An EBT consists of oral testimony under oath and includes cross-examination. A deposition, taken at an EBT, is the testimony of a witness that has been recorded in a written form. Either party may obtain a court order permitting the examination and copying of books and records such as medical records, as well as the inspection of buildings and equipment. A court order may also be obtained allowing the physical or mental examination of a party when the party's condition is important to the case.

In certain instances, it may be desirable to record a witness's testimony outside the court before the time of trial. In such a case, one party, after giving proper notice to the opposing party and to the prospective missing witness, may require a witness to appear before a person authorized to administer oaths in order to answer questions and submit to cross-examination. The testimony is recorded and filed with the court and is entered in evidence as the testimony of the missing witness. This procedure may be used when a witness is aged or infirm or too ill to testify at the time of trial.

The following are some helpful guidelines for a witness undergoing examination in a trial or a court hearing:

- Do not be antagonistic in answering the questions. The jury may already be somewhat sympathetic toward a particular party to the lawsuit; your antagonism may only serve to reinforce such an impression.
- Be organized in your thinking and recollection of the facts regarding the incident.
- Answer only the questions asked.
- Explain your testimony in simple, succinct terminology.
- Do not overdramatize the facts you are relating.
- Do not allow yourself to become overpowered by the cross-examiner.
- Be polite, sincere, and courteous at all times.
- Dress appropriately, and be neatly groomed.
- Pay close attention to any objections your attorney may have as to the line of questioning being conducted by the opposing counsel.
- Be sure to have reviewed any oral deposition that you may have participated in during EBT.
- Be straightforward with the examiner. Any answers designed to cover up or cloud an issue or fact will, if discovered, serve only to discredit any previous testimony you may have given.
- Do not show any visible signs of displeasure regarding any testimony with which you are in disagreement.
- Be sure to have questions that you did not hear repeated and questions that you did not understand rephrased.
- If you are not sure of an answer, indicate that you are not sure or that you just don't know the answer.

NOTICE OF TRIAL

The examination before trial may reveal sufficient facts that would discourage the plaintiff from continuing the case, or it may encourage one or both parties to settle out of court. Once a decision to go forward is reached, the case is placed on the court calendar. Postponement of the trial may be secured with the consent of both parties and the consent of the court. A case may not be indefinitely postponed without being dismissed by the court. Where one party is ready to proceed and another party seeks a postponement, a valid excuse must be shown. An example of a valid excuse is that the attorney for the party seeking the postponement is actually engaged in another case. Should a defendant fail to appear at trial, the judge can pass judgment against the defendant by default. A case can also be dismissed if the plaintiff fails to appear at trial.

MEMORANDUM OF LAW

A memorandum of law (or trial brief) is prepared for the court by each attorney. It presents the nature of the case, cites case decisions to substantiate arguments, and aids the court regarding points of law. Trial briefs are prepared by both the plaintiff's and the defendant's attorneys. A trial brief is not required, but it is a recommended strategy. It provides the court with a basic understanding of the position of the party submitting the brief before the commencement of the trial. It also focuses the court's attention on specific legal points that may influence the court in ruling on objections and the admissibility of evidence in the course of the trial.

THE JURY

The right to a trial by jury is a constitutional right in certain cases. Not all cases entitle the parties to a jury trial as a matter of right. For example, in many jurisdictions, a case in equity (a case seeking a specific course of conduct rather than monetary damages) may not entitle the parties to a trial by a jury. An example of an equity case would be one that seeks a declaration as to the title to real property.

An individual may waive the right to a jury trial. If this right is waived, the judge acts as judge and jury and becomes the trier of facts as well as issues of law.

Members of the jury are selected from a jury list. They are summoned to court by a paper known as the *jury process*. Impartiality is a prerequisite of all jurors. The number of jurors who sit at trial is 12 in common law. If there are fewer than 12, the number must be established by statute. Doctors, druggists, nurses, and lawyers are generally excused from sitting on a jury.

The counsels for both parties of a lawsuit question each prospective jury member for impartiality, bias, and prejudicial thinking. Once members of the jury are selected, they are sworn in to try the case. The jury makes a determination of the facts that have occurred, evaluating whether or not the plaintiff's damages were caused by the defendant's negligence and whether or not the defendant exercised due care. The jury must pay close attention to the evidence presented by both sides and decide on a verdict. The verdict must be based on the theory of wrongdoing. The jury makes a determination of the particular standard of conduct required in all cases where the judgment of reasonable people might differ. The jury also determines the extent of damages, if any, and the degree to which the plaintiff's conduct may have contributed to his or her injury, thereby mitigating the responsibility of the defendant (contributory negligence).

THE JUDGE

The judge decides questions of law and is responsible for ensuring that a trial is conducted properly in an impartial atmosphere and is fair to both parties of a lawsuit. He or she determines what constitutes the general standard of conduct required for the exercise of due care. The judge informs the jury of what the defendant's conduct should have been, thereby making a determination of the existence of a legal duty.

The judge plays the dominant role in a trial. He or she decides whether evidence is admissible, charges the jury (defines the jurors' responsibility in relation to existing law), and may, in fact, take a case away from the jury (by directed verdict or judgment notwithstanding the verdict) where he or she feels there are no issues for the jury to consider or that the jury has erred in its decision. This right on the part of the judge with respect to the role of the jury, in fact, narrows the jury's responsibility with regard to the facts of the case. The judge maintains order throughout the suit, determines issues of procedure, and is generally responsible for the conduct of the trial.

OPENING STATEMENTS

The plaintiff's attorney attempts to prove the wrongdoing of the defendant by presenting credible evidence favorable to his or her client. The opening statement by the plaintiff's attorney provides in capsule form the facts of the case, what he or she intends to prove by means of a summary of the evidence to be presented, and a description of the damages to his or her client. In some jurisdictions a list of witnesses, containing what the lawyers hope to obtain from each witness's testimony, is given to the judge and to the opposition prior to commencement of the trial. Included on this list are the names, addresses, and occupations of each witness. The order of the names indicates the order in which each witness will be called to the stand.

The defense attorney makes his or her opening statement indicating the position of the defendant and the points of the plaintiff's case he/she intends to refute. The defense attorney explains the facts as they apply to the case for the defendant.

BURDEN OF PROOF

The burden of proof in a lawsuit is the obligation of the plaintiff to persuade the jury regarding the truth of his or her case. A "fair preponderance of the credible evidence" must be presented in order for a plaintiff to recover. The burden of proof requires that the plaintiff's attorney show that the defendant violated a legal duty by not following an acceptable standard of care and that the plaintiff suffered injury because of the defendant's breach. If the evidence presented does not support the allegations made, the case is dismissed. Where a plaintiff, who has the burden of proof, fails to sustain such burden, the case may be dismissed despite the failure of the defendant to present any evidence to the contrary on his or her behalf. The burden of proof in some states shifts from the plaintiff to the defendant when it is obvious that the injury would not have occurred unless there was negligence.

The burden of proof in a criminal case lies with the prosecution. Proof of guilt "beyond a reasonable doubt" is required to convict a criminal defendant—a higher standard than that used in a civil case (which is a fair preponderance of the credible evidence presented).

Res Ipsa Loquitur

Res ipsa loquitur ("the thing speaks for itself" or "circumstances speak for themselves") is the legal doctrine that shifts the burden of proof from the plaintiff to the defendant. It is an evidentiary device that allows the plaintiff to make a case legally adequate to go to the jury on the basis of well-defined circumstantial evidence. This does not mean that the plaintiff has fully proven the defendant's negligence. It merely shifts the burden of going forward to the defendant—who must argue to dismiss the circumstantial evidence presented as "speaking for itself."

An inference of negligence is permitted from the mere occurrence of an injury when the defendant owed a duty and possessed the sole power of preventing the injury by exercise of reasonable care. For example, the mere presence of a surgical instrument in a patient's body raises the question of negligence without the need for expert testimony. Negligence is considered so obvious that expert testimony is not necessary. It lies within a layman's realm of knowledge that people are not born with surgical instruments in their abdomen. That alone is sufficient to require a defendant to come forward with a rebuttal. The three elements necessary to shift the burden of proof under the doctrine of *res ipsa loquitur* are as follows:

1. The event would not normally have occurred in the absence of negligence.
2. The defendant must have had exclusive control over the instrumentality that caused the injury.
3. The plaintiff must not have contributed to the injury.

Some common injuries that lead to the inference of negligence include burns from hot water bottles, heat lamps, steam vaporizers, chemicals, and bedside lamps and failure to take x-rays to diagnose possible fractures.

The patient in *Mack v. Lydia E. Hall Hospital*, 503 N.Y.S.2d 131 (App. Div. 1986), was properly permitted to invoke the doctrine of *res ipsa loquitur* in her suit to recover damages for a third-degree burn by an electrocoagulator on the side of her left thigh during surgery. The prerequisites for application of the doctrine were satisfied by evidence that the injury was unusual, the surgeon had exclusive control over the electrocoagulator, and the patient could not have contributed to the injury. The plaintiff's award of $75,000 was not considered excessive.

A major problem with the doctrine is abuse. To permit an inference of negligence under the doctrine of *res ipsa loquitur*, solely because an uncommon complication develops, would place too heavy a burden on the medical profession and might result in an undesirable limitation on the use of operations or new procedures involving inherent risks of injury in spite of due care. Abuse can occur when *res ipsa loquitur* is applied to cases where the facts show no more than a mistake in diagnosis (such as surgery for presumed appendicitis) or an adverse result of a medical procedure known to produce some poor results even when all precautions have been taken.

In *Myers v. Hospital Association of City of Schenectady*, 356 N.Y.S.2d 720 (App. Div. 1974), the patient's body was found lying on the ground five floors below the window of his room. The window was not locked when the body was found. The patient had been given a drug capable of causing drowsiness the night before. The court found these facts, which were entered into evidence, insufficient to invoke *res ipsa loquitur*. There was not a sufficient, causal relationship between the patient's death and the unlocked window.

SUBPOENAS

A subpoena is a legal order requiring the appearance of a person or documents before a court or administrative body. Subpoenas may be issued by lawyers, judges, and certain law enforcement and administrative officials, depending on the jurisdiction. Subpoenas generally include

- reference number
- names of plaintiff and defendant
- date, time, and place to appear
- name, address, and telephone number of opposing attorney
- documents requested if a subpoena is for records

Some jurisdictions require the service of a subpoena at a specified time in advance of the requested appearance (e.g., 24 hours). In other jurisdictions, no such time limitation exists. A subpoena can be served by a court clerk, sheriff, attorney, process server, or other person as provided by state statute.

A subpoena ad testificandum orders the appearance of a person at a trial or other investigative proceeding to give testimony. Witnesses have a duty to appear and may suffer a penalty for contempt of court should they fail to appear. They may not deny knowledge of a subpoena if they simply refused to accept it. Failure to appear may be excused if extenuating circumstances exist. Witnesses are paid nominal fees for time and travel whether they testify or not. Payment can be requested in advance. A subpoena must allow a reasonable amount of time to travel.

A subpoena for records, known as a subpoena duces tecum, is a written command to bring records, documents, or other evidence described in the subpoena to a trial or other investigative proceeding. The subpoena is served on one able to produce such records. Disobedience in answering a subpoena duces tecum is considered contempt of court and carries a penalty of a fine or imprisonment. The custodian of a record may require a record fee and mileage fee prior to appearance in court. The Appellate Division of the New York State Supreme Court in *Hernandez v. Lutheran Medical Center*, 478 N.Y.S.2d 697 (App. Div. 1984), held that a $1 per page charge for copies of medical records was reasonable within the meaning of the Public Health Law, which authorizes patients or their representatives to obtain copies of a medical record upon payment of a reasonable charge.

EXPERT WITNESSES

Expert testimony, as well as scientific data, is utilized to assist in establishing the standard of care required in any given situation. Expert witnesses may be used to assist a plaintiff in proving the wrongful act of a defendant or to assist a defendant in refuting such evidence. In addition, expert testimony may be used to show the extent of the plaintiff's damages or to show the lack of such damages.

It is the jury's function to receive testimony presented by witnesses and to draw conclusions in the determination of facts. The law does recognize that the jury is composed of ordinary men and women and that some fact finding will involve subjects beyond their knowledge. When a jury cannot otherwise obtain sufficient facts from which to draw conclusions, an expert witness who has special knowledge, skill, experience, or training can be called on to submit an opinion. Laymen are quite able to render opinions about a great variety of general subjects, but for technical questions the opinion of an expert is necessary. At the time of testifying, each expert's training, experience, and special qualifications will be explained to the jury. The experts will be asked to give an opinion concerning hypothetical questions based on the facts of the case. Should the testimony of two experts conflict, the jury will determine which expert opinion to accept.

The Supreme Court of Iowa in *Kastler v. Iowa Methodist Hospital*, 193 N.W.2d 98 (Iowa 1971), held that injuries sustained by the patient from a fall in a shower afforded by the hospital were the result of routine and not professional care. The patient was not required to introduce expert testimony on her behalf. Expert testimony was not required in *Powell v. Mullins*, 479 So. 2d 1119 (Ala. 1985), where a surgical lap sponge was left in the abdomen of a patient during the performance of a Caesarian section. The trial court committed reversible error in directing a verdict in the physician's favor because of the patient's failure to present an expert witness. Testimony of an expert witness is generally not required where an understanding of the physician's alleged lack of skill or due care requires only common knowledge or experience. The evidence in this case demonstrated that no intrasurgical x-rays were taken despite the fact the patient was high risk due to her smoking, obesity, and diabetes. The Supreme Court of Alabama held that it was the physician's responsibility to remove all sponges from inside the patient before closing the incision.

EXAMINATION OF WITNESSES

Following conclusion of the opening statements, the judge calls for the witnesses of the plaintiff. An officer of the court administers an oath to each witness, and direct examination begins. Information must be obtained from each witness in the form of questions by the attorney, not by the attorney's recitation of the story to the witness. On cross-examination by the defense, an attempt will be made to challenge or discredit the plaintiff's witness. Redirect examination by the plaintiff's attorney can follow the cross-examination, if so desired. The plaintiff's attorney may at this time wish to have his or her witness review an important point the jury may have forgotten during cross-examination. The plaintiff's attorney may ask the same witness more questions in an effort to overcome the effect of the cross-examination. Recross-examination by the defense may take place if necessary for the defense of the defendant.

The credibility of a witness may be impeached if prior statements are inconsistent with later statements and if there is bias in favor of a party or prejudice against a party to a lawsuit. Either attorney to a lawsuit may ask the judge for permission to recall a witness. After all the witnesses of the plaintiff have taken the stand, the defense may call its witnesses and the process of direct, cross-, redirect, and recross-examination is repeated until the defense rests.

EVIDENCE

Evidence consists of the facts proved or disproved during a lawsuit. The law of evidence is a body of rules under which facts are proved. Evidence must be competent, relevant, and material.

Demonstrative or "real" evidence is an object to which testimony refers, such as hospital equipment, surgical instruments, broken infusion needles, autopsy reports, birth certificates, site visits (e.g., visits to the hospital where the plaintiff was injured) that can be requested by the jury, or documentary evidence (any tangible object capable of making a truthful statement, such as a medical record). Demonstrative evidence is admissible in court if it is relevant, has probative value, and serves the interest of justice. It is not admissible if it is intended to prejudice, mislead, confuse, offend, inflame, or arouse the sympathy or passion of the jury or to be indecent. Other forms of demonstrative evidence include photographs, motion pictures, x-ray films, drawings, human bodies as exhibits, pathology slides, fetal monitoring strips, operating room logs, anesthesia logs, infection committee reports, medical staff bylaws, rules and regulations, Joint Commission on Accreditation of Healthcare Organizations standards, nursing manuals, departmental policy and procedure manuals, census data, staffing patterns, etc. The plaintiff's attorney utilizes all pertinent evidence to reconstruct chronologically the patient's care and treatment.

When presenting photographs as a form of evidence, the photographer or a reliable witness who is familiar with the object photographed must state that the picture is an accurate representation and a fair likeness of the object portrayed. The photograph must not exaggerate a client's physical condition or show coloring of injuries that is prejudicial. Photographs can be valuable legal evidence when they illustrate graphically the nature and extent of a medical injury. Motion pictures are also valuable evidence. They are helpful in re-enacting a crime. The same principles that apply to photographs apply to motion pictures. Motion pictures must not be fraudulently portrayed by destroying continuity (by either cutting or rearranging). Videotape, a modern form of recording events, is admissible in court, assuming appropriate authentication of the matter being taped, the time of the taping, and the manner in which such taping took place.

X-ray films are considered pictures of the interior of the object portrayed and are admitted under the same requirements as photographs and motion pictures. The attorney must show competent evidence that the x-rays taken are the object or body part under consideration—that the x-ray was made in a recognized manner, taken by a competent technician, and interpreted by a competent physician trained to read x-rays. The value of x-rays lies in the fact that they illustrate fractures, foreign objects, etc.

The plaintiff's injuries are admissible as an exhibit if the physical condition of the body is material. The human body is considered the best evidence of the nature and extent of the plaintiff's injury. If there is no controversy about either the nature or the extent of the injury, such evidence can be considered prejudicial material to which the defendant's attorney should object. Demonstrations are permitted in some instances to illustrate the extent of injuries.

Documentary evidence, such as medical records, must satisfy the jury as to authenticity. Proof of authenticity is not necessary if genuineness is accepted by the opposing party. In some instances, concerning wills, for example, witnesses are necessary. In the case of documentation, the original of a document must be produced unless it can be demonstrated that the original has been lost or destroyed, in which case a properly authenticated copy may be substituted. A manufacturer's drug insert or manual describing the use of equipment is admissible. In *Mueller v. Mueller*, 221 N.W.2d 39 (S.D. 1974), a physician was sued by a patient who charged that as a result of the administration of cortisone over an extended period, she had needlessly suffered a deterioration of bone structure and ultimately a collapsed hip. The jury decided that the physician's prolonged use of cortisone was negligent, and the physician appealed. The appeals court held that the manufacturer's recommendations are not only admissible, but also essential in determining a physician's possible lack of proper care.

The judicial notice rule prescribes that well-known facts (for example, that fractures need prompt attention and that two x-rays of the same patient may show different results) need not be proven. If a fact can be disputed, the rule does not apply.

The plaintiff in *Arthur v. St. Peter's Hospital*, 169 N.J. Super. 575, 405 A.2d 443 (1979), sought treatment in the emergency room of St. Peter's Hospital following an injury to his left wrist. After being examined, he was sent to the radiology department for x-rays of his wrist. He was later released after being advised that there were no fractures. The plaintiff suffered continued swelling and pain. As a result, he decided to seek care from another physician, who subsequently diagnosed a fracture of the navicular bone. The plaintiff sued, and the hospital motioned for summary judgment, stating that the physicians were independent contractors, not employees of the hospital.

Copies of the emergency room record, x-ray report, and billing record contained the logo of the hospital. There was nothing on the records to identify the physicians as being independent contractors. The court took judicial notice that generally people who seek medical help through the emergency room facilities of hospitals are unaware of the status of various professionals working there. Unless the patient had been in some manner put on notice that those physicians with whom he might come into contact during the course of his treatment were independent contractors, it would be natural to assume that they were employees of the hospital.

Evidence indicating the propensity of a defendant to commit a negligent act is admissible evidence. The Supreme Court of Suffolk County, Special Term, in *Cotgreave v. Public Administration of Imperial County*, 443 N.Y.S.2d 971 (Sup. Ct. 1981), held that medical malpractice plaintiffs would be allowed to introduce evidence of prior operations on persons other than the patient by the defendant physician, who allegedly intentionally performed unnecessary surgery on the patient. The court had been informed of other cases pending against the surgeon in which allegations were made as to the lack of indications for surgery.

Hearsay evidence is that which is based on what another has said or done and is not the result of the personal knowledge of the witness. Due to the ability to successfully challenge hearsay evidence, which rests on the credibility of the witness as well as on the competency and veracity of other persons not before the court, it is admitted as evidence in a trial only under very strict rules. The U.S.

district court in *Northeast Women's Center, Inc., v. McMonagle*, 689 F. Supp. 465 (E.D. Pa. 1988), in a civil action alleging RICO violations and trespass arising from protests at an abortion clinic, found the trial court to have properly excluded testimony of one of the witnesses. The substance of the proposed testimony was based on double hearsay and not the competent testimony of the witness. A police officer's testimony that he had overheard a drug dealer tell the informant, who was wearing a concealed transmitter, that he could obtain proof for the informant from a pharmacist friend was properly admitted in a disciplinary proceeding. *Brown v. Idaho State Board of Pharmacy*, 746 P.2d 1006 (Idaho Ct. App. 1987). The testimony was presented before the Idaho State Board of Pharmacy for proving a dealer's state of mind and explaining his subsequent visit to the pharmacy. The testimony was not subject to hearsay objection.

DEFENSES AGAINST RECOVERY

Once a plaintiff's case has been established, the defendant may put forward a defense against the claim for damages. The defendant's case is presented to discredit the plaintiff's cause of action and prevent recovery of damages.

Doctrine of Charitable Immunity

The doctrine of charitable immunity is a legal doctrine that developed out of the English court system and held charitable institutions blameless for their negligent acts. Historically, there was little consistency in the application of the doctrine in the United States. Some states permitted judgment for paying patients, while others did not hold hospitals liable even if it was shown they were negligent. Patients who were treated in charitable hospitals were said to have implicitly waived their right of suit because of negligence. Patients paying a reasonable charge were not considered to be the recipients of charity.

Today, the doctrine of charitable immunity is essentially history. Most states have abolished charitable immunity exemptions. Suits may now be brought against charitable institutions, and such institutions will be liable for their negligent acts and those of their agents.

Contributory Negligence

When the issue of contributory negligence is raised, the defendant claims that the conduct of the injured person is below the standard of care reasonably prudent persons would exercise for their own safety. In some jurisdictions, contributory negligence, no matter how slight, is sufficient to defeat a plaintiff's claim. The two elements necessary to establish contributory negligence are (1) that the plaintiff's conduct fell below the required standard of personal care, and (2) that there is a connection between the plaintiff's careless conduct and the plaintiff's injury. Thus, the defendant contends that some, if not all, liability is attributable to the plaintiff's own actions. The defendant, in order to establish a defense of contributory negligence, must show that the plaintiff's negligence was an active and efficient contributing cause of the injury. This was not the case in *Bird v. Pritchard*, 33 Ohio App. 2d 31, 291 N.E.2d 769 (1973), where the plaintiff on July 3, 1970, slipped and fell, cutting her right hand on a mayonnaise jar and thus injuring the ulnar nerve. She was taken to Hocking Valley Memorial Hospital where she requested the services of Dr. Najm, a board-certified general surgeon. However, he was not available. The defendant, an osteopathic surgeon, was available, and he treated the patient's wound. The patient had complained that the fourth and fifth fingers of her right hand were numb. The defendant cleaned the wound and advised the patient to see him on Monday, July 7. The patient did not return to the osteopathic surgeon, but went to see Dr. Najm that same Monday. A suit was filed, the court of common pleas rendered a judgment for the defendant, and the plaintiff appealed. The court of appeals held that the patient could not be found to have been contributorily negligent or to have assumed the risk where by the time of her scheduled visit it was impossible to perform primary or secondary repair of the injured nerves which had not been treated on the initial visit when she had first complained of numbness. "For contributory negligence to defeat the claim of the plaintiff, there must not only be negligent conduct by the plaintiff but also a direct and proximate causal relationship between the negligent act and the injury the plaintiff received." 291 N.E. 2d at 771.

The patient, Mr. Cammatte, in *Jenkins v. Bogalusa Community Medical Center*, 340 So. 2d 1065 (La. Ct. App. 1976), was admitted to Bogalusa Community Medical Center on September 11, 1970, for the treatment of a severe gouty arthritic condition. He had been advised not to get out of bed without first ringing for assistance. On the morning of September 16, 1970, the patient got out of bed without ringing for assistance and went to a bathroom across the hall. As he returned to his room, he fell and fractured his hip. Mr. Cammatte was transferred to Touro Infirmary in New Orleans where he underwent hip surgery and expired on October 5, 1970, during recuperation, due to an apparent pulmonary embolism. The Twenty-Second Judicial District Court entered judgment for the defendants, and the plaintiffs appealed. The court of appeals found that the patient was in full possession of his faculties at the time he fell and fractured his hip. The accident was the result of the patient's knowing failure to follow instructions not to get out of bed without ringing for assistance. The injury in this case was not the result of any breach of the hospital's duty to exercise due care.

The rationale for contributory negligence is based on the principle that all persons must be both careful and responsible for their acts. A plaintiff is required to conform to the broad standard of conduct of the reasonable person. The plaintiff's negligence will be determined and governed by the same tests and rules as the negligence of the defendant.

The Delaware Supreme Court affirmed a lower court's dismissal of a wrongful death action against a medical center's emergency room personnel in *Rochester v. Katalan*, 320 A.2d 704 (Del. 1974). The decedent, Mr. Rochester, and a friend had been brought to the emergency room at approximately 6:30 P.M. under the custody of two police officers. Rochester and his friend, claiming to be heroin addicts suffering withdrawal symptoms, requested some form of medication. The decedent stated that he had a habit requiring four to five bags of heroin a day. His actions denoted symptoms of withdrawal. He and his friend were loud, abusive, and uncooperative. Rochester complained of abdominal pains, his eyes appeared glassy, and his body was shaking, among other symptoms that he exhibited. The physician on duty in the emergency room asked whether he had ever participated in a methadone clinic program. He indicated that he had, but that he had dropped out of it because he found a new supply source for heroin. The physician then ordered the administration of 40 mg. of methadone. Rochester continued to put on an act by beating his head against a wall and claiming that he was still sick and needed more methadone. The plea was granted, and the physician ordered a second dosage of 40 mg. of methadone. After eventually calming down, Rochester was taken to a cell by the police officers. The following morning it was impossible to awaken him, and he was later pronounced dead. It was discovered that he had never been an addict or on a methadone program. Rather, the previous night he had been drinking beer and taking librium. He had not told this to hospital authorities.

His estate sued the physician, and the trial court dismissed the suit. The appellate court affirmed, saying that by his failure to give the physician accurate information, the deceased had contributed to his own death. On appeal, the plaintiff had argued that the doctor and staff could have done more to determine the truth of Rochester's assertions that he was a drug addict. The Delaware Supreme Court held that it had already assumed negligence in that respect. Rochester contributed to his own death by failing to provide a true account of the facts to the emergency room staff. He was guilty of negligent conduct, more accurately "willful" or "intentional" conduct, which was the proximate cause of his death, resulting from multiple drug intoxication. His estate was barred from recovering any monetary damages.

Assumption of the Risk

Assumption of the risk means knowing that a danger exists and voluntarily accepting the risk by taking a chance in exposing oneself to it, knowing that harm might occur. Assumption of the risk may be implicitly assumed, as in alcohol consumption, or expressly assumed, as in relation to warnings found on cigarette packaging.

This defense provides that the plaintiff has expressly given consent in advance, relieving the defendant of an obligation of conduct toward the plaintiff and taking the chances of injury from a known risk arising from the defendant's conduct. For example, one who agrees to care for a patient with a communicable disease and then contracts the disease would not be entitled to recovery from the former patient for damages suffered. In taking the job, the individual agreed to assume the risk of infection, thereby releasing the patient from all legal obligations.

The following two requirements must be established in order for a defendant to be successful in an assumption of the risk defense: (1) The plaintiff must know and understand the risk that is being incurred, and (2) the choice to incur the risk must be free and voluntary.

Comparative Negligence

The doctrine of comparative negligence provides that the degree of negligence or carelessness of each party to a lawsuit must be established by the finder of fact, and each party is then responsible for his or her proportional share of any damages awarded. For example, where a plaintiff suffers injuries of $10,000 from an accident and where the plaintiff is found 20 percent negligent and the defendant 80 percent negligent, the defendant would be required to pay $8,000 to the plaintiff. Thus, with comparative negligence the plaintiff can collect for 80 percent of the injuries, whereas an application of contributory negligence would deprive the plaintiff of any money judgment. This doctrine relieves the plaintiff from the hardship of losing an entire claim when a defendant has been successful in establishing that the plaintiff has contributed to his or her own injuries. A defense that provides that the plaintiff will forfeit an entire claim if he or she has been contributorily negligent is considered too harsh a result in jurisdictions that recognize comparative negligence.

In most states today, contributory negligence will not defeat a plaintiff's claim, but may reduce the amount of damages. A patient's negligence was permitted as a defense to lessen the damages and to reflect her personal contribution to her injury in *Heller v. Medine*, 377 N.Y.S.2d 100 (App. Div. 1975). The patient had brought a malpractice action against a physician, alleging improper treatment of a herpes infection following cataract surgery on the right eye. The physician alleged that the plaintiff contributed to her own injury by failing to make two follow-up visits. The trial court entered a verdict in favor of the physician. On appeal, the supreme court, appellate division, held that the patient's failure to follow the physician's instructions did not defeat the action where the alleged improper professional treatment occurred prior to the patient's own negligence. Damages were reduced to the degree that the plaintiff's negligence increased the extent of the injury.

The plaintiff in *Quinones v. Public Administrator of Kings County*, 373 N.Y.S.2d 224 (App. Div. 1975), sought to recover damages for the alleged negligence of the defendant's physicians for their failure to treat a fractured ankle. The plaintiff claimed that there was a nonunion of the fracture and that he was advised to put weight on his leg. As a result of this advice, the plaintiff claimed that there was an exacerbation of the original injury requiring two operative procedures, which resulted in the fusion of his left ankle. The defendant claimed that if there was any subsequent injury, it was the failure of the plaintiff to return for care. The supreme court entered a judgment in favor of the defendant hospital, and the plaintiff appealed. The supreme court, appellate division, held that a patient's failure to follow instructions does not defeat an action for malpractice where the alleged improper professional treatment occurred prior to the patient's own negligence. Damages would be reduced to the degree that the plaintiff's negligence increased the extent of the injury.

Borrowed Servant and Captain of the Ship Doctrines

The borrowed servant doctrine is a special application of the doctrine of *respondeat superior* and applies when an employer lends an employee to another for a particular employment. Although an employee remains the servant of the employer, under the borrowed servant doctrine the employer is not liable for injury negligently caused by the servant while in the special service of another. The borrowed servant rule provides that in certain situations a nurse employed by a hospital may be considered the employee of the physician. In these situations, the physician is the special or temporary employer and is liable for the negligence of the nurse. To determine whether a physician is liable for the negligence of a nurse, it must be established that the physician had the right to control and direct the nurse at the time of the negligent act. If the physician is found to be in exclusive control and if the nurse is deemed to be the physician's temporary special employee, the hospital is not generally liable for the nurse's negligent acts.

In the context of the operating room, the application of the borrowed servant doctrine is generally referred to as the captain of the ship doctrine. Under this doctrine, the surgeon is viewed as being the one in command in the operating room. The rationale for this concept was provided in the Minnesota case of *St. Paul-Mercury Indemnity Co. v. St. Joseph Hospital*, 4 N.W.2d 637 (Minn. 1942), when the court stated this:

> The desirability of the rule is obvious. The patient is completely at the mercy of the surgeon and relies upon him to see that all the acts relative to the operation are performed in a careful manner. It is the surgeon's duty to guard against any and all avoidable acts that may result in injury to his patient. In the operating room, the surgeon must be master. He cannot tolerate any other voice in the control of his assistants. In the case at bar, the evidence is clear that the doctor had exclusive control over the acts in question, and therefore the hospital cannot be said to have been a "joint master" or "comaster," even though the nurse was in its general employ and paid by it.

Id. at 638, 639.

In *Krane v. Saint Anthony Hospital Systems*, 738 P.2d 75 (Colo. App. 1987) the Colorado Court of Appeals held that even if we assume that the surgical nurse was the employee of the hospital, that she was negligent, and that such negligence caused the death of the plaintiff's husband, the so-called captain of the ship doctrine still precludes recovery against the hospital. The factual question that must be determined is whether, at the time of the alleged negligent act, the operating surgeon had assumed such control. If so, the responsibility of the surgeon supersedes that of the hospital. Since it was uncontradicted that the alleged negligent act of the surgical nurse took place over two and one-half hours into surgery, there could be no factual dispute that the surgeon had assumed control over the nurse.

Several courts have developed a distinction between a nurse's clerical or administrative acts and those involving professional skill and judgment, which are considered medical acts. The courts use this distinction in allocating liability for the acts of a nurse as between the surgeon and the hospital. If the act is characterized as administrative or clerical, it is the hospital's responsibility; if the act is considered to be medical, it is the surgeon's responsibility. This rule was followed in the Minnesota case of *Swigerd v. City of Ortonville*, 75 N.W.2d 217 (Minn. 1956), when the court found that the hospital is liable as an employer for the negligence of its nurses in performing acts that are basically administrative, such as clerical acts. Administrative acts, though constituting a component of a patient's prescribed medical treatment, do not require the application of specialized procedures and techniques or the understanding of a skilled physician or surgeon.

The distinction between administrative and other acts is occasionally stated by the courts in order to determine whether a hospital or a physician is liable for a nurse's negligent acts. However, it is regarded by some jurisdictions as lacking sound judgment. Although the courts have narrowed those situations where a nonemployee staff physician will be held liable for the negligent acts of hospital employees, there continue to be cases holding physicians responsible for the negligent acts of nurses. The court of appeal in *Schultz v. Mutch*, 211 Cal. Rptr. 455 (Cal. Ct. App. 1985), held that the jury was correctly instructed as to a physician's *respondeat superior* liability for the acts and omissions of nurses. A doctor's reliance, no matter how reasonable, on hospital nursing procedures does not extinguish his liability for the negligence of nurses under the *respondeat superior* doctrine of captain of the ship, which is founded in the doctor's power and resulting duty to direct nurses under his/her supervision.

Good Samaritan Laws

Most states have enacted good samaritan laws, which relieve physicians, nurses, dentists, and other health professionals, and in some instances laymen, from liability in certain emergency situations. Good samaritan legislation encourages health professionals to render assistance at the scene of emergencies. By offering immunity, the laws attempt to overcome the widespread notion that physicians, nurses, and others who render assistance in emergencies are likely to be held liable for negligence.

State legislatures have enacted good samaritan statutes for a variety of legal, ethical, and moral reasons. It is a generally accepted legal principle that there is no legal duty to assist a stranger in a time of distress. However, if one person has caused distress to another, there is a legal duty to assist. This principle extends to physicians. They are not legally bound to answer the call of strangers who are dying and might be saved; however, it is a generally recognized moral duty to help a person in distress.

Minnesota state law provides for fines of up to $100 for persons who fail to aid others in emergency situations. The law in this instance provides that "reasonable assistance" should be given (i.e., obtain or attempt to obtain aid from medical and/or law enforcement personnel). The law protects an individual from liability unless he or she is reckless and/or intentionally cruel when rendering aid. If an individual at the scene of an emergency would have to place himself or herself or another in danger by assisting, each would be exempt from providing assistance.

Each good samaritan statute provides a standard of care that delineates the scope of immunity for those persons eligible under the law. The standards vary widely from state to state and are sometimes ambiguous. In most states the scope of immunity is generally qualified by the statement that the person giving aid must act "in good faith." Some statutes require that a physician or the person rendering care must act with "due care," without "gross negligence," or without "willful or wanton" misconduct.

Despite problems of interpretation, it is clear that the purpose of the statutes is to encourage volunteer medical assistance in emergency situations. The language that grants immunity also supports the conclusion that the doctor, nurse, or layman who is covered by the act will be protected from liability for ordinary negligence in rendering assistance in an emergency.

Under most statutes, immunity is granted only during an emergency or when rendering emergency care. The concept of emergency usually refers to a combination of unforeseen circumstances that require spontaneous action to avoid impending danger. Some states have sought to be more precise regarding what constitutes an emergency or accident. According to the Alaska statute, the emergency circumstances must suggest that the giving of aid is the only alternative to death or serious bodily injury.

Most statutes require that emergency services be rendered without payment or expectation of payment. Apparently this provision was inserted to emphasize that the actions of a good samaritan must be voluntary. In order to be legally immune under the good samaritan laws, a physician or nurse must render help voluntarily and without expectation of later pay.

Statute of Limitations

Whether a suit for personal injury can be brought against a defendant often depends on whether the suit was commenced within a time specified by the applicable statute of limitations. The statutory period begins when an injury occurs, although in some cases (usually involving foreign objects left in the body during surgery) the statutory period commences when the injured person discovers or should have discovered the injury.

Many technical rules are associated with statutes of limitations. Statutes in each state specify that malpractice suits and other personal injury suits must be brought within fixed periods of time. The fact that an injured person is a minor or is otherwise under a legal disability may, under the laws of many states, extend the period within which an action for injury may be brought. Computation of the period when the statute begins in a particular state may be based on any of the following factors: the date that the physician terminated treatment; the time of the wrongful act; the time when the patient should have reasonably discovered the injury; the date that the injury is actually discovered; and the date when the contract between the patient and the physician ended. The running of the statute will not begin if fraud (the deliberate concealment from a patient of facts that might present a cause of action for damages) is involved. The cause of action begins at the time fraud is discovered.

In a 1949 Michigan case, *Buchanan v. Kull*, 16 C.C.H. Neg. Cases 490 (Mich. 1949), a patient who had undergone a thyroidectomy suffered paralyzed vocal cords. The patient had been told that the injury was due to a lack of calcium. The patient later learned that the vocal cords had been cut. The statute of limitations would normally have run out in this case; however, the presence of fraud did not permit the statute to commence until the patient became aware of the fraud.

A New Hampshire patient in *Shillady v. Elliot Community Hospital*, 320 A.2d 637 (N.H. 1974), sued the hospital for negligence in treatment that was administered 31 years earlier. A needle had been left in the patient's spine after a spinal tap in 1940. In 1970 an x-ray showed the needle. The patient had suffered severe pain immediately after the spinal tap, which had decreased over the intervening years to about three "spells" a year. The court held that the six-year statute of limitations does not begin "until the patient learns or in the exercise of reasonable care and diligence should have learned of its presence." *Id.* at 637. Therefore, the defendant's motion to dismiss the case on the ground that the statute of limitations had run was not granted.

In *Whack v. Seminole Memorial Hospital, Inc.*, 456 So. 2d 561 (Fla. Dist. Ct. App. 1984), summary dismissal of a suit on the basis that the statute of limitations had tolled was improperly ordered in an action for wrongful death during the performance of a Caesarean section. It was found that the cause of death could not have been determined until receipt of an autopsy report.

Ignorance of Fact and Unintentional Wrongs

Ignorance of the law is not a defense; otherwise, the ignorant would be rewarded. The fact that a negligent act is unintentional is no defense. Otherwise, defendants could never be found guilty.

Intervening Cause

Intervening cause refers to an act of an independent agency that destroys the causal connection between the negligent act of a defendant and the wrongful injury; if the independent act, not the original wrongful act, is the proximate cause of injury, damages are not recoverable.

In *Cohran v. Harper*, 154 S.E.2d 461 (Ga. Ct. App. 1967), the patient sued a physician, charging him with malpractice for an alleged staph infection she received from a hypodermic needle used by the physician's nurse. The nurse gave the patient an injection that resulted in osteomyelitis. The grounds of negligence included an allegation that the physician failed to properly sterilize the hypodermic needle that was used to administer a certain dose of penicillin. The evidence showed, without dispute, that a prepackaged, sterilized needle and syringe were used in accordance with proper and accepted medical practice. The physician was not liable. There was inadequate proof that either the physician or his nurse was negligent. The court said that even if there was evidence that the needle was contaminated and that the patient's ailment was caused thereby, there was no evidence that either the physician or his nurse or anyone in his office knew, or by the exercise of ordinary care could have discovered, that the prepackaged needle and syringe were so contaminated. The defense of intervening cause would have been an adequate defense against recovery of damages if it had been established that the needle was contaminated when packaged.

Sovereign Immunity

Sovereign immunity refers to the common law doctrine by which federal and state governments have historically been immune from liability for harm suffered by the tortious conduct of employees. Sovereign immunity has for the most part been abolished by both federal and state governments.

Congress enacted the Federal Tort Claims Act (FTCA), which provides redress for those who have been negligently injured by employees of the federal government while acting within their scope of employment. Action was brought on behalf of a minor in *Steele v. United States*, 463 F. Supp. 321 (D. Alaska 1978), who received treatment at a U.S. Army hospital and suffered injury because of the optometrist's failure to refer the child to an ophthalmologist for examination. The U.S. district court held that it was probable that an ophthalmologist would have diagnosed the child's problem and prevented the loss of his right eye. Recovery was permitted against the United States under the Federal Tort Claims Act, 28 U.S.C.A. Section 1346 (b) 2671 *et seq.*

Immunity from intentional torts, claims arising from combat, etc., are exceptions to the FTCA. A serviceman brought a claim for medical malpractice against the United States in *Luce v. United States*, 538 F. Supp. 637 (E.D. Wis. 1982), under the Federal Tort Claims Act. The district court held that the claim was barred under a doctrine prohibiting actions for injuries to a serviceman arising out of or in the course of activity incident to service. The holding was granted even though the operation was elective and the serviceman was absent from regular duty at the time of surgery. The Feres doctrine, which prohibits a serviceman from bringing an action against the United States under the Federal Tort Claims Act, was first enunciated in *Feres v. United States*, 340 U.S. 135 (1950).

Claims made are governed by the law of the state in which negligence is asserted. The state of Missouri was protected from liability by the doctrine of sovereign immunity in *Sherrill v. Wilson*, 653 S.W. 2d 661 (Mo. 1983) (en banc). Action had been brought for the wrongful death of the plaintiff's son at the hands of an involuntary patient at a state mental hospital who failed to return to the institution from a two-day pass.

The Veterans Administration Hospital of Memphis, Tennessee, in *Wooten v. United States*, 574 F. Supp. 200 (W.D. Tenn. 1982), was held negligent for injuries sustained by an 83-year-old heart patient who was found lying outside his room in a hallway of the hospital. This action was brought under the FTCA. The patient had suffered severe head injuries that required surgery. Damages in the amount of $80,000 were awarded the plaintiff. The U.S. district court held that the evidence was sufficient to raise a duty on the part of hospital personnel attending the patient to use reasonable care to protect him from getting out of bed and injuring himself. This duty was breached, and the patient was injured. The proximate cause of the patient's injuries was related to the hospital's failure to put up the patient's bedrails and its failure to remind him to call a nurse if he needed help. Evidence offered in this case indicated that the Veterans Administration hospital did not meet the standards rendered in other large Memphis hospitals.

Independent Contractor

An independent contractor is an individual who agrees to undertake work without being under the direct control or direction of another and is personally responsible for his or her negligent acts. This doctrine is used by hospitals as a defense to avoid liability caused by a physician's negligence. The mere existence of an independent contractual relationship is not sufficient to remove a hospital from liability for the acts of certain of its professional personnel where the independent contractor status is not readily known to the injured party.

The appellate division of the New York State Supreme Court in *Mduba v. Benedictine Hospital*, 384 N.Y.S.2d 527 (App. Div. 1976), held that the hospital was liable for the emergency room physician's negligence, whether or not the physician was an independent contractor, even if under contract the physician was considered to be an independent contractor. The court held that the patient had no way of knowing of the existence of a contract and relied on the relationship between the hospital and the physician in seeking treatment in the emergency room.

The appellant hospital in *Garcia v. Tarrio*, 380 So. 2d 1068 (Fla. Dist. Ct. App. 1980), claimed that the evidence presented did not establish that Dr. Garcia, a surgeon, was the hospital's agent and that the negligence established was attributable to Dr. Garcia alone. The district court of appeals held that the appellant surgeon was the hospital's agent in that he had an agreement with the hospital guaranteeing him at least 50 percent of the work at the hospital.

Whether or not a physician is an employee or an independent contractor is of primary importance in determining hospital liability. A hospital is generally not liable for injuries resulting from negligent acts or omissions of independent physicians. There is no liability on the theory of *respondeat superior* where a physician is an independent contractor and not an employee or servant of the hospital, is in no way compensated by the hospital, maintains a private practice, and is directly chosen by his or her patients.

CLOSING STATEMENTS

The judge, following completion of the plaintiff's case and the defendant's defense, calls for closing statements. The defense proceeds first, then the plaintiff. Closing statements provide lawyers an opportunity to summarize for the jury and the court what they have proven. They may point out faults in their opponent's case and emphasize points they wish the jury to remember.

If there appears to be only a question of law at the end of a case, a motion can be made for a directed verdict. A motion of this nature must be decided by the court. The court will grant the motion if there is no question of fact to be decided by the jury. The directed verdict may also be made on the ground that the plaintiff has failed to present sufficient facts to prove his/her case or that the evidence fails to establish a legal basis for a verdict in the plaintiff's favor.

Following the attorneys' summations, the court charges the jury before the jurors recess to deliberate. Since the jury determines issues of fact, it is necessary for the court to instruct the jury with regard to the applicable law. This is done by means of a charge. The charge defines the responsibility of the jury, describes the applicable law, and advises the jury of the alternatives available to it.

When a charge given by the court is not clear enough on a particular point or when it does not cover various issues in the case, it is the obligation of the attorneys for both sides to request clarification of the existing charge. When the jury retires to deliberate, the members are reminded not to discuss the case except among themselves.

It should be noted that if a verdict is against the weight of the evidence, a judge may dismiss the case, order a new trial, or set his or her own verdict. At the time judgment is rendered, the losing party has an opportunity to motion for a new trial. If the new trial is granted, the entire process is repeated; if not, the judgment becomes final, subject to a review of the trial record by an appellate court.

DAMAGES

Damages are fixed by the jury and are either nominal, compensatory, or punitive. Nominal damages are awarded as a mere token in recognition that wrong has been committed when the actual amount of compensation is insignificant. Compensatory damages are estimated reparation in money for detriment or injury sustained (including loss of earnings, medical costs, and loss of financial support). Punitive damages are additional money awards authorized when an injury is caused by gross carelessness or disregard for the safety of others. Damages cover such items as physical disability, mental anguish, loss of a spouse's services, physical suffering, injury to one's reputation, and loss of companionship.

Punitive damages have been referred to as "that mighty engine of deterrence" in *Johnson v. Terry*, No. 537-907 (Wis. Cir. Ct. Mar. 18, 1983). The Supreme Court of North Carolina in *Henry v. Deen*, 310 S.E.2d 326 (N.C. 1984), held that allegations of gross and wanton negligence incidental to wrongful death in the plaintiff's complaint gave sufficient notice of a claim against the treating physician and physician's assistant for punitive damages. The original complaint, which alleged that the treating physician, the physician's assistant, and the consulting physician agreed to create and did create false and misleading entries in the patient's medical record, was sufficient to allege a civil conspiracy. The decision of the court of appeals was reversed, and the case was remanded for further proceedings.

In *Garcia v. Kantor*, 54 Cal. App. 3d 1025, 127 Cal. Rptr. 164 (1976), the court refused to allow recovery of money damages by married children in a case where their father suffered injury because of a negligent defendant. The children had claimed that they lost the companionship of their father.

The court of appeals in *Haught v. Maceluch*, 681 F.2d 291 (5th Cir. 1982), held that under Texas law the mother was entitled to recover for her emotional distress, even though she was not conscious at the time her child was born. The mother had brought a medical malpractice action, alleging that the physician was negligent in the delivery of her child, causing her daughter to suffer permanent brain injury. The district court entered judgment of $1,160,000 for the child's medical expenses and $175,000 for her lost future earnings. The court deleted a jury award of $118,000 for the mother's mental suffering over her daughter's impaired condition. On appeal, the court of appeals permitted recovery, under Texas law, for mental suffering. The mother was conscious for more than 11 hours of labor and was aware of the physician's negligent acts, his absence in a near-emergency situation, and the overadministration of the labor-inducing drug Pitocin.

The supreme court, appellate division, in *Quijije v. Lutheran Medical Center*, 460 N.Y.S.2d 601 (App. Div. 1983), held that the plaintiff's mother may not recover for emotional injury rising solely from having to observe her baby suffer and die due to alleged denial of timely medical treatment. The plaintiff could not succeed by invoking a section of the Public Health Law that requires general hospitals to admit and provide emergency medical treatment to all in immediate need thereof without advance payment or questioning as to payment. Section 2805-b provided no basis for an action to recover money damages.

A jury verdict totaling $12,393,130 was considered an excessive award in *Merrill v. Albany Medical Center*, 512 N.Y.S.2d 519 (App. Div. 1987), where damages were sought with respect to the severe brain damage sustained by a 22-month-old infant as the result of oxygen deprivation. This occurred when the infant went into cardiac arrest during surgery for removal of a suspected malignant tumor from her right lung. Reduction of the amount to $6,143,130 was considered appropriate.

The plaintiffs in *Campbell v. Pitt County Memorial Hospital, Inc.*, 321 N.C. 260, 362 S.E.2d 273 (1987), brought an action to recover damages for personal injury suffered by an infant. The infant's mother had been admitted to the defendant hospital for delivery of her baby. The defendant physician, Dr. Deyton, determined that the baby was in a footing breech, feet first position. At 1:30 P.M. on the date of delivery, Dr. Deyton proceeded with a vaginal delivery despite the position of the baby. For several hours prior to delivery, the hospital nurses monitoring the baby observed complications which they believed were adversely affecting the condition of the fetus. One of the nurses expressed their concerns to Dr. Deyton; however, she did not contact her immediate supervisor or anyone else when Dr. Deyton failed to address her concerns. The infant's umbilical cord became wrapped around her legs. The infant sustained brain damage due to severe asphyxia from the entangled cord. Today, the child suffers from cerebral palsy and requires constant care and supervision. Damages were sought for medical expenses, mental anguish, and trauma. The plaintiffs settled with the defendant physician and his professional association in the amount of $1,500,000, leaving Pitt County Memorial Hospital as the sole defendant. The trial court was found not to have abused its discretion when, after the jury awarded the infant damages in the amount of $4,850,000, it ordered a new trial, finding the damages awarded excessive. The jury award appeared to the court to have been made under the influence of passion and prejudice and was unsupported by the evidence. The defendant's motion for a new trial on this issue was granted. This decision was upheld on appeal to both the Court of Appeals and the Supreme Court of North Carolina.

The plaintiff in *Burge v. Parker*, 510 So. 2d 538 (Ala. 1987), suffered a laceration of his right foot on April 2 and was taken to St. Margaret's Hospital. A physician in the emergency room cleaned and stitched the laceration and released the patient with instructions to keep the foot elevated. Even though reports prepared by the fire medic who arrived on the scene of the accident and by ambulance personnel had indicated the chief complaint as being a fracture of the foot, no x-rays were ordered in the emergency room. The admitting clerk had typed a statement on the admission form indicating possible fracture of the right foot. However, a handwritten note stated the chief complaint as being a laceration of the right foot. The patient returned to the hospital later in the day with his mother, complaining of pain in the right foot. His mother asked if x-rays had been taken. The physician said that it was not necessary. The wound was redressed, and the patient was sent home again with instructions to keep the foot elevated. The pain continued to get worse, and the patient was taken to see another physician on April 5. X-rays were ordered, and an orthopedic surgeon called for a consultation diagnosed three fractures and a compartment syndrome, a swelling of tissue in the muscle compartments. The swelling increased pressure on the blood vessels, thus decreasing circulation, which tends to cause muscles to die. Approximately one-half pint of clotted blood had been removed from the wound. By April 11, the big toe had to be surgically removed. It was alleged that the physician had failed to obtain a full medical history, to order the necessary x-rays, and to diagnose and treat the fractures of the foot. As a result, the patient ultimately suffered loss of his great toe. The Circuit Court of Macon County awarded damages totaling $450,000 for loss of a big toe, and the physician appealed. The Supreme Court of Alabama found the damages not to have been excessive.

JOINT AND SEVERAL LIABILITY

The doctrine of joint and several liability permits the plaintiff to bring suit against all persons who share responsibility for his/her injury. The doctrine allows the plaintiff to recover monetary damages from any one or all of the defendants. Any one defendant, even though partially responsible for the plaintiff's injury, can be required to pay the full judgment awarded by the jury. Awards tend to fall in greater amounts on defendants with the better insurance. This is the "deep pockets" concept: Whoever has the most pays the greater percentage of the award.

APPEALS

An appellate court reviews a case on the basis of the trial record as well as written briefs and, if requested, concise oral arguments by the attorneys. A brief summarizes the facts of a case, testimony of the witnesses, laws affecting the case, and arguments of counsel. The party making the appeal is the *appellant*. The party answering the appeal is the *appellee*. After hearing the oral arguments, the court takes the case under advisement until such time as the judges consider it and agree on a decision. An opinion is then prepared explaining the reasons for a decision.

Grounds for appeal may result from the following: the verdict was excessive or inadequate in the lower court, evidence was rejected that should have been accepted, inadmissible evidence was permitted, testimony was excluded that should have been admissible, the verdict was contrary to the weight of the evidence, and/or the court improperly charged the jury.

Notice of appeal must be filed with the trial court, the appellate court, and the adverse party. A *supersedeas*, a "stay of execution," should also be filed by the party wishing to prevent execution of an adverse judgment until such time as the case has been heard and decided by an appellate court.

The appellate court may modify, affirm, or reverse the judgment or reorder a new trial on an appeal. The majority ruling of the judges in the appellate court is binding on the parties of a lawsuit. If the appellate court's decision is not unanimous, the minority may render a dissenting opinion. Further appeal may be made, as set by statute, to the highest court of appeals. If an appeal involves a constitutional question, it may eventually be appealed to the U.S. Supreme Court.

When a case is decided by the highest appellate court in a state, a final judgment results, and the matter is ended. The instances when one may appeal the ruling of a state court to the Supreme Court of the United States are rare. A federal question must be involved, and even then the Supreme Court must decide whether it will hear the case. A federal question is one involving the Constitution of the United States or a statute enacted by Congress, so it is unlikely that a negligence case arising in a state court would be reviewed and decided by the Supreme Court.

EXECUTION OF JUDGMENTS

Once the amount of damages has been established and all the appeals have been heard, the defendant must comply with the judgment. If he fails to do so, a court order may be executed requiring the sheriff or other judicial officer to sell as much of the defendant's property as necessary, within statutory limitations, to satisfy the plaintiff's judgment.

Chapter 19

Restraint of Trade

SHERMAN ANTITRUST ACT

Health care expenditures are a major segment of the nation's economy and are considered a significant cause of inflation. This has resulted in a demand, from both the public and the private sectors, for the development of more cost-effective approaches to the delivery of health care. This, in turn, has led to significant competition for the health care "dollar" and is changing the very nature of how health care delivery is viewed by the courts.

Probably the most dramatic example of this is in the area of antitrust. Antitrust litigation and enforcement in the health care field were nearly nonexistent prior to 1975; since that time, it has become a major legal issue with health care providers.

The increasing number of health care professionals and alternative delivery systems and the resultant competition create the potential for illegal activities to restrain trade. The emphasis on free enterprise and a competitive marketplace have caused careful scrutiny by the Federal Trade Commission, the federal agency responsible for monitoring the marketplace and enforcing federal antitrust laws.

The primary federal law that comes into play in the health care area is the Sherman Antitrust Act. The Sherman Act proscribes the following:

> Section 1. Every contract, combination in the form of trust or otherwise, or conspiracy, in restraint of trade or commerce among the several states . . . is declared to be illegal.
>
> Section 2. Every person who shall monopolize, or attempt to monopolize, or combine or conspire with any other person or persons, to monopolize any part of the trade or commerce among the several states . . . shall be deemed . . . guilty of a felony . . . .

15 U.S.C. §1 (1982).

Areas of concern for hospitals include mergers that reduce market competition, price fixing, actions that bar or limit new entrants to the field, preferred provider arrangements, exclusive contracts, and the like.

For example, hospitals must be cognizant of the potential problems that may exist in limiting the number of physicians that it will admit to its medical staff. Since closed staff determinations can effectively limit competition from other physicians, medical groups, health maintenance organizations, etc., the governing board must ensure that the decision-making process in granting hospital privileges is based on legislative, objective criteria and is not dominated by those who have the most to gain competitively by denying privileges.

Physicians have attempted to use state and federal antitrust laws to challenge hospital determinations denying or limiting medical staff privileges. Generally these actions claim that the hospital conspired with other physicians to ensure that the complaining physician would not get privileges so that competition among the physicians would be reduced. To date, physicians have generally been unsuccessful in pursuing these antitrust claims.

However, in a landmark decision, the U.S. Supreme Court upheld a $2 million jury verdict in favor of a surgeon, practicing in Astoria, Oregon, who claimed that other doctors had conspired to terminate his staff privileges at the only hospital in town, and thus drove him out of practice. *Patrick v. Burget*, 108 S. Ct. 1658 (1988). The defendant doctors argued that their conduct should be immune from liability under the state action doctrine since Oregon, like many states, has state agencies that generally regulate the procedures hospitals may use to grant or deny staff privileges. This state action defense was rejected by the Supreme Court in light of the egregious facts of the case (the defendant doctors were also participants in the state processes) and the fact that Oregon's statutory scheme did not actively supervise medical staff determinations.

Significantly, the *Patrick* case was decided prior to the effective date of the Federal Health Care Quality Improvement Act of 1986, 42 U.S.C.A. Sections 11101–11152, which insulates certain medical peer-review activities affecting medical staff privileges from antitrust liability. In essence, such an activity is protected so long as it is taken "in the reasonable belief that [it] was in the furtherance of quality health care." In enacting this legislation, Congress recognized that without such antitrust immunity, effective peer review may not be possible.

EXCLUSIVE CONTRACTS

Hospitals often enter into an exclusive contract with physicians and/or medical groups for the purpose of providing a specific service to the hospitals. Exclusive contracts generally occur within the hospital's ancillary services (i.e., radiology, anesthesiology, and pathology).

Physicians who seek to practice at hospitals in these ancillary areas, but who are not part of the exclusive group, have attempted to invoke the federal antitrust laws to challenge these exclusive contracts. These challenges have generally been unsuccessful.

In *Jefferson Parish Hospital v. Hyde*, 466 U.S. 2 (1984), the defendant hospital had a contract with a firm of anesthesiologists that required that all anesthesia services for the hospital's patients be performed by that firm. Because of this contract, the plaintiff anesthesiologist's application for admission to the hospital's medical staff was denied. Dr. Hyde commenced an action in the federal district court, claiming the exclusive contract violated Section 1 of the Sherman Antitrust Act. The district court rejected the plaintiff's complaint, but the U.S. Court of Appeals for the Fifth Circuit reversed, finding the contract illegal per se. The Supreme Court reversed the Fifth Circuit, holding that the exclusive contract in question does not violate Section 1 of the Sherman Antitrust Act. The Supreme Court's holding was based on the fact that the defendant hospital did not possess "market power" and therefore patients were free to enter a competing hospital and to use another anesthesiologist instead of the firm. Thus, the Court concluded that the evidence was insufficient to provide a basis for finding that the contract, as it actually operates in the market, had unreasonably restrained competition.

Similarly, the anesthesiologists in *Belmar v. Cipolla*, 96 N.J. 199, 475 A.2d 533 (1984), brought an action challenging a hospital's exclusive contract with a different group of anesthesiologists. The Supreme Court of New Jersey held that under state law the hospital's exclusive contract was reasonable and did not violate public policy.

MORATORIUM AND CLOSED MEDICAL STAFF

Moratorium and *closed medical staff*, as used in the health care field, describe a hospital's policy of prohibiting further appointments to its medical staff. A moratorium is generally for a specified period of time. It is lifted at such time as the purpose for which it was instituted no longer exists. A closed staff is of a more permanent nature and relates to the mission of the institution, such as a commitment to teaching and research. Such institutions are very selective in their medical staff appointments. Physicians who are appointed generally have high academic interests and abilities as well as national recognition for expertise in their specialties.

Hospital boards have adopted a moratorium policy in certain instances because of a high inpatient census and the difficulties that would be encountered in accommodating new physicians. If left unchecked, the closing of hospital medical staffs could eventually have the effect of discouraging a competitive environment in the physician marketplace.

Hospital boards that adopt a closed staff policy must do so on a rational basis and take the following into consideration before closing the medical staff to new applicants:

- the effect on the quality of patient care
- the effect on the hospital census

- hospital and community needs for additional physicians in certain medical and surgical specialties and subspecialties
- the strain that additional staff will put on the hospital's supporting departments (e.g., radiology and laboratory services)
- the effect of denying medical staff privileges to applicants who are presently located within the geographical area of the hospital and serving community residents
- the effect on any contracts the hospital may have with other health care delivery systems, such as health maintenance organizations
- the effect a moratorium will have on physician groups that may desire to add a partner
- the effect additional staff may have on the quality of care rendered at the hospital
- whether closing the staff will confine control of the hospital's beds to the existing medical staff, allowing them to enhance their economic interests at the expense of other qualified physicians and their patients
- the effect of a limited moratorium by specialty as opposed to a comprehensive one involving all specialties (Closing a staff in all departments and sections indiscriminately without a review could be considered an action in restraint of trade.)
- the existence of a mechanism for periodic review of the need to continue a moratorium
- the effect that medical staff resignations during the moratorium may have on the hospital's census
- the existence of a mechanism for notifying potential medical staff candidates at such time that the hospital determines there is a need for an expanded medical staff
- characteristics of the medical staff (that is, is the staff aging and in need of new membership?)
- the potential for restraint of trade legal action under the antitrust laws
- the effect of increasing competition from free-standing surgicenters, emergency care centers, hospice programs, nursing homes, etc., on the hospital census
- the long-term effects
- the effect on physicians without staff privileges whose patients are admitted to a hospital's emergency room
- the formation of a committee composed of representatives from the board of managers, medical staff, administration, and legal counsel to develop an appropriate moratorium policy
- the selection of a consultant who would study the demographics marketplace, physician referral patterns, literature, and hospital utilization; conduct a

medical staff opinion poll; develop patient-physician population ratios; determine population shifts; develop a formula to determine optimal staffing levels by department and section; and provide this information to the board for use in determining the appropriateness of closing the staff in selected departments

The continuing pressure of new technology, government, third party payers, a host of regulations (e.g., utilization reviews, length of stay reviews, appropriateness of care reviews, alternate levels of care, diagnostic related groupings, and professional review organizations), and an increasing number of physicians demand that hospitals review the fast-changing health care delivery systems and seriously consider ways they can effectively expand and compete in the marketplace. In light of this, the imposition of a moratorium or the closing of a hospital's medical staff may prove to be counterproductive to the long-term survival of an institution.

A moratorium must be applied with consistency and nondiscrimination. In *Walsky v. Pascack Valley Hospital*, 367 A.2d 1204 (N.J. 1976), the New Jersey Supreme Court held that the moratorium discriminated against newly admitted members of the staff who were required to agree not to seek staff privileges elsewhere, while those admitted to the staff prior to the moratorium were not subject to the same restriction, and that the moratorium represented an arbitrary and capricious exercise of discretion on the part of the board of trustees and defendant hospital.

Medical staff privileges in *Desai v. St. Barnabas Medical Center*, 510 A.2d 662 (N.J. 1986), were closed to new applicants with the exception of physicians who had become affiliated with current staff members. This was considered arbitrary and discriminatory against otherwise competent physicians. The hospital argued that the exception was necessary to help cover the practices of physicians who were already on the hospital's medical staff. It was decided that such arguments involved mere supposition.

The New Jersey Supreme Court in *Berman v. Valley Hospital*, 103 N.J. 100, 510 A.2d 673 (1986), held that a policy denying medical staff privileges to doctors who practiced in the hospital's service area for more than two years was arbitrary and not enforceable. The hospital had claimed that it was overcrowded and overutilized and that this was attributable to physicians from surrounding areas obtaining medical staff privileges. The hospital stated that its medical/surgical bed occupancy rate in 1977 had reached 89 percent and that the number of doctors increased from 172 in 1968 to 260 in 1977. It is of great interest to note that the hospital conceded that it would have empty beds if it limited admissions to its primary service area.

The governing board must ensure that any proposed action to close a hospital's medical staff is based on objective criteria. In several states, state agencies monitor the actions of a hospital's governing board with respect to the granting or denial of clinical privileges. Unless the hospital can demonstrate that its actions are based on legitimate patient care concerns or concerns related to the objectives of the hospital, physicians may be successful in employing antitrust and tort law to challenge the hospital's actions.

CONCLUSION

Hospital privileges are both professionally and economically important to health professionals in the practice of their chosen professions. Hospital trustees must be selective in the granting of hospital privileges in order to maintain quality standards. Every effort must be made to prevent anticompetitive abuses. As competition increases between podiatrists and orthopedic surgeons, psychologists and psychiatrists, nurse midwives and obstetricians, nurse anesthetists and anesthesiologists, chiropractors and orthopedic surgeons, nurse practitioners and family practice physicians, etc., it must be understood that there is a clear difference in denying hospital privileges to an individual on a quality basis and denying such privileges to an entire group of professionals; the latter will serve only to raise a red flag and increase the chances of scrutiny by the courts. The stage has been set for tough competition for a dwindling number of patients which in turn increases the potential for denial of staff privileges to prevent competitors from effectively entering the marketplace and practicing their respective professions.

Chapter 20

Hospital Reorganization

INTRODUCTION

Traditionally, hospitals have functioned as independent, free-standing corporate entities or as units or divisions of multihospital systems. Until recently, a free-standing hospital functioned as a single corporate entity with most programs and activities carried out within such entity to meet increasing competition.

Dependence on government funding and related programs (e.g., Medicare, Medicaid, and Blue Cross) and the continuous shrinkage occurring in such revenues have forced hospitals to seek alternative sources of revenue. Greater competition from nonhospital sources has also contributed to this need to seek alternative revenue sources. It has become apparent that traditional corporate structures may no longer be appropriate to accommodate both normal hospital activities and those additional activities undertaken to provide alternative sources of revenue.

EXISTING STRUCTURES

The typical hospital is incorporated under state law as a free-standing for-profit or not-for-profit corporation. The corporation has a governing body (generally known as a board of directors, or board of trustees). Such governing body has overall responsibility for the operation and management of the hospital with a necessary delegation of appropriate responsibility to administrative employees and the medical staff.

Not-for-profit hospitals are usually exempt from federal taxation under Section 501(c)(3) of the U.S. Internal Revenue Code of 1986 as amended. Such federal exemption usually entitles the organization to an automatic exemption from state taxes as well. Such tax exemption not only relieves the hospital from the payment of income taxes, sales taxes, and the like, but also permits the hospital to receive contributions from donors who then may obtain charitable deductions on their personal tax returns.

CONSIDERATIONS LEADING TO CORPORATE REORGANIZATION

Given the need to obtain income and to meet competition, hospitals have begun to consider establishing business enterprises. They may also consider other nonbusiness operations, such as the establishment of additional nonexempt undertakings (e.g., hospices and long-term care facilities). Since hospitals have resources including the physical plant, administrative talent, and technical expertise in areas that are potentially profitable, the first option usually considered is direct participation by the hospital in health-related business enterprises. There are, however, regulatory and legal pressures that present substantial impediments.

Taxation

Income earned by tax-exempt organizations from nonexempt activities is subject to unrelated business income taxes under the Internal Revenue Code. These taxes are similar to those paid by profit-making organizations. In addition, tax-exempt status may be lost if a substantial portion of the corporation's activities are related to nonexempt activities and/or if the benefits of the tax-exempt status accrue to individuals who control the entity either directly or indirectly (private inurement). Care must also be taken to avoid use of facilities exempt from real estate taxation because this may lead to a partial or complete loss of such exemption.

Third Party Reimbursement

Medicare, Medicaid, Blue Cross, and other third parties that reimburse hospitals directly for patient care require that no reimbursement be available for activities unrelated to the provision of such care. Thus, costs associated with unrelated activities must be deducted from costs submitted to third party payers for reimbursement. The "carving out" of these costs can be detrimental to the hospital unless alternative revenues are found. Under a case payment (DRG) system, costs may not seem as important. However, cost reporting remains significant for the establishment of capital reimbursement and for the potential change of the base year used for rate-setting purposes.

Certificate of Need

Generally, hospitals may not add additional programs or services, nor may they expend monies for the acquisition of capital in excess of specified threshold limits without first obtaining approval from appropriate state regulatory agencies. The process by which this approval is granted is generally referred to as the certificate of need (CON) process. This process can be lengthy and expensive. Further, it may not always result in approval of the request to offer the new program or service or to make the capital expenditure. In addition, the process is somewhat competitive in nature. New programs and services may not be permitted to a number of institutions in the same geographic locale. Thus, where one hospital successfully obtains permission to add a new program or service, a nearby hospital may be denied the same request because the perceived public need for such program or service has already been met.

Financing

Even where a hospital has determined that it can and should add a program or service and where it is allowed to do so, it may lack the necessary capital financing. The hospital could join with private investors (who may, in fact, be members of the medical staff) in order to gain greater access to capital. Care must be taken, however, that no venture that includes physicians who refer to the hospital can be construed as providing an incentive or a reward for such referrals. Federal antifraud and abuse laws and regulations and similar state regulations impose severe penalties for such violations.

Recognizing the problems enumerated above and further recognizing the need to develop alternate sources of revenue, hospitals have determined that the establishment of an additional or a restructured organization is necessary. In addition to the need to develop alternate sources of capital, some restructurings come about simply because of the evolution of a multi-institutional system. Thus, where hospitals merge or consolidate, restructuring is virtually automatic. Also, where a number of hospitals fall under common ownership or where additional health enterprises are undertaken, restructuring usually evolves as more institutions are added to the system. In these instances, general legal principles applicable to corporations, as well as proper management considerations, will control the development of the appropriate corporate structure.

RESTRUCTURING ALTERNATIVES

Assuming the existence of a single not-for-profit, tax-exempt hospital, any restructuring that is undertaken will normally involve the creation of at least one additional not-for-profit, tax-exempt entity. This entity may be referred to as a *parent* or *holding company* or *foundation*. Its general function is to serve as the corporate vehicle to receive the ultimate benefits from the revenue-producing activities and to confer some or all of these benefits on the hospital. Under current rules regarding income taxation, income received directly (by providing goods or services) or indirectly (by means of dividends or other investment income) does not give rise to any tax obligation if the receiver of such benefit is exempt from taxation under any of several subsections of Section 501(c) of the Internal Revenue Code, provided that exempt activities are the organization's major source of income and expense.

Parent Holding Company Model

Under this model, a new not-for-profit corporation is formed in conformity with the laws of the state in which the hospital is located. This corporation can then seek to obtain a tax exemption under the Internal Revenue Code. The overall purposes of the corporation are general in nature, but involve a promotion of the health and welfare of the public and may also directly involve benefit to a named hospital or hospitals. In some states, where one organization exists to benefit a licensed hospital, such organization must itself be approved through a CON or similar process. The government of the parent holding company is usually derived from the governing body of the hospital. Qualifications for certain categories of exempt status under the Internal Revenue Code may, in fact, require overlapping governing bodies between the hospital and the new entity. Section 509(a) of the Internal Revenue Code deals with the qualification of a tax-exempt entity as a "private and/ or non-private" foundation. "Non-private" is the preferred status, and the qualification for such status may depend in part on the relationship between the entity seeking tax exemption and the already exempt entity (i.e., the hospital).

Since there is no stock involved in a not-for-profit corporation (the ownership of which would confer control by one corporation over another), control of the not-for-profit hospital by the not-for-profit parent holding company generally arises when the parent holding company is the sole "member" of the hospital corporation. Membership carries with it the right to elect directors and thus creates the necessary linkage for the "parent-subsidiary" relationship.

As a tax-exempt entity, the parent holding company may also own one or more for-profit subsidiaries. While such ownership cannot represent the majority of the activities of the parent holding company, the ownership of such entities would not in and of itself disqualify the parent holding company from achieving and maintaining a tax-exempt status. It is through the subsidiaries that for-profit activities are carried on. The for-profit ventures (which may be independent corporations, joint ventures with other investors, etc.) are tax-paying entities. The net revenues (after payment of taxes) are paid out as dividends to the entity owning the stock or other ownership interest (the parent holding company), which, being tax exempt, pays no taxes on the receipt of such dividends. The parent holding company may then, as a donation, confer benefits directly on the hospital or any other entity intended to benefit from the parent holding company. Again, it is important to closely monitor the activities of this corporation so that its participation in or ownership of for-profit entities does not destroy its tax-exempt status. The Internal Revenue Service is becoming increasingly concerned about this issue and has dramatically stepped up its auditing activities.

Controlled Foundation

An alternative structure to the parent holding company model is one in which the new not-for-profit entity is directly controlled by the hospital. Instead of the parent holding company's being a member of the hospital corporation, the reverse is true. The hospital is the member of the new entity. The structure described above to carry out for-profit activities would then fall under the controlled foundation. In many states the regulators would view such a controlled foundation as nothing more than the alter ego of the hospital and therefore impose on this entity all regulatory restrictions, reimbursement restrictions, and the like.

Independent Foundation

The establishment of a separate not-for-profit corporation and the substructure below it for carrying out for-profit activities may be accomplished independent of the hospital. Even though members of the hospital's governing body are involved in the creation of the new not-for-profit entity, the two corporations themselves may not necessarily be linked. This "brother-sister" relationship is frequently found to be desirable where the governing body of a hospital does not favor the creation of a parent organization to control the hospital, but nevertheless seeks to create a viable structure within which for-profit activities may be carried on outside the hospital. A concern that is frequently expressed in this brother-sister relationship is that the new entity, not being controlled directly by the hospital or in the alternative not controlling the hospital, may "run away" and not necessarily ultimately benefit the hospital as was originally intended. Whether or not such a concern will materialize is naturally dependent on the degree to which the governing bodies of the two organizations overlap and the degree to which each organization remains responsive to the other. The use of this model may also have certain reimbursement advantages regarding earnings on donated monies. If reimbursement regulations ever change to offset charitable gifts from reimbursable activities, an "independent" organization may also prove useful. While no such proposal is being seriously entertained at this time, this could change in the future.

GENERAL CONSIDERATIONS

None of the structures described above is intended to alter the way the hospital is managed or the way the hospital delivers care. The driving force behind the creation of alternative structures is the desire to develop alternate sources of revenue and/or to streamline management of multi-institutional systems. In many states substantial changes in the governance of a hospital require regulatory approval. The establishment of the alternative structures previously described normally does not require such regulatory approval so long as the hospital continues to be governed by a governing body and so long as the hospital continues to carry out its functions in accordance with applicable laws, rules, and regulations.

Once restructuring has taken place, obviously numerous additional entities will require legal and accounting attention. These entities (normally corporations) must maintain minutes, books, and records; file tax returns; and make such other filings as are required by state laws and by federal and state income tax laws and regulations. It is important that the structures be viewed as running independently, one from the other. This includes the establishment of separate bank accounts, the holding of regular meetings among officers and directors, and the maintenance of appropriate minutes. Too often the activities and records of one entity are difficult to discern from those of another, and then the benefits of the separate organizations may be lost. The concept of "piercing the corporate veil" may come in to play where each corporate entity is not maintained separate and apart from every other entity. The corporate veil will be pierced where a court determines that the activities of the corporation are indistinguishable from the activities of either another corporation or the corporation's directors, officers, or members.

The parent corporation in *Boafo v. Hospital Corp. of America*, 338 S.E.2d 477 (Ga. Ct. App. 1985), was held not liable for injuries sustained by a patient at a subsidiary hospital. Even though the parent corporation shared some officers with the subsidiary and furnished it with substantial administrative services, there was no basis for piercing the corporate veil of the parent absent some showing that the subsidiary was a sham formed for the purpose of promoting fraud, defeating justice, concealing crime, or evading contractual or tort responsibility. Although the hospital was a wholly owned subsidiary of a national management corporation, it was a fully capitalized corporate entity that was insured, owned the hospital property, autonomously managed and operated the hospital on a day-to-day basis, maintained its own payroll, and employed its own employees. There was therefore no basis for holding the parent corporation liable.

INVOLVEMENT OF THE MEDICAL STAFF IN RESTRUCTURING

Any discussion of corporate reorganization undertaken by a hospital must necessarily involve the medical staff. While a reorganization may have little or no direct impact on the medical staff, the perception of major change requires, at the very least, a full explanation and involvement in the process.

Many hospitals have come to realize that the medical staff presents a fertile area for developing relationships and projects leading to additional revenues. Projects such as imaging centers, laboratories, durable medical equipment businesses, and the like may be organized in conjunction with one or more members of the medical staff. Other likely candidates to participate in joint ventures include existing laboratories, home care companies, durable medical equipment companies, drug companies, surgical supply houses, and the like. As previously noted, ventures involving physicians are coming under significantly greater scrutiny and regulation. Laws and regulations have been designed to curb the practice of physicians and other health professionals of referring patients to facilities or enterprises in which they have a financial interest. See, e.g., Social Security Act, 18 U.S.C. Section 6204 (amended 1989).

Joint ventures with physician groups are not without risk, as was demonstrated in *Arango v. Reyka*, 507 So. 2d 1211 (Fla. Dist. Ct. App. 1987), where a hospital entered into a joint venture with an anesthesiology group and thus was vicariously liable for the malpractice of the members of that group. The hospital billed patients for anesthesiological services, retained 12 percent of all collections, owned and furnished anesthesiology equipment and medications utilized by the group, scheduled patients, and referred to the group as the hospital's Department of Anesthesiology. As a result, there existed a common purpose to provide anesthesiological services to hospital patients. Control was shared between the hospital and the group over the provision of anesthesia services, and there was a joint interest in the financial benefits and profits generated by the combination of their resources and services. The fact that the physicians had an obligation to maintain control over their medical judgment did not prevent the creation of a joint venture contract.

Development of a business involving equity participation must be considered in light of state and federal securities laws and other relevant laws, rules, and regulations to determine that there is full compliance. Shares of stock, shares in linked partnerships, and other similar equity participation interests may fall within the definition of a public offering of securities requiring filings and/or registrations under state and federal securities laws.

FUND RAISING

A not-for-profit hospital generally raises funds. Any new not-for-profit corporation formed as part of restructuring may also be able to engage in fund raising if such entity obtains a tax exemption under the Internal Revenue Code.

In addition, as part of a reorganization and despite the creation of a new entity as indicated, hospitals frequently determine that it is desirable to create an additional foundation the sole purpose of which is fund raising for the hospital. This may therefore lead to as many as three organizations with both the capability and the intent to engage in fund raising to benefit the hospital. Obvious confusion may arise in the minds of the public being asked to give to these organizations. A coordinated approach to fund raising is critical to avoid such confusion.

Any organization engaged in fund raising may have local filing requirements at the state or other governmental level. Care must be taken that the public is completely informed as to the ultimate beneficiary of such fund raising and the manner in which the monies raised will be spent. A donor to a charity may have a claim against that charity if the donor can demonstrate that he or she was misled as to the ultimate beneficiary of the gift or as to the purposes for which the gift would be used. Members of the public may be reluctant to donate where capital is to be used to fund for-profit enterprises. The overall charitable purposes of the entity must be carried out, and the activities may not be so concentrated on the operation or participation in for-profit ventures that either the tax exemption is jeopardized or it is determined (usually by the state attorney general) that the funds have been raised improperly from the public.

REGULATORY AUTHORITY CHECKLIST

In considering restructuring, the following regulatory authority checklist may be helpful:

- Not-for-profit corporations
  —not-for-profit corporation law
  —Internal Revenue Code (exemption and taxpayer identification number)
  —state and local tax laws on exemptions (including real property)
  —attorney general or similar charitable registration requirements
  —bylaws, organization minutes, minutes of first governing board meeting
  —bank account
- For-profit corporations
  —business corporation law
  —taxpayer identification number
  —bylaws, organization minutes, minutes of first board meeting, issuance of stock
  —bank account
- Hospitals
  —reimbursement regulations
  —certificate of need regulations
  —governing board bylaws and relationship to additional corporations
  —fraud and abuse laws, rules, and regulations

ANTICOMPETITION

Because a hospital exerts a certain amount of influence and dominance over its patient population, the participation in for-profit enterprises to which hospital patients are referred may give rise to anticompetitive activities and antitrust claims. Patients must be permitted a free choice in connection with goods and services. For example, if the hospital (through its reorganized structure) participates in a durable medical equipment (DME) business and seeks to recommend such business to its patients upon discharge, such patients must be allowed to choose an alternate supplier. Patients must be advised that they are not required to use the vendor recommended by the hospital. It may also be wise for the hospital to disclose its relationship to the DME company so that the patient knows the hospital's involvement in advance of making a choice.

Care must be taken that local vendors and merchants who have a traditional relationship with the hospital or with the patients are not so affected by the proposed for-profit activity that not only is ill will generated within the community, but also a potential legal claim regarding anticompetitive activity may evolve.

Restructuring requires a multidisciplinary approach. The issues to be considered include legal, financial, accounting, tax, regulatory, and reimbursement concerns. These disciplines must provide input on an ongoing basis, not merely at inception. Changing requirements and interpretations, especially in the areas of taxation and Medicare/Medicaid fraud and abuse regulations, mandate a continuous process of review and modification so that desired goals are not subverted by legal and financial problems.

> Nonetheless, a word of caution. Today's ventures require additional planning for the possibility that some, or part of an enterprise might ultimately be found illegal. Therefore, potential buyers, and hopefully arrangements with them, as well as appropriate dissolution and unwinding provisions, now more than ever, need to be part of the fabric and documentation of any new joint venture. As well, the documentation of existing ventures must be reviewed in the light of current considerations and where necessary, needed revisions crafted.[1]

The Federal Trade Commission (FTC) determined that the Hospital Corporation of America (HCA), a proprietary hospital chain, violated Section 7 of the Clayton Act, as amended, 15 U.S.C. § 18 (1982), by acquiring two hospital corporations, Hospital Affiliates International, Inc., and Health Care Corporation, in the Chattanooga area for $700 million. HCA already owned one hospital in the area. Hospital Affiliates International held management contracts with two other area hospitals. This in effect gave HCA control over 5 of the 11 hospitals in the Chattanooga area. The management contract with one of the hospitals was canceled after the FTC began investigating HCA's acquisition of Hospital Affiliates. HCA sought judicial review by petitioning the court of appeals to set aside the decision of the FTC. The court of appeals held that there was substantial evidence to support the commission's determination that the acquisitions were likely to foster collusive practices harmful to consumers. *Hospital Corp. of America v. Federal Trade Commission*, 807 F.2d 1381 (7th Cir. 1986).

Restructuring is an undertaking that requires careful planning and legal and accounting advice and should be undertaken not because it is "fashionable," but rather because it will provide the hospital with opportunities not available under its current structure.

NOTE

1. Weissburg, *Joint Ventures: To Be or Not To Be*, FEDERATION OF AMERICAN HEALTH SYSTEMS REVIEW, May–June 1989, at 50.

Chapter 21

Miscellaneous Topics

The Oath of Hippocrates has been passed on to us as a living and workable statement of ideals to be cherished by the physician. This oath protects rights of the patient and appeals to the finer instincts of the physician without imposing sanctions or penalties. Other civilizations have developed written principles, but the Oath of Hippocrates has remained in Western civilization as an expression of ideal conduct for the physician. Adherence to professional medical ethics will go a long way in the prevention of lawsuits and the development of good physician-patient relationships.

The following topics describe the continuing efforts by both public and private entities to resolve the malpractice crisis.

DEFENSIVE MEDICINE

Defensive medicine is believed to be one of the most harmful effects produced by the threat of malpractice litigation. It is practiced to forestall potential litigation and provide a good legal defense should a lawsuit be instituted. Medical records are becoming more defensive and will become even more so with closer scrutiny by insurance carriers. Because of the calculated risk and potential for liability in most diagnostic and therapeutic procedures, physicians are practicing both negative and positive defensive medicine.

Negative defensive medicine avoids the performance of high-risk tests and/or procedures. This avoidance has led to what has been termed undertreatment. Positive defensive medicine includes the excessive utilization of x-rays and other diagnostic tests. It has been referred to as overtreatment.

COLLATERAL SOURCE RULE

The collateral source rule is a common law principle that prohibits the court or jury from taking into account when setting an award the fact that part, or even all, of the plaintiff's damages have already been covered by other sources of payment such as health insurance, disability, and compensation. Several states have modified the collateral source rule so that evidence regarding other sources of payment to the plaintiff may be introduced, and this may affect the amount of the award to the plaintiff. The jury is then permitted to assign the evidence such weight as it chooses.

Imposition of the collateral source rule can often result in recoveries to plaintiffs far in excess of their economic loss. Such excessive payments contribute significantly to the high cost of malpractice insurance and the high cost of medicine to the public. Where evidence regarding collateral sources of payment can be introduced in order to mitigate the damages payable to a plaintiff, excessive recoveries may be discouraged.

The malpractice litigants in *Baker v. Vanderbilt University*, 616 F. Supp. 330 (D.C. Tenn. 1985), sought a court order declaring the provisions of the Tennessee statute abrogating the collateral source rule in medical malpractice cases to be unconstitutional. The district court held that the Tennessee statute did not deny the litigants equal protection as compared with victims of other torts.

CONTINGENCY FEES

Contingency fees result when an attorney agrees to accept payment for a malpractice case that is dependent on its favorable outcome. Payment is based on a pre-established percentage of the total award. Some states set this percentage by statute or court rule.

Physicians argue that the contingency fee arrangement serves to encourage frivolous prosecution and an inordinate number of lawsuits. Lawyers reason that if they or their clients must bear the initial cost of a lawsuit, only those with obvious merit would be brought. The contingency fee structure also allows those unable to bear the cost of litigation to initiate a suit for damages.

COUNTERSUITS

Physicians, in some instances, are filing countersuits after being named in what they believe to be malicious, libelous, slanderous, frivolous, and nonmeritorious medical malpractice suits. Remedies for such actions vary from one jurisdiction to the next. In order for a physician to prevail in a suit against a plaintiff and/or plaintiff's attorney, the physician must show that the suit was frivolous, that the motivation of the plaintiff was not to recover for a legitimate injury, and that the physician has suffered damages as a result of the suit. The plaintiff's attorney has a legal and ethical responsibility to make sure that any suits filed are backed by sufficient and reasonable facts.

In *Berlin v. Nathan*, 64 Ill. App. 3d 940, 381 N.E.2d 1367 (1978), a radiologist, a surgeon, and a hospital were sued for alleged malpractice by a patient who sought $250,000 because the defendants did not properly diagnose a fracture of her little finger. The radiologist missed the break, but he claimed that it was not evident on the x-ray taken at the hospital and that there was no error on his part. Furthermore, the finger was placed in a splint just as if it had been broken, so the treatment was correct regardless of the diagnosis. The radiologist countersued, so that the malpractice suit and countersuit were tried together. When the jury was selected, the patient withdrew the malpractice suit, but the radiologist persisted with his case. The jury awarded the radiologist $2,000 as compensation and $6,000 in punitive damages, presumably convinced that the patient and her attorneys acted improperly in bringing the lawsuit and that the lawyers were negligent in their investigation of the patient's case before filing suit.

When the case was taken to an appellate court, the decision of the lower court was reversed on the grounds that the physician had failed to plead special damages and (because the countersuit had been filed prematurely) had failed to plead a favorable result in the original suit. The appellate court went on to say that a showing of special damages is essential in a case of this type in order that the public's right to free access to the court system not be impeded by the threat of counterlitigation. The court reasoned that persons who feel they have legitimate claims should not be dissuaded from using the court system solely because of the fear of liability in the event their claim is unsuccessful.

The appellate court holding in the *Berlin* case represents the majority judicial view across the country regarding countersuits. Courts generally do not find in favor of the countersuing party because they fear that persons who would otherwise bring such suits will be discouraged simply because of a concern over the possibility of a countersuit.

AWARD LIMITATIONS

Jury awards for economic and noneconomic damages have skyrocketed to astronomical heights. As a result, negligence attorneys often prefer to try negligence cases in those jurisdictions where a jury is likely to grant a higher award. Various states are attempting to stem the tide of rising malpractice costs by passing laws that impose restrictions on the total dollar damages allowable in malpractice actions.

While only a few states have enacted such legislation and there have been challenges to such enactments, it would appear that limitations on malpractice recoveries are not unconstitutional. The Supreme Court of Idaho in *Jones v. State Board of Medicine*, 97 Idaho 859, 555 P.2d 399 (1976), held that the state's limitation on malpractice recoveries ($150,000) need not necessarily be unconstitutional. The court held that there was no inherent right to an unlimited amount of damages and that the state had a legitimate interest in controlling excessive medical costs caused by large malpractice recoveries, and thus the statute could be held constitutional.

The Supreme Court of California in *Fein v. Permanente Medical Group*, 38 Cal. 3d 137, 695 P.2d 665, 211 Cal. Rptr. 368 (1985), found that provisions in the Medical Injury Compensation Reform Act of 1975 (MICRA), Civil Code Section 3333.2, that limit noneconomic damages for pain and suffering in medical malpractice cases to $250,000 are not unconstitutional. The legislature did not place limits on a plaintiff's right to recover for economic damages, such as medical expenses and lost earnings resulting from an injury. The plaintiff in this case had brought a medical malpractice action against the Permanente Medical Group, alleging that he was injured by failure of the group to promptly diagnose an impending heart attack.

A Virginia statute that places a cap of $750,000 on damages recoverable in a malpractice action was found not to violate Seventh Amendment separation of powers principles or Fourteenth Amendment due process or equal protection clauses. *Boyd v. Bulala* No. 8-205L (4th Cir. June 12, 1989), *reversing* 56 U.S. L.W. 2285.

Some states have sought to deal with award limitations either by limiting the amount of recovery except in the most serious cases or by mandating so-called structured recoveries where recoveries exceed a certain dollar amount. Structured recoveries are those requiring that money awarded to the plaintiff be placed in a trust fund and invested appropriately so that money will be available to the plaintiff over a long period of time. The rationale behind such legislation is that a plaintiff need not be awarded a large sum of money immediately in order to be well taken care of because of injuries suffered at the hands of the defendant. The prudent investment of a smaller amount of money can produce a recovery commensurate with the needs and the rights of the plaintiff. This, in turn, requires a smaller cash outlay by the defendant or the defendant's insurance company, thereby holding down the costs of malpractice insurance and the ultimate cost of medical care to the consumer.

MEDIATION PANELS

Arbitration is the process by which parties to a dispute submit their differences to the judgment of an impartial mediation panel. Mediation is a means to evaluate, screen, and resolve medical malpractice disputes before they reach the courts. A panel can be appointed by mutual consent or statutory provision.

Among the many factors contributing to the malpractice crisis is the high cost of litigation. Trial by jury is lengthy and expensive. If case disputes can be handled out of court, the process and expense of a lawsuit can be greatly reduced. Arbitration is one means for simplifying and expediting the settlement of claims.

RISK MANAGEMENT

Increasing insurance costs and general financial constraints are putting pressure on hospitals to assume leadership in the prevention of medically related injuries. Risk management is the identification of potential accidents with an emphasis on claims prevention. In risk management, steps are taken on a team-effort basis to improve the quality of care and eliminate or minimize the number of accidents that become potential lawsuits. Rhode Island adopted the following risk management legislation in 1976:

3-28.10-39. INTERNAL RISK MANAGEMENT PROGRAM

Every hospital licensed in this state and its insurance carrier shall cooperatively as part of their administrative functions establish an internal risk management program which shall include at least the following components:

(1) an in-hospital grievance or complaint mechanism designed to process and resolve as promptly and effectively as possible grievances by patients or their representatives related to incidents, billing, inadequacies in treatment, and other factors known to influence malpractice claims and suits. Such mechanism shall include appointment of a representative accountable to the hospital administration who shall anticipate and monitor on a day-to-day basis such grievances and administer said mechanism;

(2) the continuous collection of data by each hospital with respect to its negative health care outcomes (whether or not they give rise to claims), patient grievances, claims, suits, professional liability premiums, settlements, awards, allocated and administrative costs of claims handling, costs of patient injury prevention and safety engineering activities, and other relevant statistics and information;

(3) medical care evaluation mechanisms, which shall include but not be limited to, tissue committees or medical audit committees, to review the appropriateness of procedures performed, to periodically assess the quality of medical care being provided at the institution and to pass on the necessity of surgery;

(4) education programs for the hospital's staff personnel engaged in patient care activities dealing with patient safety, medical injury prevention, the legal aspects of patient care, problems of communication and rapport with patients, and other relevant factors known to influence malpractice claims and suits.

Board of Directors

The hospital board must concern itself with reviewing the competence of the medical staff as well as with auditing the hospital's financial status. Standards of performance must be set against which medical care can be evaluated. Standards must also be set to measure the quality of sophisticated equipment being utilized, and a preventative maintenance program must be established to correct deficiencies. Public expectations place a broad responsibility on the hospital to ensure safe, adequate care, whether that care involves administrative, nursing, or physician activities. Hospital emergency rooms are becoming the centers to which the public turns in time of crisis, and, as a result, patients look to the hospital as a focal point for their grievances as well as their expectations. The hospital board's ultimate responsibility for adequate patient care mandates its involvement in the risk management process.

Administration

There must be cooperation among all levels of personnel. The medical staff must be encouraged to present their problems. The administrator must listen to patient care status reports. An administrative representative should be present at all medical staff meetings. All incident reports should be reviewed by an administrative representative. A continuing effort must be made on the part of management to provide an educational program in risk management to board members, physicians, and employees.

Medical Staff

The medical staff must establish and enforce professional performance standards. The conduct of each physician must then be evaluated against these established standards. Appropriate committees of the medical staff should support the risk management process.

National Organizations

National organizations, such as the American Hospital Association and the American Medical Association, must become involved in developing comprehensive risk management programs.

Elements of a Risk Management Program

Valuable components of a risk management program include

- preparation of incident reports
- evaluation of the frequency and severity of incident exposure
- definition of the cause of each incident

- formulation and implementation of corrective actions to reduce risk and exposure to liability
- training and education of hospital staff to assist in reducing exposure
- continuing attention of a safety committee
- use of a suggestion box
- a public relations program (Employees should be trained in completing timely incident reports that document the facts and that are not utilized to cover up unfortunate incidents, but to train personnel and identify problems.)
- prompt investigation and sympathetic care following accidental injury to a patient

Incident reports should be directed to counsel for legal advice. This will help prevent discovery on the basis of client-attorney privilege. They should not be placed in patients' medical records.

The New York State Public Health Law requires hospitals to investigate incidents regarding patient care and report them to the department of health.

> Any incident required to be reported . . . shall be reported to the department's Office of Health Systems Management on a telephone number maintained for such purpose. Hospitals shall report such incidents within 24 hours of when the incident occurred or when the hospital has reasonable cause to believe that such an incident has occurred and shall take no more than seven calendar days to determine whether an incident defined . . . is reportable and subject to the requirements of this section. The hospital shall give written notification within seven calendar days of the initial notification. This notification shall be submitted in a format specified by the department and shall record the nature, classification and location of the incident; medical record numbers of all patients directly affected by the incident; the full name and title of physicians and hospital staff directly involved in the incident as well as their license, permit, certification or registration numbers; the effect of the incident on the patient; follow-up treatments and evaluations planned; the expected completion date for the hospital's investigation and identification information required by the department.

Official compilation of Rules and Regulations of the State of New York, Title 10(c), Chapter V, Part 400, Section 405.8, 12/31/88.

Section 405.8 requires the reporting of the following incidents within 24 hours of occurrence to the Office Health Systems Management:

- patients' deaths in circumstances other than those related to the natural course of illness
- fires or internal disasters in the facility

- equipment malfunction or equipment user error during treatment or diagnosis of a patient which did or could have adversely affected a patient or personnel
- poisoning occurring within facility
- reportable infection outbreaks
- patient elopements and kidnapings
- strikes by personnel
- disasters or other emergency situations external to the hospital environment that affect facility operations
- unscheduled termination of any services vital to the continued safe operation of the facility.

Risk Management Committee

A risk management committee with representation from a hospital's medical staff and appropriate hospital departments should be established. The committee should be chaired by a person trained in medical audits and the risk management process. The risk manager should be responsible for the development and coordination of strategic prevention programs. Information from all hospital committees (i.e., pharmacy, transfusion, infections, safety, audit, utilization, tissue, medical records, personnel, credentials, continuing education, product review, etc.) regarding potential liability hazards should be funneled into this committee for review, evaluation, and appropriate action. This committee serves to monitor all potential hazards. The hospital's attorney should be readily available for legal counsel.

Privileged Communications

Many states have enacted various privilege and nondiscovery statutes protecting the recorded minutes and proceedings of such committees as risk management, quality assurance, and utilization review. Such minutes, however, can often be subpoenaed after showing good cause due to extraordinary circumstances. Privileged communications statutes do not protect from discovery the records maintained in the ordinary course of doing business and rendering inpatient care.

The surgeon in *Robinson v. Magovern*, 83 F.R.D. 79, 521 F. Supp. 842 (W.D. Pa. 1981), brought an action under the Sherman Antitrust Act, as well as under state law, seeking recovery because he had been denied hospital privileges. The plaintiff moved in the U.S. district court for an order compelling the defendants and certain third-party witnesses to respond to discovery requests and deposition questions. The defendants had objected, claiming the information sought was privileged and that the Pennsylvania Peer Review Protection Act seeks to foster candor and discussion at medical review committee meetings through grants of immunity and confidentiality. The court held that although there was a powerful interest in confidentiality embodied in the Pennsylvania Peer Review Protection

Act, the act would not be applied to shield from discovery events surrounding the denial of staff privileges, including what occurred at meetings of the hospital's credentials committee and executive committee. The need for evidence was greater than the need for confidentiality in this case. The defendant's objections were overruled, and the motion to compel was granted.

The physician in *Ott v. St. Luke Hospital of Campbell County, Inc.*, 522 F. Supp. 706 (E.D. Ky. 1981), had brought a civil rights suit because his application for medical staff privileges was denied. The physician contended that he was not invited to several peer review committee meetings or given an opportunity to be heard. The hospital filed for a protective order that would bar discovery of the proceedings of the peer review committee. The hospital argued that such committees would become ineffective if their deliberations were discoverable and that the privilege claimed by the hospital is recognized in the Kentucky Revised Statutes, Section 311.377.

The U.S. district court held that where there was no real showing that the peer review committee's functions would be substantially impaired and where the benefit gained for correct disposal of the litigation by denying privilege was overwhelming, the hospital would not be permitted to assert privilege. The hospital's motion was therefore denied. The court reasoned that the efficiency of such committees may be fostered by an atmosphere of openness, and there may be less likelihood of reliance on bias, hearsay, and prejudice. A potential Louis Pasteur (French chemist and microbiologist), Joseph Lister (British surgeon), or Philipp Semmelweis (Hungarian physician) who advocates salutary changes in procedures may be excluded simply because he or she makes waves. The court, in concluding, indicated that it cannot permit the discharge of its responsibility to conduct a search for the truth to be thwarted by rules of privilege in the absence of strong countervailing public policies.

The physician in *Dorsten v. Lapeer County General Hospital*, 88 F.R.D. 583 (E.D. Mich. 1980), had brought an action against a hospital and certain physicians on the medical board, alleging wrongful denial of her application for medical staff privileges. The plaintiff asserted claims under 42 U.S.C. Section 1983 for sex discrimination, violations of the Sherman Antitrust Act, and pendent claims for defamation and interference with advantageous business relations. The plaintiff had filed a motion to compel discovery of peer review reports to support her case. The U.S. district court granted the motion, holding that the plaintiff was entitled to discovery of peer review reports in spite of a state law, Michigan Compiled Laws Annotated, Section 333.21515, purporting to establish an absolute privilege for peer review reports conducted by hospital review boards.

The California Court of Appeals in *Mt. Diablo Hospital District v. Superior Court*, 227 Cal. Rptr. 790 (Ct. App. 1986), held that the trial court erred in requiring the hospital to produce minutes of five medical staff committees that had been charged with establishing standards for granting physicians authority to use a procedure known as chemonucleolysis. The patient, in an action involving the hospital, allegedly suffered injuries as a result of this procedure for lower back pain in which a drug substance known as chymopapain or chymodiactin was injected into the patient. The court held that the documents in question so clearly fell within statutory privilege that there was no occasion to order in camera review to determine whether they should be produced.

PEER REVIEW ORGANIZATIONS

Public Law 92-603 of the 92d Congress and Public Law 94-182 of the 94th Congress created a nationwide review agency known as Professional Standard Review Organizations (PSROs) under Title XI of the Social Security Act. Their purpose is to assure that medical care provided to patients is of high quality and reflects the most appropriate and efficient utilization of institutional health care services.

The PSRO norms, standards, and criteria were to be utilized as guidelines of acceptable medical care to measure the standard of care rendered to beneficiaries of Medicare, Medicaid, and maternal and child health programs. PSROs compiled and studied physician profiles of care to determine if services rendered in a given area were consistent with the standards of learning and skill of the average reputable physician, either nationwide or in communities similar to those under examination.

In 1982 Congress repealed the PSRO program, replacing it with the Peer Review Improvement Act (Title XI, Sec. 143, Part B). Under this act, peer review organizations (PROs) perform functions similar to those of the PSROs. Hospitals must have agreements with PROs as a condition of receiving Medicare payments under the prospective payment system (PPS), as required by the Deficit Reduction Act of 1984 (Pub. L. 98-369). PROs can deny reimbursement for substandard care. They can also recommend that a practitioner be suspended from the Medicare and Medicaid programs, as well as fined for a pattern of poor performance.

Peer review documents are generally protected from discovery. The superior court in *Sanderson v. Bryan*, 522 A.2d 1138 (Pa. Super. Ct. 1987), held that the Peer Review Protection Act of 1974, Pub. L. 564, No. 193, as amended October 5, 1978, Pub. L. 1121, No. 262, was violated by an order giving a plaintiff access through the discovery process to peer review information that was not directly related to his case. The act does not prevent the plaintiffs from gaining access to their own medical records or other relevant business records of the hospital or from compelling persons with firsthand knowledge of the incident to testify.

The U.S. Supreme Court in *Patrick v. Burget*, 108 S. Ct. 1658 (1988), by an 8–0 vote reversed the decision of the U.S. Court of Appeals for the Ninth Circuit, which had held that the hospital peer review process was exempt from antitrust scrutiny under the so-called state action doctrine. The result is that compliance with the Health Care Quality Improvement Act is the only way hospitals and their medical staffs can hope to protect credentialing and peer review activities from antitrust liability. The Supreme Court endorsed the Act in the *Patrick* opinion, holding that the Home Care Quality Improvement Act "essentially immunizes peer review action from liability if the action was taken in the reasonable belief that [it] was in the furtherance of quality health care." *Id.* at 1665.

A physician who resigned following evaluation of his suspected alcohol, drug, or emotional problem filed a complaint against the hospital and the assistant administrator on the theories of slander, coercion, intentional infliction of emotional distress, and intentional interference with his employment contract as Medical Director of the hospital's Department of Perinatology. Alcohol had been detected on the physician's breath while he was performing certain medical procedures. Interviews were conducted by a chemical dependency specialist with members of the hospital's staff who had contact with the plaintiff. According to the witnesses, the plaintiff was subject to mood swings, became abrupt and tactless with patients, boasted of becoming intoxicated, and would occasionally leave work and return "wired." The plaintiff had been described as bizarre and paranoid. In conducting the interviews with the hospital staff, the witnesses believed that something was wrong with the plaintiff, but they were reluctant to speak because of their fondness for him.

Acting on the advice of the chemical dependency specialist, the vice president of medical staff affairs for the hospital formed a committee which met for the purpose of confronting the physician regarding the alleged behavior problem. The physician reluctantly agreed to an evaluation by a physician experienced in treating impaired physicians. The plaintiff was evaluated later that day at a nearby hospital. The record is silent as to the results of that evaluation except to indicate that the plaintiff did not require hospitalization. The circuit court dismissed the complaint, and the physician appealed. On appeal, the appellate court held that the Hospital Licensing Act provided the defendants with absolute immunity from liability for the hospital peer review committee's investigation of the physician's conduct. *Cardwell v. Rockford Memorial Hospital Association*, 183 Ill. App. 3d 1072, 132 Ill. Dec. 516, 539 N.E.2d 1322 (1989).

PROFESSIONAL MISCONDUCT

State boards of medical misconduct have been established in several states. New York has a panel within the state department of health to deal with issues of medical misconduct. The panel is appointed by the commissioner of health. Committees are appointed from among the members to investigate each complaint of professional misconduct received, regardless of the source.

Professional misconduct generally includes

- obtaining a license fraudulently
- practicing a profession fraudulently, beyond its authorized scope, with gross incompetence on a particular occasion, or with negligence or incompetence on more than one occasion
- practicing a profession while the ability to practice is impaired by alcohol, drugs, physical disability, or mental disability

- refusing to provide professional service to a person because of such person's race, creed, color, or national origin
- permitting, aiding, or abetting an unlicensed person to perform activities requiring a license
- being convicted of committing an act constituting a crime

The penalties that may be imposed on a licensee found guilty of professional misconduct include

- suspension of the license to practice
- revocation of the license to practice
- limitation on registration or issuance of any further licenses
- a fine

In New York, the board of regents may stay such penalties and place the licensee on probation, or it may restore a license that has been revoked. New York State Education Law, Section 6509.

The chief executive officer, the chief of the medical staff, and the department chairpersons of every institution established pursuant to Article 2803-e, as amended, of the New York State Public Health Law shall, and any other person may, report without malice any information to the board that reasonably appears to show that a physician is guilty of professional misconduct. Section 2803-e of the law provides that hospitals must report within 60 days the termination or curtailment of privileges of physicians for alleged malpractice, incompetence, misconduct, or alleged mental or physical impairment; resignation or withdrawal of association or privileges from a facility to avoid disciplinary action; and/or the facility's receipt of information that indicates that a professional licensee has been convicted of a crime.

The physician in *Gunduy v. Commissioner of Education*, 460 N.Y.S.2d 664 (App. Div. 1983), appealed the commissioner of education's decision to revoke his license for being convicted under federal law of seven counts of an indictment. The physician was involved in the possession and distribution of large amounts of amphetamines and furnished false information in required reports and records. The supreme court, appellate division, confirmed the commissioner's decision and noted that there is considerable responsibility on the part of professionals not to abuse the trust that licensure places on them by violating the laws controlling dangerous drugs.

NATIONAL DATA BANK

The Health Care Quality Improvement Act of 1986, signed by President Reagan on November 14, 1986, establishes a central national data bank to be operated under the authority of the secretary of health and human services.[1] State medical licensing authorities will be required to report disciplinary actions and malpractice claims paid on behalf of physicians and dentists. A nationwide computer record of this information will be maintained in the data bank. The information in the data bank will be available to hospitals and other entities appointing physicians to their staffs.

MEDICAL MALPRACTICE LEGISLATION

The traditional negligence-based system for adverse medical outcomes has seriously broken down. Compensation as a deterrent to malpractice has failed to hold the number of claims to a reasonable level. As jury awards and malpractice insurance premiums continue to increase, the health care system comes ever closer to a day of reckoning with financial disaster. Tort reform may well be the only alternative. The following proposals have been offered by various organizations, as well as by federal and state legislative bodies, as a more reasonable way to reduce and adjudicate the ever-increasing number of medical malpractice cases:

- Strictly regulate insurance practices.
- Require coordinated malpractice prevention programs that would identify and assist in preventing negligent acts.
- Scrutinize health professionals more closely prior to granting hospital privileges.
- Resolve patient complaints promptly.
- Require precalendar conferences to encourage settlements prior to trial.
- Establish and set guidelines for medical malpractice panels to facilitate professional malpractice actions.
- Expedite the adjudication of malpractice cases by limiting the time allotted for discovery proceedings.
- Legislate a statute of limitations that prescribes a time frame within which a lawsuit must be initiated that could begin to run when the injury is discovered and the physician-patient relationship has ended.
- Require that a certificate of merit be filed by the plaintiff, prior to initiating a suit, indicating that the plaintiff consulted with an expert medical witness who established that a negligent act was committed (legislation could be enacted that would impose a penalty against those filing frivolous claims).
- Disclose qualifications of any expert witness, and mandate that only experts in an appropriate field be allowed to present admissible testimony in court.
- Provide defendants with access to the medical records of the plaintiff.
- Set a cap on the amount of awards for pain and suffering.
- Limit contingency fees on a sliding scale basis with the percentage decreasing as the award to the plaintiff increases, and/or provide for a lesser fee if a claim is settled without going to trial.

- Establish guidelines that juries must follow in setting punitive damage awards.

- Provide structured awards for the periodic payment of judgments by establishing a reversible trust fund for specified parts of awards due patients (this would provide compensation during a patient's lifetime and would eliminate an unwarranted windfall to the patient's beneficiaries in the event of death).

- Limit liability awards. "More than 20 states have already enacted laws that limit malpractice awards."[2]

- Revise the doctrine of joint and several liability by limiting each defendant's responsibility, in a multidefendant action, for payment to the percentage of fault ascribed to each defendant.

- Allow the defendant(s) to recover court costs and damage awards from both the plaintiff(s) and their attorneys for frivolous claims and counterclaims.

- Reduce the award if the plaintiff(s) received compensation from other sources.

- Generate malpractice reform, from a legislative viewpoint, on a national basis.

- Establish quality assurance committees having responsibility for reviewing services rendered in the hospital with a goal of improving care (the committee should include representation from the governing board, administration, and medical staff).

- Periodically review the credentials, physical and mental capacity, and competency of health professionals employed or associated with a hospital.

- Institute continuing education programs for health professionals in their areas of responsibility.

- Institute general education programs that include patient safety, fire prevention, etc.

- Require hospitals that provide emergency medical care to purchase a policy for excess malpractice insurance coverage for physicians who identify a particular hospital as being their primary affiliation. This idea was tried in New York. It is likely that this sort of legislation will tend to increase the number of malpractice claims and not reduce them.

- Introduce a no-fault system of compensating injured parties for economic losses without regard to fault.

Frivolous and unscrupulous malpractice actions have caused physicians to place limitations on their scope of practice. Many obstetricians/gynecologists, for example, have dropped the high-risk obstetrics portion of their practices in order to reduce their malpractice premiums. There is also an ever-increasing reluctance by physicians to perform heroic measures on accident victims due to the high risks of malpractice exposure. Neurosurgeons, for example, are reluctant to treat patients with spinal cord injuries and prefer to stabilize and transfer them to specialty care centers.

Given the above-described changes in the practice of "medicine," we have become victims of its failures as opposed to beneficiaries of its numerous successes. Physicians have lost in that they have changed, limited, or closed their practices after having spent the most energetic years of their lives training for such work. Patients have lost in that the physicians of their choice, with whom they have developed trusting relationships, are no longer available to care for them. It is certain that the malpractice problem and its effects are truly a societal problem.

The distress of physicians is illustrated in a $15 million malpractice award in West Virginia, where, "Seven Charleston obstetricians stopped accepting new patients . . . and others say they may leave the state in reaction to a $15 million malpractice decision against another Charleston obstetrician . . . . 'The award may further worsen the increasing shortage of obstetricians in the state,' said Ben E. Lusk, associate director of the West Virginia State Medical Association. He explained that, largely because of the high cost of malpractice insurance, the number of obstetricians in West Virginia has dropped by about one-half during the last five years.[3]

HOSPITAL WASTE AND POLLUTION

The wash-up of medical wastes on the East Coast placed the seriousness of waste disposal in the public spotlight. Judges, lawyers and regulators are just beginning to grapple with the appropriate parameters of this litigation. There are an "estimated 20,000 hazardous-waste dump sites in the country, with ever-widening chemical contamination, and . . . no end in sight of the constant parade of state and federal rules in this area . . . ."[4] The fear of AIDS has only served to exacerbate the problem. This has resulted in costly legislation and government scrutiny.

The regulation and cleanup of hazardous waste, along with tort liability arising from exposure to toxic substances, are major environmental problems facing the health care industry. Pollution issues have generated costly legislative and regulatory responses on the federal level [e.g., by the Environmental Protection Agency (EPA), the Occupational Safety and Health Administration (OSHA), and the Centers for Disease Control (CDC)] and on the state and local levels, and they have resulted in numerous lawsuits nationwide in the areas of enforcement, toxic torts, and products liability. Hospitals—through their representative councils and their state and national associations—and physicians—through their medical societies and associations—should become more involved in the regulatory process to identify what wastes should be regulated and the methods most appropriate for their disposal.

The federal "Medical Waste Tracking Act" passed in late 1988 established a pilot program to be administered by EPA for tracking medical waste in three states—New York, New Jersey and Connecticut—and made the program optional for other states. The federal legislation and the increasing state regulation are multiplying restrictions on generators of wastes, haulers and landfills and causing confusion as to which of the regulators is the final authority.[5]

EPA reporting requirements are mandated by Title III of the Superfund Amendment and Reauthorization Act of 1986 (SARA), which imposes significant penalties for noncompliance.

> Hospitals in North Carolina are being forced to change the way they dispose of waste under the state's new waste-disposal regulations. On Nov. 21 [1989], the state began regulating a new category of waste, called "mixed waste," which is both hazardous and radioactive. . . . The new rules will necessitate finding larger storage facilities to hold the additional waste until the radioactivity decays and then securing contracts to have it hauled away. . . . Just obtaining the permits to transport, store and dispose of mixed waste could easily cost $250,000.[6]

Refuse generated by hospitals can be divided into "five separate categories: infectious, biohazardous, hazardous, radioactive and general (solid) waste. Each category poses its own particular problems—with no easy solutions available for any or all forms of waste."[7] However, potential polluters must keep in mind that "existing fines are stiff. One Minnesota hospital recently paid a $35,000 fine for improper incineration, and violators in states implementing the tracking systems face fines of up to $25,000 per day for each violation and criminal penalties of up to $50,000 a day per violation."[8]

Compliance

Hospitals and physicians must be aware of what regulations apply to them. Hospitals should develop a plan of action and organize an effective program by working through an appropriate committee, such as the Safety Committee, to review the needs of both the hospital and the physicians. Membership should include a director of environmental services and representation from finance, administration, medical staff, housekeeping, nursing (infection control nurse), and engineering. The committee should identify infectious wastes (e.g., cultures, blood and blood byproducts, needles, and pathological wastes); review and develop appropriate protocols for disposal of wastes; review the various methods of disposal (carting, incineration, recycling, etc.) from a cost point of view; review recycling options (disposal methods vary depending on the kind of waste); identify waste-handling costs when purchasing; develop employee safety programs to determine what handling, storage, and disposal procedures should be implemented for both employee and patient safety; and develop a monitoring system to assure that the various classifications of wastes are disposed of properly and that the hospital complies with the ever-expanding body of law regulating the disposal of medical waste.

Insurance

Hospitals and physicians should review their insurance policies to determine if they have (1) liability coverage for cleanup and disposal of hazardous wastes, environmental impairment, property damage claims, future injury claims, and demands for medical monitoring by claimants; (2) comprehensive general liability; (3) pollution exclusion clauses; and (4) provisions covering the number of occurrences. Health care providers without such coverage should evaluate the need for its inclusion in their policies.

NOTES

1. Pub. L. No. 99-660, tit. IV, 100 Stat. 3743, 3784–94 (codified at 42 U.S.C. §§ 11101–11152).

2. Congressman Robert J. Mrazek (3d District, New York), correspondence dated July 11, 1989, at 1.

3. *U.S. Wrap-up, West Virginia/$15 Million Malpractice Award*, AHA NEWS 26(12), March 26, 1990, at 7.

4. M. LAUCHHEIMER, HAZARDOUS WASTE AND TOXIC TORTS 1 (1989).

5. Fields, *Containing Waste Disposal Costs*, FED'N AM. HEALTH SYSTEMS REV. May–June 1989, at 53.

6. *Waste Disposal Rules*, AHA NEWS, Dec. 11, 1989, at 7.

7. Charlton, *Medical Hazardous Waste Issues Demand Attention*, FED'N AM. HEALTH SYSTEMS REV. July–Aug. 1989, at 46.

8. Fields, *supra* note 4, at 55.

Chapter 22

Criminal Aspects of Health Care

INTRODUCTION

Criminal law is society's expression of the limits of acceptable human and institutional behavior. This chapter presents a variety of criminal cases that have occurred in the health care industry. They are by no means exhaustive for a particular profession.

Peculiar to the hospital setting is the fact that patients are helpless and at the mercy of others. Health care facilities are far too often places where the morally weak and mentally deficient prey on the physically and sometimes mentally helpless. The very institutions that are designed to make you well and feel safe can provide the setting for criminal conduct. The objectives of criminal law are to maintain public order and safety, protect the individual, utilize punishment as a deterrent to crime, and rehabilitate the criminal for return to society.

ARREST

A crime is any social harm defined and made punishable by law.[1] Prosecutions for crimes generally begin with the arrest of a defendant by a police officer or the filing of a formal action in a court of law and the issuance of an arrest warrant or summons. Detectives are assigned to cases where investigations are necessary to gather evidence and prepare a case for trial.

A misdemeanor is an offense punishable by less than one year in jail and/or a fine.

A felony is a much more serious crime generally punishable by imprisonment in a penitentiary, state or federal, for more than one year. A felony complaint commences a criminal proceeding; however, an individual may not be tried for a felony without indictment by a grand jury or a court prescribed by statute unless the defendant waives presentment to the grand jury and pleads guilty by way of a superior statute. Felony cases are presented to a grand jury by a district attorney or an assistant district attorney. The jury is presented with the prosecution's evidence and then charged that they may indict the target if they find reasonable cause to believe from the evidence that was presented to them that all of the elements of a particular crime are present. The grand jury may request that witnesses be subpoenaed to testify. Actions of a grand jury are handed up to a judge.

ARRAIGNMENT

The arraignment is a formal reading of the accusatory instrument and includes the setting of bail. The accused should appear with counsel or have counsel appointed by the court if he or she cannot afford his or her own. After the defendant is arraigned, the judge will set a date for the defendant to return to court. Between the time of arraignment and the next court date, the defense attorney and the prosecutor will confer about the charges and evidence in possession of the prosecutor.

CONFERENCE

Both felony and misdemeanor cases are conferenced, and plea bargaining commences with the goal of an agreed-on disposition. If no disposition can be reached, the case is adjourned, motions are made, and further plea bargaining takes place. Generally after several adjournments, a case is assigned to a trial court.

THE PROSECUTOR

The role of the prosecutor in the criminal justice system is well defined in *Berger v. United States*, 295 U.S. 88 (1935).

> The United States Attorney is the representative not of an ordinary party to a controversy, but of a sovereignty whose obligation to govern at all; and whose interest, therefore, in a criminal prosecution is not that it shall win a case, but that justice will be done. As such, he is in a peculiar and very definite sense the servant of the law, the twofold aim of which is that guilt shall not escape or innocence suffer.

The potential of the prosecutor's office is not always fully realized in many jurisdictions. "In many cities the prosecutor must operate under such staggering cases with a small staff of assistants that sufficient attention cannot be given to each case."[2]

THE DEFENSE ATTORNEY

The defense attorney generally sits in the proverbial hot seat of being perceived as the "bad guy." While everyone seems to understand his/her function in protecting the rights of those he/she represents, the defense attorney is often not very popular.

> There is a substantial difference in the problem of representing the "run-of-the-mill" criminal defendant and one whose alleged crimes have aroused great public outcry. The difficulties in providing representation for the ordinary criminal defendant are simple compared with the difficulties of obtaining counsel for one who is charged with a crime which by its nature or circumstances incites strong public condemnation.[3]

PROCESSES OF A CRIMINAL TRIAL

The processes of a criminal trial are, as outlined below, very similar to those of a civil trial, as discussed in Chapter 18.

- Jurors are selected.
- Jury is sworn.
- Prosecutor (representing the people) opens.
- Defendant opens (optional).
- Prosecutor calls witnesses.
- Defense attorney cross-examines.
- Defendant calls witnesses.
- Prosecutor cross-examines.
- Defendant sums up.
- Prosecutor sums up.
- Judge charges the jury by explaining the legal aspects of the case.
- Jury deliberates and returns a verdict.
- Appeals go to a higher court.

DRUGS

Drug abuse has been described as the number one problem facing the United States today. It is no surprise that hospitals and health professionals are affected by the theft of drugs, drug abuse, and the illegal sale of drugs. There appears to be no end to the stream of cases entering the nation's courtrooms.

The ophthalmologist in *Bouquett v. St. Elizabeth's Corporation*, 538 N.E.2d 113 (Ohio 1989), brought an action to challenge suspension of his medical staff privileges after a felony conviction in a federal court for conspiracy to distribute Dilaudid. He was subsequently sentenced to five years of incarceration. The court of common pleas upheld the hospital's summary suspension, and the court of appeals upheld in part and remanded in part. On further appeal, the supreme court held that the conviction of the ophthalmologist justified summary suspension of his staff privileges pursuant to a hospital bylaw permitting summary suspension in the best interest of patient care in the hospital. Hospital boards of trustees of private hospitals have broad discretion in determining who shall be granted medical staff privileges. Unless a hospital has been arbitrary and capricious or has abused its discretion, the courts will not generally interfere with a hospital's decision to suspend physicians convicted on drug-related felony charges. Summary suspension of a physician extends beyond technical skills and medical competence. It encompasses the perceived integrity of a physician which becomes suspect after conviction of a felony.

The pharmacists in *Brown v. Idaho State Board of Pharmacy*, 746 P.2d 1006 (Idaho App. 1987), had admitted to using marijuana approximately twice a week. During a hearing by the Idaho State Board of Pharmacy, the hearing officer admitted into evidence a copy of a judgment of a conviction on Brown's plea of guilty to a criminal charge of possession of drug paraphernalia. Brown's license was suspended by the Idaho State Board of Pharmacy. On appeal, the Court of Appeals of Idaho held that revocation of his license was supported by evidence that he engaged in the illegal use of marijuana and that he also had participated in the sale and delivery of a misbranded drug.

CHILD ABUSE

Child abuse statutes provide protection from civil suits for those making or participating in a good faith report of suspected child abuse. Most states also provide immunity from criminal liability. The New York State Social Services Law provides that "Any person, official, or institution participating in good faith in the making of a report, the taking of photographs, or the removal or keeping of a child pursuant to this title shall have immunity from any liability, civil or criminal, that might otherwise result by reason of such actions."[4] Even in states that do not provide immunity, it is unlikely that anyone making a good faith report of suspected child abuse would be subject to criminal liability. State laws generally specify what persons (e.g., physicians, nurses, and social workers) are required to report suspected child abuse that comes before them in their official capacity. In some states, failure to report a case of suspected child abuse carries criminal penalties, as well as civil liability for the damages resulting from such failure.[5]

The pediatrician in *Satler v. Larsen*, 520 N.Y.S.2d 378 (App. Div. 1987), had reported the possibility of child abuse to the Bureau of Child Welfare. The report of suspected child abuse was held not actionable in the absence of a persuasive showing that the report was made in bad faith. Summary dismissal was appropriate with respect to defamation claims brought against the pediatrician for reporting suspected child abuse. The four-month-old infant had been brought to the physician's office in a comatose state with a bilateral subdural hematoma. This occurred one day after the child had been discharged from the hospital.

The psychologist in *E.S. by D.S. v. Seitz*, 413 N.W.2d 670 (Wis. Ct. App. 1987), was immune from liability in a suit charging her with negligence in formulating and reporting her professional opinion to a social worker that a father had sexually abused his three-year-old daughter. It was undisputed that the psychologist had made the report in compliance with the Wisconsin statute, after having examined the child in the course of her professional duties as a mental health professional.

The Minnesota Board of Psychology in *In the Matter of Schroeder*, 415 N.W.2d 436 (Minn. Ct. App. 1987), was found to have acted properly when it placed the license of a psychologist on conditional status. The psychologist had failed to report incidents of the sexual abuse of a child. The court held that there was no merit to the psychologist's contentions that the child abuse reporting laws were not clear and that they did not apply to one patient who was a grandfather and who had been charged with the child's care at the time of the incident in question. The psychologist had argued that he was not required to report past abuse which was not ongoing, that a report made five weeks after the incident was not untimely, and that the reporting laws were not constitutional in that the laws violated the privacy rights of clients and the privilege against self-incrimination.

The criminal and civil risks for health professionals lie not in reporting in good faith suspected incidents of child abuse, but in failing to report such incidents. The New York State Social Services Law, Article 6, Title 6, Section 420, provides for the following civil and criminal penalties for failure to report suspected child abuse incidents:

1. Any person, official or institution required by this title to report a case of suspected child abuse or maltreatment who willfully fails to do so shall be guilty of a class A misdemeanor.
2. Any person, official or institution required by this title to report a case of suspected child abuse or maltreatment who knowingly and willfully fails to do so shall be civilly liable for the damages proximately caused by such failure.

CRIMINAL NEGLIGENCE

Criminal negligence is the reckless disregard for the safety of others. It is the willful indifference to an injury that could follow an act.

FALSIFICATION OF RECORDS

All professionals should be aware that falsification of medical and/or business records is grounds for criminal indictment, as well as for civil liability for damages suffered.

Two of the defendants, orthopedic surgeons, Drs. Lipton and Massoff, in *People v. Smithtown General Hospital*, 93 Misc. 736, 402 N.Y.S.2d 318 (Sup. Ct. 1978), on the morning of July 3, 1975, performed an orthopedic procedure on a patient. The prosthesis utilized during surgery was supplied by a general sales manager, Mr. MacKay, who was present in the operating room during most of the operation, which began at 8:00 A.M. and ended at 11:30 A.M. After completion of the operation, the patient was x-rayed, revealing that the "head of the femur popped out of the acetabulum." At the request of Dr. Lipton, the salesman was located at a golf course and requested to return to the hospital. Upon arriving back in the operating room, he found Dr. Massoff reopening the hip. Dr. Massoff attempted to remove the prosthesis. Mr. MacKay offered his assistance and was successful in removing the prosthesis. Dr. Massoff then left and returned to his office. With the consent of Dr. Lipton, Mr. MacKay removed the cement from the bone shaft and reinserted the prosthesis. An indictment charged Dr. Lipton with the intent to defraud and to conceal crimes of "Unauthorized Practice of Medicine and Assault," for omitting to make a true entry in his operative report in that he did not refer to the fact that a nonphysician assisted in the patient's surgery. A similar indictment was returned against a supervising nurse and the hospital for failure to make a true entry in the operating room register. Section 175.00 of the Penal Law of the State of New York defines a business record as "any writing or article, including computer data or a computer program, kept or maintained by an enterprise for the purpose of evidencing or reflecting its condition or activity." In each indictment, it was charged that the defendants were in violation of a duty imposed on them by law or by the nature of their positions.

Section 175.05 of the Penal Law of the State of New York provides:

> A person is guilty of falsifying business records in the second degree when, with the intent to defraud, he: . . .
> 3. Omits to make a true entry in the business records of an enterprise in violation of a duty to do so which he knows to be imposed upon him by law or by the nature of his position; or
> 4. Prevents the making of a true entry or causes the omission thereof in the business records of an enterprise.

Section 175.10 of the Penal Law of the State of New York provides: "A person is guilty of falsifying business records in the first degree when he commits the crime of falsifying business records in the second degree, and when his intent to defraud includes the intent to commit another crime or to aid or conceal the commission thereof."

The supreme court held that the salesman could be found guilty of unlawfully engaging in the practice of medicine without the prior informed consent of a patient under circumstances that did not constitute an emergency. Dr. Lipton should have sought the assistance of another surgeon before turning a surgical case over to a layman. A motion to dismiss the indictments against the physicians and nurse charged with falsifying business records in the first degree were denied. A motion to dismiss the indictments for assault in the second degree was granted.

FRAUD

The Office of Inspector General was established at the Department of Health and Human Services (HHS) by Congress in 1976 to identify and eliminate fraud, abuse, and waste in HHS programs and to promote efficiency and economy in departmental operations. It carries out this mission through a nationwide network of audits, investigations, and inspections. To help reduce fraud in the Medicare and Medicaid programs, the Office of Inspector General is actively investigating violations of the Medicare and Medicaid antikickback statute, 42 U.S.C. Section 1320a-7b(b). Violators are subject to criminal penalties or exclusion from participation in the Medicare and Medicaid programs.[6]

The following are examples of questionable features, identified by the inspector general, which separately or taken together could be construed as a business arrangement that violates the antikickback statute:

- Investors are chosen because they are in a position to make referrals.
- Physicians who are expected to make a large number of referrals may be offered a greater investment opportunity in the joint venture than are those anticipated to make fewer referrals.
- Physician investors may be actively encouraged to make referrals to the joint venture and may be encouraged to divest their ownership interest if they fail to sustain an "acceptable" level of referrals.
- The joint venture tracks its source of referrals and distributes this information to investors.
- Investors may be required to divest their ownership interest if they cease to practice in the service area—for example, if they move, become disabled, or retire.
- Investment interests may be nontransferable.[7]

There is a price to be paid by those who dare to make a fast dollar through fraudulent activities. Health professionals must be aware of criminal liability common to their profession. The following cases describe several areas where health professionals have been involved in criminal fraud.

Pharmacist

The pharmacist in the *State v. Heath*, 513 So. 2d 493, (La. Ct. App. 1987), was convicted on three counts of Medicaid fraud where the pharmacist had submitted claims for reimbursement on brand name medications rather than on the less expensive generic drugs that were actually dispensed to Medicaid patients.

The court of appeals in *State v. Beatty*, 308 S.E.2d 65 (N.C. Ct. App. 1983), upheld the superior court's finding that the evidence submitted against a defendant pharmacist was sufficient to sustain a conviction for Medicaid fraud. The state was billed for medications that had never been dispensed, for more medications than some patients received, and in some instances for the more expensive trade name drugs when cheaper generic drugs had been dispensed.

Physician and Office Manager

A physician and his office manager in *United States v. Larm*, 824 F.2d 780 (9th Cir. 1987), were convicted of charges that they violated 42 U.S.C. Section 139h (a)1 by submitting false Medicaid claims for medical services they never rendered to patients. Claims were sometimes submitted even when patients administered allergy injections themselves. In addition, more expensive serums were sometimes billed for, rather than those actually given.

The physician in *State v. Cargille*, 507 So. 2d 1254 (La. Ct. App. 1987), was found to have submitted false information for the purpose of obtaining greater compensation than was otherwise permitted under the Medicaid program. Sufficient evidence had been presented to sustain a conviction of Medicaid fraud. The physician had argued that he felt justified for multiple billings for single office visits because of the actual amount of time that he saw a patient. He believed that his method of reimbursement was more equitable than was that of Medicaid.

Stockholder/Nursing Home

The principal stockholder of a nursing home corporation in *Chapman v. United States, Department of Health and Human Services*, 821 F.2d 523 (10th Cir. 1987), was convicted of making 19 false line item cost entries in reports to the Kansas Medicaid agency. HHS did not act unreasonably when it imposed a $2,000 penalty for each of the 19 false Medicaid claims and proposed an additional settlement of $118,136 even though the state had already recovered the $21,115 in excessive reimbursement by setoff. The administrative law judge did not err in concluding that the setoff did not make up for the other injuries suffered by the government, such as the cost of investigating the fraud and the cost of pursuing administrative sanctions.

Medicare Kickbacks

An osteopathic physician, board certified in cardiology, was president of Cardio-Med, Inc., an organization that he formed. The company provides physicians with diagnostic services, one of which was Holter monitoring, a method of recording a patient's cardiac activity on tape, generally for a period of 24 hours. Cardio-Med billed Medicare for the monitoring service and, when payment was received, forwarded a portion to the referring physician. The government charged that the referral fee exceeded that permitted by Medicare and that there was evidence physicians received "interpretation fees" even though the defendant actually evaluated the monitoring data. After a trial by jury, the physician was convicted on 20 of 23 counts in an indictment charging mail fraud, Medicare fraud, and false statement. On appeal in *United States v. Greber*, 760 F.2d 68 (3d Cir. 1985), the physician contended that the evidence was insufficient to support the guilty verdict. The court of appeals held that to the extent that payments made to a physician were made to induce referrals by that physician of Medicare patients to use payor laboratory services, Medicare fraud was established even if the payments were also intended to compensate the physician for professional services in connection with tests performed by the lab. Even if only "one" purpose of the payment was to induce future referrals, the Medicare statute has been violated.

The owner of Tech Diagnostic Medical Lab agreed to kick back 50 percent of the Medicare payments received by Tech-Lab as a consequence of referrals from Total Health Care, a medical service company. Under the scheme, Total Health Care collected blood and urine samples from medical offices and clinics in southern California and sent them to Tech-Lab for testing. Tech-Lab billed Total Health Care, which in turn billed the private insurance carrier or the government-funded insurance programs Medi-Cal and Medicare for reimbursement. Tech-Lab then kicked back half of its receipts to Total Health Care. The owners of Tech-Lab and Total Health Care arranged an identical scheme with a community medical clinic; Kats, the appellant, subsequently purchased a 25 percent interest in the clinic and began collecting payments under the scheme. Kats was convicted of conspiracy to commit Medicare fraud and of receipt of kickbacks in exchange for referral of Medicare patients. He appealed the decision, and the court of appeals in *United States v. Kats*, 871 F.2d 105 (9th Cir. 1989), affirmed the charges against him.

SOLICITATION AND RECEIPT OF KICKBACKS

The solicitation and receipt of kickbacks are not new to the health care industry, as is demonstrated in the following cases.

Architectural Contract Kickback

Three members of a county council, which served as the governing body of a county hospital, were convicted by a jury of soliciting and receiving a $6,000 kickback from architects. The architects had testified that the appellants and others sought a 1 percent kickback on the hospital project, financed by federal funds, in return for being awarded the architectural contract. The $6,000 was delivered by Mr. Galloway, of the architectural firm of Galloway and Guthrey, to appellant Campbell at the Knoxville airport. The FBI had been informed by the architects, and an investigation was conducted. Following the investigation, indictments, and trial by jury, the defendants were each sentenced to one year in prison. On appeal, the U.S. Court of Appeals for the Sixth Circuit, in *United States v. Thompson*, 366 F.2d 167 (6th Cir. 1966), held that the receipt of a kickback constituted an overt act in furtherance of a conspiracy to obstruct lawful government function and was a violation of the general conspiracy statute and a crime against the United States. "To conspire to defraud the United States means primarily to cheat the government out of property or money, but it also means to interfere with or obstruct one of its lawful governmental functions by deceit, craft or trickery, or at least by means that are dishonest." *Hammerschmidt v. United States*, 265 U.S. 182, 188 (1924). Proof that part of the architects' fee was reimbursed with federal funds was not necessary for a conviction. The criminal convictions were affirmed.

Ambulance Service Kickback

A city official was convicted in a U.S. district court for conspiring to commit Medicare fraud. Some defendants were also convicted of making illegal payments. Bay State Ambulance and Hospital Rental Service, Inc., a privately owned ambulance company, had given cash and two automobiles to an official of a city-owned hospital. The gifts were given as an inducement to the city official for his recommendation that Bay State be awarded the Quincy City Hospital ambulance service contract, for which Bay State received some Medicare funds as reimbursement. The defendants appealed, and the U.S. Court of Appeals for the First Circuit held that the evidence was sufficient to sustain a conviction. *United States v. Bay State Ambulance & Hospital Rental Services, Inc.*, 874 F.2d 20 (1st Cir. 1989).

MURDER

The tragedy of murder in institutions that are dedicated to the healing of the sick has been an all too frequent occurrence. A recent case involved Richard Angelo, a registered nurse on the cardiac/intensive care unit at a Long Island, New York, hospital, who was found guilty of second-degree murder on December 14, 1989, for injecting two patients with the drug Pavulon. Further, he was found guilty of the lesser charges of manslaughter and criminally negligent homicide in the deaths of two other patients. Angelo had committed the murders in a bizarre scheme to revive the patients and be thought of as a hero. The attorney for the estate of one of the alleged victims had filed a wrongful death suit against Angelo and the hospital a day before the verdict was rendered by the jury.[8]

In another case, the petitioner, a nurse's aide, in *Hargrave v. Landon*, 584 F. Supp. 302 (E.D. Va. 1984), was convicted of murder in the first degree when he was found to have injected an elderly patient with a fatal dose of the drug lidocaine. He was sentenced to life imprisonment by the circuit court. The petitioner appealed the judgment of the circuit court, alleging that his due process rights were violated during the trial, in that

1. The trial court failed to grant petitioner's motion for change of venue;
2. Because of a "carnival atmosphere" surrounding the trial, the trial court should have, but did not, sequester the jury sua sponte;
3. The trial court improperly admitted evidence of other crimes;
4. The evidence was insufficient as a matter of law to sustain petitioner's conviction.

Id. at 305.

The U.S. district court held that the petitioner failed to establish that he was denied an impartial jury due to adverse pretrial publicity, especially in view of the facts that the tenor of newspaper articles prior to his trial were primarily informative and factual and that the articles treated the story objectively. The evidence was found to have been sufficient to support petitioner's conviction for murder.

As pointed out in the following case, indictments for murder by health professionals are not limited to the hospital setting. A licensed dentist and oral surgeon, in *People v. Protopappas*, 201 Cal. App. 3d 152, 246 Cal. Rptr. 915 (1988), was convicted in the superior court of second-degree murder for the deaths of three of his patients, who died after receiving general anesthesia. The record revealed that the three patients received massive doses of drugs, which resulted in their deaths. The dosages had not been tailored to the patients' individual conditions. The dentist had improperly instructed surrogate dentists, who were neither licensed nor qualified to administer general anesthesia, to administer preset dosages for extended periods of time with little or no personal supervision, and the dentist had been habitually slow in reacting to resulting overdoses. In one of the cases, the patient's general physician informed the defendant that the 24-year-old, 88-pound patient suffered from lupus, total kidney failure, high blood pressure, anemia, heart murmur, and chronic seizure disorder and should not be placed under anesthesia even for a short time. The defendant consciously elected to ignore that medical opinion. On appeal, the court of appeals found that there was sufficient evidence of implied malice to support the jury's findings that the dentist and oral surgeon was guilty of second-degree murder. "This is more than gross negligence. These are the acts of a person who knows that his conduct endangers the life of another and who acts with conscious disregard for life. . . . Many murders are committed to satisfy a feeling of a hatred or grudge, it is true, but this crime may be perpetrated without the slightest trace of personal ill-will." *Id.* at 927. To illustrate this point, Professors Perkins and Boyce supply a number of examples, including the mother who kills an illegitimate infant out of shame even though she may be filled with maternal love, a mercy killing carried out at the victim's own request, and the shooting of a person with the intent to wound, but not to kill, without justification or provocation. *Id.* at 927, 928. The conduct of the defendant "is not meaningfully distinguishable from any of the acts described above. No reasonable person, much less a dentist trained in the use of anesthesia, could have failed to appreciate the risk of death posed by the procedures he utilized. It is not a question of whether a fatality would occur, only a question of when; and ultimately there were three of them." *Id.*, 246 Cal. Rptr. at 928.

As the following case points out, not every charge of suspected murder ends in a conviction; however, there is a heavy price to be paid in terms of the mental anguish suffered by those charged with the crime. Two government nurses in *United States v. Narciso*, 446 F. Supp. 252 (E.D. Mich. 1977), were indicted for and convicted of certain offenses arising out of multiple cardiopulmonary arrests in a two-month period at Ann Arbor Veterans Administration Hospital. During the months of July and August of 1975, 35 patients had suffered 51 cardiac arrests. Following an intensive investigation, the defendants were charged in June of 1976 with five counts of murder by injecting a powerful muscle relaxant, Pavulon, into the patients' intravenous apparatus. The government presented 89 witnesses over a nearly three-month period. The massive set of proofs was entirely circumstantial in nature. The government had sought to show through numerous witnesses that certain breathing failures were criminal in nature, that the defendants had the opportunity to commit these crimes, that they were present during a critical time period, that the drug had to have been injected in order to produce the observed effect, and that this presence during the critical time period was exclusive. There was no direct proof of guilt on any count. No witnesses testified that the defendants had Pavulon in their possession, nor was there any testimony that the defendants injected anything into the patients. The district court granted the defendants' motion for a new trial in the interests of justice and judicial conscience. The defendants were eventually found not guilty of the murders of which they were accused.

Euthanasia

Although there may be a duty to provide life-sustaining machinery in the immediate aftermath of cardiopulmonary arrest, there is no duty to continue its use once it has become futile and ineffective to do so in the opinion of qualified medical personnel. Two physicians in *Barber v. Superior Court*, 147 Cal. App. 3d 1006, 195 Cal. Rptr. 484 (1983), were charged with the crimes of murder and conspiracy to commit murder. The charges were based on their acceding to requests of the patient's family to discontinue life-support equipment and intravenous tubes. The patient had suffered a cardiopulmonary arrest in the recovery room following surgery. A team of physicians and nurses revived the patient and placed him on life-support equipment. The patient had suffered severe brain damage which placed him in a comatose and vegetative state, from which, according to tests and examinations by other specialists, he was unlikely to recover. The patient, upon the written request of the family, was taken off life-support equipment. The family, his wife and eight children, made the decision together after consultation with the physicians. Evidence had been presented that the patient, prior to his incapacitation, had expressed to his wife that he would not want to be kept alive by machine or "become another Karen Ann Quinlan." There was no evidence indicating that the family was motivated in their decision by anything other than love and concern for the dignity of their loved one. The patient continued to breathe on his own. Showing no signs of improvement, the physicians again discussed the patient's poor prognosis with the family. The IVs were removed, and the patient expired sometime thereafter.

A complaint was then filed against the two physicians. The magistrate who heard the evidence determined that the physicians did not kill the deceased since their conduct was not the proximate cause of the patient's death. On motion of the people, the superior court determined as a matter of law that the evidence required the magistrate to hold the physicians to answer and ordered the complaint reinstated. The physicians then filed a writ of prohibition with the court of appeals. The court of appeals held that the doctors' omission to continue treatment, though intentional and with knowledge that the patient would die, was not an unlawful failure to perform a legal duty. The evidence amply supported the magistrate's decision. The superior court erred in determining that as a matter of law the evidence required the magistrate to hold the physicians to answer. The peremptory writ of prohibition to restrain the Superior Court of Los Angeles from taking any further action in this matter, other than to vacate its order reinstating the complaint and to enter a new and different order denying the People's motion, was granted.

PATIENT ABUSE

The nurse in *People v. Coe*, 501 N.Y.S.2d 997 (1986), was charged with a willful violation of the Public Health Law in connection with an allegedly abusive search of an 86-year-old patient at a geriatric center and with falsifying business records in the first degree. The patient, Mr. Gersh, had heart disease and difficulty in expressing himself verbally. Another resident claimed that two $5 bills were missing. Nurse Coe assumed that it was Mr. Gersh because he had been known to take things in the past. The nurse proceeded to search Mr. Gersh, who resisted. A security guard was summoned, and another search was undertaken. The patient again resisted, and the security guard slammed a chair down in front of the patient and pinned his arms while the defendant nurse searched the patient's pockets, failing to retrieve the two $5 bills. The patient, five minutes later, collapsed in a chair gasping for air. Nurse Coe administered CPR, but was unsuccessful, and the patient expired.

The defendant was charged with violation of Section 175.10 of the Penal Law for falsification of records, which is said to have occurred by reason of the defendant's "omission" to state any of the facts relating to the search of Mr. Gersh. These facts were considered relevant and should have been included in the nurse's notes in order to make the note regarding this incident more accurate. "The first sentence states, 'Observed resident was extremely confused and talks incoherently. Suddenly became unresponsive. . .' This statement is simply false. It could only be true if some reference to the search and the loud noise was included." *Id*. at 1001. A motion was made to dismiss the indictment at the end of the trial.

The supreme court, criminal term, held that the search became an act of physical abuse and mistreatment, the evidence was sufficient to warrant a finding of guilt on both charges, and the fact that searches took place quite frequently did not excuse an otherwise illegal procedure. "It may well be that this incident reached the attention of the criminal justice system only because, in the end, a man had died. In those instances which are equally violative of residents' rights and equally contrary to standards of common decency but which do not result in visible harm to a patient, the acts are nevertheless illegal and subject to prosecution. A criminal act is not legitimized by the fact that others have, with impunity, engaged in that act."

PETTY THEFT

Hospitals must be alert to the potential ongoing threat of theft by unscrupulous employees, physicians, patients, visitors, and trespassers. The theft of hospital supplies and equipment is substantial and costs hospitals millions of dollars a year.

The physician in *Eufemio v. University of the State of New York*, 516 N.Y.S.2d 129 (App. Div. 1987), was convicted in Maryland for the crime of petty theft which arose out of financial irregularities at a nursing home which was owned by the physician. The physician moved to New York before the Maryland Commission of Medical Discipline could impose a penalty on him because of his conviction. The commissioner of education's determination that the physician's license to practice medicine should be suspended for three years was upheld by a New York court. The commissioner's determination was subject to confirmation notwithstanding the physician's assertion that the sanctions were too harsh.

RAPE

Murder and rape are by no means foreign to hospitals. In recent years both have occurred within hospitals by employees. Section 2805-i of the New York State Public Health Law requires hospitals to maintain sexual offense evidence in a locked, separate, and secure area for a period not less than 96 hours. The evidence shall include, but not be limited to, cotton swabs, clothing, and other items. Each item of evidence must be marked and logged with a code number corresponding to the patient's medical record. The patient must be notified after 96 hours that the evidence will be destroyed with the exception of clothing, which must be returned to the patient upon request.

SEXUAL IMPROPRIETIES

A significant number of cases address health professionals who have been involved in sexual relationships with patients in a hospital setting and with clients in private offices. Such cases are being presented, in many instances, on both civil and criminal grounds. Health professionals finding themselves in such unprofessional relationships must seek help for themselves as well as refer their patients to other appropriate professionals.

A defense that sexual improprieties with patients/clients did not take place during treatment sessions will not generally be upheld by the courts. In addition to civil and criminal litigation, health professionals are subject to having their licenses revoked.

The license of a psychologist was revoked in *Gilmore v. Board of Psychologist Examiners*, 725 P.2d 400 (Ore. Ct. App. 1986), for engaging in sexual improprieties with clients. A defense that the misconduct did not occur during treatment sessions was not upheld. Further, the physician in *Goomar v. Ambach*, 523 N.Y.S.2d 238 (App. Div. 1988), had his license revoked for professional misconduct and the fraudulent and incompetent practice of medicine. The decision was supported by evidence where four female patients testified as to the sexual improprieties of the physician.

California Civil Code Section 43.5, abolishing causes of action for alienation of affection, criminal conversation, and seduction of a person over the age of consent, did not bar damages in *Richard v. Larry*, 243 Cal. Rptr. 807 (Ct. App. 1988), for emotional distress caused by the alleged professional negligence of a psychiatrist who had sexual relations with the plaintiff's wife. The psychiatrist owed a special duty to use due care for his patient's health. The statute was not intended to lower the standard of care that psychiatrists owed their patients.

TRESPASS AND CRIMINAL MISCHIEF

An abortion clinic, Northeast Women's Center, Inc., brought an action against antiabortion demonstrators who allegedly disrupted its operations by harassing its patients and employees and by trespassing on the clinic's property. The defendants who were found guilty of trespass were liable for injury to the clinic's business and property. The district court found the defendants liable under the Racketeer Influenced and Corrupt Organizations Act and assessed $887 in damages, which was trebled by the court to $2,661.

The First Amendment rights of a Catholic priest in *Markley v. State*, 507 So. 2d 1043 (Ala. Crim. App. 1987), were found not to have been violated when the circuit court placed him on conditional probation and prohibited his antiabortion protest activities during his period of probation, following his conviction on charges of burglary in the second degree and criminal mischief in the first degree. The charges stemmed from antiabortion demonstrations, which took place at a medical clinic specializing in pregnancy testing, counseling, and abortions. The court of criminal appeals held that limitation of protest activities as a term of probation did not violate the priest's First Amendment rights.

NOTES

1. R.M. PERKINS, CRIMINAL LAW AND PROCEDURE 2 (1972).
2. J. KAPLAN, CRIMINAL JUSTICE: INTRODUCTORY CASES AND MATERIALS 228 (1973).
3. *Id.* at 259.
4. New York State Social Services Law, art. 6, tit. 6, § 419.
5. *Id.* at § 402.
6. OFFICE OF INSPECTOR GENERAL, DEPARTMENT OF HEALTH AND HUMAN SERVICES, SPECIAL FRAUD ALERT, JOINT VENTURE ARRANGEMENTS 1(1) (May 1989).
7. *Id.* at 2(2).
8. Colwell, *The Verdict of Angelo*, NEWSDAY, 50(103), Dec. 15, 1989, at 3.

Chapter 23

Teaching Techniques

The study of law can be drudgery, or it can be an adventure. This chapter provides the instructor with proven classroom techniques, which will make the study of health law an exciting endeavor. The techniques described below have been successfully applied in health law classes and seminars around the country. They have been successful in bringing the legal aspects of health care to life in the classroom, while at the same time increasing the students' knowledge, interest, and enthusiasm for learning the law.

THE PRE-POST TEST

This short-answer exam should be taken prior to reading the text. The scores will give the student an indication of his or her knowledge and understanding of the topics examined in each chapter. The test should be retaken again after the book has been read and discussed. Each student will show a marked increase in knowledge, as exemplified by higher scores. (See Appendix 23-A for the Pre-Post Test.)

GROUP ADVOCACY DISCUSSIONS

Divide the class into two groups for study purposes. Assign each group opposing views on a selected topic (e.g., waste disposal, euthanasia, abortion, and AIDS). Students can be assigned to argue the view opposite their own personal beliefs for greater group dynamics. Allow several weeks for the students to research their assigned topic. On the assigned date of the class discussion, select three students to sit as judges to lead the classroom discussion. If, for example, the topic selected for debate is abortion, one of the judges would be assigned to be a freedom-of-choice advocate, the second a pro-life advocate, and the third undecided. The judges should be seated in the front of the classroom with the opposing teams seated to the left and right of the judges in semicircles. Following the debate, a closed ballot vote should be taken to determine which team presented the most convincing arguments.

WRITTEN AND ORAL CASE PRESENTATIONS

Divide the class into teams of two. Select two students to represent the plaintiff(s) and two students to represent the defendant(s) in an assigned case. The cases can be selected from the text, or the students can be provided with a case from a regional legal reporter or other source. The students should then research their assigned case. After their research is completed, student teams should submit a typed brief of the case. The brief does not have to be longer than two pages in length and should follow this format:

Students' names (two-member team)
Case citation
Brief for Defendant (or Plaintiff)
Facts: These should be summarized in clear, concise, chronological statements, numerically ordered. Only the major facts, important to the issues in the case, should be included.
Issue(s): Students should phrase the issue(s) of the case in the form of one or two brief statements (e.g., the issue is whether or not a woman's right to privacy allows her to have an abortion).
Conclusions: The court's conclusion regarding the issue(s) in the case should be phrased in the form of a summary statement.
Reasons: Students should summarize in numerical steps the reasoning of the court in deciding the case.

On the assigned date, the plaintiff team should be prepared to orally argue against the defendant team. Each team should be given a specified amount of time to argue its case. Three students should sit as judges and probe each side regarding its arguments. After the judges are finished questioning, half of the remaining members of the class should sit as a jury to deliberate and determine a verdict, while the other half of the class observes the deliberations. No comments should be permitted by the observers during the course of jury deliberations. The students observing the jury discussions will want to say something, but must not. This is an opportunity for them to experience the frustrations of the attorneys and judges, as well as the public, "patiently" awaiting their verdict outside the jury room. The judges and attorneys should be excused while the jury discusses the case. This provides them with an opportunity to experience the anxiety of being uncertain as to how their case is being argued by members of the jury.

ROLE PLAYING

In order to assist students in gaining a deeper understanding of the problems and conflicts that health care providers face, role playing should be encouraged. Below are two real-life situations that lend themselves quite easily to role playing. Note that the various topics contained in this text also lend themselves to a variety of problem-solving situations. Students should take the described roles, act out the situation, and develop plausible solutions. After each episode is presented, have the class discuss other options. Role playing can be extremely stressful, and it is therefore important to monitor it closely with strict time limitations.

1. Two nurses complain to the hospital administrator that a doctor has harassed them. They refuse to put their complaint in writing.

Potential role players include the administrator, the nurses, the physician, and the medical staff director.

2. A comatose patient had formerly expressed a desire to have the respirator turned off if she is ever on one. Her parents don't want it shut off, but her husband does. They go to present their arguments to the administrator, the chief of the medical staff, and the director of nursing.

Potential role players include the director of nursing, the administrator, the physician, the family members, the chaplain, the attorneys, and the judge.

TRIAL

Students should select a case of general interest to them as a class. They can then be divided into two teams of equal numbers. One team chooses two plaintiff's attorneys, and the other team chooses two defense attorneys. After the two teams research an agreed-on case, they then develop it by assigning witness parts. A full trial would then be conducted, beginning with the opening statements by the plaintiff's attorney and followed by the opening statements by the defendant's attorney. The trial should then proceed in the following order:

- direct examination of plaintiff's witnesses
- cross-examination by defendant of plaintiff's witnesses as each takes the stand
- redirect by the plaintiff, if necessary
- recross by the defendant, if necessary

Witnesses should not be permitted in the classroom during the trial except for their specific testimony, nor should witnesses be permitted to prompt each other as to what happened to them while on the witness stand, for purposes of "keeping the story straight." This will provide opportunity for impeachment of the credibility of a witness's testimony which could be based on contradictory testimony by a previous witness. This should prove to be a dynamic time in the classroom.

The defendant's case would then be presented after the plaintiff's witnesses have testified. At the conclusion of the defendant's case, closing arguments should be made. A verdict, after deliberation, can then be rendered by chosen members of the class sitting as jurors.

CLASSROOM DISCUSSION CASES

The following two examples illustrate the potential for review and analysis of cases in the classroom setting. Selected questions have been provided as a basis for initiating classroom participation.

1. A patient died after her third cerebral hemorrhage. When the patient was admitted to the hospital following a cerebral hemorrhage, her physician determined that she should be given a specific drug to reduce her blood pressure and make her condition operable, and he directed its administration. For an unexplained reason, the drug was not administered. The patient's blood pressure rose, and after another hemorrhage she passed away.

2. Following an automobile accident, a 16-year-old boy, who had recently escaped from a detention center, was brought to the hospital emergency room by ambulance. The patient seemed to be alert and claimed to be suffering withdrawal symptoms from a drug habit. The patient claimed that he participated in a methadone treatment program. The physician administered 40 mg of methadone. The patient needed blood but refused it. After being observed in the emergency room for several hours, the patient was later placed on a medical-surgical unit for observation. The following morning, it was not possible to awaken him, and he was later pronounced dead. It was discovered that he had never been an addict or in a methadone treatment program. Rather, the previous night he had been drinking beer and taking librium. He had not told this to hospital authorities. His estate sued the physician. Consider the possible outcomes if death was the result of: 1) an overdose, 2) the failure to administer blood, or 3) a subdural hematoma. Consider the possible outcomes if the patient was an adult as opposed to a minor.

Selected Questions for Case Discussions

1. What are the facts of the case?
2. Are all the elements required in a negligence suit present?
3. What standard of care is required?
4. Who would you consider the potential plaintiff(s) and defendant(s)?
5. How would you argue for the plaintiff(s)?
6. What evidence would you present?
7. How would you defend the defendant(s)?
8. What are your defense options?
9. If you were on the jury, what would your finding be, based on only the facts as presented and the classroom discussion?
10. If you find the defendant(s) responsible, what damages would you award, and for what reasons?
11. What are your options if you, as plaintiff or defendant, are unhappy with the jury decision?

UNDERSTANDING CASE CITATIONS

Students should be encouraged to research cases cited in this text in order to gain a deeper understanding of the topics covered. A case citation tells the reader the identity of the parties in the case, the text in which the case can be found, and the year in which the case was decided.

Example

Bouvia v. Superior Court (Glenchur), 225 Cal. Rptr. 297 (Ct. App. 1986).

- *Bouvia v. Superior Court (Glenchur)*—Identifies the basic parties involved in the lawsuit.
- 225 Cal. Rptr. 297—Identifies the case as being reported in volume 225 of the California Reporter at page 297.
- Ct. App. 1986—Identifies the case as being in the California Court of Appeals in 1986.

Students who wish to research a specific case should visit a law school library, which will contain various state and regional reporters.

COMMUNITY RESOURCES

People who work in the administrative, legal, or medical profession in a given community are excellent sources of information. Students are encouraged to contact these professionals in order to enrich and expand on what they learn in this text. They should first determine who will be interviewed and then formulate their questions accordingly. Some potential interviewees include judges, attorneys, expert witnesses, plaintiffs, defendants, jurors (after trial), and court clerks.

On completion of an interview and/or courtroom observation, each student should be prepared to discuss with the class his or her experiences. Classroom participation in this manner will serve to enhance the learning process.

Local bar associations have speakers on various topics who are ready to address groups on request. Potential speakers for the classroom include representatives from the medical, legal, administrative, government, and insurance professions.

The Pre-Post Test

MULTIPLE CHOICE

General directions: Write the most correct answer to each question on a sheet of paper numbered 1 though 25.

1. The type of law that consists of principles derived from court decisions is

a. statutory law

b. common law

c. natural law

d. criminal law

2. A civil wrong committed by one person against the person or property of another is a

a. crime

b. misdemeanor

c. tort

d. trespass

3. The commission or omission of an act that a reasonably prudent person would not or would do is

a. negligence

b. vengeance

c. retribution

d. self-help

4. A threat coupled with the apparent present ability to do immediate physical harm to another is

a. battery

b. menacing

c. extortion

d. assault

326

5. A person who is physically restrained from leaving a hospital for not paying a bill is said to be a victim of

a. kidnapping

b. false imprisonment

c. lawful confinement

d. false arrest

6. When a person is publicly, wrongfully accused of committing a crime, that constitutes the offense of

a. malicious prosecution

b. libel

c. slander per se

d. false light privacy invasion

7. A complete defense to a defamation action is

a. consent

b. truth

c. retraction

d. written apology

8. The policy that temporarily denies new appointments to a hospital medical staff is called

a. moratorium

b. exclusive contract

c. restraint of trade

d. reduced market approach

9. The hospital, as an employer, is liable for the negligent acts of its nurses under the doctrine of

a. res ipsa loquitur

b. umbrella liability

c. respondeat superior

d. caveat emptor

10. The sworn statement made by a witness that can be used as evidence in court is a/an

a. witness transcript

b. affidavit

c. subpoena

d. deposition

11. The term referring to adults who stand in the place of a parent with responsibility over a child is

a. in loco parentis

b. parens patriae

c. custodialship

d. lex loci parentis

12. If an x-ray machine is entered as evidence, it is a form of

a. direct evidence

b. real evidence

c. documentary evidence

d. circumstantial evidence

13. The law that made it mandatory for a hospital receiving funds to provide reasonable services to indigents is the

a. Hill-Burton Act

b. Fair Trade Act

c. Simkins Act

d. Health and Hospital Fair Standards Act

14. The case that paved the way for women to have the right to choose an abortion was

a. *Doe v. Bolton*

b. *Danforth v. Planned Parenthood*

c. *Canterbury v. Spence*

d. *Roe v. Wade*

15. The court decides

a. questions of fact

b. the guilt of a party

c. questions of evidence

d. questions of law

16. Comparative negligence requires that damages among multiple defendants be divided

a. equally

b. according to fault

c. 60/40

d. as the patient decides

17. The order that calls for a document to be produced by a hospital is called a

a. summons

b. subpoena duces tecum

c. writ

d. bench order

18. Which of the following involves an intentional wrong?

a. battery

b. false imprisonment

c. invasion of privacy

d. all of the above

19. Malpractice is negligence by a

a. physician

b. registered nurse

c. pharmacist

d. all of the above

20. The taking of property from another by force or violence is

a. larceny

b. burglary

c. robbery

d. pick pocketing

21. The most important factor in determining the negligence of a health care professional is

a. education

b. age

c. years of experience

d. experience and training

22. The removal of nasogastric feeding tubes from a mentally competent patient to legally hasten death is an example of

a. informed consent

b. active euthanasia

c. passive euthanasia

d. aiding suicide

23. A preferred defense in a negligence suit is

a. ignorance

b. unintentional act

c. assumption of the risk

d. right to life

24. Damages that are awarded to compensate for gross negligence and to deter the wrongdoer are known as

a. special damages

b. general damages

c. exorbitant damages

d. punitive damages

25. An unconsented-to touching by one person upon the person of another is

a. jostling

b. assault

c. battery

d. menacing

MATCHING

General directions: Use a separate sheet of paper, numbered 1 through 25. Select the alphabetical letter of the definition from Column II that best describes each numbered word in Column I.

Column I

1. Common law
2. Liability
3. Tort
4. Nonfeasance
5. Direct evidence
6. Subpoena duces tecum
7. Tort-feasor
8. Stare decisis
9. Statutory Law
10. Malice
11. Libel
12. Circumstantial evidence
13. Perjury
14. Slander
15. Homicide
16. Res ispa loquitur
17. Governmental immunity
18. Consent
19. Captain of the ship
20. Borrowed servant doctrine
21. Respondeat superior
22. Defendant
23. Plaintiff
24. Malpractice
25. Summary judgment

Column II

a. Let it stand as decided
b. A wrongdoer
c. Testifying falsely
d. An obligation incurred for a wrong
e. Unwritten law based on court decisions
f. Criminal intent, ill will
g. A wrong committed against a person or property
h. An order for records
i. Failure to act
j. The killing of one human being by another
k. An oral expression of defamation of character
l. Proof offered through direct testimony
m. Written law based on enactments of legislative bodies
n. Evidence based on conclusions by inference
o. A written method of defamation of character
p. Permission to perform an agreed-on procedure
q. Let the superior respond
r. The person who brings a suit
s. The person who is called on to make satisfaction for an injury
t. The king can do no wrong
u. The failure of a physician to treat his or her patient with reasonable and ordinary care

    v. A legal doctrine developed in common law which permits the transference of liability for wrongful acts of an employee in certain instances from one employer to another (e.g., hospital to physician)

   w. A motion for an immediate decision by the judge

   x. The thing speaks for itself

   y. Refers to the situation in which an employer lends his or her employee to another for a particular employment

TRUE/FALSE

General directions: On a separate sheet of paper, numbered 1 through 50, write in your answer for each question.

1. Statutory law is synonymous with common law.
2. A hospital is liable for the negligent acts of an employee on vacation who assists an injured party in an automobile accident.
3. Hospital board members are always responsible individually for the negligent acts of nursing personnel.
4. Murder and rape are considered crimes against society.
5. The decisions of one jurisdiction are always binding on other jurisdictions with similar cases.
6. Every case is decided on common law principles unless a statute governs.
7. A parent's release of a claim surrenders only the parental claim.
8. A summons cannot be served by a sheriff.
9. A trial brief is prepared by the judge.
10. Only persons who wish to be subpoenaed by a court may be subpoenaed.
11. Criminal negligence is the flagrant and reckless disregard for the safety of others.
12. The court decides questions of fact during a jury trial.
13. The right to trial by jury in certain cases is a constitutional right.
14. Insufficiency of evidence is never a ground for dismissal of a case.
15. A prima facie case indicates that sufficient evidence is present to prove the facts alleged in a case.
16. Facts based on what another has said are hearsay evidence.
17. A contract to pay a physician pending the outcome of a case is a valid contract.

18. The employment-at-will doctrine has both pros and cons for employer and employee alike.
19. Common law is the result of a legislative enactment.
20. Criminal law deals with conduct considered offensive to society as a whole.
21. A layman can be held liable for malpractice.
22. A prisoner has a constitutional right to reject a blood test for AIDS, and this right outweighs the rights of the prison to require testing even if the prison's purpose is to prevent the spread of AIDS among inmates.
23. Employment is at the will of the employee who may not be discharged except for cause.
24. A recently promulgated Army regulation denying a homosexual the right to re-enlist does not violate the soldier's First Amendment right to freedom of speech, according to the U.S. Court of Appeals for the Seventh Circuit.
25. Recovery of damages is generally permitted for wrongful birth, but not for wrongful life.
26. A misdemeanor is an act one level of severity above that of a felony.
27. A physician who refers his/her patient to a community hospital for physical therapy is generally responsible for any injuries the patient might sustain as the result of the negligent treatment of a physical therapist.
28. An orderly, since he is not classified as a professional, is not liable for his own negligent conduct.
29. Nurses are not authorized to challenge a physician's order.
30. Only private, for-profit hospitals can be sued on the basis of *respondeat superior*.
31. Nurses must never attempt to diagnose a patient's complaint.
32. Health professionals can be held liable for attempting to carry out a procedure clearly beyond their capabilities.
33. A nurse who fails to check a label on a drug can be considered to have been negligent if the drug is administered to a patient and the patient suffers injury.
34. A physician does not have the right to assume that a hypodermic handed to him by a health professional contains the proper drug.
35. Medication errors are a common cause of malpractice claims against a nurse.
36. A specialist is held to the same standard of care as a nonspecialist.
37. Proof of deviation from the required standard of care is not necessary in a malpractice case. It is, however, necessary in a case of false imprisonment.
38. The law requires that a malpractice suit be instituted only by the injured patient.
39. There may be several plaintiffs in a lawsuit against a single defendant.
40. Questions of fact are resolved by the jury.
41. The credibility of a witness can generally be challenged if his/her statements are overly consistent.
42. In an alleged negligence case, the burden is on the defendant to prove negligence.

43. Under the doctrine of *res ipsa loquitur,* the burden of proof shifts to the defendant.
44. Hostility in the hospital setting is generally limited to the housekeeping department.
45. The more rigid and impersonal health professionals are, the more likely they will be sued by suit-prone patients.
46. Every unfavorable medical event affords a basis for a malpractice suit.
47. Paperwork takes precedence over treating difficult patients.
48. It is preferable that a patient's consent be procured by the operating physician.
49. At trial, the plaintiff's attorney presents all opening statements, and the defense attorney delivers all closing arguments.
50. The doctrine of charitable immunity is the latest legislative fad and just might be the solution to the malpractice crisis.

PRE-POST TEST ANSWERS

Multiple Choice

1. b	10. d	19. d
2. c	11. a	20. c
3. a	12. b	21. d
4. d	13. a	22. b
5. b	14. d	23. c
6. c	15. d	24. d
7. b	16. b	25. c
8. a	17. b	
9. c	18. d	

Matching

1. e	10. f	19. v
2. d	11. o	20. y
3. g	12. n	21. q
4. i	13. c	22. s
5. l	14. k	23. r
6. h	15. j	24. u
7. b	16. x	25. w
8. a	17. t	
9. m	18. p	

True/False

1. F	18. T	35. T
2. F	19. F	36. F
3. F	20. T	37. F
4. T	21. F	38. F
5. F	22. F	39. T
6. T	23. F	40. T
7. T	24. T	41. F
8. F	25. T	42. F
9. F	26. F	43. T
10. F	27. F	44. F
11. T	28. F	45. T
12. F	29. F	46. F
13. T	30. F	47. F
14. F	31. F	48. T
15. T	32. T	49. F
16. T	33. T	50. F
17. F	34. F	

Glossary of Legal Terms

Abandonment: The unilateral severance by the physician of the professional relationship between himself or herself and the patient without reasonable notice at a time when the patient still needs continuing attention.

Abortion: The premature termination of pregnancy at a time when the fetus is incapable of sustaining life independent of the mother.

Administrative agency: A government body charged with administering or implementing particular legislation.

Admissibility (of evidence): Refers to the issue of whether a court, applying the rules of evidence, is bound to receive or permit introduction of a particular piece of proof.

Affidavit: A voluntary statement of facts, or a voluntary declaration in writing of facts, that a person swears to be true before an official authorized to administer an oath.

Agency: The relationship in which one person acts for or represents another— by the latter's authority, for example, insurance agent and insurance company.

Allegation: A statement that a person expects to be able to prove.

Appellant: The party who appeals the decision of a lower court to a court of higher jurisdiction.

Appellee: The party against whom an appeal to a higher court is taken.

Assault: An intentional act that is designed to make the victim fearful and produces reasonable apprehension of harm.

Assignment: The transfer of rights, responsibilities, or property from one party to another.

Attestation: The act of witnessing a document in writing.

Battery: The touching of one person by another without the consent of the person being touched.

Best evidence rule: A legal doctrine requiring that primary evidence of a fact (such as an original document) be introduced, or that an acceptable explanation be given before a copy can be introduced or testimony given concerning the fact.

Bona fide: In good faith; openly, honestly, or innocently; without knowledge or intent of fraud.

Borrowed servant doctrine: Refers to a situation where an employee is temporarily under the control of another. The traditional example is that of a nurse employed by a hospital who is "borrowed" and under the control of the attending surgeon during a procedure in the operating room. The temporary employer of the borrowed servant can be held responsible for the negligent acts of the borrowed servant under the doctrine of *respondeat superior*.

Charitable immunity: A legal doctrine that developed out of the English court system and held charitable institutions blameless for their negligent acts.

Civil law: The body of law, sometimes referred to as municipal law, adopted in a county or state, which describes private rights and responsibilities. It is that part of American law that does not deal with crimes.

Closed shop contract: A labor-management agreement that provides that only members of a particular union may be hired.

Common law: The body of principles that has evolved and continues to evolve and expand from court decisions. Many of the legal principles and rules applied by courts in the United States had their origins in English common law.

Complaint: In a negligence action, the first pleading which is filed by the plaintiff's attorney. It is the first statement of a case by the plaintiff against the defendant and states a cause of action, notifying the defendant as to the basis for the suit.

Concurring opinion: *See* Opinion of the court.

Confidentiality: *See* Privileged communication.

Consent: Simply stated, a voluntary act by which one person agrees to allow someone else to do something.

Coroner's jury: A special jury called by the coroner to determine whether the evidence concerning the cause of death indicated that death was brought about by criminal means.

Counterclaim: A defendant's claim in opposition to a claim of the plaintiff.

Crime: An act against society in violation of the law. Crimes are prosecuted by and in the name of the state.

Criminal law: The division of the law dealing with crime and punishment.

Decedent: A deceased person.

Defamation: The injury of a person's reputation or character caused by the false statements of another made to a third person. Defamation includes both libel and slander.

Defendant: In a criminal case, the person accused of committing a crime. In a civil suit, the party against whom the suit is brought, demanding that he or she pay the other party legal relief.

Demurrer: A formal objection by one of the parties to a lawsuit that the evidence presented by the other party is insufficient to sustain an issue or case.

Deposition: A sworn statement, made out of court, that may be admitted into evidence if it is impossible for a witness to attend a trial in person.

Directed verdict: When a trial judge decides that the evidence and/or law is clearly in favor of one party or the plaintiff has failed to establish a case and that it is pointless for the trial to proceed further, the judge may direct the jury to return a verdict for the appropriate party. The conclusion of the judge must be so clear and obvious that reasonable minds could not arrive at a different conclusion.

Discovery: The ascertainment of that which was previously unknown through a pretrial investigation; it includes testimony and documents that may be under the exclusive control of the other party. Discovery facilitates out-of-court settlements.

Dissenting opinion: *See* Opinion of the court.

Emergency: A sudden unexpected occurrence or event causing a threat to life or health. The legal responsibilities of those involved in an emergency situation are measured according to the occurrence.

Employee: One who works for another in return for pay.

Employer: A person or firm that selects employees, pays their salaries or wages, retains the power to dismiss them, and can control their conduct during working hours.

Expert witness: A person who has special training, experience, skill, and knowledge in a relevant area and who is allowed to offer an opinion as testimony in court.

Federal question: A legal question involving the U.S. Constitution or a statute enacted by Congress.

Felony: A serious crime usually punishable by imprisonment for a period of longer than one year or by death.

Good samaritan laws: Laws designed to protect those who stop to render aid in an emergency. These laws generally provide immunity for specified persons from any civil suit arising out of care rendered at the scene of an emergency, provided that the one rendering assistance has not done so in a grossly negligent manner.

Grand jury: A jury called to determine whether there is sufficient evidence that a crime has been committed to justify bringing a case to trial. It is not the jury before which the case is tried to determine guilt or innocence.

Grand larceny: The theft of property valued at more than a specified amount (usually $50), thus constituting a felony instead of a misdemeanor.

Health: According to the World Health Organization, "[a] state of complete physical, mental, and social well-being and not merely the absence of disease or infirmity."

Hearsay rule: A rule of evidence that restricts the admissibility of evidence that is not the personal knowledge of the witness. Hearsay evidence is admissible only under strict rules.

Holographic will: A will handwritten by the testator.

In loco parentis: A legal doctrine that permits the courts to assign a person to stand in the place of parents and possess their legal rights, duties, and responsibilities toward a child.

Independent contractor: One who agrees to undertake work without being under the direct control or direction of the employer.

Indictment: A formal written accusation, found and presented by a grand jury, charging a person therein named with criminal conduct.

Injunction: A court order either requiring one to do a certain act or prohibiting one from doing a certain act.

Interrogatories: A list of questions sent from one party in a lawsuit to the other party to be answered under oath.

Judge: An officer who guides court proceedings to ensure impartiality and enforces the rules of evidence. The trial judge determines the applicable law and states it to the jury. The appellate judge hears appeals and renders decisions concerning the correctness of the actions of the trial judge, the law of the case, and the sufficiency of the evidence.

Jurisdiction: The right of a court to administer justice by hearing and deciding controversies.

Jurisprudence: The philosophy or science of law on which a particular legal system is built.

Jury: A certain number of persons selected and sworn to hear the evidence and determine the facts in a case.

Larceny: The taking of another person's property without consent with the intent to permanently deprive the owner of its use and ownership.

Liability: As it relates to damages, an obligation one has incurred or might incur through a negligent act.

Liability insurance: A contract to have someone else pay for any liability or loss thereby in return for the payment of premiums.

Libel: A false or malicious writing that is intended to defame or dishonor another person and is published so that someone other than the one defamed will observe it.

License: A permit from the state allowing certain acts to be performed, usually for a specific period of time.

Litigation: A trial in court to determine legal issues, rights, and duties between the parties to the litigation.

Malpractice: Professional misconduct, improper discharge of professional duties, or failure to meet the standard of care of a professional that resulted in harm to another.

Mayhem: The crime of intentionally disfiguring or dismembering another.

Misdemeanor: An unlawful act of a less serious nature than a felony, usually punishable by a jail sentence for a term of less than one year and/or a fine.

Negligence: The omission or commission of an act that a reasonably prudent person would or would not do under given circumstances. It is a form of heedlessness or carelessness that constitutes a departure from the standard of care generally imposed on members of society.

Next of kin: Those persons who by the law of descent would be adjudged the closest blood relatives of the decedent.

Non compos mentis: "Not of sound mind"; suffering from some form of mental defect.

Notary public: A public official who administers oaths and certifies the validity of documents.

Nuncupative will: An oral statement intended as a last will made in anticipation of death.

Opinion of the court: In an appellate court decision, the reasons for the decision. One judge writes the opinion for the majority of the court. Judges who agree with the result, but for different reasons, may write concurring opinions explaining their reasons. Judges who disagree with the majority may write dissenting opinions.

Ordinance: A law passed by a municipal legislative body.

Perjury: The willful act of giving false testimony under oath.

Petit (petty) larceny: The theft of property valued below a set monetary amount. This offense is usually classified as a misdemeanor.

Plaintiff: The party who brings a civil suit seeking damages or other legal relief.

Police power: The power of the state to protect the health, safety, morals, and general welfare of the people.

Privileged communication: A statement made to an attorney, physician, spouse, or anyone else in a position of trust. Because of the confidential nature of such information, the law protects it from being revealed even in court. The term is applied in two distinct situations. First, the communications between certain persons, such as physician and patient, cannot be divulged without consent of the patient. Second, in some situations the law provides an exemption from liability for disclosing information where there is a higher duty to speak, such as statutory reporting requirements.

Probate: The judicial proceeding that determines the existence and validity of a will.

Probate court: A court with jurisdiction over wills. Its powers range from deciding the validity of a will to distributing property.

Proximate: In immediate relation with something else. In negligence cases, the careless act must be the proximate cause of injury.

Real evidence: That evidence furnished by tangible things, such as weapons, bullets, and equipment.

Rebuttal: The giving of evidence to contradict the effect of evidence introduced by the opposing party.

Regulatory agency: An arm of the government that enforces legislation regulating an act or activity in a particular area—for example, the federal Food and Drug Administration.

Release: A statement signed by one person relinquishing a right or claim against another person.

Remand: The referral of a case by an appeals court back to the original court, out of which it came, for the purpose of having some action taken there.

Res gestae: "The thing done"; all of the surrounding events that become part of an incident. If statements are made as part of the incident, they are admissible in court as *res gestae* in spite of the hearsay rule.

Res ipsa loquitur: "The thing speaks for itself"; a doctrine of law applicable to cases where the defendant had exclusive control of the thing that caused the harm and where the harm ordinarily could not have occurred without negligent conduct.

Res judicata: That which has been acted on or decided by the courts.

Respondeat superior: "Let the master answer"; an aphorism meaning that the employer is responsible for the legal consequences of the acts of the servant or employee who is acting within the scope of his/her employment.

Slander: A false oral statement, made in the presence of a third person, that injures the character or reputation of another.

Standard of care: A description of what conduct is expected of an individual in a given situation. It is a measure against which a defendant's conduct is compared.

Stare decisis: "Let the decision stand"; the legal principle indicating that courts should apply previous decisions to subsequent cases involving similar facts and questions.

Statute of limitations: A legal limit on the time allowed for filing suit in civil matters, usually measured from the time of the wrong or from the time when a reasonable person would have discovered the wrong.

Subpoena ad testificandum: A court order requiring one to appear in court to give testimony.

Subpoena duces tecum: A court order that commands a person to come to court and to produce whatever documents are named in the order.

Subrogation: The substitution of one person for another in reference to a lawful claim or right.

Suit: A court proceeding where one person seeks damages or other legal remedies from another.

Summary judgment: Generally, an immediate decision by a judge, without jury deliberation.

Summons: A court order directed to the sheriff or other appropriate official to notify the defendant in a civil suit that a suit has been filed and when and where to appear.

Testimony: An oral statement of a witness given under oath at a trial.

Tort: A civil wrong. Torts may be intentional or unintentional.

Tort-feasor: A person who commits a tort.

Trial court: The court in which evidence is presented to a judge or jury for decision.

Union shop contract: A labor-management agreement making continued employment contingent on joining the union.

Verdict: The formal declaration of a jury's findings of fact, signed by the jury foreman and presented to the court.

Waiver: The intentional giving up of a right, such as allowing another person to testify to information that would ordinarily be protected as a privileged communication.

Will: A legal declaration of the intentions a person wishes to have carried out after death concerning property, children, or estate.

Witness: A person who is called to give testimony in a court of law.

Writ: A written order that is issued to a person or persons, requiring the performance of some specified act or giving authority to have it done.

Index of Cases

Index

351

About the Author

George D. Pozgar received his MBA in Health Care Administration from The George Washington University, Washington, D.C. Mr. Pozgar served an administrative residency at the Baptist Memorial Hospital in Jacksonville, Florida. He also served on the administrative staff of Huntington Hospital, Huntington, New York, for more than seven years. He was the administrator of the St. John's Episcopal Hospital, a 300-bed hospital in Smithtown, New York. Mr. Pozgar is presently Vice President for Corporate Affairs for Episcopal Health Services, Inc., a multifacility health care system. He is also an instructor in the legal aspects of health care administration at the Pilgrim State branch of the New School for Social Research, Graduate School of Management and Urban Professions in New York City.

He has served as an instructor in the legal aspects of health care at both the St. Francis College and the St. Joseph College of Brooklyn, New York. Mr. Pozgar has also served as an instructor at various conferences on the legal aspects of health care administration, including conferences held at Molloy College and the C.W. Post College of Long Island University.

Mr. Pozgar is a member of the American Hospital Association, the American Public Health Association, and the American College of Health Care Executives. He has also served as a member of the Nassau/Suffolk Hospital Council, as Vice President of the Nassau/Suffolk Health Care Associates, as President of the Huntington Township Emergency Medical Services Committee, and as an on-site faculty member of The George Washington University, Washington, D.C.